Human Security and the Environment

International Comparisons

Edited by
Edward A. Page

Research Fellow in Environmental Sustainability, Keele University, UK

Michael Redclift

Professor of International Environmental Policy, King's College, University of London, UK

Edward Elgar
Cheltenham, UK • Northampton, MA, USA

Published by
Edward Elgar Publishing Limited
Glensanda House
Montpellier Parade
Cheltenham
Glos GL50 1UA
UK

Edward Elgar Publishing, Inc.
136 West Street
Suite 202
Northampton
Massachusetts 01060
USA

A catalogue record for this book
is available from the British Library

Library of Congress Cataloguing in Publication Data
Human security and the environment : international comparisons / edited by Edward A. Page and Michael Redclift.
    p. cm.
    Includes bibliographical references and index.
    1. Environmental policy—International cooperation. 2. Security, International. I. Page, Edward, 1968– II. Redclift, M. R.

GE170 .H88 2002
363.7—dc21

2001054308

ISBN 1 84064 458 3

Typeset by Manton Typesetters, Louth, Lincolnshire, UK.
Printed and bound in Great Britain by MPG Books Ltd, Bodmin, Cornwall.

Contents

Figures, tables and boxes

FIGURES

TABLES

BOXES

Contributors

Viviana Blanco-Barboza, University of Costa Rica
Chris Cocklin, Monash University, Australia
Álvaro Fernández-González, University of Costa Rica
Oscar Forero, Wye College, London, UK
Nils Petter Gleditsch, International Peace Research Institute, Oslo, Norway
Edgar E. Gutiérrez-Espeleta, University of Costa Rica
Henk Hilderink, University of Victoria, Canada
Fred Langeweg, University of Victoria, Canada
Steve Lonergan, University of Victoria, Canada
Richard Matthew, University of California at Irvine, USA
Kwasi Nsiah-Gyabaah, Sunyani Polytechnic, Ghana
Edward Page, Keele University, UK
Michael Redclift, King's College, London, UK
Colin Sage, University College, Cork, Ireland
Johannes Stripple, Lund University, Sweden
Bjørn Otto Sverdrup, International Peace Research Institute, Oslo, Norway
John Vogler, Keele University, UK
Graham Woodgate, Wye College, London, UK

Introduction: Human security and the environment at the new millennium

Edward Page and Michael Redclift

---

1 HUMAN SECURITY AND THE ENVIRONMENT IN THE TWENTIETH CENTURY

This book examines the meaning of 'security' and the 'environment' in the post-Cold War era, and the ways in which the activities of human societies are shifting the balance with nature. Throughout the twentieth century, many of the conflicts between human societies and the natural environment have reflected differences in the capacities and wealth of human societies. In the developed world, ecological movements grew up which expressed concern about the implications for nature of unfettered economic growth. Rising levels of personal consumption, and unsustainable systems of natural resource and energy procurement, were taking a heavy toll on the planet (Redclift, 1996).

Awareness of the possible implications of global climate change only served to highlight divisions between the North and the South. In the North, the pursuit of higher living standards was, paradoxically, threatening the quality of life of many people caught up in the momentum of 'getting and spending'. In the South, countries intent on achieving the benefits of economic development have been faced by contradictory pressures. Increased dependence on fossil fuels, rising living standards and population pressures are serving to exacerbate the 'forcing' of world climate change. At the same time, threats to their domestic environments – to tropical forests, vulnerable coastal areas and wetlands – have forced developing countries to re-examine the more immediate environmental security of their own populations.

In 1987 the term 'security' was still defined solely in terms of military preparedness. This was the year that the Brundtland Commission published its report, 'Our Common Future', which introduced the term 'sustainable development' into our vocabulary (WCED, 1987). In 1987 there were still four years before the Cold War ended: on 24 August 1991, in a message from President Gorbachev that the Soviet Union would be abolished. Some two years later one of us recalls visiting a Chinese village and, at a village market, being confronted by a plastic globe among the rubber boots and vegetables. 'This is a globe of the world' – it read in Chinese – 'Germany is now one country and the Soviet Union no longer exists.'

The history of 'sustainable development' – at least in the modern period – started over a decade before with the oil crises of the 1970s, the growth of 'petrodollars' in Western banks, and the Mexican and Brazilian debt crises that this provoked, beginning in August 1982. But the roots of this twentieth century 'environmental crisis' were laid earlier. Clearly the key decade for the emergence of hydrocarbons on the global stage was the 1970s, when oil prices rose dramatically in two bursts, and the power of OPEC was born. These difficulties led, in turn, to a public re-examination of the relationship between what came to be known as the 'North' and the 'South', in the form of the Brandt Report in 1980 (Brandt Commission, 1980).

The Brandt Report charted a future for development that relied heavily on raising demand in the South for the goods and services provided in the North. In 1980 the development of the Asian 'Tiger' economies was not yet fully underway, and the so-called 'newly-industrialising countries' were still taking faltering steps towards development. Few people would have predicted, in 1980, that China would maintain an annual growth rate of between 7 and 10 per cent throughout much of the 1990s, and that by 2020 it would be expected to have a gross domestic product (at purchasing power parity) 20 per cent larger than that of the United States.

In the early 1980s a number of reports were published that were to mark an important stage in the way that environmental problems were perceived. First there was the World Conservation Strategy (1983). The evidence of serious environmental problems, many of them on a global scale and linked to discernible 'global' systems, was becoming clearer, and the second World Conservation Strategy (1991) developed a stronger focus on their interaction with human systems.

The second significant report from the early 1980s was the Global 2000 Report (1982) ('commissioned by President Carter and published under President Reagan' as the blurb read). This document, of over 1000 pages, barely mentioned climate, but it did bring modelling to bear on global issues. Building upon the innovative science and breadth of the Man and the Biosphere programme (MAB) these reports, and the work of UNEP (United Nations Environment Program), made loud warning noises to the international policy community. These assessments, like others at the time, were broadly influenced by the idea that *limitations in the resource base* would make it increasingly difficult to support economic and social development. This was the era, almost quaint from an historical perspective, of 'Limits to Growth'.

Two decades ago the environment and development were still seen as parallel but distinct discourses and the 'problems' of development were seen as caused by the limits this placed on human ingenuity. The human individual was set apart from the 'problem'. This was an era of modernist aspiration, in which 'development' was problematic in one sense only – that it seemed to be denied to some. The 'problem' with development was that there were structural obstacles that prevented its benefits from being shared more widely. As yet there were few root and branch critiques of the whole 'development' project, as seen from Green or postmodern perspectives.

Not until the Brundtland Commission reported, in 1987, after pioneering and exhaustive 'consultations' throughout the globe, was there an intellectual attempt to integrate the environment and development discourses.

2   LATE TWENTIETH-CENTURY CONCERNS

The first late twentieth-century concern was almost prompted by accident. British scientists working in Antarctica 'discovered' the ozone hole, an observation which was to drive political pressures for dramatic reductions in CFC gas emissions, pressures which culminated in the Montreal Protocol of 16 September 1987.

The first generation of multilateral environmental agreements date back to the early twentieth century, although most were signed in the 1970s and 1980s. They were largely single issue, sectoral agreements, primarily addressing the allocation and exploitation of natural resources, particularly wildlife, the atmosphere and marine environments – the so-called 'global commons'.

The second generation of multilateral environmental agreements have tended to bridge sectors, and to be based more on 'systems'; they are more holistic in design. This second generation really commenced with the Earth Summit held in Rio de Janeiro in 1992. Unlike many earlier agreements, the two conventions to which Rio gave rise (the UN Convention on Climate Change and the Convention on Biological Diversity) were highly contested, and involved diplomatic battles and posturing throughout the negotiations, as witnessed in the meeting of the Conference of the Parties (COP6) in the Netherlands in November 2000.

Both climate and biodiversity present major problems for a 'traditional' view of environment and development. After the early climate assessments of the Intergovernmental Panel on Climate Change (IPCC) it was more difficult to view traditional economic activity as an unproblematic 'good'. In the year 2000, we were told by UNEP (Global Environment Outlook, 1999), governments spent more than $700 000 million a year in subsidising environmentally unsound practices in the use of water, energy, agriculture and road transport. Many of these practices reflect 'underlying social commitments' – unquestioned social practices – with serious environmental consequences. They include our everyday uses of domestic energy, waste disposal and motorised transport. In the wake of UNCED (United Nations Commission on Environment and Development), these everyday practices have attracted closer examination and a more concerted effort to identify sustainable alternatives.

The fallout from Rio in 1992 was not *only* 'material', however, it was conceptual as well. Climate change was a 'problem' apparently caused not by scarcity but by 'plenty' – by high levels of personal and collective consumption polluting the medium through which we dispose of our waste (water, air and land). Most obviously, carbon emissions contributed to greenhouse gas concentrations in the atmosphere.

The 'discovery' that we lived in a 'global village', illustrated most vividly by the Chernobyl disaster in the Ukraine, was prompted by unforeseen problems in the *systems* through which we breathe, eat and reproduce. The reality of globalisation was revealed in the major food scares of the 1980s and 1990s, such as BSE/CJD, and the even larger, and more complex issues, prompted by the spread of HIV and AIDS.

BSE and AIDS are examples of systemic problems, which prompt unease with the links we have established between humans and 'nature', and the reliability and risks of 'science'. These problems were global in both senses: they occurred, and were transmitted globally, and they were part of *systems* that were difficult to access, or even fully understand. They brought scientific uncertainty into the realms of intimacy, of our most intimate social experiences.

The occurrence of these types of problems also served to undermine an earlier, more confident, view of 'mastering' nature through science. The modernist impulse to conquer and consume seemed to have been stopped in its tracks. It was difficult to stand 'inside' or 'outside' global issues like climate change, BSE or AIDS – since they permeated territorial boundaries and space. Significantly, they also permeated the body.

The heightened environmental concern that led to the Earth Summit of 1992 also produced an important stimulus for civil society (a much neglected concern in the previous decade, when some thought it did not exist at all!). It is easy to belittle the importance of Agenda 21 after apparently endless local committee meetings in countless halls and meeting rooms throughout the globe. But who spoke the language of sustainability, or local/global linkages before these thousands of local-level Agenda 21 initiatives were embarked upon? Who would have listened to the victims of fuel explosions in Mexico, or damaged pipelines in Nigeria, if there had been no 'global' template against which unsustainable practices, and corrupt governments, could be measured, and found wanting?

The raft of policy initiatives after the 1992 Earth Summit also introduced another important element into thinking about sustainable development at the global level. This was the new thinking that had begun to develop about 'environmental regimes', to use an example of late twentieth-century jargon. Multilateral environmental agreements were increasingly based on 'a holistic approach under which all species should be exploited sustainably or not at all' in the words of UNEP's Global Environmental Outlook (1999). However holistic, multi-sectoral agreements involve so many different and cross-cutting areas of law, policy and international politics, that they invariably engender unprecedented conflict. Much more was at stake for contracting parties who signed up to the Framework Convention on Climate Change than was the case with most agreements 20 years earlier.

It was in this context that non-binding instruments have come to play a large part in international environmental negotiations. National governments and the media pay more attention to binding instruments, but agreements that work only with the voluntary consent of the parties are just as important. At their best they provide a looser framework for action, which helps to foster discussion and attention to policy gains and new ways of thinking about human societies and nature. It was argued that, before we can move forward on the big issues such as carbon emissions or endangered species, we needed to change the behaviour of some target groups, such as business, and protect and enhance others, such as endangered peoples.

It is possible to favour non-binding agreements without ignoring the importance of compliance. Only when the costs of non-compliance are high enough to act as a deterrent will enough resources and attention be given to compliance. That is the paradox that lies behind much of the so-called 'soft law' that is literally being created as we enter the twenty-first century.

Other policy moves have taken important directions. The effort to establish the 'value' of nature has become an area of enormous controversy, in which even the charmed models of economists have been questioned, and they have broken into various camps virtually unknown 20 years ago. Even for those who take a 'radical' view of the imperfections of the market (often termed 'ecological economists') the challenge has been to find ways of internalising environmental costs, and the movement to do so even has a name, derived from the German, 'Ecological Modernisation' (Giorgi and Redclift, 2000).

The other major conceptual, and policy, area that opened up to an unprecedented degree at the close of the old century was that of 'managing' risks and uncertainties. The unbound copies of Ulrich Beck's *Risk Society* (Beck, 1992) arrived in an unsuspecting academic world just as the British were beginning to recognise the realities, and perils, of CJD/BSE. Beck's work, and that of others, laid bare the problems of 'high consequence' risks that could not be contained by better 'reactive' environmental management (the name for most of the environmental policy that had marked the twentieth century). In future, the bywords would be 'precautionary principle' and the limitations of 'expert witness'.

Valuation of nature, like much else, seemed trapped by patterns of thought which neglected things we could not count – largely because we had not tried to count them. The neoclassical solution was to draw nature into the ambit of individual choice and markets. This, in turn, raised problems both in terms of public understanding and the usefulness of 'willingness to pay' when applied to very different publics.

In response to the injunction to quantify environmental damage, and express it in terms of 'external costs', a highly sceptical extreme constructionist backlash set in among many in the humanities and social sciences. The existence of policy uncertainties as well as scientific uncertainties was, in their view, a condition of modernity itself. We lived in a world of increasingly fragmented sites that were the product of the way we understood problems. In seeking the price of everything, in Wilde's epigram, we risked knowing the value of nothing.

By the end of the twentieth century, then, it had become recognised that any agreement about 'sustainable development' told us more about the advocates than the process itself. Sustainable development was not a convergent, manageable, process, but a set of contradictions. Problems were emerging with nature and science, as well as with global management of the environment, that left us suspicious of scientists, and those who read the news to them, the politicians. These problems told us more about 'society' and the way that we arrive at decisions, than about 'science'. Meanwhile, the individual seemed to be located in a new kind of 'reflexive modernity'.

3 CARBON POLITICS

Looked at differently (post IPCC, post Earth Summit) many, if not most, of the twentieth century's concerns had environmental causes. The war in the Pacific is one example: in which Japan pursued a quest for control over much needed energy supplies. The collapse of the Soviet Union was another: in which the weight of energy subsidies hindered the modernisation of the economy and the systems of allocation through central planning. A third example is the growing divergence between the so-called 'Third World' today, and the inability of large numbers of people to maintain a livelihood without forsaking their own environments as refugees.

Security issues were increasingly linked to a chain of 'natural' processes and unanticipated consequences of human demand – biodiversity losses, hydrocarbon supplies, water and likely climate change impacts. International agreements over greenhouse gases (GHGs), and trade (World Trade Organisation, WTO), seemed to undermine national borders, or led to borders being contested (EU expansion eastwards, NAFTA in North America). Responsibility for climate change – which was a principle implicit in the climate change negotiations – has led to an examination of the individual levels of per capita carbon emissions and the role of carbon sinks.

Carbon emissions have become part of the currency of international politics and environmental security. Countries like to be credited with reducing their levels of emission, and new systems of market trading are beginning to grow up around *trading* in carbon (trading in the *unsustainable*, some have objected). Businesses do not know the cost of carbon, and it is unlikely that they ever will if penalties are not imposed on companies that produce it. The new dawn under which business is subjected to penalties is already being anticipated by some, and proving to be a profitable business in itself.

In anticipation of an agreement at COP6 in The Hague in November 2000, Garth Edward of Natsource, an emissions broker already trading in GHGs, estimated the cost of carbon (to its producers) at between US$1 and US$3 a tonne. *The Economist* reported that a pre-compliance market had already sprung up around carbon trading, and as the market developed the price was likely to rise. The World Bank's carbon fund (PCF) has been given the role of 'independently verifying' reductions in carbon emissions, and transferring credits from renewable energy schemes to the fund's investors. These are mainly energy utilities in Japan and Scandinavia. For example, some Japanese utilities, which cannot reduce their carbon emissions much more, are expected to 'buy' credits in projects for carbon reduction and substitution. Of course, the higher the price of carbon the greater the interest in cutting emissions.

In this respect, transnational corporations are *anticipating* governments by entering into agreements which help them attain their own business objectives, while providing a blueprint for much more extensive future negotiations. Shell, for example, has promised to cut GHG emissions by at least 10 per cent below 1990 levels by 2003. Carbon credits are one way of making these aspirations a reality, while also educating both buyers and sellers.

The other important dimension of this process of carbon accounting is accounting for carbon sinks. Many of the supposed carbon 'sinks' are in the developing world, and in areas such as tropical forests, which are under threat from a number of directions, including transnational corporations themselves. According to some recent models of sustainable development 'community mobilisation' can be undertaken through 'conservation-with-development'. Development is pursued, more sustainably, by tying it to the conservation of the environment. This approach emphasises the need to secure community access to valuable natural resources. However, the more we learn about the 'local' the more we realise that it is rarely *purely* local – it is created in part by extra-local influences and practices over time (Watts and Peet, 1996). Communities need to be situated within a broader institutional context (Agarwal, 1999, p. 640).

Defenders of carbon sinks as a future means of income generation in poor rural communities argue that in future the valuation of carbon sequestration (which is pressed particularly by the United States) can enhance community development efforts. Future accords, they argue, will provide such communities with a much valued bargaining tool in negotiations with governments and transnational companies. This will serve to transform theoretical 'willingness-to-pay' estimates into increased income opportunities (Fearnside, 1997; 2000).

As so often in the real world, however, these kinds of innovative mechanisms could also have perverse effects. In Brazil, for example, the biggest players are likely to be sugar-cane and paper-pulp industries, which are busily reinventing themselves as 'green' industries, positioning themselves for future carbon credits. Poor rural communities are still outside the policy 'loop' and unlikely to benefit in the short term.

4 BEYOND CARBON

Table I.1 illustrates the growth of dependence on carbon during the last century. This suggests that the use of biomass fuels, such as firewood and animal dung, has almost doubled in the two centuries since 1800. On the other hand, coal consumption increased five-fold in the twentieth century alone. The growth in oil consumption was even more dramatic, especially in the second half of the twentieth century. At the same time, global energy consumption is very unevenly distributed. Each individual in North America consumed almost three times as much energy as in Europe, and over ten times as much as in Sub-Saharan Africa and South Asia. These estimates include data from developing countries for non-commercial energy.

Table I.1   World fuel production (million tonnes)

Year	1800	1900	1990
Biomass	1000	1400	1800
Coal	10	1000	5000
Oil	0	20	3000
World energy use	21	100	1580

Source: McNeill (2000).

If we are to advance towards a cleaner, more sustainable, future the 'playing field' clearly needs to be levelled. At the moment energy consumption figures disguise huge, and largely hidden, subsidies to fossil fuels. These subsidies need to be made more transparent, and steps taken to reduce them dramatically. One policy measure that will help achieve this is the introduction of carbon taxes, to ensure that the price of fossil fuels reflects the true costs that they impose on human health and the environment.

At the same time, more progress needs to be made on renewable sources of energy. Some renewable energy technologies, such as wind power, are already becoming commercially viable, even in the absence of the level playing field. Denmark, for example, now produces sophisticated wind turbines that can compete in the world market. In some parts of Denmark, Germany and Spain almost 30 per cent of the energy used is from wind power. The principal problem of utilising wind power is that in the absence of cheap and efficient ways to store energy it is not readily dispatched. As energy markets have become liberalised this can present a serious problem – since green energy sources cannot compete effectively at peak rates. The next few decades should see technological breakthroughs in fuel cell technologies and in storage technologies, both of which should help overcome some of these problems in supply.

However, the greatest challenge, and opportunity, for renewable sources of energy, lies in the South where, during the next two decades, two-thirds of future energy demand will take place. Where the electric grid does not exist, or it is prohibitively expensive, renewable sources of energy can offer excellent *local* energy sources. If governments in the North do more to invest in, and support, renewables, the benefits flowing to the developing world are likely to increase substantially.

In the North, too, there are indications that our dependence on hydrocarbons can, gradually, be eased. A century ago, Thomas Edison built a plant near Wall Street, in New York, which was designed to provide a network of decentralised power plants, near people's homes. Economic development during the twentieth century took us closer towards the centralised grid; but at last the wheel is turning full-circle. There is growing awareness of the social and environmental costs of using fossil fuels: two million infant deaths in India are caused from the 'indoor' pollution of cooking stoves. Micro-power units enable power to be generated closer to home, closer to the end-user, and provide a real alternative where the central grid is not a feasible option.

Micro-power can also benefit from advances in software and electronics, and should enable a *combination* of power sources to be used. In the industrialised world new power plants can be built which use both natural gas and renewable energy. It is possible to foresee a future in which the national grid is used as a back-up to more localised sources of supply. 'Micro-grids' might be built which link together dozens of micro-power units, based on fuel cells and wind turbines, which themselves combine heat and power, providing a decentralised and locally-responsive source of energy with few adverse environmental consequences.

As we look towards developments in energy technology and rising levels of consumption in the twenty-first century, it is clear that our 'addiction' to carbon is not an intractable obstacle to improvements in human security. Indeed our dependence on fossil fuels was itself symptomatic of the view we took of 'external nature', of the biomass on which we depended for our life support systems. In the twenty-first century our definition of 'security' will have enlarged to include the *relationship* that obtains between human societies and nature, in which the growth of fossil fuels has been an essential part. Sustainability in the twenty-first century means not only internalising *external* environmental costs, through cleaner technologies for managing energy and waste production, but developing a clearer role for human beings which places individual needs within a broader, more future-oriented, perspective.

5　OUTLINE OF THE BOOK

The chapters in this book bear testimony to the way in which both 'security' and 'sustainability' are being reworked as concepts and increasingly linked to social, economic and cultural factors. The concept of human security has partly emerged in response to the neglect of human dimensions in thinking about environmental issues. Following Barnett (2001), a distinction can be made between threats to national security that arise from environmental degradation ('environmental security') and the impacts of human societies on the environment itself ('ecological security'). The importance of emphasising *human* security is that it suggests cognate areas of policy and discourse, such as environmental justice and human rights, which serve to broaden our understanding of environmental concerns. Of course, the link between human security on the one hand, and environmental security on the other, is itself quite subtle. It is the view of the editors that the latter is best viewed as a species of the former; that environmental threats such as those associated with global climate change are significant, but not exhaustive, determinants of human insecurity. Thus, when we talk of environmental insecurity we presuppose some degree of human insecurity, but not vice versa: some threats to human security arise through socio-economic variables which have little or no connection to environmental stress or degradation.

For the sake of simplicity, in what remains of this introduction we refer mainly to environmental (in)security and its determinants. However, it is worth observing that both *human* security and *environmental* security are relatively new and somewhat under-theorised concepts. They are also highly controversial, complex and contested. They are *controversial* mainly because these ideas cannot be easily accommodated into the traditional security discourses of international relations and political science. Human security, according to one of its most influential proponents, 'applies most at the level of the citizen. It amounts to human well-being: not only protection from harm and injury, but access to water, food, shelter, health, employment, and other basic requisites that are the due of every person on Earth' (Myers, 1993, p. 31). In focusing on the condition of individuals, and in emphasising the rights and moral standing of individuals in contrast to the states to which they belong, human/environmental security is not easily reconciled with traditional, state-centric accounts of security that focus on internal and external military threats to the territorial integrity of national states. That is, human/ environmental security is inconsistent with the well-entrenched view in international relations scholarship that security concerns 'the effort to protect a population and territory against organised force while advancing state interests through competitive behaviour' (Dabelko and Dabelko, 1995, p. 3).

The notion of environmental security is *complex* as a result of there being at least three plausible accounts of the nature of environmental security. What we might refer to as environmental security(1) focuses on the way in which environmental stress causes violent conflict (and thereby *in*security); environmental security(2) focuses on the way in which violent conflict exacerbates environmental stress (and thereby *in*security); and environmental security(3) encompasses both the way in which environmental stress causes violent conflict and the way in which violent conflict exacerbates environmental stress. The central focus of most of the papers in this book is the first of these accounts, although much ground is covered that is also relevant to the second and third understandings of security.

The notion of environmental security is *contested* as a result of it being prone to endless, irresolvable dispute regarding its meaning and application. This is not because the concept attracts alternative and conflicting accounts put forward in 'bad faith'. As W.B. Gallie has argued in the context of a discussion of political theorising, it is because disputes centred on concepts such as environmental security 'although not resolvable by argument of any kind, are nevertheless sustained by perfectly respectable arguments and evidence' (Gallie, 1956, p. 169). Put a different way, to say that a concept is essentially contested 'is to contend that the universal criteria of reason, as we can now understand them, do not suffice to settle these contests definitively' (Gallie, 1956, p. 169). Consider the disputes in security studies between the proponents of environmental security and their critics. The idea is that, while these writers appeal to a shared concept of environmental security in the sense that they will agree in

regarding a number of environmental variables as either potential or actual
threats to security, in many other situations they will disagree over the application of the concept. One interesting example of this contestedness, given by
Barnett, concerns the example of Australia (Barnett, 2001, pp. 24–5). He notes
that the different perceptions of military threats and environmental threats are
such that support for military budgets still far outweighs that for funding for
environmental preservation measures, despite the fact that any 'objective' analysis
of the Australian situation would suggest that the security of the population
would better be safeguarded by more resources being targeted towards the
latter than the former. Barnett goes on to point out that the problems of risk and
uncertainty, and their impact on people's perceptions of security threats, make
objective judgements of environmental security difficult to sustain. The idea is
that disputes between those who view environmental preservation as peripheral
to (national) security and those who view it as central are not necessarily driven
by bad faith or poorly constructed arguments on one or both sides, but rather
reflect features of the concept of security itself, namely, that its structure is
irreducibly complex and subjective.

5.1   Part I: Concepts

In the first section of the book, a number of conceptual issues surrounding the
link between environment and security are discussed. The starting point of
Edward Page's chapter 'Human Security and the Environment' is the claim
that global environmental change raises a number of questions for researchers engaged with the problems of the scope and content of security. Page
seeks to provide a conceptual overview of recent contributions to the notion
of 'environmental security' in order to bring into clearer focus the key issues
on which contributors to this important debate disagree. In particular, he
examines the claim that the concept of security should be extended in order
to accommodate (i) 'non-military threats' such as environmental degradation,
and (ii) the security status of entities other than the state. Page goes on to
outline a typology of views on the connection between environmental change
and security, which turns on the way we approach two key questions. First,
he asks what are the *subjects* of security discourse? (He goes on to call this
the *scope* question.) Second, he asks what sorts of things can be threats to
security? (He goes on to call this the *content* question.) In essence, the
argument of the chapter is that any cogent account of environmental security
must provide clear, and defensible, answers to these two questions. In the
course of his argument, Page raises some serious objections to what he calls
the 'moralised' nature of recent accounts of human security, before proposing
a methodological approach to issues of environmental security that draws on
the political theory of John Rawls.

Even if it is supposed that clear, and defensible, accounts can be given of the scope and content of environmental security, there are a host of other theoretical issues raised by this concept. Some of the most intriguing of these concern the relationship between environmental security and a range of other political ideals, such as democracy, civil society, social justice, freedom, community and equality. Perhaps the most discussed conceptual relationship concerns security and democracy. The recent wave of democratisation, for example in Eastern Europe, has stimulated much research on the beneficial effects of democracy on international affairs, notably on conflict resolution and economic development. Since most democracies are highly developed, and embrace free-market ideology, environmentalists have often been sceptical about the prospects for environmental preservation in democratic countries. While some have assumed that preserving the environment requires a strong, possibly authoritarian state, and that democracies seem incapable of solving 'tragedy of the commons' type dilemmas, recent literature suggests a more optimistic view. In Chapter 2, Nils-Petter Gleditsch and Bjørn Otto Sverdrup argue that despite the fact that democratic states have adopted patterns of development that have often been disastrous for the natural environment, they have a range of resources which can be mobilized in the future in order to manage environmental change. The heart of the paper is a ground-breaking empirical analysis which shows the generally positive bivariate effects of democracy on environmental performance, and more uniformly positive effects when controlling for the level of development. The authors conclude that democracies, in addition to overcoming national environmental degradation more efficiently, are also more effective conduits for cooperative solutions to international environmental problems.

As noted above, much of the discussion of environmental security has confused the implications of environmental problems for the human condition with the effects of human activities on the natural environment. This is the basis of the need to distinguish between *environmental security* and *ecological security.* In Chapter 3, Michael Redclift examines the way in which literature on the international dimension of sustainability has also confused the rights to 'manage' nature with the civil rights of populations, most of which are faced with difficult environmental problems and choices. It is suggested that we need to look hard at the basis for the legitimacy of our actions, and avoid confusing human rights in civil society with our obligations to environmental sustainability. The chapter goes on to argue that, before we can fully explain many of the paradoxes surrounding sustainability, we will need to disentangle some of the terms that have entered the discursive terrain.

One of the pre-eminent goals of recent social-scientific research on environmental sustainability has been the construction of scientifically robust and policy relevant indicators and indices covering a broad range of environmental and developmental variables. Research on development and poverty indices under the auspices of the United Nations Development Programme is a good example. In an attempt to assess progress toward achieving sustainability and human security, a number of analysts are working hard to identify indicators that measure both the state of (and people's access to) economic, social and natural resources. In Chapter 4, Steve Lonergan and associates, who are acknowledged leaders in this field of concern, address the problem of developing cross-national indices of human security that might provide the basis for more effective environmental policymaking. They explore the challenges associated with constructing robust indices of human (in)security, where human security is seen to focus on a secure livelihood for individuals and society and an absence of (armed) conflict. The authors review a selection of these indicator frameworks and various attempts that have been used to model indicators in order to identify future research opportunities.

5.2 Part II: Challenges

In the second section of the book, three particularly important challenges to environmental security are discussed. These are climate change, food security and water security. In Chapter 5, Johannes Stripple explains why global climate change is an issue of human *in*security *par excellence*. As he observes, climate change has been an issue on the scientific agenda for over a century, but has only recently become a focus for research in international relations and environmental politics. The implications of global climate change for patterns of international order and disorder have, therefore, yet to be revealed. As Stripple observes, scholars have in general viewed climate change as both a source of cooperation and as a source of insecurity, although the latter view has gained increasing support in the light of recent Intergovernmental Panel on Climate Change research reports on global warming (and its largely negative future impacts on human health and well-being). Stripple defends what he terms a 'constructivist' interpretation of climate change as a security issue. Constructivism in this context implies that neither what is counted as a security threat, nor the entities that we view as the focus of security discourse, can be determined prior to empirical analysis. Instead, questions can be asked about these issues, such as what are the reference objects of climate change: *who* or *what* might be threatened by it? Here, Stripple's discussion has interesting points of contact with Page's contribution on the environment–security relation. He also goes on to present a detailed summary of the climate change issue and how it may be approached, and an overview of the natural and human systems that are perceived to be sensitive and/or vulnerable to climate change.

In Chapter 6, Colin Sage discusses various issues surrounding the question of food security, which he takes to mean 'adequate access to food that is culturally and nutritionally appropriate throughout the year and from year to year'. There are two critical features of food security that have raised its profile in the discussion of human/environmental security in recent years. The first is the issue of world hunger and malnutrition. Drawing on research conducted by the UN, Sage notes that at least 800 million people in the world do not have enough food to eat, whereas over 30 million people in the developed world suffer from chronic food insecurity. The second feature is the way in which food security links to all of the key dimensions of human security (that is, political, economic, health and environment). Sage sets out to explore the concept of food security, to relate it to other dimensions of human security, and to see how it is applied at different geographical levels. After outlining recent developments in food security scholarship, for example the way in which it has been critical of the focus on calorific intake as being synonomous with nutrition, Sage goes on to outline the connection between environment and food security at different geographical levels. Particularly interesting, here, is his discussion of the food security impacts of climatic change (at the global level), civil conflict (at the national level) and gender inequality (at the local level). Finally, he discusses the limitations of recent food security interventions in Pakistan and Central America. He argues that these interventions have had limited success because they have failed to engage sufficiently with indigenous understandings and beliefs about food security, as well as with local-level experience of technology, production and other socio-economic variables. It is worth noting that Sage comes to similar conclusions in this regard to the other contributors to the volume who look at environmental security in the context of indigenous communities (Matthew in Chapter 9, Cocklin in Chapter 7 and Fernández-González et al. in Chapter 12).

Discussions of the link between environment and security often make reference to water. This is not surprising given that there are widespread scarcities of supply, water is essential to human survival, it has value in economic terms, and that some water management institutions are of strategic political significance. It seems that the extent and intensity of social, environmental, economic and strategic problems associated with water are bound to increase in the future. Numerous articles have addressed the link between competition for shared water resources and violent conflict. The view defended by Barandat and Kaplan is typical of many contributions to the 'water as a security issue' debate. The authors argue that

One area of regional conflict that is of global importance is access to fresh water. In the future, it will not only be a limiting factor in the production of food, but also a key to the development of industry. Hence, fresh water will become a major element that defines national security policy. Thus it is necessary to expand the definition of the term 'aggression' to include the deliberate withholding of water from a state. (Barandat and Kaplan, 1998, p. 12)

Consider the much discussed case of water supplies in the volatile Middle East region (see Myers, 1989, pp. 28ff; Homer-Dixon, 1991, pp. 13–14; Scheumann, 1998, pp. 113–34). At the heart of much, if not all, inter-state conflict in this region is the fact that 15 states compete with each other for fresh water supplies contained in just three river systems: the Nile, the Jordan, and the Euphrates. The demand for fresh water in the region consistently threatens to outstrip its supply, with the result that hostility and violent conflicts over water resources are a constant cause for concern. Aside from simple demand–supply issues, other factors have contributed to water insecurity in the region. One important factor is that a number of Middle-Eastern states are contemplating 'unilateral' dam projects which, although their primary purpose is to facilitate irrigation in order to increase agricultural output, threaten to divert water away from neighbouring states. A second factor is that the Middle East region is subject to significant population growth.

In the first of two chapters in the volume that address the link between water and human security, Chris Cocklin considers the under-researched question of the way in which access to, and quality of, water resources impacts upon cultural values and relationships. The point of departure in the discussion is the thought that 'inappropriate' uses of water, environmental degradation in water management, or competition-induced scarcity in water resources, can have just as pernicious an effect on the ability of cultural groups to sustain their livelihoods as they have on human and animal health. The analysis builds upon a well-established literature on the cultural significance (and the social construction) of the notions of 'nature' and 'environment'. Cocklin goes on to argue that decisions taken about the use and development of water resources can have the effect of undermining cultural security. This in turn rests on claims about the social construction of nature and the inseparability of nature/culture, and recent research on the nature/culture relation among indigenous peoples of New Zealand and Australia.

5.3   Part III: International Cases

The ending of the Cold War in Europe destroyed many of the old certainties about the character of threats, the meaning of security and the identity of the providers of security. It also coincided with the upsurge of public and political interest in global environmental change. As noted by both Page and Stripple, one consequence of this was an ongoing academic debate on the redefinition or extension of existing security concepts with particular reference to environmental threats. Although much of the recent research has been conducted in North America, there have also been significant European contributions.

Most academic work within Europe has avoided a radical re-conceptualisation of security along the lines proposed by writers such as Ullman (1983) and Myers (1989), and has instead focused on extending existing security concerns with armed conflict to encompass the consequences of environmental change. One example mentioned by John Vogler in Chapter 8 on European contributions to human/environmental security is EU-funded research that seeks to model the relationships between physical and socio-economic change and conflict behaviour. Such work has supported the insight offered by North American writers, such as Thomas Homer-Dixon (1991), that there exists no simple causal connection between environmental stress/degradation and violent conflict within, or between, states. Another example is the EU-funded Network on Environmental Security (NES) which provided the impetus for the present volume. The NES project brought together an international and multi-disciplinary group of researchers concerned with human/environmental security issues from across Europe in order to exchange ideas and facilitate pan-European research in the field. After outlining the political context into which ideas about environmental security were introduced at the European level, Vogler sets out to investigate how the EU has framed the question of environmental security, and to what extent the EU might become involved in environmental security politics. Much of the investigation is pursued in terms of the concept of 'securitisation'.

The relationship between environment and security has generated an enormous amount of interest in the academic community in recent decades. Although the scholarly interest in environmental security issues is truly international, it seems fair to say that the most distinguished contributions to the debate have originated in North America, and particularly in the US. As Richard Matthew argues in his chapter on the North American perspective on human/environmental security, researchers and policymakers in North America have been interested in the linkages between environmental change, conflict and security for over two decades. According to Matthew, the interest in these issues can be traced to research and policy opportunities created by the ending of the Cold War. As Myers (1989) argues, the US has been a fertile environment for scholars on all sides of the environment–security debate. Prominent defenders of the notion of environmental security (such as Norman Myers (1989), Thomas Homer-Dixon (1991) and Robert Kaplan (1996)) as well as prominent sceptics of it (such as Daniel Deudney (1993)) are all based in North America. It seems safe to say, then, that whatever the future of environmental security discourse, this future will be shaped profoundly by developments, and fashions, in American research and scholarship. In his chapter, Richard Matthew addresses the questions of why the notion of environmental security has generated such a following in North America, as well as what it means for the United States and for the rest of the world. He offers a brief overview of environmental security research and policy activities in North America, a review and assessment of principal areas of controversy and critique, and goes on to defend his own account that situates environmental security scholarship within the context of the unique status of both the US and environmentalism in contemporary world affairs.

Although the bulk of environmental security research being carried out today is being conducted in North America and the European Union, much of the focus of this research is on insecurities within the developing world. The well-being and human security of those belonging to developing countries is consistently undermined by a range of socio-economic and environmental factors which have much less threatening, and subtler, effects in the North. Just some of these factors are overpopulation, human rights abuses, civil war, political oppression, desertification, deforestation, human rights abuses, toxic contamination, soil degradation, pollution and loss of biodiversity. These natural and socio-economic factors represent the most significant threats to sustainable development and human security in the developing world. As Kwasi Nsiah-Gyabaah observes in Chapter 10, the importance of these factors is no more obvious than in the context of Sub-Saharan Africa (SSA), which is not only the poorest region in the world, but also the fastest growing. SSA is an interesting case study for scholars of human/environmental security for a variety of reasons. Many observers hold that it will be an increasingly important region of the world for international relations (Kaplan, 1994). The sheer scale of the environmental problems that the region faces also singles it out as a critical recipient – and test of the usefulness of – the rubric of human/ environmental security. Finally, as Gyabaah goes on to argue, recent developments in SSA suggest that some progress towards greater human security might be possible in the future given the appropriate balance of international investment/support, and local-level coordination. As a result, the rather pessimistic audit of environmental and other problems outlined in the early sections of his chapter (concerning, for example, food shortages, declining international investment, deforestation, land degradation, and post-1960s economic stagnation) is mitigated somewhat by other more positive developments such as increasing democratisation and local-level sustainable agriculture initiatives.

The increasing profile of environmental and human security, in both academic and policymaking circles, has been accompanied by a variety of political actors seeking to legitimise policy decisions in their name. Of course, such moves have attracted as much cynicism as they have support. In Chapter 11[1], Oscar Forero and Graham Woodgate pose an interesting question for analysts of environmental security that builds on this development. In what circumstances, they ask, would it be justifiable for policy elites to appeal to considerations of human/environmental security when the policies they advocate involve large-scale disruption to the lives of the populations of the states they are directed at? They observe that the circumstances, and policies, are unlikely to be similar to those of France's continued nuclear testing in the South Pacific, or the continued bombing of Iraq by NATO forces in February 2001. The articulation of a human/environmental security agenda to justify such actions seems wholly rhetorical, and even a little perverse. Other examples of foreign policy coordination, however, seem potentially more authentic attempts to reduce human insecurity. The authors seek to investigate one such attempt, which concerns the continuing effort to control the drug-trafficking industry in South America. Here, under 'Plan Colombia', a broad range of actions have been devised to reduce the capacity of Colombian cartels to export drugs to the US and elsewhere (one example given is the aerial application of herbicides chosen specifically to eradicate coca crops from large parts of the country, another is the threat of military action against farmers). As the authors argue, Plan Colombia reflects a complex and contradictory mixture of local, national and international initiatives that seek to promote human and environmental security. As they also observe, however, these initiatives are often very unpopular with the local population, seem to exacerbate existing inequities in the region, and are not uniformly effective as weapons against the drugs' cartels. The authors go on to examine the extent to which Plan Colombia, and other initiatives that involve the use of military force, might be justified on human/environmental security grounds and thereby rendered more acceptable to the civil societies of affected countries. This not only leads the authors to ask what the concepts of human/environmental security mean for the indigenous people of Northwest Amazonia, but also to ask what ideological grounds these people (individually and collectively) might accept as legitimating policies such as those mentioned above.

One interesting, and under researched, issue raised by Forero and Woodgate's analysis (and also raised in the earlier chapters by Cocklin and Sage) is the connection between culture on the one hand, and human/environmental security on the other. It is a fairly well-established principle in contemporary liberal political theory that cultural membership is a critical factor in the development and maintenance of a political system which treats people as deserving of equal concern and respect. This is because individuals need to operate within a well-established set of cultural norms and practices in order for them to flourish and act autonomously. To assume otherwise, it is argued, is to presuppose a wholly unrealistic view of human freedom according to which people can make sense of the opportunities they have in life completely free of cultural ties and roles. The reality, so it goes, is that culture and community provide a 'meaningful context for choice', as Kymlicka has put it (Kymlicka, 1990). Forero and Woodgate provide an illuminating discussion of the way in which cultural and aesthetic beliefs provide the background for the quite sophisticated 'agro-ecological' practices adopted by indigenous Amazonion peoples. They also discuss the way in which the complex political situation in the region has undermined the ability of these peoples to maintain their traditional ways of life. The importance of the Church and environmental conservationists, as well as other socio-economic variables, are highlighted in this regard. Finally, the authors make the interesting observation that these ways of life have developed free of the Western belief in a dichotomy between society and nature. As a result, it is more difficult than ever in this context to separate the discourse of human security on the one side, and environmental security on the other for, as they argue, these peoples 'do not see themselves as distinct from the environment in which they live, they are part of the "world" and in managing it they instinctively manage themselves'. It might strike some as odd, therefore, that policies such as Plan Columbia, which effectively exclude indigenous peoples from the management of lands they have farmed for centuries, can be justified on the grounds that they improve the security of the very people they displace.

As noted in relation to Chris Cocklin's chapter on water and cultural security, the health and well-being of humans and other species is critically dependent on the quality and availability of fresh water supplies. Degraded water stocks are a significant source of mortality and morbidity, particularly in the developing world. Threats to water resources will also have a range of effects on other socio-economic variables that can be expected to affect human well-being for the worse, such as economic development, population migration, political stability and competitiveness. As a result, the risks to public and environmental health stemming from the degradation or depletion of water resources constitute perhaps the greatest contemporary challenge to human/environmental security. One reason for this is that conflicts between users of the resource, and between different uses of it, can produce escalating costs and disturbances that have regional and international consequences. Some of these international consequences, it is argued, will relate to increasing violent conflict and war. Although inter-state competition for fresh water supplies are at their keenest in the Middle East, such competition, and the insecurities it threatens, are global in nature. According to Scheumann and Schiffler, approximately '40% of the world's population live in the watersheds of international rivers' (Scheumann and Schiffler, 1998, p. 1). The overwhelming importance of water as a life-sustaining resource, and the high population densities of communities living adjacent to the major river systems of the world, emphasise the massive potential for violent conflict over fresh water supplies.

It is within this context that Álvaro Fernández-González and associates provide a valuable contribution to the growing literature on water and human (in)security. The focus of this chapter is on the critical role that water resources play in the maintenance of human security in Costa Rica. The authors outline the current state of water resources in the country and go on to sketch some of the implications of the resource for human security, giving examples of the nature of conflicts arising in this context. The main focus of the chapter is on water quality and availability, with reference to three pivotal issues: population dynamics, water resource impacts, and institutional/policy responses. The point of departure of the chapter is the observation that, though water is generally abundant, there are signs that pollution and over-exploitation might pose a serious threat to the country's supplies of fresh water over the coming decades. In particular, they warn that tensions and contradictions will arise as a result of the alternative uses of water as a source and a sink. The authors report that conflicts over water pollution and over-exploitation have provoked a number of legal battles in the nation's courts, as well as tending to follow unconventional, occasionally violent, paths as a consequence of the shortcomings of the country's legal institutions and water management arrangements. They conclude their study with the thought that such conflicts are unlikely to go away given the pressures of future development and population growth.

NOTE

1. At the time this chapter was written three different events, which are of crucial importance to our analysis, had not yet taken place: 1. The terrorist attacks on the World Trade Center, which made explicit the switch from the politics of sustainability to the politics of security in the international globalisation discourse – something we had only discussed theoretically in our chapter, but now seem obvious post-September 11th 2001. 2. In May 2001, after much international pressure, the government of the U.S.A. finally included the rightwing paramilitaries of Colombia on their list of international terrorist groups, although the military actions of Plan Colombia continue to focus on the war against leftwing narco-guerrillas. 3. A revealing in-depth interview with Carlos Castaño, leader of the rightwing paramilitaries in Colombia, has recently been published (Aranguren-Molina M. 2001 "Mi Confesión. Carlos Castaño revela sus secretos". Oveja Negra. Bogotá). Our chapter suggests that an earlier television interview with Castaño represented a manoeuvre in his search for political recognition and national support for his regimen of terror, in the more recent interview this has become self-evident.

BIBLIOGRAPHY

Agarwal, A. (1999) 'Community and Natural Resource Conservation', in Fred Gale and Michael McGonigle (eds) *Nature, Power and Production*, Cheltenham, UK: Edward Elgar.

Barandat, J. and Kaplan, A. (1998) 'International Water Law: Regulations for Cooperation and the Discussion of the International Water Convention', in W. Scheumann and M. Schiffler (eds) *Water in the Middle East*, Heidelberg: Springer-Verlag, pp. 11–30.

Barnett, J. (2001) *The Meaning of Environmental Security*, London: Zed Books.

Beck, U. (1992) *Risk Society: Towards a New Modernity*, London: Sage.

Brandt Commission (1980) *North–South: a Programme for Survival*, London: Pan Books.

Brandt Commission (1983) *Common Crisis*, London: Pan Books.

Brock, L. (1991) 'Peace through Parks: The Environment on the Peace Research Agenda', *Journal of Peace Research*, Vol. 28, No. 4, pp. 407–23.

Brock, L. (1997) 'The Environment and Security: Conceptual and Theoretical Issues', in N.P. Gleditsch (ed.) *Conflict and the Environment*, Dordrecht: Kluwer Academic Publishers, pp. 17–34.

Dabelko, G. and Dabelko, D. (1995) 'Environmental Security: Issues of Conflict and Redefinition', *Environmental Change and Security Project Report*, Spring, pp. 3–13.

Dalby, S. (1992) 'Ecopolitical Discourse: "Environmental Security" and Political Geography', *Progress in Human Geography*, Vol. 16, No. 4, pp. 503–22.

Darier, E. (ed.) (1999) *Discourses of the Environment*, Oxford: Blackwells.

Deudney, D. (1993) 'Environment and Security: Muddled Thinking', *Bulletin of the Atomic Scientists*, April, pp. 22–8.

Diehl, P.F. (1998) 'Environmental Conflict: An Introduction', *Journal of Peace Research*, Vol. 35, No. 3, pp. 275–7.

Elliot. L. (1996) 'Environmental Conflict: Reviewing the Arguments', *Journal of Environment and Development*, Vol. 5, No. 2, June, pp. 149–67.

Fearnside, P. (1997) 'Environmental services as a strategy for sustainable development in rural Amazonia', *Ecological Economics*, Vol. 20, No. 1.

Finkler, K. (2000) *Experiencing the New Genetics*, Philadelphia: University of Pennsylvania Press.

Gallie, W.B. (1956) 'Essentially Contested Concepts', *Proceeding of the Aristotelian Society*, Vol. 56, pp. 167–98.

Ginsburg, F. and Rapp, R. (1995) *Conceiving the New World Order*, Berkeley: University of California Press.

Giorgi, L. and Redclift, M. (2000) 'European Environmental Research in the Social Sciences: research into Ecological Modernisation as a "Boundary Object"', *European Environment*, Vol. 10, No. 1, Jan/Feb, 12–23.

Gleditsch, N.P. (1997) 'Environmental Conflict and the Democratic Peace', in N.P. Gleditsch (ed.) *Conflict and the Environment*, Dordrecht: Kluwer Academic Publishers, pp. 91–106.

Gleditsch, N.P. (1998) 'Armed Conflict and the Environment: A Critique of the Literature', Vol. 35, No. 3, pp. 381–400.

Global 2000 Report (1982) *Report to the President*, London: Penguin Books.

Global Environment Outlook (1999) International Union for Conservation of Nature (IUCN) and United Nations Environment Program (UNEP), New York: Oxford University Press.

Goodman, D.E and Redclift, M.R (1991) *Refashioning Nature: Food, Ecology, Culture*, London: Routledge.

Graeger, N. (1996) 'Environmental Security?', *Journal of Peace Research*, Vol. 33, No. 1, pp. 109–16.

Homer-Dixon, T.F. (1991) 'On the Threshold: Environmental Changes as Causes of Acute Conflict', *International Security*, Vol. 16, No. 2, Fall, pp. 76–116.

Homer-Dixon, T.F. (1994) 'Environmental Scarcities and Violent Conflict: Evidence from Cases', *International Security*, Vol. 19, No.1, Summer, pp. 5–40.

Jordomara, L (ed.) (1986) *Languages of Nature*, London: Free Association Books.

Kaplan, R.D. (1994) 'The Coming Anarchy', *Atlantic Monthly*, Vol. 273, No. 3, February, pp. 44–76 (page numbers in text refer to reprinted version at atlantic.com/politics/foreign/anarchy.htm (pp. 1–35).

Kymlicka, W. (1990) *Contemporary Political Philosophy*, Oxford: Clarendon Press.

Latour, B. (1993) *We Have Never Been Modern*, Cambridge, MA: Harvard University Press.

Levy, M. (1995a) 'Is the Environment a National Security Issue?', *International Security*, Vol. 20, No. 2, Fall, pp. 35–62.

Levy, M. (1995b) 'Time for a Third Wave of Environment and Security Scholarship?', *Environmental Change and Security Project Report*, Spring, pp. 44–6.

Lipschutz, R.D. (1997) 'Environmental Conflict and Environmental Determinism: The Relative Importance of Social and Natural Factors', in N.P. Gleditsch (ed.) *Conflict and the Environment*, Dordrecht: Kluwer Academic Publishers, pp. 35–50.

Lonergan, S. (1997) 'Water Resources and Conflict: Examples from the Middle East', in N.P. Gleditsch (ed.) *Conflict and the Environment*, Dordrecht: Kluwer Academic Publishers, pp. 37–84.

Luke T.W. (1999) 'Environmentality as Green Governmentability', in E. Darnier (ed.) *Discourses of the Environment*, Oxford: Basil Blackwell.

Matthew, R. (1995) 'Environmental Security: Demystifying the Concept, Clarifying the Stakes', *Environmental Change and Security Project Report*, Spring, pp. 14–23.

Matthew, R.A. (1997) 'Rethinking Environmental Security', in N.P. Gleditsch (ed.) *Conflict and the Environment*, Dordrecht: Kluwer Academic Publishers, pp. 71–90.

McNeill, J. (2000) *Something New under the Sun: An Environmental History of the 20th Century*, Harmondsworth: Penguin.

Meadows, D.C., Randers, D.H and Behrens,W.W. (1972) *The Limits to Growth*, London: Pan Books.

Myers, N.S. (1989) 'Environment and Security', *Foreign Policy*, Vol. 74, Spring, pp. 23–41.

Myers, N. (1993) *Ultimate Security*, New York: W.W. Norton & Company.

Ohlsson, L. (ed.) (1995) *Hydropolitics: Conflicts over Water as a Development Constraint*, London: Zed Books.

Redclift, M.R. (1983) *Development and the Environmental Crisis*, London: Methuen.

Redclift, M.R. (1987) *Sustainable Development: Exploring the Contradictions*, London: Methuen.

Redclift,M.R. (1996) *Wasted: Counting the Costs of Global Consumption*, London: Earthscan.

Renger, J. (1998) 'The Middle East Peace Process: Obstacles to Cooperation over Shared Waters', in W. Scheumann and M. Schiffler (eds) *Water in the Middle East*, Heidelberg: Springer-Verlag, pp. 47–55.

Ronnfeldt, C. (1997) 'Three Generations of Environment and Security Research', *Journal of Peace Research*, Vol. 34, No. 4, pp. 473–82.

Sachs, W. (ed.) (1993) *Global Ecology: A New Arena of Political Conflict*, London: Zed Books.

Scheumann, W. (1998) 'Conflicts on the Euphrates: An Analysis of Water and Non-water Issues', in W. Scheumann and M. Schiffler (eds) *Water in the Middle East*, Heidelberg: Springer-Verlag, pp. 113–34.

Scheumann and Schiffler, M. (eds) (1998) *Water in the Middle East*, Heidelberg: Springer-Verlag.

Schiffler, M. (1998) 'Conflicts over the Nile or Conflicts on the Nile?', in W. Scheumann and M. Schiffler (eds) *Water in the Middle East*, Heidelberg: Springer-Verlag, pp. 137–50.

Simonis, I. (1989) 'Ecological Modernisation of Industrial Society: Three Strategic Elements', *International Social Science Journal*, vol. 121, pp. 347–61.

Soroos, M.S. (1994) 'Global Change, Environmental Security, and the Prisoner's Dilemma', *Journal of Peace Research*, Vol. 31, No. 3, pp. 317–32.

Ullman, R. (1983) 'Redefining Security', *International Security*, Vol. 8, No. 1, Summer, pp. 129–53.

Vogler, J.(2000) *The Global Commons: Environmental and Technological Governance*, Chichester: John Wiley.

Waever, O. (1995) 'Securitization and Desecuritization', in R.D. Lipschutz (ed.) *On Security*, New York, Columbia University Press, pp. 46–86.

Watts, M. and Peet, R. (1996) 'Towards a Theory of Liberation Ecology', in R. Peet and M. Watts (eds) *Liberation Ecologies*, London: Routledge.

WCED (World Commission on Environment and Development) (1987) *Our Common Future*, Oxford: Oxford University Press.

Westing, A.H. (1989) *Global Resources and International Conflict: Environmental Factors in Strategic Policy and Action*, Oxford: Oxford University Press.

World Conservation Strategy (1983) *Living Resource Conservation for Sustainable Development*, Gland, Switzerland: IUCN, UNEP.

World Conservation Strategy (1991) *Caring for Nature* (the Second World Conservation Strategy), Gland, Switzerland: IUCN, UNEP.

PART I

Concepts

1. Human security and the environment

Edward Page

1 INTRODUCTION

The phenomenon of global environmental change (that is, of natural and human induced changes in the Earth's environment, affecting land use and land cover, biodiversity, atmospheric composition and climate) raises a number of interesting questions for scholars of political science and international relations. Some of these concern the way in which states might cooperate in order to mitigate, or adapt to, the environmental stresses associated with climatic change, deforestation, declining species diversity and so on. Others relate to the way in which global environmental change may exacerbate existing inequalities across space and time. In this chapter, I want to pursue the question of links between environmental change and some rival conceptions of security.

On the face of it, the prospect of securing a full reconciliation between the notions of environmental change and security are not encouraging. This is because the traditional focus of work on security has been on the investigation of military threats to the territorial integrity of a given state that arise either *externally* (from the military activities of other states) or *internally* (from the subversive, and generally violent, activities of terrorist groups). The security studies literature usually, though not exclusively, views individual states as sovereign entities that pursue their own advantage in a context where other states do the same. That is, this literature is on the whole shaped by *neo-liberal* and *neo-realist* assumptions, such as the assumption that the behaviour of states is determined by the structure of power relations in the international environment.

The problem is that it is not easy to see how any non-military phenomena, not least those arising from highly complex and unpredictable biological and physical systems associated with environmental change, might threaten a state's security when security is viewed in this rather restricted sense. Traditional accounts of security during the Cold War period held that the paradigmatic threat to national security was the capacity of another state to mount a decisive nuclear attack. This reflected the fact that Cold War security theorists were preoccupied with the thought that a decisive strike against the people and institutions of any state could be translated from threat to reality in a matter of minutes. The consequence of this preoccupation was that the politics of nuclear confrontation, and nuclear weapons proliferation, became the key focus of security scholarship during this period. Threats to national security that did not have the special characteristics of nuclear attack – in short, immediacy and decisiveness – were often neglected.

However, several considerations have combined in recent years to under-mine the view that security studies should be restricted to considering military threats, such as nuclear attacks. Three of these considerations are particularly worth mentioning (Matthew, 1997, pp. 75ff). First, the break-up of the Soviet Union had the consequence that the threat of full-scale nuclear confrontation between the superpowers diminished. As the credibility of the paradigmatic threat to national security receded, many security scholars, and the security community in general, warmed to the idea that there might be non-military threats to national security. Second, awareness of the increasing interdepend-ence of economic relations throughout the world, as manifested in a series of global economic and financial crises, has led to an awareness that destabilising changes in economic variables in one part of the world can lead to significant levels of instability and insecurity in distant states. Third, increasing evidence has emerged that certain environmental changes could well endanger the existence of whole communities, as well as exacerbating already existing social evils such as poverty, mortality, morbidity, overpopulation and so on. This consideration has gained particular salience in the light of successive internationally authored reports on the scientific basis, and likely human impact, of global climate change (McMichael et al., 1996, pp. 564ff).

In this chapter, I set out to illuminate the considerations mentioned above and to provide a conceptual overview which brings into clearer focus the key issues on which contributors to the debate on environmental security differ. Section 2 considers the claim that the concept of security should be extended (i) in order to cover non-military threats and (ii) in order to cover the security of non-state entities. In Section 3 I outline a new typology of views on the connection between environmental change and security. I conclude by outlin-ing a methodological approach to issues of environmental security that draws on the political theory of John Rawls.

2   COMPREHENSIVE AND DE-MILITARISED SECURITY

A popular assumption in the security literature is that conflicts over natural resources are a perennial source of war (Gleditsch, 1997, p. 91; Elliot, 1996, pp. 152ff; Brock, 1991, pp. 408ff). Ullman, for example, argues that resource conflict is at the root of most violent conflicts in history (Ullman, 1983, p. 290; World Commission on Environment and Development, 1997, p. 290; Brock, 1991, p. 409). As well as investigating alleged past and present instances of resource-driven conflicts, much of the literature on environmental security seeks to defend the claim that environmental stress is a major, and growing, cause of violent conflict and insecurity – particularly in the developing world. That this is a distinct claim to be defended and criticised independently of the resource-war issue is evident in the fact that the origins of resource wars cannot always be traced to conflicts over transboundary environmental stresses (such as pollution, for example) but rather to conflicts which arise purely over the possession of scarce resources. This suggests that there may be two key understandings of environmental conflict, and thus environmental security (Gleditsch, 1998, pp. 38ff). The first concerns the way in which conflicts over natural resources threaten to undermine the security of states. The second concerns the way in which degradations of the environment threaten to undermine the security of states, and possibly other entities. This chapter concentrates on the latter understanding because I assume that this is the issue we are mostly concerned about when discussing the link between environmental change and security.

Environmental change is often assumed to be a much more indirect cause of violent conflict than inter-state rivalry for precious resource ownership. According to Elliot, for example, to the extent that environmental change gives rise to violent conflict, it does this by 'interacting with other social, economic, political and cultural drivers which (taken together) reduce instability in a given domain' (Elliot, 1996, p. 159). Moreover, according to the World Commission on Environment and Development, 'poverty, injustice, environmental degradation, and conflict interact in complex and potent ways' (World Commission on Environment and Development, 1987, p. 291). The sorts of socio-economic drivers which have attracted most interest in the literature concern the impact of growing environmental stress on demographic variables, such as mass migrations and refugee crises; economic variables such as total employment; and civil strife and unrest (Elliot, 1996, pp. 159ff; World Commission on Environment and Development, 1997, pp. 291ff).

Perhaps the most sophisticated research on the link between environmental change and violent conflict has emerged from the work carried out at Toronto University by Thomas Homer-Dixon et al. This research was, above all, motivated by a lack of satisfaction with the level of abstraction that permeated early debates on the re-conceptualisation of security, which attempted to accommodate non-military threats into discussions of security on the basis of 'anecdotal' evidence of the importance of these threats. As Lonergan et al. have put it, the conceptual debates about the broadening of security had given rise to 'a number of plausible hypotheses, but rigorous studies were lacking' (Lonergan et al., 1999, p. 29). I think we can explain the frustration with the early conceptual debates about the extension of the concept of security with recourse to the idea of essential contestedness. The concept of security appears to be a clear example of a concept that is prone to endless, irresolvable dispute regarding its meaning and application. This is not because such concepts attract interpretations put forward in bad faith. As W.B. Gallie has argued, this is because disputes centred on concepts such as security 'although not resolvable by argument of any kind, are nevertheless sustained by perfectly respectable arguments and evidence' (Gallie, 1956, p. 169).

In response to the irresolvable conflicts which come as an inevitable consequence of conceptual discussions of the meaning, value, scope and content of security, the strategy of Homer-Dixon and associates was to employ a much narrower, and empirically driven, focus on the way in which environmental stress gives rise, either directly or indirectly, to violent conflict in various parts of the world.[1] These researchers identified several case studies which appeared to demonstrate a link between environmental change and violent conflict, and went on to investigate the underlying resource scarcities and environmental stresses (Homer-Dixon, 1994, p. 7).

It is worth outlining the four key interim findings of this research. First, that the most important variables concerned in environmental causes of violent conflict are land, forests, water and fish. (Homer-Dixon found, however, that undue attention has been placed hitherto on the potential of ozone depletion and global climate change to cause violent conflicts.) Second, that there are three main sources of environmental stress: environmental change, population growth and social inequality (Homer-Dixon, 1994, p. 8). Third, that these three sources of environmental resource scarcity interact with (and reinforce) each other (Homer-Dixon, 1994, pp. 8–16ff). Fourth, that societies that are able to adapt to environmental stress are more likely to avoid significant turmoil and conflict than those that are not (Homer-Dixon, 1994, pp. 16–17).

Pulling these findings together, they found that there was 'substantial evidence' for the claim that environmental scarcity causes violent conflict. They argue that 'although more study is needed, the multiple effects of environmental scarcity, including large population movements and economic decline, appear likely to weaken sharply the capacity and legitimacy of the state in some poor countries' (Homer-Dixon, 1994, p. 25).

2.1   Environmental Change, National Security, and Human Security

Granted that environmental variables are factors in both resource conflicts and certain disputes either between people living in the same state, or between people living in different states, or between states as such, what is the exact nature of the connection between environmental change and security? Does the fact that environmental change leads *indirectly* to a certain amount of conflict within, and between, states mean that such changes are significant threats to national (or some other conception of) security? Are environmental changes the sorts of phenomena that can threaten security? It is my view that these questions do not simply reflect hypotheses which are raised by conceptual analyses of the general proposition that non-military threats can affect security – the answers we give to them will often *depend* on the coherence of such propositions. As a result, we have more reason to investigate the conceptual-level debates about the scope of security discourse than Homer-Dixon and associates realise. In the remainder of this section I survey some of the seminal contributions to these debates

A number of writers have defended the view that many things are threatening in security terms aside from military threats. These writers can be divided into two camps depending on the account they offer of the scope of security discourse. The first camp seeks to include non-military threats in discussion of security but only insofar as these threats undermine the security of states; the second camp seeks to include non-military threats in discussion of security insofar as these threats undermine the security of both states and certain other entities. The key difference between the camps, then, is that members of the former camp retain the traditional rubric of national security whereas member of the latter embrace the more radical rubric of human security.

An early, and influential, example of first camp thinking is to be found in the work of Richard Ullman. He argues that

> Defining national security merely (or even primarily) in military terms conveys a profoundly false image of reality. That false image is doubly misleading and therefore doubly dangerous. First, it causes states to concentrate on military threats and to ignore other and perhaps even more harmful dangers. Thus it reduces their security. And second, it contributes to a pervasive militarization of international relations that in the long run can only increase global insecurity. (Ullman, 1983, p. 129)

Ullman goes on to propose a broader definition of security according to which

> a threat to national security is an action or sequence of events that (1) threatens drastically and over a relatively brief spell of time to degrade the quality of life for the inhabitants of a state, or (2) threatens significantly to narrow the range of policy choices available to the government of a state or to private, nongovernmental entities (persons, groups, corporations) within the state. (Ullman, 1983, p. 133)

One problem for de-militarised views of security, such as Ullman's, is that instances of organised violence and environmental degradation quite often pose very different sorts of threats to human communities. Environmental problems such as climate change, ozone depletion, deforestation and so forth undoubtedly contribute massively to mortality and morbidity rates throughout the world, but to say that in so doing they undermine the security of the states where they hit hardest in the same way as wars and other violent conflicts seems problematic. The problem is that labelling anything that causes a decline in human well-being a security threat may result in the term losing 'any analytical usefulness', as Deudney has put it (Waever, 1995, p. 63; Deudney, 1991, p. 24).

Suppose that wars and environmental stresses gave rise to an identical incidence of morbidity and mortality in a given state in a given year. Would they pose equally prominent threats to national security? There are at least three reasons to think that they would not. First, at the heart of the traditional literature on security is the plausible, though largely unexamined, assumption that there is an important *intentional* aspect to the sorts of threats which undermine a state's security. Wars between states seem to have an inherent intentional aspect, at least on the side of the aggressor, whereas the environmental changes which *appear* to bring about insecurity are more often than not either (i) the unintended, and unwelcome, by-products of human action, (ii) the products of natural forces, or (iii) some combination of (i) and (ii) (Waever, 1995, p. 63; Deudney, 1991, p. 24).

Consider the issue of global climate change. It seems fair to say that most scientists believe that human action is responsible for at least some of the climatic changes that they have detected in recent decades. However, no one seriously believes that people intentionally set out to increase greenhouse gas (GHG) concentrations in the atmosphere for the hell of it. Rather we believe that, to the extent that human actions are responsible for increasing concentrations of GHGs, this is an unfortunate side effect of other intentional action (for example, the widespread use of vehicles with petrol engines). To the extent that we think an environmental change, X, has to have been brought about intentionally for it to threaten an agent, Y's, security we will not view many of the climatic changes projected by the Intergovernmental Panel on Climate Change as threatening to Y in security terms (though of course, this is not to say that we cannot claim that such changes harm or worsen the condition of that agent in some way that doesn't connect to questions of security).

Second, environmental threats and threats of violence have very different sources and impacts. No one state is responsible for the majority of the anthropogenic GHG emissions that drive global climatic change, and no single state will be the sole recipient of the predominantly bad effects of climatic change. Rather, the causes and effects, costs and benefits, of climate change (as well as many other environmental changes) cannot be entirely explained in terms of national states. The causes and effects of organised violence, however, are much more readily investigated through the lens of the state and its security.

Third, the traditional focus of security studies has been on violent conflict of a particular kind, namely, violence directed towards State A from State B. As both Weaver and Deudney have observed, this 'insider vs. outsider' thinking is deeply ingrained in the security studies literature (Waever, 1995, p. 63; Deudney, 1991, p. 24). According to the traditional view, a threat of violence must have at least some external dimension to be a credible threat to national security; this is true even of threats which emanate from individuals and groups within the state, who are generally regarded as being 'outsiders' or 'the enemy within'. The proponents of de-militarised, or non-statist, conceptions of security often point to examples of environmental stress giving rise to civil, political and economic discontent and violence in various regions. In the vast majority of cases, these stresses have emerged as a result of the behaviour of both the government and population of those regions. But, in this case, where does the external aspect of such threats arise? As Deudney writes: 'existing groups of opponents in world politics do not match the causal lines of environmental degradation' (Deudney, 1991, p. 24).

Let us now turn to the second camp of thinking on the scope of security discourse. An influential source of this thinking is research being carried out under the auspices of the Global Environmental Change and Human Security (GECHS) project.[2] According to GECHS,

> human security is achieved when and where individuals and communities have the options necessary to end, mitigate, or adapt to threats to their human, environmental, and social rights; [and] have the capacity and freedom to exercise these options and actively participate in attaining these options. (Lonergan et al., 1999, p. 29)

A similar view is also held by Myers, who argues that

> in essence, and little though this is generally recognised by governments, security applies most at the level of the individual citizen. It amounts to human wellbeing: not only protection from harm and injury but access to other basic requisites that are the due of every person on earth. (Myers, 1993, p. 31)

One question that both the Myers and the GECHS conceptions of human security raise is whether human security can obtain in the context of states which either have not fully entrenched basic welfare systems to guarantee some level of economic equality, or political rights to guarantee equality of democratic citizenship. This is because these rather broad definitions of human security incorporate fairly sophisticated notions of human autonomy and well-being, the implication being that we cannot discuss the security or insecurity of entities without considering the question of whether these entities operate in conditions conducive to their autonomy or overall well-being. The GECHS definition, for example, assumes that democracy is a necessary condition of security, and in doing so it plays down the importance of geographical, demographic, ethnic, and historical factors that influence the political and socio-economic significance of environmental events. These factors are at the very least partly independent of the political system they relate to, and would seem far more relevant to the issue of environmental insecurity than issues of democracy or autonomy. Consider the example of climate change. The Intergovernmental Panel on Climate Change (IPCC) suggest that the developed countries will be in a much better position to adapt to (and mitigate certain aspects of) climate change than developing states.[3] However, much of the final distribution of the insecurities brought about by climate change will be shaped by non-political variables, such as geography and demography. It is not the fact that the Bangladeshi state has perennial problems guaranteeing its citizens equal political rights and freedoms that may bring about its destruction in the light of rising sea-levels, but rather the fact that much of its population and industry is located along its low-lying coast.[4]

The highly moralised understandings of security defended by GECHS and Myers raises at least three further problems. First, they raise the question of the link between the concept of security and the value of security. Most discussions of security attempt to keep these two issues apart, and claim that insightful judgements can be made about the extent to which an entity, such as the state, is secure without taking a stand on the issue of whether this security is ethically valuable. These accounts are narrow in the sense that they seek only to put forward an account of the necessary and sufficient conditions of a certain entity being secure from external or internal threats, rather than a moralised account of the higher ethical purpose which security might serve.

The second problem is that these understandings run up against the consideration that many states, groups or individuals seem to maintain a fairly high degree of security in the absence of at least some social and political freedom. This seems a fair reflection of the situation of the Soviet Union in the Cold War period, for example; and it might also be a fair reflection of the situation that the Chinese enjoy at present. Are we to say that individuals living in an economically and militarily secure society are insecure if the only reasons we can come up with to explain this is that the conditions of democracy and autonomy are not protected in that society? Is it really the case that individuals or communities which operate within a non-democratic context should always be viewed as less secure than those individuals or communities which are fortunate enough to exist within the context of social or liberal democracy?

Third, to have any point of contact with traditional understandings of security, as well as avoiding being subsumed into the concept of well-being, human security must be restricted to a few basic conditions which enable individuals, and communities, to pursue the values which they affirm (whatever they may be). As some of these values might not be consistent with the ideal of autonomy, or indeed equality of democratic citizenship, we cannot build these predominantly liberal values into the definition of human security. In effect, the problem is that the Myers–GECHS view fails to keep apart the meaning of security and the value of security.

3 TOWARDS A TYPOLOGY OF ENVIRONMENTAL SECURITY

There are three key aspects of the debate between proponents of the national security and human security paradigms (and their off-shoots) regarding the extension of the concept of security. These are brought into focus when three questions are posed:

- What is the nature of the entity whose security matters from the point of view of security discourse? (*The scope question*)
- From what phenomena is such an entity at risk of being rendered insecure? (*The content question*)
- Is environmental change a threat to the subjects of security discourse? (*The environment question*)

In essence, the response of Ullman and other proponents of what I will call the (narrow) comprehensive view of national security is that while we do not need to revise the traditional view's insistence that it is the state which is the subject of security discourse, we do need to revise the traditional view's insistence that it is only external military threats to (and the domestic order of) the state that mark out the appropriate objects of security discourse. That is, these writers answer 'state' in response to the first question; and 'military and non-military threats' in response to the second question. If these writers also view environmental changes and stresses as bona fide non-military threats to a state's security I will refer to them as proponents of *environmental national security*.

The response of Myers and other proponents of what I will call the (wide) comprehensive view of human security is that we need to drop both the claim that it is the state which is the sole subject of security discourse and the claim that it is only military threats to states that are the appropriate objects of security discourse. That is, these writers answer 'state or other relevant entity' in response to the first question; and 'military and non-military threats' in response to the second question. If these writers also view environmental changes and stresses as bona fide non-military threats to a state's security I will refer to them as proponents of *environmental human security*.

3.1   The Scope of Security

There are a number of entities, other than the national state, which might be the subjects of security discourse. For example, a key necessary condition of an entity being the prima facie subject of security or insecurity is that alternative developments in the world at large render that entity more or less insecure. Consider Wolfer's influential definition of security, according to which security 'in an objective sense, measures the absence of threats to acquired values, in a subjective sense, the absence of fear that such values must be attacked' (Wolfers, 1962, p. 150; and quoted in Scanlon, 1996, p. 131). Several entities other than the state would seem to pass this test, the most obvious of these being individual human beings, sub-statal groups (such as ethnic or linguistic minorities), supra-national organisations (such as the EU), and perhaps the Earth's population considered as a whole. Moreover, if we were to embrace either a zoocentric or ecocentric (as opposed to the standard anthropocentric) approach to security we might go on to suggest more radical suggestions for the subjects of security studies, such as the biosphere itself or other animal species.[5]

It is true that some scholars appear to rule out the possibility of extending the scope of security by assuming that the only coherent and useful understanding of security is that of national security. But this assumption is rarely examined. In an otherwise illuminating discussion of the problems of defining both environment and security, for example, Levy fails to consider definitions of anything other than national security (Levy, 1995). This might not be such a defect if he at any stage provided an argument for why the scope of security studies should be restricted to cover national states only, but he does not do so. A similar objection can be made to Deudney's work (Deudney, 1991, pp. 23–4). Deudney shares Levy's scepticism of the notion of environmental security, and outlines several dissimilarities between traditional security threats and the environmental security threats outlined by proponents of de-militarised, or non state-centric, conceptions of security such as Myers. However, these dissimilarities themselves rest on an under-

		What are the subjects of security discourse?	
		Only states	States & other entities
What sorts of things can threaten the subjects of security discourse?	Military threats only	Narrow statist security	Narrow comprehensive security
	Military & non-military threats	Wide statist security	Wide comprehensive security

Figure 1.1   Rethinking the scope and content of security discourse

standing of security discourse as being concerned essentially with national security and threats of organisational violence. (See Figure 1.1)

3.2   The Content of Security

According to proponents of *comprehensive security*, the notion of security should be amended to incorporate a sensitivity to various non-military threats to national security. The threats which the comprehensive conception seeks to introduce into security debates will usually arise out of circumstances which endanger certain entrenched societal values or goals, but where the values concerned are not themselves threatened as a result of organised violence but rather as a result of some alternative cultural, social, environmental or political process. However, these threats might be conceived of as threatening values that underpin either human or national security (or both). Among the multitude of national security-affecting values which are discussed in the literature are the following: respect for individual/collective human rights and norms of justice; income, wealth generation and international competitiveness; population control; respect for cultural diversity; gender related inequalities; health; respect for law and order; and, of course, environmental change. (See also Figure 1.1)

3.3   Environment and Security

We have already looked in detail at some of the arguments in favour of extending security discourse to include within its remit environmental threats. Suffice it to say that the typology put forward in Figure 1.1 makes a crucial distinction between versions of comprehensive security which embrace environmental threats to security and those that are state-centric. I call these state-centric versions *environmental national security views*, and those that are not state-centric I call *environmental human security views*.

4   ENVIRONMENTAL SECURITY, REFLECTIVE EQUILIBRIUM AND COMMON POOL RESOURCES

In this concluding section I want to defend the view that a fruitful 'way of investigating the link between environmental change and security is to adopt the methodological strategy of seeking a balance between empirical data about the conflicts which environmental change brings about and theoretical insights into (environmental) security. According to this view, a cogent theory of national security (as in the case of other political concepts such as social justice or democracy) must cohere with at least some of our most deeply held convictions about (environmental) security and other empirical evidence that bears on this matter. This is not to say, however, that this methodological strategy requires us to evaluate the theories considered solely according to the extent to which they reflect empirical work on the conflictual outcomes caused by environmental change. However, it does mean that we seek to take empirical data seriously in our investigation of the concept of security.

There are a number of ways in which this 'coherentist' approach might be developed, but perhaps the most obvious is captured by the notion of reflective equilibrium. The notion of reflective equilibrium was introduced by Rawls (Rawls, 1971, pp. 20 and 48ff). In *A Theory of Justice*, Rawls addresses the issue of how we might best characterize the relation between our common-sense beliefs and our ethical or political theories. Do the former stand in need of the latter for their justification? Or is the acceptability of these beliefs constrained by considerations of theory? Or is the justifiability of ethics constrained in some way by our considered common-sense beliefs? Rawls suggests that, rather than privileging either side of the equation, we should attempt to find a balance, or equilibrium, between pre-theoretical and theoretical ethical beliefs. The basic procedure for doing this is as follows. First, we start with our most considered pre-theoretical beliefs about a political or ethical issue purged of basic inconsistencies. Second, we attempt to construct a theory that will explain and give unity to these beliefs. Third, we ask whether this theory implies that we ought to change or modify some of our pre-theoretical beliefs. Fourth, and depending on our answer to this question, we have basically two options: (a) to return to theory and adjust it until it delivers acceptable results, or (b) to give up some elements of the pre-theoretical position. Whether we choose (a) or (b), Rawls thinks, depends on the circumstances of the case. If the theory is particularly attractive, and any modifications to it appear arbitrary, then we may decide to reject the common-sense beliefs that we started with (an approach which we might refer to as 'biting the bullet'). This is an attractive move if we can give a good explanation of why the common-sense view is obviously unsound which is independent of the theory we give. If, however, the common-sense view is very firmly held, then we might wish to modify the theory. Basically, the overall aim is to reach a point with which we are, on balance, satisfied; where we have reached a 'reflective equilibrium' between common-sense beliefs about particular practices and our best candidate political or ethical theory.

Of course, the raw data we will be appealing to in the context of (environmental) security debates will be empirical research on the link between environmental change and violent conflict, or cooperation, rather than the pre-theoretical beliefs people have about the nature of security (although these may prove relevant at some point in the procedure). Nonetheless, the method of reflective equilibrium appears well suited to issues of environmental security for, as Homer-Dixon and associates have demonstrated, there is much empirical data that can be collected, and which is relevant, to the link between environmental change and alternative understandings of security. This empirical research has addressed the issue of the socio-economic and socio-political impacts of international resource conflicts and transboundary environmental problems, and as a result contrasting theories of the environment–security link can at least in principle be tested against the results of this research. This does not, of course, imply that the findings of these empirical projects should be viewed uncritically, for the nature of reflective equilibrium as an approach to political and ethical issues is that of seeking a balance between the importance of gathering raw data which has a bearing on the matters at hand and the fact that these findings will need to be constantly interpreted in the light of fresh theoretical insights, as well as fresh empirical findings. However, it does suggest that an approach to security issues that takes empirical research seriously will have a rich source of empirical data to draw upon.

One interesting application of the reflective equilibrium approach in this context is that it seems to undermine recent taxonomies of environmental security which refer to the existence of three distinct 'generations' or 'waves' of work on environment–security links, such as those proposed by Ronnfeldt and Levy (Ronnfeldt, 1997, pp. 473ff; Levy, 1995, pp. 44–6). According to

Ronnfeldt, for example, the first generation of environmental security research 'refers to an ongoing interdisciplinary debate in the academic and political community on whether and how environmental issues should be incorporated into security concerns'; the second generation refers to the attempt to 'deviate from the conceptual polemic and to base research on firm empirical ground'; and the third generation refers to the attempt to place environment and security research on firmer methodological ground (Ronnfeldt, 1997, pp. 473ff). The flaw in such typologies, though, is that they do not take adequate account of the fact that the different approaches to environmental security referred to do not come in and out of existence (and more to the point, they do not come in and out of relevance) in any linear fashion. Rather a real grasp of the issues surrounding the security–environment debate requires constant reciprocal interaction between them. For this reason I prefer to view the categories described by Ronnfeldt as 'levels' of environmental security thinking – though with the rider that I am not convinced either that there really exists a 'third level' of discourse which is independent of the first and second levels.

There is another interesting application of reflective equilibrium that is worth raising. As was explained above, this methodological approach stresses the importance of both empirical studies of environmental conflict and theoretical conceptual work on the nature and scope of security discourse. No one side is privileged over the other: the method requires bringing both of these approaches into coherence with each other, not maintaining the priority of one over the other. One way of putting this is to observe that it is the conceptual work of theorists that give rise to hypotheses which empirical research can test; and it is the empirical findings of this empirical research which will often, though not always, result in a particular conceptual view being amended. The empirical work of Homer-Dixon and associates has, for example, given theorists much food for thought. For example, it seems to put a certain amount of pressure on defenders of traditional militarised conceptions of security to reformulate their views. As we have seen, however, the research on environmental stress and violent conflict conducted by Homer-Dixon and associates is to a certain extent flawed. The main problem with it is the lack of any control group associated with their case study analyses; they are looking for links between environmental variables and violent conflicts only in cases where conflicts have already emerged. If we are to make a serious attempt at pursuing a reflective equilibrium between environmental security theory and environmental security practice, we really need a fresh impetus on the empirical side.

Aside from recommending more research which involves variability across both the independent variable (environmental change) and the dependent variable (violent conflict), what else might we suggest? It is my view that the next breakthrough in environmental security research will be achieved by seeking and developing linkages between research on environmental causes of violent conflict and research on the emergence of cooperative solutions to environmental resource dilemmas, such as those surrounding the issue of Common Pool Resources. According to the seminal definition proposed by Elinor Ostrom, Common Pool Resources (CPRs) are 'natural and human-constructed resources in which (i) exclusion of beneficiaries through physical and institutional means is especially costly, and (ii) exploitation by one user reduces availability for others' (Ostrom et al., 1999, pp. 278ff). CPR resource systems are particularly prone to dilemmas in which people acting within the paradigm of unconstrained self-interest become trapped in a set of behaviours that lead to the overuse, and eventual destruction, of the resources they depend upon. This is because instrumentally rational agents faced with a finite resource which is open to all will over-exploit this resource as a result of the fact that each receives the benefits of his own actions, while only bearing a share of the costs resulting from the resource's over-exploitation. Typical CPR systems would be constructed around agricultural land or marine ecosystems.

According to early work on CPRs, pioneered by Garrett Hardin, the potential tragedy of overuse and destruction of common resources could only be avoided by two developments: either (1) the resources must be taken into private ownership, or (2) the state must take over ownership and control of the resources (Hardin, 1968; 1998). At the heart of Ostrom's approach, however, is the thought that Hardin's 'tragedy of the commons' model is not inescapable. Rather, it is her view that in a number of cases CPR dilemmas can be solved, though this depends on certain preconditions obtaining. The most important of these conditions concern the emergence of reciprocity and trust between those who operate within any given CPR system. In cases where norms of reciprocity and trust cannot emerge, such as in contexts where there is little communication between those who operate within the system, Ostrom concedes that Hardin's 'tragedy of the commons' will continue to apply. At the time of writing, however, it is worth noting that there is a large, and ever expanding, database of documented cases of CPR systems that are managed efficiently in the absence of either privatisation or socialism.[6]

What has this got to do with environmental security? It appears that successful CPR systems offer an important bulwark against the environmental insecurity of the individuals and groups that participate in them. By reducing conflict within the state, they may also, indirectly, increase the security of the state itself. As Ostrom observes, 'protecting institutional diversity related to how diverse peoples cope with CPRs may be as important for our long-run survival as the protection of biological diversity' (Ostrom, 1999, p. 282). The other side of the coin is that CPR systems are peculiarly vulnerable to the effects of civil and international wars. The question arises whether successful CPR strategies can also be used by states to reduce international environmental conflicts, such as those associated with the much discussed case of fresh water supplies or those which are expected to arise as a result of future climate change.

One consideration that bears on this issue is that there is some evidence that governmental attempts to create successful CPR systems hinder, rather than facilitate, the emergence of local cooperation (Ostrom et al., 1999, p. 281). This suggests not only that state intervention may not be the ideal vehicle for the development of successful CPR systems in intra-national contexts, but also that CPR solutions may not be applicable to environmental resource dilemmas at the international level. The research of Ostrom and others has identified literally thousands of cases where CPRs are managed effectively, but these are almost all to be found at the local and regional levels. Part of the reason for this is that norms of trust and reciprocity emerge more readily in contexts where those involved live in the same locality. But, as Ostrom observes, it is also because the greater the population associated with a CPR the more difficult it is for rules of organisation, and enforcement, to emerge (Ostrom et al., p. 281). The upshot of such considerations might seem to be that research into CPR systems and solutions are of limited relevance to issues of national environmental security, or indeed to issues pertaining to the management of global environmental changes such as those associated with climatic change, biodiversity, atmospheric composition and so forth – Ostrom refers to this as the 'scaling-up problem' (Ostrom et al., p. 282). However, it might be that future collaborative research between these related, but distinct, approaches to environmental issues, will provide a common approach to both national insecurity and CPR dilemmas.

NOTES

1. Following Levy, environmental stress brings about national insecurity *directly* when it 'results directly in the significant loss of life or welfare ... or otherwise impairs our most important national values'; and *indirectly* when it degrades a state's most important values through an intervening degradation of political and economic variables (Levy, 1995, p. 46). See also Homer-Dixon (1991, pp. 76–116); Percival and Homer-Dixon (1998, pp. 297–8). The *Project on Environment, Population, and Security* has an extensive WWW site at: (http://utl2.library.utoronto.ca/www/pcs/eps.htm).
2. Global Environmental Change and Human Security (GECHS) is an international interdisciplinary research project designed to advance research and policy efforts in the area of human security and global environmental change. It has an extensive WWW site at (http://www.gechs.org).
3. The IPCC suggest that countries which possess a 'diversified industrial economy and an educated and flexible labour force' will suffer least from the economic effects of climate change, whereas countries which possess specialised, and natural resource-based econo-

mies and 'a poorly developed and land-tied labour force' will be expected to fare much worse (Bruce et al., 1996, p. 11).

4. According to one study, for example, a 1 metre sea-level rise on the Bay of Bengal coastline would bring about a loss of up to 15% of the total land surface area of the country – on the assumption that coastal protection measures are not established. See McMichael et al. (1996b, p. 156).

5. According to an elegant typology provided by Brian Barry, anthropocentric theories are those which attribute value only to states of human beings; zoocentric theories attribute value only to states of sentient creatures, including human beings; and ecocentric theories hold that components of the natural world such as plant life, and possibly the biotic community as a whole, possess value independently of humans or animals (Barry, 1995, pp. 20ff).

6. To get an idea of the tremendous amount of research in this area, see the WWW site for the International Association for the Study of Common Property (IASCP): (http://www.indiana.edu/~iascp).

BIBLIOGRAPHY

Barry, B. (1995) *Justice as Impartiality* (Oxford: Oxford University Press).

Brock, Lothar (1991) 'Peace Through Parks: The Environment on the Peace Research Agenda', *Journal of Peace Research*, 28(4), pp. 407–24.

Bruce, J.P., Lee, H. and Haites, E.F. (eds) (1996) *Climate Change 1995: Economic and Social Dimensions of Climate Change* (Cambridge: Cambridge University Press).

Dabelko, G. and Dabelko, D. (1995) 'Environmental Security: Issues of Conflict and Redefinition', *Environmental Change and Security Project Report*, Spring 1995, pp. 3–13.

Deudney, D. (1991) 'Environment and Security: Muddled Thinking', *Bulletin of the Atomic Scientists*, April, pp. 22–8.

Elliot, L. (1996) 'Environmental Conflict: Reviewing the Arguments', *Journal of Environment and Development*, 5(2), pp. 149–67.

Gallie, W.B. (1956) 'Essentially Contested Concepts', *Proceedings of the Aristotelian Society*, 56, pp. 167–98.

Gleditsch, N.P. (1997) 'Environmental Conflict and the Democratic Peace', in Nils Petter Gleditsch (ed.) *Conflict and the Environment* (Dordrecht: Kluwer Academic Publishers, pp. 91–106.

Gleditsch, N.P. (1998) 'Armed Conflict and the Environment: A Critique of the Literature', *Journal of Peace Research*, 35(3), pp. 381–400.

Hardin, G. (1968) 'The Tragedy of the Commons', *Science*, 162, 13 December, pp. 1243–8.

Hardin, G. (1998) 'Extensions of "The Tragedy of the Commons"', *Science*, 280, 1 May, pp. 682–4.

Homer-Dixon, T. (1991) 'On the Threshold: Environmental Changes a Cause of Acute Conflict', *International Security*, 16(2), pp. 76–116.

Homer-Dixon, T. (1994) 'Environmental Scarcities and Violent Conflict: Evidence from Cases', *International Security*, 19(1), Summer, pp. 5–40.

Houghton, J., Meira Filho, L.G., Callander, B.A., Harris, N., Kattenberg, A. and Maskell, K. (eds) (1996) *Climate Change 1995: The Science of Climate Change* (Cambridge: Cambridge University Press).

Levy, M. (1995) 'Time for a Third Wave of Environment and Security Scholarship?',

Environmental Change and Security Project Report, Washington DC: The Woodrow Wilson Center, Spring, pp. 44–6.

Lonergan, S. (1999) *Global Environmental Change and Human Security (GECHS) Science Plan* (Bonn, International Human Dimensions Programme (IHDP)).

Matthew, R. (1997) 'Rethinking Environmental Security', in Nils Petter Gleditsch (ed.) *Conflict and the Environment* (Dordrecht: Kluwer Academic Publishers).

McMichael, A.J. (1996) 'Human Population Health', in R.T. Watson, M.C. Zinyowera and R.H. Moss (eds), *Climate Change 1995: Impacts, Adaptations, and Mitigation of Climate Change* (Cambridge: Cambridge University Press), pp. 561–84.

McMichael, A.J., Haines, A., Slooff, R. and Kovats, S. (eds) (1996), *Climate Change and Human Health* (Geneva: World Health Organisation).

Myers, N. (1989) 'Environment and Security', *Foreign Policy*, 74, Spring, pp. 23–41.

Myers, N. (1993) *Ultimate Security* (New York: W.W. Norton & Company).

Ostrom, E. (1990) *Governing the Commons: The Evolution of Institutions for Collective Action* (Cambridge: Cambridge University Press).

Ostrom, E., Burger, J., Field, C.B., Norgaard, R.B. and Policansky, D. (1999) 'Revisiting the Commons: Local Lessons, Global Changes', *Science*, 284, 9 April, pp. 278–82.

Percival, V. and Homer-Dixon, T. (1998) 'Environmental Scarcity and Violent Conflict: The Case of South Africa', *Journal of Peace Research*, 35(3), pp. 279–98.

Rawls, J. (1971) *A Theory of Justice* (Harvard: Harvard University Press).

Ronnfeldt, C.F. (1997) 'Three Generations of Environment and Security Research', *Journal of Peace Research*, 34(4), pp. 473–82.

Scanlon, T.C. (1996) 'The Nature of International Security', in Roger Carey and Trevor C. Salmon (eds), *International Security in the Modern World* (Basingstoke: Macmillan Press), pp. 1–20.

Scheumann, W. (1998) 'Conflicts on the Euphrates: An Analysis of Water and Non-water Issues', in W. Scheumann and M. Schiffler (eds) *Water in the Middle East* (Heidelberg: Springer-Verlag), pp. 113–35.

Ullman, R. (1983) 'Redefining Security', *International Security*, 8(1), Summer, pp. 129–53.

Waever, O. (1995) 'Securitization and Desecuritization', in Ronald Lipschutz (ed.) *On Security* (New York: Columbia University Press), pp. 46–86.

Wolfers, Arnold (1962) *Discord and Collaboration* (Baltimore: Johns Hopkins University Press).

World Commission on Environment and Development (1987) *Our Common Future* (Oxford: Oxford University Press).

2. Democracy and the environment[1]

Nils Petter Gleditsch and Bjørn Otto Sverdrup

1   INTRODUCTION

The recent wave of democratisation has rekindled interest in liberal propositions about the beneficial effects of democracy on international affairs, notably
on peace and development. Much of the literature on the environment has
ignored the effects of the political system, while other parts have suggested that
development, industrialisation, and capitalism are particularly apt to lead to
environmental degradation. Since most democracies are highly developed, industrialised and capitalist, many environmentalists have taken a dim view of
the prospects for environmental protection in democratic countries. While some
have assumed that saving the environment requires a strong state, even an
authoritarian regime, and that democracies are incapable of handling the 'tragedy of the commons', recent literature suggests a more optimistic view. The
end of the Cold War has also occasioned a more critical look at the environmental policies under socialism. This article suggests that although many
democracies have permitted development at the expense of environmental protection, democracies are also likely to mobilise counter-forces to such
degradation. An empirical analysis shows generally positive bivariate effects of
democracy on environmental performance, and more uniformly positive effects
when controlling for the level of development. Many environmental problems
have transnational effects, but few are exclusively international. Democracies,
in addition to overcoming national environmental degradation more efficiently,
are also better at developing cooperative solutions to international environmental problems.

2   THE RENAISSANCE OF DEMOCRACY IN
     INTERNATIONAL AFFAIRS

During 'the third wave of democratization' (Huntington, 1991), interest has
been rekindled in liberal propositions about the beneficial effects of democracy on international affairs. A great deal of attention has been focused on its

effects on peace (Gleditsch and Hegre, 1997) and on development (Lipset, 1959; Burkhart and Lewis-Beck, 1994). The question is increasingly being raised what effect, if any, democracy may have on environmental practice.

Despite the high priority now given to environmental issues, there are few systematic empirical studies on the influence of the political system on environmental performance. In the environmental field, more emphasis has been put on the impact of the economic system, on environmental negotiations and diplomacy, and on the formation of international regimes. Even the seminal report from the World Commission on Environment and Development, *Our Common Future*, lacks a comprehensive discussion of the effects of the political system. The importance of making governments accountable for environmental degradation is noted (Brundtland et al., 1988, p. 314), but the report does not explore how accountability is ensured in various types of political systems. The report contains formulations such as 'the pursuit of sustainable development requires a political system that secures effective citizen participation in decision making' (p. 65) and stresses that it is important to 'promote citizen initiatives, empowering people's organizations and strengthening local democracy' (p. 63), but overall the role of the political system receives only modest attention. A major study from the United Nations Environment Programme (UNEP), *The World Environment 1972–1992* (Tolba et al., 1992) discusses consequences, causes, and appropriate responses to environmental degradation, but does not include a discussion of the role of the political system. Neither does *The State of the World Report* discuss the significance of political democracy for the environment. The 1995 edition, for example, advocates involving people and promoting citizens' groups as key success factors for improved environmental quality. In addition, it discusses the various political obstacles for organized interests at the international level (French, 1995, pp. 185–8). However, the national level is hardly mentioned, and the relationship between democracy and the right of citizens to organize and promote their interests is not discussed. Nor does the report consider whether the removal of political obstacles at the international level is meaningful if similar obstacles at the national level have not been eliminated first. The Brundtland report and *The State of the World Report* have been extremely influential in shaping the rhetoric of Western environment-conscious politicians and they have largely directed their attention towards factors other than the character of the political system.

The impact of democracy on the environment is also absent from most of the literature on democracy. Terms like 'environment' and 'pollution' are not found in the subject indexes of important books on democracy such as Dahl (1989), Huntington (1991), Marks and Diamond (1992), Rueschemeyer et al. (1992), and Sørensen (1992).

Some historians and social scientists have come close to the issue of the possible effects of democracy on environmental performance. In an influential book, Kennedy (1993) puts the population explosion and environmental degradation very high on his list of world problems and concludes that 'political leadership' is crucial for the future of humanity, even though 'our endeavour might have only marginal effect on the profound driving forces of today's world' (p. 348). A few studies, such as Dahl (1993), have looked at how various aspects of democracy have affected environmental politics in a handful of Western countries and concluded that political systems that emphasise participation tend to pursue less harmful environmental policies. The same author shows that environmental movements with little influence in the domestic political system tend to support regional and international integration in order to increase their political power (Dahl, 1994). Even if such studies take into account political organization, their focus has been primarily on minor variations of democracy, rather than on the issue of democracy vs. non-democracy, and their empirical domain has been limited to a small group of European countries. The issue of democratic governance is not addressed.

Among those who have made explicit attempts to explore the relationship between democracy and the environment, we find two sharply diverging schools of thought. We first summarise the case for the position that democracy is likely to have a positive influence on the environment. We next examine a counterargument that has been influential in the Western environmental movement before we move on to our empirical study.

3   HOW DEMOCRACIES MAY PROTECT THE ENVIRONMENT

To make the positive case, we follow Payne (1995), who identified five reasons why democratic regimes should be less harmful to the environment than non-democracies.

First, *democracies support individual political rights and a free flow of information*. This favours the growth of opposition and is fundamental for the formation of environmental pressure groups. Moreover, free flow of information is important for technological innovation, the improved utilisation of scientific knowledge, and the development of new legal instruments for environmental protection.

Second, *democracies are more responsive than non-democracies*. Through a system of checks and balances, a free press, organised interest groups, and other social forces, democratic governments will have to take environmental concerns more seriously than non-democracies. Thus, democracies allow more freedom for politicisation of new issues. It might be argued that this point holds only if voters are strongly in favour of environmentally-sound action over other concerns such as jobs, wealth and so on. However, self-interest or group interest is not the only basis for changing political agendas. The public sphere in democracies plays a constructive role in identifying issues and mobilising support for these issues above and beyond narrow group interest.

Third, *democracies are better learners than non-democracies.* The openness of democracies advances the flow of information on environmental success and failure, at home and abroad. This permits democracies to be more flexible and better at inter-state environmental learning.

Fourth, *democracies participate more willingly in global environmental cooperation.* Payne argues that democracies will be more sensitive to rule and norm compliance than non-democracies and thus more likely to adjust to the standards and rules agreed on in environmental treaties and decisions by international organizations. However, successful international cooperation may also set a standard that shapes the behaviour of even non-democratic states.

Finally, according to Payne, *an open market economy – a feature of any democracy – provides the best incentives for responsible environmental policies.* Such incentives may be introduced through legal or quasi-legal standards such as the 'polluter pays' principle, by regulatory politics, or by direct bargaining between polluter and polluted. The latter model has proved successful in Japan (Leane, 1991). 'Green consumerism' and 'market-based incentives' are ways of handling environmental problems within a market-oriented economy. The overall effect of these five mechanisms leads Payne to conclude that democracies are more likely to recognise and act upon environmental interests than non-democracies.

One argument not discussed by Payne is the greater value that democracies place on human life, as evident from their absence of genocide (Rummel, 1994) and of famines (Sen, 1994) and the rare occurrence of civil war in established democracies (Hegre et al., 2001). If serious environmental problems take on a life-threatening character, or seem as if they might, we would expect democracies to respond with particular urgency to such problems, whereas in authoritarian states they would get lower priority than the ideological or power-political aims of the regime.

Payne's is not a lone voice. Schultz and Crockett (1990, p. 62) find the lack of information within the Communist regimes to be one of the fundamental problems of their environmental policy. Increasing openness and market-oriented reforms have improved the flow of environmental data. Berge (1994) argues, on theoretical grounds, that human rights and democracy are essential components in a process aimed at sustainable development, and that a property rights regime governing resource utilisation represents the key to institutional implementation of human rights and democracy in relation to a specific resource. Mann (1991) finds that nation-to-nation learning is crucial for achieving the paradigm shift necessary for an ecological balance. Such learning is easier in 'open societies', hence 'the rapid growth of democratic governments throughout the world would seem to augur well for great acceptance of environmental issues' (p. 330). In the political arena, Bill Clinton and Al Gore have both suggested that non-democratic governments are more likely to cause environmental problems than democracies (Kane, 1993, p. 390; Payne, 1995, pp. 41, 54). In a study of Russia's environmental policy, Kotov and Nikitina (1995, p. 27) maintained that democratisation is a necessary prerequisite for improved environmental policies in Russia since there is still little environmental consciousness in the political and administrative leadership. They also suggested (p. 26) that the decentralisation that followed the democratisation in Russia improved the conditions for international regional cooperation, for instance between Russian regions and the Scandinavian countries. Such cooperation facilitates the import of solutions and the spread of knowledge and increases environmental consciousness through new channels. The literature on the democratic peace has found that not only do democracies feud less among themselves but they also cooperate more than other regimes, and this makes it likely that environmental cooperation will also be higher.

In a study of factors promoting compliance with international environmental accords, Weiss and Jacobsen (1999) hypothesise that transparency may promote compliance because it makes non-compliance more apparent and makes it easier for domestic and international actors to take appropriate action (p. 10). Democratic actors are normally more transparent (p. 21).

Finally, Bailey (1998) argues that the negative effects of environmental disruption are likely to be exacerbated in non-democratic political systems by war, famine, and excessive population growth. *War* is immensely destructive for the environment (Westing, 1980). Thus, if increasing democratisation leads to less war, it will also promote the environment. The importance of this factor is probably increasing, given the increasing physical destructiveness of major war in the modern world, with global nuclear war at the extreme end. *Famine* puts pressure on the environment because people become desperate for survival and will be insensitive to long-term arguments about the responsible management of resources. Moreover, as Sen (1994) has argued, democracies rarely if ever experience major famines. *Population pressure* is also likely to increase pressure on the resources, but the link between and democracy and low population growth may be more tenuous.

4   HOW DEMOCRACIES MAY HARM THE ENVIRONMENT

The classic case of the tragedy of the commons (Hardin, 1968) is the story of independent citizens each acting in their individual self-interest and producing a result ultimately negative to all. It is not a story to inspire confidence in political or economic freedom: 'Freedom in a commons brings ruin to all' (p. 1244). In the environmental movement of the 1970s, such views were explicitly followed up by sceptical pronouncements about the ability of democracies to overcome individual egoism and to act with sufficient resolve to deal with the critical environmental problems facing mankind. Environmental theorists such as Ophuls (1977) and Heilbroner (1974) declared the age of liberty and democracy to be over and called for a social order which would blend religious orientation and military discipline (for a review of such views, see Paehlke 1988, 1989). Similarly, Passmore (1974), seeing democratic practice as a powerful weapon against ecological destruction, feared that environmentalists who favoured strong leadership in politics would undermine democracy.

Paehlke argues that such attitudes are rare today. However, similar arguments have been voiced more recently by Lafferty (1993), who argues that there is 'an inherent conflict between democracy and the solution of the environmental crisis',[2] and by Wyller (1994, 1999), who concludes that it is highly improbable that any solutions to major environmental problems can be found through democratic procedure, and that 'a value conflict might ensue, between the safeguarding of democracy and the environment' (1994, p. 19).

Another argument against democracy is its close association with a market economy. (All democracies are market economies, although not all market economies are democracies.) Dryzek (1987), among many others, sees the business interests that dominate democracies as harmful to the environment.

A middle ground is occupied by, for example, Hartmann (1992) who asserts that the relationship between democracy, development, and environmental protection 'is an extremely complicated one' (p. 49), and concludes that there 'is little correlation between democracy and protection of the environment' (p. 57). This conclusion is not built on any statistical or comparative study, but rather on impressionistic evidence to the effect that 'democratic countries of the North also contribute to pollution'.

On the whole, we find the case for a positive influence of democracy on the environment more persuasive than the opposite argument. The pessimistic case may well be correct in suggesting that the individualism of democratic societies is likely to give rise to environmental problems. At the same time, democracies seem more likely to take corrective action to reduce the problem or mitigate its effects.

5 SOME ALTERNATIVE HYPOTHESES

While we are not trying to develop a fully specified theory of environmental behaviour, it is useful to discuss a few alternative interpretations of national differences in environmental performance.

5.1 Development

Since its first appearance, industrialisation has been associated with human and material degradation. The famous report from the Club of Rome, *The Limits to Growth* (Meadows et al., 1972), put the question of the environmental effects of economic growth squarely on the environmental agenda. Fifteen years later, the Brundtland report formulated the slogan of 'sustainable development' as a formula for reconciling the two goals of economic development and environmental protection. In the environmental movement, there is a widespread belief that comprehensive environmental protection is incompatible with continued industrial development, capitalist development in particular, or even with any kind of economic growth.

Many environmental economists now believe that the relationship between pollution and similar forms of environmental degradation follows an inverted U-shaped curve, usually called the environmental Kuznets curve. While the development of heavy industry (such as metals, chemicals and paper) was associated with extensive pollution, the later development of high-technology industry (for example, micro-electronics and pharmaceuticals) is environmentally much less harmful. In a study of the toxic intensity of industrial production, Hettige et al. (1992) found clear confirmation of the inverted U and they also found toxicity to increase more strongly in economies that were relatively closed to international trade. Lomborg (2001a, b) has amassed a great deal of empirical evidence of the decline of traditional pollution problems in advanced economies. Karshenas (1994, p. 731) has suggested that it might be useful to distinguish between two kinds of environmental problems: those related to the use of technology, economic growth, and high consumption and those related to economic backwardness, poverty, and low growth in general. Karshenas suggests that some economic growth is necessary in order to avoid environmental degradation.

It has been suggested that relative production costs and increasing environmental restrictions in the mature industrialised economies will lead to a displacement of polluting industries to the industrialising developing countries. If this were true, highly-developed economies would have found a way to obscure the true environmental costs of their economic system. O'Neill (2000), in a study of the hazardous waste trade, takes the opposite starting point. She expects advanced industrial democracies to be restrictive with regard to the domestic handling of toxic waste. She finds that Germany conforms to this standard, but not Britain. In a study of the international toxic waste trade, Hilz (1992, p. 21) concluded that only between 10–20 per cent of the toxic waste produced by OECD countries was exported and that nearly 80 per cent of this was exported within the OECD area. Only 5–10 per cent of the exports went to the developing countries and a slightly higher share to Eastern Europe. According to Hilz's estimate, of the 300–500 millions tons generated annually in the OECD region,[3] only between 1.5 million and 10 million tons a year is exported to the developing countries. The major share of the toxic waste remains in the waste-producing country or region. Other studies have shown that national political participation and political mobilisation have contributed to make the toxic waste industry less harmful (Szasz, 1994).

Lauber (1978) is among those who argue that economic growth is the key to environmental deterioration, although not all growth is incompatible with ecological balance. He notes the view expressed by Heilbroner (1974), Ophuls (1977) and others that 'the ecological imperative' is incompatible with democracy. And although he largely accepts the link between growth and environmental destruction, he disputes the contention that liberal democracy is to be blamed for (or credited with) the spectacular growth rates of the postwar period; rather, he asserts that these are due to 'nascent authoritarian politics'. Among other pieces of evidence, he cites studies that show that economic modernisation is controversial among the general public, if not outright unpopular. Economic growth is a power-enhancing project undertaken by the elite. On the whole it seems that Lauber has reached the correct conclusion about the relationship between democracy and the environment, on the basis of two incorrect premises about economic growth.

5.2   Socialism vs. Capitalism

Much of the criticism regarding economic development and its environmental consequences has a clear anti-capitalist tone. This literature generally – implicitly or explicitly – offers some sort of socialism as an alternative. Increasingly, however, it has become clear that Soviet-style socialism did not provide a good example of enlightened stewardship of the environment. On the contrary, pollution from industry, military activities, industrial blight, and resource waste seemed to be even worse under 'real existing socialism'. After glasnost, and even more so after the fall of the Soviet empire, it became evident that the former Soviet Union was an ecological disaster area.[4] The planning system did not achieve the rational allocation of resources necessary to achieve satisfactory economic development; it should not come as a great surprise that it also failed in the preservation of environmental resources.

Moreover, the closed nature of the society under state socialism seems to have contributed to the lack of corrective action once environmental problems developed.

Mirovitskaya and Soroos (1995), however, maintain that socialism may be a 'fourth solution' to Hardin's tragedy of the commons. Basing their claim on what they call a Marxist doctrine of human–nature interaction, they characterise the 'command-administrative system' as 'a rather efficient mechanism for concentrating limited resources available for undertaking critical national tasks' (p. 5). Unfortunately, in the former Soviet Union, no national authority was charged with environmental protection, so environmental values did not benefit from this system. Mirovitskaya and Soroos propose that Soviet environmental practice may be seen in a more favourable light if one takes into account that the country was in an earlier phase of industrialisation than mature Western economies, that it faces adverse climatic conditions in most of its territory, and that war and insecurity have led to excessive concentrations of industry in secure areas such as the Urals and Siberia.

However, other late industrialisers, notably in East Asia, have avoided the environmental disasters of the Soviet Union. Moreover, climatic conditions are adverse in other countries as well (low temperature is just one climatic problem among several) and the low population density of the Soviet Union might be considered a balance to the problems resulting from the climate. The concentration of military industry behind the Ural mountains should not be a major problem either, given the size of the available area. Finally, other parts of the former Soviet Union are no less polluted. On the whole, the experience of Soviet Russian, East European and Communist Chinese environmental policies tends to support the argument that a lack of democracy promotes environmentally malign behaviour. Although the effects of the political and economic system cannot easily be separated, the ideologically-driven nature of these regimes makes it reasonable to give primacy to the political factors.

Other writers find capitalism to be more adjustable to the demands of environmentalism than a command economy, emphasising how 'green consumers' can influence producers to become 'green capitalists'. For such capitalists, competition in the marketplace has simply been modified to include the preferences of the consumers for environmentally-sound products. Martell (1994, ch. 2), while not dismissing such views, finds them inadequate for maintaining environmental sustainability. This is in part because he argues from a wide ('eco-centric') view of the environment, as opposed to a narrower anthropocentric view that places human well-being at the centre of the environmental debate. He also questions whether the market can take into account the long-term (and most serious) environmental problems. Martell concludes that the global and interventionist approaches are more appropriate for securing sustainability than decentralisation and economic liberalism.

5.3   War and War Preparations

Critics of the military establishment frequently argue that 'armed forces all over the world are among the greatest polluters' (Altes, 1992, p. 65). This literature has been reviewed elsewhere (Gleditsch, 1994); one major criticism being that the environmental effects of alternative resource use resulting from disarmament have not been considered. If curtailing the size of the military establishment reduces military pollution but increases private consumption with extensive civilian pollution, the net result is not necessarily favourable for the environment. A macroeconomic simulation for Norway shows, however, that disarmament with counter-measures such as tax reduction or increased public spending for health would reduce the emission of greenhouse gases while preserving the level of employment and the rate of economic growth (Gleditsch et al., 1994). Although we are not aware of similar analyses for other countries, it seems likely that disarmament would have a similar effect for most military establishments. Of course, the disposal of the radioactive and toxic substances associated with weapons of mass destruction involves the risk of particularly serious peacetime pollution. The destruction of these weapons is also very costly. There is a great deal of disagreement, however, with regard to the seriousness of these problems in peacetime. Locally, such problems may overshadow other environmental problems, as when early nuclear weapons were tested in airbursts over land, with scant regard for the effects on soldiers and civilian neighbours. But as the subsequent history of nuclear testing has shown, while some environmental effects may be inevitable, they can be reduced substantially by underground testing. In fact, the Partial Test Ban Treaty of 1963 can be seen as an early environmental measure as much as an arms control effort (Soroos, 1995). War preparations in themselves are hardly decisive for environmental degradation. The crucial point is whether the environmental effects are taken into account in military planning – and that is a question of politics.

5.4   The Question of Internationalism

It is frequently argued that because environmental problems do not respect national boundaries, they must be solved by international agreement. For instance, Schultz and Crockett (1990, p. 59), though recognising that problems like air pollution have local effects, state that 'most environmental contamination finally is being recognized as an international problem addressable only by international solutions', since 'pollutants do not respect political boundaries'. Hence, the strong emphasis on 'environmental diplomacy' (Susskind, 1994) in recent environmental literature.

However, most environmental problems are felt more strongly close to the source. Pollution from a factory or a leaking nuclear reactor generally tapers off in a monotonic relationship with distance, although not necessarily in a linear fashion.[5] A large proportion of the pollution can be exported out of the local area by building a high smokestack or by discharging the waste into a river or into the sea, but heavier concentrations of pollution will nevertheless affect local areas more than distant parts. By far the most serious effects of Chernobyl were borne by the local residents, even if reindeer meat and mushrooms were affected as far away as in Scandinavia. Even in cases where a majority of the pollutants may be exported out of the country, the exports will be distributed over a wider area in several countries, and the polluter will still generally be affected more on a per capita basis. This is not well modelled by the analogy of the tragedy of the commons, which assumes that the actions of one affect everyone in the same degree. Pollution generally affects the polluting country more than its neighbouring countries, and this ensures that an environmental benefit may be derived from unilateral action. Thus, a country is motivated to clean up on a unilateral basis if the costs are not prohibitive. A democratic polity may ensure that the political costs of inaction rise to the point where the costs of cleanup appear manageable in comparison.

Many studies have looked at the conditions for establishing effective international regimes for international environmental cooperation (Haas et al., 1993; List and Rittberger, 1992; Young, 1989). Without denying the importance of environmental treaties, compliance with such arrangements depends heavily on the capability of each state to establish and enforce a domestic regime (Chayes and Chayes, 1993, p. 193). Studies of environmental treaties have shown that an overwhelming majority of them regulate issues considered to be under national control. For instance, 85 per cent of the international treaties seek to regulate domestic actions for the benefit of oneself and others, rather than to create supranational authorities or arrangements (Haas and Sundgren, 1993, p. 408). Coordinated regulations and reporting between governments is by far the most common type of environmental cooperation. Environmental treaty-making is moving from an emphasis on global treaties towards an emphasis on the regional and the national. To ensure that citizens and companies do not violate international agreements requires a comprehensive set of domestic bureaucratic and legal regulations, scientific and technical judgments, as well as resources and incentives. Thus, the question of the effectiveness of international regimes and environmental cooperation cannot be studied in isolation from the ability of a state to establish a domestic regime. A government's legitimacy to regulate and its accountability to its

citizens are essential for the success of international environmental cooperation. Unilateral action motivated by domestic pressure may also pave the way
for a system of multilateral management of shared resources.

But surely *some* environmental degradation is *essentially* international?
The greenhouse effect is the classic case of an environmental problem that is
neither generated nor solvable at the national level. In fact, the effect may be
positive for some countries, while spelling disaster for others. Siberia may
bloom, but the Maldives will vanish off the map. Nevertheless, the same
gases that are assumed to produce a global greenhouse effect also contribute
to local air pollution in cities. Hence, there is a local self-interest in acting
against greenhouse gas emissions, even if the most serious long-term threat is
global. Finally, many environmental groups exert strong pressure for the
unilateral fulfilment of global goals. The strong pressure on first world governments from environmental groups in support of limiting CO_2 emissions is
a case in point. Such activity can hardly be explained in terms of national
self-interest, but neither is it caused exclusively by international pressure.
Rather, there is a strong domestic feeling of moral responsibility towards the
fulfilment of global goals, and a sense that unilateral examples can contribute
effectively to raising international standards and encouraging compliance
with them.

6   EMPIRICAL STUDY

There is little previous systematic empirical work on this issue. Indeed, Payne
(1995) complains that few have directly addressed the possibility of a connection between political regime type and the environment, and several literature
reviews (Knoepfel et al., 1987; Vogel and Kun, 1987) have found that most
previous research has concentrated on case studies or studies of a small number
of states. For instance, Mirovitskaya and Soroos (1995) show that in pairwise
comparisons between the Soviet Union and the United States on such indicators as emissions of carbon, sulphur, and nitrogen oxides, the Soviet Union
does not generally show a poorer performance. However, unlike the United
States, the Soviet Union (and since 1992, Russia) has suffered a serious decline
in health indicators that seems at least partially due to environmental factors.
This did not show up in the comparison, which raises serious questions about
the validity of the environmental indicators used by Mirovitskaya and Soroos.
In their study of factors promoting compliance with international treaties on the
environment, Weiss and Jacobsen (1999) use data on the compliance of eight
countries with six treaties. They find that democratic countries are generally
ahead in compliance. However, in Russia democratisation has resulted in a
decline in compliance with the Convention on International Trade in Endan-

gered Species (CITES) due to Moscow's loss of control over local authorities. The empirical base used by Weiss and Jacobsen is rather limited.

Because of the scarcity of systematic empirical studies, the environmental debate has been heavily influenced by instances of environmental degradation in the open societies where information was readily available. More recently, more attention has been focused on the revelations of environmental malpractice in the former socialist countries. In this chapter we try to move beyond single case studies, pairwise comparison, and regional studies.

6.1 Research Design

The unit of analysis is the nation. Even though many environmental problems are local, regional or global, environmental performance can be more easily evaluated at the level of the nation. This is not merely a question of data availability, but also a recognition that most of the environmental decision-making occurs at the national level.

The temporal domain is the late Cold War world, that is, the world in the late 1980s and up to the early 1990s. We have stayed away from the post-Cold War world partly because we lack updated information. A more important reason is that while political variables can change very quickly – democratic institutions can be built quickly (although to nurture a stable democratic culture takes longer) and they can crumble overnight – most environmental and developmental variables are not prone to such rapid change. Hence, an analysis for a later year would include many new democracies with extensive environmental problems inherited from previous regimes, and this would seriously distort the analysis.

6.2 Measuring Environmental Performance

The selection of indicators of environmental quality is not a simple matter. Despite greatly increased attention to environmental issues, complete, comparable, and valid data sets are still hard to find. Compared to existing data sets for economic performance, demographic developments, political rights, democratisation, or armed conflict, international data sets for environmental issues are still in their infancy. For many aspects of environmental performance, such as biodiversity and urban pollution, data for more than 50 per cent of nations are missing. In this study, we have made an effort to find valid indicators for the most central aspects of the environment that also include data for as many countries as possible. We have attempted not to include variables that would be biased for or against our main hypotheses.

Environmental performance cannot be easily summed up in one or two indicators of overall performance. According to the comprehensive UNEP-sponsored volume, *The World Environment* (Tolba et al., 1992), the key environmental issues include air pollution, ozone depletion and climate change, fresh water access, coastal and marine degradation, land degradation and deforestation, biodiversity, environmental hazards, and toxic chemicals. This is a rather mixed bag. We have sought to include a sufficient number of variables to create as representative as possible a picture of environmental quality without yielding a systematic bias in favour of our hypotheses. We include positive as well as negative indicators of environmental quality. However, lack of data has forced us to omit some central aspects of negative performance such as urban air pollution and coastal and marine degradation.

Since environmental issues and problems are so diverse, we cannot assume a high correlation between all our different environmental indicators. To construct an overall index for environmental quality is premature until we have a much clearer idea of the main dimensions of environmental performance. Instead, we examine the effect of democracy on each of the environmental indicators. The following indicators were selected:

Direct problem indicators
- emissions of climate gases per capita
- emissions of CO_2 per capita
- deforestation
- threats to biodiversity
- lack of safe drinking water

Indirect problem indicators
- lack of sanitary services
- population growth
- population density
- urban population change

Solution-oriented indicators
- signed and ratified environmental treaties
- environmental organisations

Many potentially interesting variables had to be dropped because it was impossible to find data for a sufficient number of countries. For instance, data on the emissions on sulphur dioxide (SO_2) – crucial to the acid rain debate – were available only for the OECD countries and a handful of other countries. Using this as an indicator of environmental behaviour, we would be unable to distinguish between democracies and non-democracies. Judging from the environmental literature, our list nevertheless seems to include the most important aspects of the environment. The central issue of climate change is captured through the emissions of climate gases generally and CO_2 specifically. While climate change is a global problem, we measure contributions to it in terms of national levels of emissions. The other indicators of environmental disruption are at the national level. In addition to the *direct* environmental problems measured by the first indicators, we have included two indicators on *indirect* problems: the level of population density and the rate of population growth. We are not suggesting that a high population density or rate of growth are in themselves negative. But, everything else being equal, a high or rising population represents an increased load on the environment and a potential for environmental disruption. Finally, we have included two solution-oriented indicators on international environmental action (also measured at the national level): support for environmental treaties and tolerance of the presence of international environmental organisations. If democracies are more environment-friendly, we would expect them to contribute more to international protective action than non-democracies. We do not have adequate data to examine the *implementation* of these treaties; the variables measure declared policy rather than actions taken to conform to the rules. In the subsequent correlation analysis, the results for the problem-oriented indicators have been reversed, with a high score indicating favourable environmental performance.

We have relied primarily on three reputable collections of statistics: World Resources Institute (1994), United Nations (1993), and UNDP (1993). A more complete description of the variables is found in an Appendix posted on the World Wide Web (see note 1).

6.3 Measuring Democracy

To measure democracy we use the Polity III index of Institutionalised Democracy (Jaggers and Gurr, 1995), and define a country as a democracy if it obtains a score of 6 or higher. The cut-off is fairly arbitrary – higher than the middle value – but not so high as to restrict democracy to the twentieth century. We use the democracy score for 1990 in this study, that is, the level of democracy at the end of the Cold War. Countries in political transition were excluded from the analysis.

6.4 Measuring Development

We use two indicators of development: GDP per capita and the Human Development Index (HDI), a measure constructed by the UNDP (annual), which includes life expectancy, knowledge (adult literacy and years of schooling) and income. The index provides a more comprehensive measure of development and is more sensitive to the distribution of wealth, but is not particularly well grounded in any theory of development.

6.5   Democracy and the Environment

Table 2.1 shows the bivariate relationship between democracy and the environmental variables. Positive numbers indicate that a high value on democracy goes together with good environmental performance (for example, low CO_2 emissions, and a high number of treaties signed). While we observe a clear and significant relationship between democracy and most of the environmen-

Table 2.1   Democracy and good environmental performance

	r	Percentage difference	(n)
Climate gas emissions[a]			
Climate gas overall	–0.30**	–36	(129)
Emissions of CO_2	–0.32**	–40	(124)
Deforestation[a]	0.17**	27	(91)
Biodiversity			
Mammals	0.25**	24	(109)
Birds	–0.10	–23	(107)
Water and sanitary services			
Drinking water	0.21*	20	(77)
Sanitary services	0.23*	19	(60)
Population growth[a]	0.49**	43	(123)
Population density[a]	–0.02	–11	(123)
Urban population growth[a]	0.51**	52	(121)
Environmental treaties			
Signed	0.52**	40	(121)
Ratified	0.53**	36	(121)
Environmental organisations	0.63**	54	(117)

Notes:
** significant at the 0.05 level; * significant at the 0.10 level.
a. The variable is reversed, that is, we measure lack of deforestation rather than deforestation, low rather than high climate gas emissions and so on.
The first column gives correlation coefficients (Pearson's r), whereas the second shows percentage differences between dichotomized variables. The correlations for environmental degradation have been reversed; thus a correlation greater than zero implies a positive association between democracy and good environmental performance.

Sources: The democracy data are for 1990, the other variables for years close to 1990.

tal indicators, the effect is negative on the emission of climate gases and in particular on the emission of CO_2. As one might expect, the strongest relationships are found between democracy and the solution-oriented indicators of environmental performance.

One odd finding is that democracies seem to have fewer threatened mammal species than non-democracies, but more threatened bird species, than non-democracies. One explanation for this discrepancy may be that mammal species receive a great deal of attention in the media and occupy a central position in many environmental campaigns. The visibility of large or cuddly mammals and their commonly noted similarities with humans have given them a special status. Mammal species, notably whales and pandas, have become important symbols in the environmental debate. Hence, the attention of policy-makers has been directed toward the living conditions of mammals, and efforts have been made to halt the shrinking of stocks. Insects or birds, on the other hand, are less visible and less appealing and have not received as much attention. In cross-tabulating democracy against a variable for threatened higher plant species we found a similar negative pattern. This provides additional support for the attention hypothesis. However, the variable higher plant species had to be omitted from further analysis due to the low number of units. The idea that the most visible problems, rather than the most serious ones, receive the most attention, finds some support in the environmental literature. For instance, Haas and Sundgren (1993, p. 407) found that most environmental treaties concern highly visible problems like oil pollution. A US study found little relation between actual risk and public perceptions.[6]

There is little variation between the results of the two methods of analysis. Positive correlations correspond to positive percentage differences. This suggests that the findings are fairly robust.

6.6   Multivariate Analysis

In a separate analysis, not included here, we found a positive relationship between development and environmental problems such as climate gas emissions and one of the biodiversity variables. However, high development was also associated with lack of deforestation, good water and sanitary conditions, and with the positive environmental indicators. When controlling for the level of development, we found a positive relationship between democracy and several of the environmental indicators. But the results were weaker than in the bivariate analysis. For the emission of greenhouse gases, they were somewhat ambiguous. Since the emission of climate gases, and in particular emission of CO_2, has recently gained much attention in the environmental debate, and since our earlier findings did not point clearly in one direction, we have singled out the CO_2 variable for special attention in a multivariate analysis.

In a multiple regression analysis of the emissions, with CO_2 per capita in 1990 as the dependent variable (Table 2.2), we included four independent variables: GDP per capita, oil production, the HDI and democracy (the latter in dichotomous form only). Based on the assumption of a tapering-off effect, we also included a variable with GDP per capita squared. Liquid fuel production is the only genuinely new variable, relative to our earlier analysis. It is included because oil-producing states are assumed to contribute heavily to CO_2 emissions. A negative sign implies a greater contribution to CO_2 emissions.

Table 2.2   Regression analysis of the limitation of CO_2 emissions

	Beta
Democracy	0.24
HDI	–0.24
Oil-producing country	–0.18
GDP per capita	–1.31
Squared GDP per capita	0.66

Adjusted $R^2 = 0.67$, n = 108

A coefficient less than zero implies a contribution to *increased* CO_2 emissions and thus to environmental disruption. The beta value is the standardised regression coefficient for each of the independent variables. All coefficients are significant at the 0.01 level.

The analysis suggests that democracies have lower CO_2 emissions than non-democracies after the effects of the level of development and oil production have been isolated. The importance of political regime type is less than that of development and wealth, but slightly stronger than that of liquid fuel production. The coefficient on GDP per capita squared tends in the predicted direction, indicating that there is indeed a tapering-off effect between GDP and CO_2 emissions. In other words, highly-developed countries emit more CO_2, but very highly-developed countries do not emit as much as one would expect from a linear relationship. The explanatory power of the model is quite respectable, and it increased after the introduction of democracy.

A similar analysis with the variable for climate gas emission generally yielded a similar pattern with respect to the effect of democracy, but with an insignificant and much lower beta value (0.05) and much lower overall explanatory power ($R^2 = 0.28$). Nevertheless, this analysis confirms the pattern found earlier: democracies tend to be less harmful to the environment than non-democracies. An analysis of the interaction between democracy and development indicates that the effect of democracy is much stronger for the most highly-developed countries.

7 CONCLUSIONS OF EMPIRICAL STUDY

If our analysis holds, a high level of development promotes some environmental problems and alleviates others. Since most democracies are highly developed, they are likely to experience some environmental stress. However, democracy tends to mobilise counter-forces that will work to lessen these problems. The two are not, however, necessarily in balance; for some indicators, the relationship comes out negative, in other cases, positive. Thus, for some environmental indicators, development may create more problems than democracy is able to solve. However, given that environmental problems are relatively new on the international – and even the national – political agenda, it is permissible to be optimistic about the ability of humankind to tackle these problems through political means.[7]

A major problem, which this chapter cannot answer directly, is whether a solution to the global environmental problems will require a *decrease* in development in the wealthiest countries, as many environmental movements argue, or whether the technological optimists are right in saying that there are ways of reconciling a continued increase in development with a decrease in the load on the environment. An illustration of this dilemma is provided by the *State of the World Report* (Brown et al., 1995): rapid Chinese economic development is predicted to be a major threat if the supply of food, raw materials and so on stays constant while demand rises. A technologically more optimistic argument would take into account how the supply would be affected by the demand through rising prices, mobilisation of resources which at today's price levels are not economic, new technology, increased imports and so on. But is this enough to compensate for the problems generated by rapid growth?

8 WHY HAS DEMOCRACY BEEN IGNORED?

Given the political composition and mandate of the Brundtland commission, UNEP and other UN bodies, it should not come as a great surprise that these groups tread carefully when commenting on the effects of different political systems. This caution was largely an effect of the Cold War, a period when a clear majority of countries were non-democracies and when the Soviet bloc provided a 'second centre' of world power with which representatives of other authoritarian ideologies could form temporary alliances whenever convenient. The commitment to democracy can now be stated much more openly in international bodies, and those who represent nations with little or no democracy may prefer to keep quiet rather than to object or try to promote 'people's democracy' or some alternative professedly democratic ideology.

On the other hand, many analysts take democracy for granted. In analysing contributing and restraining factors, they discuss environmental policy as if it concerns only the countries where there are environmental movements and an environmental debate. In fact, countries with little public attention directed to the environment probably need it even more. Under the Soviet system, even centrally placed advisers were ignorant of the true state of environmental disruption. Openness leads to disclosures, even scandals. But the number of exposed environmental scandals is not a good measure of environmental degradation; the number of cover-ups, if measurable, would have been more relevant.

Finally, much of the environmental debate has been marred by catastrophe scenarios; bad news tends to overshadow good news, and problems are translated into disasters (Bailey, 1993; Easterbrook, 1995; Myers and Simon, 1994). Predictions of future calamities may promote cataclysmic visions of environmental degradation in the West and eventually the end of the civilisation that generated them. Such thinking leads easily to absolutism and rejection of gradualist ideologies such as democracy. A risk assessment based on probabilities is replaced by one based on possibilities. Assertions of possible environmental damage cannot be disproved by scientific means. 'The precautionary principle' assumes the role that 'worst-case analysis' has held in national security affairs, as an obstacle to enlightened public policies for human betterment (Wildavsky, 1995, p. 427). Democracy is a method for those who are patient. Environmental concern frequently takes on an absolute value, much like national security thinking or religious fundamentalism. Such single-minded enthusiasm for the environment, coupled with ignorance of physical laws governing environmental processes, is particularly objectionable to scientists (Hoffman, 1990). This may cause scientists to turn away from the public debate in distaste, leading to further damage to the democratic process.

A strong environmental movement is an asset in a democracy, and by raising issues of great popular concern it can also serve as an instrument for democratisation in an authoritarian country. NGO activity provides an important explanation for the generally superior performance of democracies in environmental management. Indeed, the question is increasingly being asked whether many democracies have not gone *too* far in adapting to the concerns of environmentalists. Environmentalism in quasi-religious form (Liebich, 1993) is as much of a challenge to democratic decision-making as other forms of fundamentalism. The increasingly positive view of the effects of democracy in the environmental literature is a sign of maturity in the movement as well as in the society it reflects.

NOTES

1. We would like to express our gratitude to the Norwegian Ministry of Defence, the Fridtjof Nansen Foundation for Science and the Humanities, the United States Institute for Peace, and the Research Council of Norway for financial support of the research reported here. We are grateful to Robert Engelmann and Thomas Homer-Dixon, who were among the first to provide us with advice on environmental indicators. They bear, however, no responsibility for the way we have used (and sometimes ignored) their advice. Earlier versions of this article were presented to the 36th Annual Convention of the International Studies Association Chicago, IL, 21–25 February 1995 and a number of subsequent meetings. Håvard Hegre assisted with data processing and provided a stimulating critique. Jennifer Bailey, Robert Bathurst, Agnethe Dahl, Paul Dunne, Andreas Føllesdal, Leonard Hirsch, Oluf Langhelle, Eric Neumauer, Rodger Payne, Arvid Raknerud, Dan Smith, Marvin Soroos, Veronica Ward, and Arthur H. Westing have also contributed valuable comments and suggestions. The usual disclaimers apply. A detailed description of the data collection for the empirical part of the study can be found on (http://www.prio.no/cwp/datasets.asp).
2. See also Lafferty and Meadowcroft (1996).
3. A later update on the transfrontier movements of hazardous wastes for the OECD countries suggests that the minimum estimate (1.5 million tons) is the more likely one. The estimate for the annual generation of hazardous waste in the OECD region was 258 million tons for 1991 (OECD, 1994), that is, a bit lower than Hilz's lowest estimate.
4. Strong indictments of Soviet environmental practice are found in Feshbach and Friendly (1992), Jancar (1990), Kaffka (1997), Klötzli (1997), Pearce (1993), and Åhlander (1994). A more detailed study of the environmental degradation of the Aral Sea Basin is found in Glantz et al. (1993). Critical examinations of China's environmental policies are found in Smil (1993) and Stranks (1997).
5. For instance, air dispersion models are generally based on the normal distribution with the source at the highest point of the curve, and adjusted for factors like wind direction, air turbulence, terrain features, and so on (Lape, 1994, pp. 229ff.).
6. US EPA (1987), as cited in Levy (1995, p. 45).
7. Somewhat more pessimistic results with regard to the effect of democracy have been reported by Midlarsky (1998). However, his data exclude East European countries. He also includes a variable for 'European location', which generally has a positive impact. Since this variable measures mostly West European democratic countries, this variable may proxy a democracy effect among highly developed countries. Barrett and Graddy (2000) also report that for several pollution variables, an increase in civil and political freedom improves environmental quality.

BIBLIOGRAPHY

Åhlander, A.-M.S. (1994), *Environmental Problems in the Shortage Economy. The Legacy of Soviet Environmental Policy*, Aldershot: Edward Elgar.
Altes, E.J.K. (1992), 'The Arms Race, Development and the Environment in Peace

Time', in Nils Petter Gleditsch (ed.), *Conversion and the Environment*, Proceedings of a Seminar in Perm, Russia, 24–27 November, 1991, PRIO Report (2), Oslo: International Peace Research Institute, pp. 65–79.

Bailey, R. (1993), *Eco-Scam. The False Prophets of Ecological Apocalypse*, New York: St Martin's Press.

Bailey, J. (1998), 'Demokrati som politisk betingelse for miljøvern' [Democracy as a Political Condition for Environmental Protection], in N.P. Gleditsch et al., *Det nye sikkerhetsbildet. Mot en demokratisk og fredelig verden?*, Trondheim: Tapir, pp. 29–42.

Barrett, S. and Graddy, K. (2000), 'Freedom, Growth, and the Environment', *Environment and Development Economics*, **5**(4), pp. 433–56.

Berge, E. (1994), 'Democracy and Human Rights: Conditions for Sustainable Resource Utilization', in B.R. Johnston (ed.), *Who Pays the Price? The Sociocultural Context of Environmental Crisis*, Covelo, CA: Island Press, pp. 187–93.

Bergesen, H.O. and Parmann, G. (eds) (annual), *Green Globe Yearbook of International Co-operation on Environment and Development*, Oxford: Oxford University Press, for Fridtjof Nansen's Institute.

Brown, L. et al. (1995), *State of the World. A World Watch Institute Report on Progress toward a Sustainable Society*, New York and London: Norton.

Brundtland, G. et al. (1988), *Our Common Future*, New York: Oxford University Press.

Burkhart, R.E. and Lewis-Beck, M.S. (1994), 'Comparative Democracy: The Economic Development Thesis', *American Political Science Review*, **88**(4), pp. 903–10.

Chayes, A. and Chayes, A. (1993), 'On Compliance', *International Organization*, **47**(2), pp. 175–205.

D'Souza, F. (1994), 'Focus On: Democracy as a Cure for Famine', *Journal of Peace Research*, **31**(3), pp. 369–73.

Dahl, A. (1993), 'Miljøhensyn i vest-europeisk energipolitikk: Reserver av fossile brensler, miljøbevegelsens styrke og statlig styring av energisektoren som forklarende faktorer?' [Environmental Concerns in West European Energy Policy: Fossile Fuel Reserves, a Strong Environmental Movement and Government Control of the Energy Sector as Explanatory Factors?] EED Report no. 9, Lysaker: Fridtjof Nansen Institute.

Dahl, A. (1994), *Environmental Actors and European Integration: Attitudes towards Further Integration*, EED Report, no. 6, Oslo and Lysaker: Fridtjof Nansen Institute.

Dahl, R.A. (1989), *Democracy and Its Critics*, New Haven, CT and London: Yale University Press.

Dahl, R.A. (1992), 'Why Free Markets Are Not Enough', *Journal of Democracy*, **3**(1), pp. 82–9.

Diehl, P.F. and Gleditsch, N.P. (eds) (2001), *Environmental Conflict*, Boulder, CO: Westview.

Dierkes, M., Weiler, H.N. and Berthoin, Antal A. (eds) (1987), *Comparative Policy Research: Learning from Experience*, New York: St. Martin's Press.

Dryzek, J.S. (1987), *Rational Ecology. Environment and Political Economy*, Oxford: Blackwell.

Dupuy, T.N. (1964), 'Quantification of Factors Related to Weapon Lethality', Annex III-H, in R. Sunderland et al. (eds), 'Historical Trends Related to Weapon Lethality', Report Prepared Under Contract for the Advanced Tactics Project of the Combat Development Command, HQ US Army. Washington, DC.

Easterbrook, G. (1995), *A Moment on the Earth. The Coming Age of Environmental Optimism*, New York: Viking Penguin. (Paperback edition, New York: Penguin, 1996).

Engelmann, R. (1994), *Stabilizing the Atmosphere: Population, Consumption and Greenhouse Gases*, Population and Environment Program, Washington, DC: Population Action International.

Feshbach, M. and Friendly, A. (1992), *Ecocide in the USSR: Health and Nature under Siege*, New York: Basic Books.

French, H.F. (1995), 'Forging a New Global Partnership', in L. Brown et al. (eds), *State of the World. A World Watch Institute Report on Progress Toward a Sustainable Society*, New York and London: Norton, pp. 170–89.

Glantz, M.H., Rubinstein, A.Z. and Zonn, I. (1993), 'Tragedy in the Aral Sea Basin. Looking Back to Plan Ahead', *Global Environmental Change*, **3**(2), pp. 174–98.

Gleditsch, N.P. (1994), 'Conversion and the Environment', in J. Käkönen (ed.), *Green Security or Militarized Environment*, Aldershot and Brookfield: Dartmouth, pp. 131–54.

Gleditsch, N.P. (1997a), 'Environmental Conflict and the Democratic Peace' in N.P. Gleditsch (ed.), *Conflict and the Environment*, Dordrecht: Kluwer, pp. 91–106.

Gleditsch, N.P. (ed.) (1997b), *Conflict and the Environment*, Dordrecht: Kluwer.

Gleditsch, N.P., Bjerkholt, O. and Cappelen, Å. (1994), *The Wages of Peace. Disarmament in a Small Industrialized Economy*, London: Sage.

Gleditsch, N.P. and Hegre, H. (1997), 'Peace and Democracy: Three Levels of Analysis', *Journal of Conflict Resolution*, **41**(2), pp. 283–310.

Haas, P.M., Keohane, R.O. and Levy, M. (eds) (1993), *Institutions for the Earth. Sources of Effective Environmental Protection*, Cambridge, MA and London: MIT Press.

Haas, P.M. and Sundgren, J. (1993), 'Evolving International Environmental Law: Changing Practices of National Sovereignty', in N. Choucri (ed.), *Global Accord: Environmental Challenges and International Responses*, Cambridge, MA: MIT Press, pp. 401–29.

Hardin, G. (1968), 'The Tragedy of the Commons', *Science*, 162, pp. 1243–8.

Hartmann, J. (1992), 'Democracy, Development, and Environmental Sustainability', in H.O. Bergesen and G. Parmann (eds), *Green Globe Yearbook of International Co-operation on Environment and Development*, Oxford: Oxford University Press, for Fridtjof Nansen's Institute, pp. 49–57.

Hegre, H., Ellingsen, T., Gleditsch, N.P. and Gates, S. (2001), 'Toward a Democratic Civil Peace? Democracy, Political Change, and Civil War 1816–1992', *American Political Science Review*, **95**(1), pp. 35–48.

Heilbroner, R.L. (1991), *An Inquiry into the Human Prospect. Looked at again for the 1990s*, New York: Norton. (First published in 1974).

Hellevik, O. (1988), *Introduction to Causal Analysis: Exploring Survey Data by Cross Tabulation*, Oslo: Norwegian University Press.

Hettige, H., Lucas, J., Robert, E. and Wheeler, D. (1992), 'The Toxic Intensity of Industrial Production: Global Patterns, Trends, and Trade Policy', *American Economic Review*, **82**(2), pp. 478–81.

Hilz, C. (1992), *The International Toxic Waste Trade*, New York: Van Nostrand Reinhold.

Hoffman, R. (1990), 'Chemistry, Democracy, and a Response to the Environment', Priestley Medal Address, *Chemical and Engineering News*, **68**(17), pp. 25–9.

Huntington, S.P. (1991), *The Third Wave: Democratization in the Late Twentieth Century*, Norman, OK and London: University of Oklahoma Press.

Jaggers, K. and Gurr, T.R. (1995), 'Tracking Democracy's Third Wave with the Polity III Data', *Journal of Peace Research*, **32**(4), pp. 469–82.

Jancar, B. (1990), 'Democracy and Environment in Eastern Europe and the Soviet Union', *Harvard International Review*, **12**(Summer), pp. 13–14, 16–118 and 158–62.

Jänicke, M. and Weidner, H. (1994), 'Successful Environmental Policy: An Introduction', Paper Presented at the Sixteenth World Congress of Political Science, Berlin, 21–25 August.

Kaffka, A.V. (1997), 'Threats to Security: Environmental Degradation in the Former Soviet Union', in N.P. Gleditsch (ed.), *Conflict and the Environment*, Dordrecht: Kluwer, pp. 177–90.

Kane, M.J. (1993), 'Promoting Political Rights to Protect the Environment', *Yale Journal of International Law*, **18**, pp. 389–411.

Karshenas, M. (1994), 'Environment, Technology and Employment: Towards a New Definition of Sustainable Development', *Development and Change*, **25**(4), pp. 723–56.

Kennedy, P. (1993), *Preparing for the Twenty-First Century*, New York: Random House. (Page references from the 1994 paperback edition, New York: Vintage).

Klötzli, S. (1997), 'The "Aral Sea Syndrome" and Regional Cooperation in Central Asia: Opportunity or Obstacle?', in N.P. Gleditsch (ed.), *Conflict and the Environment*, Dordrecht: Kluwer, pp. 417–34.

Knoepfel, P., Lundquist, L., Prud'homme, R. and Wagner, P. (1987), 'Comparing Environmental Policies: Different Styles, Similar Content', in M. Dierkes, H.N. Weiler and A. Berthoin Antal (eds), *Comparative Policy Research: Learning from Experience*, New York: St. Martin's Press, pp. 171–85.

Kotov, V. and Nikitina, E. (1995), 'Russia and International Environmental Co-operation', in H.O. Bergesen and G. Parmann (eds), *Green Globe Yearbook of International Co-operation on Environment and Development*, Oxford: Oxford University Press, for Fridtjof Nansen's Institute, pp. 17–27.

Lafferty, W.M. (1993), 'Interview', *Natur & Miljø*, (1), pp. 23–4.

Lafferty, W.M. and Meadowcroft, J. (eds) (1996), *Democracy and the Environment: Problems and Prospects*, Cheltenham: Edward Elgar.

Lape, J.F. (1994), 'Air Dispersion and Deposition Models', in D.R. Patrick (ed.), *Toxic Air Pollution Handbook*, New York: Van Nostrand Reinhold, pp. 226–40.

Lauber, V. (1978), 'Ecology Politics and Liberal Democracy', *Government and Opposition*, **13**(2), pp. 199–217.

Leane, G.W.G. (1991), 'Environmental Contracts – A Lesson in Democracy from the Japanese', *University of British Columbia Law Review*, **25**(2), pp. 361–85.

Levy, M. (1995) 'Is the Environment a National Security Issue?', *International Security*, **20**(2), pp. 35–62.

Liebich, H. (1993), 'Naturvern som religion', *Humanist*, (3), pp. 22–5.

Lipset, S.M. (1959), 'Some Social Requisites of Democracy: Economic Development and Political Legitimacy', *American Political Science Review*, **53**, pp. 69–105. (Reprinted as ch. 2 of Lipset, *Political Man*, New York: Doubleday, 1960).

List, M. and Rittberger, V. (1992), 'Regime Theory and International Environmental Management', in A. Hurrell and B. Kingsbury (eds), *The International Politics of the Environment*, Oxford: Clarendon, pp. 85–110.

Lomborg, B. (2001a), 'Resource Constraints or Abundance?', in P.F. Diehl and N.P. Gleditsch (eds), *Environmental Conflict*, Boulder, CO: Westview, pp. 125–52.

Lomborg, B. (2001b), *The Skeptical Environmentalist: Measuring the Real State of the World*, Cambridge: Cambridge University Press.

Mann, D.E. (1991), 'Environmental Learning in a Decentralized Political World', *Journal of International Affairs*, **44**(2), pp. 301–37.

Maoz, Z. and Russett, B.M. (1993), 'Normative and Structural Causes of Democratic Peace', *American Political Science Review*, **87**(3), pp. 624–38.

Marks, G. and Diamond, L. (1992), *Reexamining Democracy. Essays in Honour of Seymour Martin Lipset*, Newbury Park, CA: Sage.

Martell, L. (1994), *Ecology and Society. An Introduction*, Cambridge: Polity.

Meadows, D.H., Meadows, D.L., Randers, J. and Behrens, III, W.W. (1972), *The Limits to Growth: A Report for the Club of Rome's Project on the Predicament of Mankind*, London and New York: Earth Island and Universe Books.

Midlarsky, M.I. (1998), 'Democracy and the Environment', *Journal of Peace Research*, **35**(3), pp. 341–61. (Revised version in P.F. Diehl and N.P. Gleditsch (eds) (2001), *Environmental Conflict*, Boulder, CO: Westview).

Mirovitskaya, N. and Soroos, M.S. (1995), 'Socialism and the Tragedy of the Commons: Reflections on Environmental Practice in the Soviet Union and Russia', *Journal of Environment and Development*, **4**(1), pp. 77–109.

Myers, N. and Simon, J. (1994), *Scarcity and Abundance? A Debate on the Environment*, New York and London: Norton.

Neumayer, E. (2001), 'Democracy and International Environmental Commitment', *Journal of Peace Research*, **39**, in press.

O'Neill, K. (2000), *Waste Trading among Rich Nations: Building a New Theory of Environmental Regulation*, Cambridge, MA: MIT Press.

OECD (1994), *Transfrontier Movements of Hazardous Wastes. 1991 Statistics*, Paris: Organisation for Economic Co-operation and Development.

Ophuls, W. (1977), *Ecology and the Politics of Scarcity. Prologue to a Political Theory of the Steady State*, San Francisco, CA: Freeman.

Paehlke, R. (1988), 'Democracy, Bureaucracy and Environmentalism', *Environmental Ethics*, **10**(4), pp. 291–308.

Paehlke, R. (1989), *Environmentalism and the Future of Progressive Politics*, New Haven, CT: Yale University Press.

Passmore, J. (1974), *Man's Responsibility for Nature*, London: Duckworth.

Payne, R.A. (1995), 'Freedom and the Environment', *Journal of Democracy*, **6**(3), pp. 41–55.

Pearce, F. (1993), 'The Scandal of Siberia', *New Scientist*, **140**(1901), pp. 28–33.

Pickering, K.T. and Owen, L.A. (1994), *An Introduction to Global Environmental Issues*, London and New York: Routledge.

Rayner, S. (1993), 'Special Issue: National Case Studies of Institutional Capabilities to Implement Greenhouse Gas Reductions: Introduction', *Global Environmental Change*, **3**(1), pp. 7–11.

Rueschemeyer, D., Stephens, E.H. and Stephens, J.D. (1992), *Capitalist Development and Democracy*, Chicago: University of Chicago Press.

Rummel, R.J. (1994), 'Power, Genocide and Mass Murder', *Journal of Peace Research*, **31**(1), pp. 1–10.

Schultz, C.B. and Crockett, T.R. (1990), 'Economic Development, Democratization, and Environmental Protection in Eastern Europe', *Boston College Environmental Affairs Law Review*, **18**(1), pp. 53–84.

Sen, A. (1994), 'Liberty and Poverty: Political Rights and Economics', *New Republic*, **210**(10 January), pp. 31–7.

Smil, V. (1993), *China's Environmental Crisis: An Inquiry Into the Limits of National Development*, Armonk, NY and London: Sharpe.

Sørensen, G. (1992), *Democracy and Democratization: Processes and Prospects in a Changing World*, Boulder, CO: Westview.

Soroos, M.S. (1995), 'The Test Ban Treaty of 1963: A Case Study of a Successful International Environmental Regime', Paper Presented at the 36th Annual Convention of the International Studies Association, Chicago, IL, 21–25 February.

Stranks, R.T. (1997) 'China: Environmental Stress and Violent Conflict', in N.P. Gleditsch (ed.), *Conflict and the Environment*, Dordrecht: Kluwer, pp. 157–75.

Susskind, L.E. (1994), *Environmental Diplomacy: Negotiating More Effective Global Agreements*, New York: Oxford University Press.

Szasz, A. (1994), *Ecopopulism: Toxic Waste and the Movement for Environmental Justice*, Minneapolis, MI: University of Minnesota Press.

Tolba, M. et al. (eds) (1992), *The World Environment 1972–1992 – Two Decades of Challenge*, London and New York: Chapman & Hall, for the United Nations Environment Programme.

UN (Annual), *Statistical Yearbook*, New York: United Nations.

UNDP (Annual), *Human Development Report*, New York and Oxford: Oxford University Press, for United Nations Development Programme.

US EPA (1987), *Unfinished Business: A Comparative Assessment of Environmental Problems*, Washington, DC: US Environmental Protection Agency, Office of Policy Analysis.

Vogel, D. and Kun, V. (1987), 'The Comparative Study of Environmental Policy: A Review of the Literature', in M. Dierkes, H.N. Weiler and A. Berthoin Antal (eds), *Comparative Policy Research: Learning from Experience*, New York: St. Martin's Press, pp. 99–170.

Weiss, E.B. and Jacobsen, H.K. (1999), 'Getting Countries to Comply with International Agreements', *Environment*, **41**(6), pp. 16ff.

Westing, A.H. (1980), *Warfare in a Fragile World: Military Impact on the Environment*, London: Taylor & Francis, for SIPRI.

Wildavsky, A. (1995), *But Is It True? A Citizen's Guide to Environmental Health and Safety Issues*, Cambridge, MA and London: Harvard University Press.

World Resources Institute (Annual), *World Resources. A Guide to the Global Environment*, New York and Oxford: Oxford University Press.

Wyller, T.C. (1994), 'The Ecological Crisis: A Problem of Democratic Political Power', Paper Presented at the Sixteenth World Congress of Political Science, Berlin, 21–25 August.

Wyller, T.C. (1999), *Demokratiet og miljøkrisen: En problemskisse* [Democracy and the Environment Crisis: A Problem Sketch], Oslo: Norwegian University Press.

Young, O.R. (1989), 'The Politics of International Regime Formation: Managing Natural Resources and the Environment', *International Organization*, **43**(3), pp. 349–75.

3. The environment and civil society: the rights to nature, and the rights of nature

Michael Redclift

1 INTRODUCTION

Much of the discussion of environmental security has confused the implications of environmental problems for the human condition with the effects of human activities on the natural environment. In the Introduction it was suggested that we might begin by distinguishing between *ecological security* and *environmental security*. This chapter examines the way in which the international dimensions of sustainability have also confused the rights to 'manage' nature, which is largely informed by a science paradigm, with the civil rights of populations, most of which are faced with difficult environmental problems and choices. It is suggested that we need to look hard at the basis for the legitimacy of our actions, and avoid confusing human rights in civil society with our obligations to environmental sustainability.

For some time now the term 'sustainability' has only existed within quotation marks. Like the transition from feminism to 'gender studies', the attention to *what* is sustainable, and *how* it is measured, has had a profoundly depoliticising effect. This is not to argue that measuring sustainability is a purposeless activity, merely that sustainability discourses frequently mark the point at which the idea of sustainability loses its radical edge (Redclift, 1999).

The re-emergence of market economics and neo-liberal policies in the 1980s, with which the measurement of sustainability is associated, clearly marked a watershed for environmental politics. Increasingly 'sustainability' was detached from the *environment*, and environmental sustainability was confused with wider questions of equity, governance and social justice, which were themselves given weight in the arguments about sustainability. Earlier discussion of 'sustainability' and 'sustainable development' had been preoccupied with *needs*, particularly (but not exclusively) human needs. As the sustainability debate became more mainstream, much of it was influenced by neoclassical economics, and the translation of environmental choices into market preferences. Increasing attention to measurement was a necessary corollary of this trend. A search had begun for practical ways in which sustainability could be built into existing policies and planning.

Perhaps in response to the incorporation of environmental economics into more 'mainstream' policy, perhaps to compensate for a history of neglect, much of the discussion of sustainability as a political process was taken up by disciplines other than environmental economics. One consequence is that the sustainability discussion has moved, almost imperceptibly, away from human needs, the original focus of the Brundtland Commission's report, to that of *rights*. The emphasis on human rights in much of the subsequent discussion can be seen as an attempt to draw the discussion of sustainability towards other concerns of the social sciences: questions of power, of distribution and equity.

However, today the links between the environment, social justice and governance have become increasingly vague and, in some cases, the structural relationships between power, consciousness and the environment have become blurred. In the search for a more inclusive view of sustainability, rhetoric has often replaced the rigorous analysis of sustainability and sustainable development.

The mainstreaming of the sustainability debate came about as environmental and other campaigning groups sought to distance themselves from neo-liberal solutions. This stance requires little explanation. However, this chapter argues that environmental discourses which claim precedence for 'rights', and which are conducted at high levels of abstraction and geographical aggregation are only loosely connected with cultural choices and political decisions on the ground.

At the same time the criticism of market economics, which has characterised international non-governmental organisations (NGOs), however justifiable, presents problems of its own. Opposition to neo-liberalism is at its most effective when it moves beyond a critique of institutions, to embrace new networks of global communication. This was evident in the 'virtual', but very *material*, opposition to the World Trade Organisation (WTO) talks in Seattle in 1999, and later in the Washington street protests. Contemporary environmental protest raises questions of accountability for oppositional groups, as well as dominant economic forces.

These 'oppositional' discourses on the environment represent the communicability of different codes. They mark *practices* of communication, which themselves carry symbolic and political meanings – 'democratic power', 'empowerment', 'natural justice' – and which are seen by their advocates as an alternative to elective democracy (Esteva, 1999). However, these new environmental discourses, which reflect recent changes in globalisation, and the communicability of information, are no less subject to the spatial inequalities introduced by access to the information technologies themselves.

There are other sources of disquiet in the land of 'sustainability'. As species boundaries become subverted, and the human individual becomes characterised as a 'genetically modified being', the relationship of the individual to society changes (Finkler, 2000). The new biology, together with the revolution in information technology, may be altering what it means to be an 'individual', what it means to be 'socially connected' and to 'participate' in civil society.

The formal challenge of the Earth Summit in Rio de Janeiro in 1992 was nothing less than to transform the governance of the global system. At the time this meant the global environment, and the institutions that are used to exploit and manage it. However, within the last decades the global system has been, and is being, reconstituted, and institutions such as the World Trade Organization (WTO), the human genome project and the World Wide Web, are now integral to it. They are as integral to globalisation today as the Global Environment Facility or the United Nations General Assembly.

In this new global system territoriality is no longer a necessary property of the environment, but often simply a conditional feature of it. Calls for 'natural' rights to be protected, and for better governance of the environment, need to be understood as part of the wider, and contentious, discourses surrounding sustainability. This chapter argues that before we can fully explain many of the paradoxes surrounding sustainability, we will need to disentangle some of the terms that have entered the discursive terrain. The first of these elements is 'globalisation'.

2 GLOBALISATION DISCOURSES

According to Castells globalisation is linked to a *new technological paradigm* with roots in micro-electronics, new information and communication technologies and genetic engineering (Castells, 2000). The two key elements of this paradigm are 'universal interactive communication and the design and manipulation of living organisms, including human parts' (Castells, 2000, p. 10). These changes are destined to penetrate 'every domain of our eco-social system' through the development of the 'instrumental codes and cultural flows embedded in networks' that constitute what Castells terms the *network society*. The 'new economy' according to Castells is *informational, global and networked*.

The processes to which Castells refers place the environment at the centre of globalisation: since it is material nature which is being 'manipulated' and 'designed', and symbolic 'nature' which is communicated interactively, immediately and universally. The environmental 'regimes' which have become established since the Earth Summit in 1992, provide examples of these processes.

The Rio Declaration (Agenda 21) in 1992 reflected an increasing concern with global environmental issues: a concern that was to lead to the establishment of a number of institutional mechanisms to try and ensure that environmental problems could be managed more effectively. Behind this concern were a number of assumptions. The first was that international environmental problems – notably climate change and biodiversity loss – were '*anomalies* to the existing institutional arrangements of politics and science, and their capability of dealing with problems' (Becker and Jahn, 1999, p. 284; emphasis added). Environmental problems had eluded the international system, since they had not been predicted (in the main) and were difficult to control through the orthodox instruments of financial institutions.

The second assumption, on which the 1992 Earth Summit itself was based, was that both North and South had a *shared* interest in ensuring that future economic development was not prejudicial to the environment. At one level this normative framework was very attractive – it marked a departure from the divisions of the Cold War, as pointed out in the Introduction to this book, and marked an acknowledgement of the vulnerability of the globe itself. This consensus-based approach still represents the dominant discourse surrounding key concepts like 'sustainable development', 'human security' and 'global environmental change', taken up by institutions like the European Commission and nation states.

According to Law and Barnett (2000, p. 55), globalisation 'constructs the present as a moment, which is part of a fundamental historical transformation. Globalisation has become the grand narrative which justifies the end of all the other master narratives of social change.' Globalisation has thus taken on the mantle of modernity itself – it is the name given to both the journey and the destination, as far as most of its apologists are concerned. Policy discourses of this kind are essential ideological underpinnings for concerted action by national governments and international organisations (Baumann, 1998). They translate ideas, such as 'sustainability', into discursive terrain, providing a framework that is largely absent from traditional international diplomacy. They also suggest opportunities for different actors and groups to mobilise around policies and, in the process, provide them with legitimacy.

Different actors are also able to elaborate and embroider these discourses, providing ways in which the discourse itself can be redefined, or deflected. These *discourse narratives* are the stuff of international environmental policy today, and are exchanged and negotiated at distinct spatial levels.

To take one common example, within international nature conservation the word *nature* is used in a variety of different ways, to express social and economic interests in the environment. Conservationists use it to mean 'object', such as a habitat, a field, a forest, wetland or reef. Environmental groups, however, have adopted 'nature' to express place-based identity – their own legitimate (natural) environment. Finally, 'nature' is used in policy discourses to express a professional judgement on the type or value of a resource, as in the terms 'critical natural capital', 'biodiversity hotspots', 'common-pool resources', 'natural sinks' and so on. Each of these definitions of nature provides symbolic meaning for different groups of people and reflects their different interests.

Tropical forest management is one example where we can identify several contrasting discourses and alliances through which nature is characterised and conservation objectives are expressed. Protecting 'nature' becomes synonymous with protecting environments and endangered ecological systems, as well as the 'indigenous people' who inhabit these environments. It is not always clear where these discrete interests overlap or diverge.

Under globalisation, too, discourse narratives frequently obscure *spatialised* social processes, which remove and redirect biological resources from one location to another. The tropical forest becomes, literally, a global resource, to be exploited at several removes, and in the interest of 'science' as well as the market. Before the benefits of biodiversity can be commoditised and traded, they must first be privatised, and their ownership clarified. This is the important, and highly contested, domain of intellectual property rights.

According to McAfee (1999, p. 133) it is built on shifting sand: 'Contrary to the premise of the global economic paradigm there can be no universal metric for comparing and exchanging the real values of nature among different groups of people from different cultures, and with vastly different degrees of political and economic power.'

The processes through which globalisation is undertaken, and environmental agreements made, involves highly unequal capital and information systems, to which groups of people, and governments, have unequal access. For example, Vogler (2000, p. 209) shows how some members of the international community wield disproportionate power: 'In most ... regimes ... there [is] fairly marked evidence of the way in which norms and rules emanating from United States practices and legislation [are] translated to the international level.' It is a paradox of globalisation that the deliberations that accompany decisions to exploit genetic material in the wild, for example, are rarely public property in the way that political decisions were in the past. A basic unease with these new realities has, in turn, stimulated new forms of social protest, and new legitimacy practices.

After 1992 new environmental *regimes* were established to help implement the principles of sustainable development (Vogler, 2000). These regimes are legal, institutional and political processes, and provide testimony to the ubiquitous nature of discourse alliances. Today there are several hundred such 'environmental regimes', seeking to regulate, or control, virtually every facet of the natural environment, in the (supposed) interest of different coalitions of social groups and interests.

The *effectiveness* of the new environmental regimes depends, critically, on the way they are perceived by a variety of interested groups. As Vogler (2000, p. 208) argues: 'Looking across the spread of commons regimes a utilitarian hypothesis would appear to provide the best explanation for the incidence of well developed, and effective, institutions. There is clearly a relationship between mutual vulnerability, interdependence and effective regimes.' To aid their acceptance, and legitimacy, a number of measures are taken to provide both incentives, and disincentives, to comply with the regime. These include external debt cancellation, technology transfer and international 'exchanges' such as tradable permits or forest offsets. Such measures make up an armoury of 'soft law', which is undertaken to compensate for global 'distortions' in inequality between states, and within them. As suggested at the beginning of this section, they are a logical outcome of the view that global inequalities are 'distorting', in some sense an aberration of the global system, rather than a true manifestation of it.

The existence of environmental regimes, then, can obscure some key features of the new global environmental politics. Behind the facade of consensus-based environmental agreements lie fundamental questions of justice and equity, which regimes themselves do not address. What constitutes a 'fair' level of carbon emissions? Should cuts in levels of emission be 'equal', as between different nation states, and at what spatial level? Should they be linked to inward investment?

There is another major flaw with the international environmental regimes, which have come into being during the last decade. It is argued that 'soft law', of this kind, contributes to social learning, in that it engages everyone in the process. However, it can also be argued that 'soft law', such as that of environmental regimes, also risks *weakening* existing international obligations, particularly those of the industrialised world. The more that 'consultation' precedes non-compliance, the less that legally enforceable sanctions are effective. The problems of the compliance of the United States with the Kyoto Agreement, provide a case in point.

The current interest in 'human security' and the environment closely parallels that of environmental regimes. It has broadened the compass of sustainable development discourse, and provided the necessary ethical underpinning for global environmental policy.

Many of the features of the human security discourse are exemplified by former United States Vice-President Al Gore's advocacy of a 'Global Marshall Plan' (Gore, 1992). In Gore's submission: 'The task of restoring the natural balance of the Earth's ecological system ... might be viewed as a new mission for America's long-standing interest in *social justice, democratic government and free market economics*' (Gore, 1992, p. 270, emphasis added). In this account the environment becomes the means of achieving other social and political goals consistent with liberal democracy and the interests of international capital, and its protection, appears to answer to universal properties rather than 'political' values.

There are six main points in the Gore Marshall Plan:

1. the stabilisation of the world population,
2. the deployment of appropriate technology, from an environmental standpoint,
3. techniques for environmental accounting, which can help audit the environmental impact of industrial production,
4. improved regulatory frameworks,
5. the re-education of the global population about environmental necessities, and,
6. the establishment of models for sustainable development.

Some critics of the Gore approach, following Foucault, argue that: 'producing discourses of ecological living, articulating design of sustainable development, and propagating definitions of environmental literacy for contemporary individuals, simply adds new twists to the very specific pattern by which the state formation constitutes ... a modern matrix of individualisation' (Luke, 1999, p. 149). The political significance of globalisation discourses is not confined to the individual, however. The environment, seen as a strategic resource, can be managed in much the same way as 'non-aligned' status was negotiated during the Cold War. To increase human security, supra-national organisations might be expected to act with 'the global interest' in mind, since environmental stability is perceived as a 'shared' problem, for the developed and less developed world. The human security discourse is one of qualified support for interventions which reduce environmental vulnerabilities, and in which the political nature of this intervention is obscured.

A central principle of the new global 'environmentalism', as we have seen, is the role it affords the state and supra-national institutions. Ecological systems and 'environments' leave the moral domain, under this perspective, and become things which the state, and supra state, must administer. This represents a major shift away from the principle of national sovereignty, beloved by traditional theorists of international relations.

At the same time, the new paradigm advocates shared responsibility for the environment, as we saw above. Ideologies of 'co-partnership' emphasise the benefits of better management to both 'endangered populations' and ecosystems. Finally, the environmental security discourse builds upon the post-Cold War liberal consensus, by advocating planning and intervention. Terms like 'wise use', 'wise stewardship' and 'sovereign property rights' echo the principles of ecology for specific audiences, particularly those in North America.

Before examining some of the ways in which materiality and consciousness are changing global discourses and politics we turn to the way in which
the 'environment', and in particular 'nature management', is weighed against
other factors in what we might term the new *scale of international justice.*

3   NATURE MANAGEMENT AND THE SCALE OF JUSTICE

It is an assumption of international environmental agreements post Rio 1992,
that objective 'scientific assessment' will lead to an enhanced profile for
protected areas and species. Agenda 21 speaks of 'strengthening the *scientific*
basis for sustainable management ... enhanced *scientific* understanding ...
building up *scientific* capacity and capability' (UNCED, Agenda 21, 1992,
emphasis added).

This, in turn, has led to increased efforts to protect the environment through
binding agreements. An example is that of the Universal Declaration of
Human Responsibilities, which was prepared for the fifty-third United Nations General Assembly, in conjunction with the Assembly's commemoration
of the golden anniversary of the UN Declaration of Human Rights. Two of
the 19 principles of the Universal Declaration of Human Responsibilities
have particular bearing on the environment:

1.   Article 7 states 'All people have a responsibility to protect the air, water
     and soil of the earth for the sake of present inhabitants and future genera-
     tions'; and
2.   Article 9 states '[all people] should promote sustainable development all
     over the world to assure dignity, freedom, security and justice for all
     people.'

Westing (1999) argues that the UN Declaration of Human Responsibilities
should be a binding covenant in much less than the 18 years it took the UN
Declaration of Human Rights (1948–66) and that the World Charter for
Nature (1982) should be transformed into 'a binding international covenant
that explicitly guarantees appropriate rights for nature *per se*' (Westing, 1999,
p. 157).

In this chapter I want to argue that both these issues – the scientific basis of
the 'sustainability' discourse and the use of this discourse on behalf of 'natural rights'– requires closer attention. Misunderstanding the issues at stake has
led to widespread confusion.

4   THE SCIENTIFIC BASIS OF ENVIRONMENTAL MANAGEMENT

The belief in a global science, implicit in Agenda 21, is highly contested, not least by many scientists themselves. What is brought to bear on global problems is a combination of different, discrete, scientific traditions, rooted in different disciplinary traditions. For example, environmental chemistry is used to research pollution, botanical knowledge is used to identify endangered species. These traditions usually insist (compare Locke's view of 'natural kinds') that they are *carving nature at the joints*, marking boundaries that already exist in nature.

Most of these discrete scientific disciplines have nothing to say about the key issues, correctly identified in Agenda 21, as 'the *linkages* ... between human and natural environmental systems', and they are neither predictive nor prescriptive. The idea of 'sustainability' is invoked in policy discourses, as speaking to objective scientific method, without the complications of human judgement, although in practice it is routinely used as a way of guiding human actions. The very parts of the scientific tradition that have driven forward the frontiers of knowledge heuristically, have imposed boundaries, taxonomies and categories on nature, and have been used to make judgements which reflect human concerns and political interests.

The management of nature and natural resources, then, is linked to questions of human needs and values, rather than to abstract 'scientific' understanding. It is sometimes asserted, usually by 'disinterested' outsiders, that the 'community' or 'group' should be the unit of management in protected areas because these groups equate with ecological functions. For example, the Amazonian *caboclos* are interpreted as the essential ingredient for reconciling forest extraction and forest management, because these social groups populate the Amazon region.

However, as a recent review of deforestation in Latin America has argued, global paradigms are used for analysing local environmental problems, as well as specifically global concerns. Deforestation is 'understood' in terms of generic theories of development and the environment, whether neoclassical, neo-Malthusian or derived from political economy. The author concludes that 'it remains useful that *local* variations are emphasised over global patterns' (Browder, 1995, p. 135). The existence of global discourses on the environment and sustainability is frequently used to obscure the evidence and by obfuscating understanding such discourses provide few clues to local meanings of environmental degradation.

Similarly, much of the rhetoric accompanying sustainability fails to acknowledge that environmental and social objectives are frequently different, and sometimes at odds with each other. Can effective nature management be based on assumptions that we can 'read off' from the characteristics of societies and ecological systems?

5   NATURAL 'RIGHTS' AND THE ENVIRONMENT

These problems pervade the growing literature on 'rights' and the environment, as some commentators have noted (Dobson, 1998; Miller, 1998). Today, 'natural rights' are usually translated as 'human rights'. The idea that nature endows us with natural, inalienable rights, which governments in some cases wish to deprive us of, is deeply embedded in the political consciousness. The idea is there in the UN Universal Declaration of Human Rights, as we have seen, and has a history that extends backwards to the French Declaration of Rights 1789, the United States' Declaration of Independence 1776 and the Bill of Rights 1791.

The problem, however, is that this sense of 'rights' in a political sense is derived from natural law and is routinely confused in environmental discourses with 'the laws *of* nature'. These laws – the canon of science – include the idea of homeostasis in both biology and cybernetics, and the laws of thermodynamics, which express the principle that physical processes are irreversible. Once they are regarded as 'natural' such laws tend to be confused with the political and social implications that follow from their adoption.

Sustainability is a case in point. Andy Dobson notes that theories of sustainability 'sometimes make it subordinate to justice, but often the reverse is the case', and justice is looked upon as subordinate to sustainability (Dobson, 1998). This subordinate position of justice in relation to sustainability is concealed by the language of 'functionality', and it only comes to light when the 'win–win' relationship commonly found in theories of sustainable development is replaced by a potential 'win–lose' relationship. It also comes to light when examining actual cases, existing places and communities.

Dobson also observes that, since neither sustainability nor social justice has determinate meanings, this 'opens the way to legitimising one of them in terms of the other' (Dobson, 1998, p. 242). If you view sustainability as sustaining households and people, then the distribution of resources and rights in them is central to your objectives. If, however, you view 'sustainability' as the protection and conservation of the environment, then 'justice' consists primarily of ensuring it continues to play its vital ecological function. At the moment we cannot say whether justice is either a necessary or a sufficient condition for environmental sustainability.

In an analysis of forest discourses in Africa, Melissa Leach and James Fairhead compare the 'orthodox' enlightened view of forest management with that of local people. In the orthodox view the forest is portrayed as original and 'natural' cover, which is being progressively destroyed as population presses on land, and 'modernity transforms cultures which were once more forest benign' (Leach and Fairhead, 2000, p. 43).

Leach and Fairhead contest this dominant view and suggest that 'the persistence of such representations, even despite the existence of counter-interpretations and evidence for these, suggests that a certain "systematicity" is at work in science-policy processes' (Leach and Fairhead, 2000, p. 43). They attribute the dominance of the science-policy approach to dominant economic and administrative structures, and the financial mechanisms that operate within development planning. The 'global discourse' surrounding deforestation is a good example of what they argue is a 'pattern of representation', from which it is difficult to disentangle the arguments or the evidence. In policy circumstances such discourses have 'material effects', which are easily diffused, without the analytical assumptions of the discourse being subjected to any rigorous analysis. A number of changes are taking place, in the contemporary world, which are changing both the symbolic and the material ways in which environments change, and civil societies are recreated.

5.1 The Human Subject as Genetics

The first set of changes are in biology and genetics. In a sense 'security' questions have shifted towards 'nature', forcing us to reconsider what we mean by both 'sustainability' and 'security'. The protection of 'nature' is now used to legitimate military action. As we have seen, assumptions about the global reach of nature management have become enshrined in 'soft law', to which governments have signed up. Sustainability is no longer primarily a question of maintaining, and enhancing, existing environmental resources; it is about engineering new ones. The publication of the first results from the Human Genome project marks a watershed in the largely 'taken-for-granted' biology that underpins most environmental politics: individual entitlements, citizenship and governance. Some authors even argue that the new genetics is altering what it means to be *socially connected*, to *participate* in civil society (Finkler, 2000).

We already live in a global society where selecting a co-parent for genetic characteristics is a reality, and where surrogate motherhood is commonly practised. The research community has forced genetic cloning of animals onto the political agenda, and politicians, wary of something they have not begun to think about, have reacted warily. 'Patenting' nature *in vitro* has provoked mixed responses, as it appears to give transnational companies carte blanche to invade and remove genetic materials from 'other people's' environments. Many of these moves follow directly from the impasse created by the efforts at global 'management' under the Biodiversity Convention. In other quarters, genetic manipulation is defended by medical researchers investigating ways of correcting human disability, and working under increasing public pressure. So called 'smart' cards, holding vital genetic 'prints' are foreseen as the future biological equivalent to identity cards. Like the creatures of Aldous Huxley's imagination, we may soon inhabit a 'brave new world' without ever really knowing how it came about.

As species boundaries are eroded, and genetic choice dictates policy, are the 'environment' and 'sustainability' even valid categories any longer?

5.2   The Human Subject as Informatics

The second major shift in the way the global environment is constituted is linked to the development of information technology and, in particular, the changes being wrought by the Internet. These extend beyond the communication of information to the very nature of materiality, as 'virtual reality' comes to replace, or supplement material reality.

When Tim Berners-Lee invented the Internet he imagined a world free from regulation; one in which information flowed freely between sites, like currencies on a free market. To some extent this has given rise to a myth that has its own power – that the Internet is 'anarchic', and subject to no controlling forces. In many ways this is the opposite of the truth, since the forces that control the Internet are those that exert control in human societies and the market.

The regulation of the Internet is unique among global institutions in that it merged from the 'bottom up', rather than 'top down'. A comparison with global institutions like the United Nations agencies, or the World Trade Organisation, is instructive. What distinguishes global communication, via the net, is that online processes started as global processes, while most other institutions ended globally. As a result it was easier to gain agreement for policy formation on the Internet; a process which most users do not recognise.

Unlike offline organisations online ones are made up of like-minded individuals, who share a common (computer) culture, and common interests. What they do not share, in common with offline groups, is a common geography. Defenders of the 'openness' of on-line communication argue that the very criteria for success militate against secrecy and hierarchy. They argue that it is difficult to manipulate decision-making since anybody can gain immediate access to any proposal. In place of 'smoke-filled rooms' decision-making about virtual communication takes place in very public cyberspace.

None of this detracts from the fact that, with the Internet, we have a new type of global organisation that seeks to regulate itself, rather than a body that exists in order to regulate others. It is expressly, and self-consciously, free from the interference of national governments. It remains to be seen how far the practices and realities of the virtual world will influence those of the 'real' world. The Internet appears to be consensus-driven, but its message (coded and uncoded) is about markets and material success. In no sense can this be politically, or environmentally, neutral.

The *Zapatistas* in Chiapas were one of the first groups to use the Internet for global communication, over the 'heads' of politicians and local *caciques*. Some commentators have argued that this ability to communicate globally has served to undermine the hegemony of the global marketplace:

> a new internationalism is in the process of making itself. This new international-ism is not the adaptation to a preconceived idea, to an ideology which serves as a recomposing factor. Instead, the recomposition of the diversity of social subjects seems to originate out of practical necessity by different movements in their reciprocal interaction within the context of the global economy and their strug-gles. (De Angelis, 2000, p. 10)

This type of argument is used most persuasively in relation to the protests over the World Trade Organisation's meeting in Seattle. While the WTO debated measures to advance economic liberalisation, outside the hall pro-tests were mounted through the agency of Internet communication. Many of these protests were deliberative, and consensual, and politically accountable in a way common to non-governmental organisations, but to few political parties. Echoing Esteva (1999) again, perhaps these protests were more in-dicative of the democratic impulse than the battery of 'democratic' institutions, parties, governments and international organisations with which they were locked in conflict?

6   CONCLUSION

This chapter began by asserting that 'sustainability' discourses had reached mainstream international environmental policy at the cost of diluting, and confusing, the relationship between the physical environment and civil society.

The chapter then went on to examine the discourses through which sustainability, and the rights to, and of, nature, were expressed. It was sug-gested that although sustainability travelled with rather less baggage than sustainable development, as a mainstream concept it had often disguised in newer vestments the conflicts and agendas of the past. As Habermas (1981) has argued, the way that we understand 'nature' today is framed by the past. The 'new' sustainability discourses were often clothed in new language – deliberation, citizenship, even the rights of species – but they hid, or marginalised, the inequalities and cultural distinctions that had driven the 'environmental' agenda internationally.

REFERENCES

Baumann, Z. (1998) *Globalisation*, Polity Press, Cambridge.

Becker, E. (1999) 'Exploring Uncommon Ground: Sustainability and the Social Sciences' in Becker, E. and Jahn, T. (eds) *Sustainability and the Social Sciences*, Zed Press, London, pp. 1–22.

Becker, E. and Jahn, T. (eds) (1999) *Sustainability and the Social Sciences*, UNESCO and Zed Press, London.

Browder, J. (1995) 'Deforestation and the Environmental Crisis in Latin America', *Latin American Research Review*, 30 (3), 213–29.

Brundtland Commission (1987) *Our Common Future*, Oxford University Press, New York.

Castells, M. (2000) 'Materials for an Exploratory Theory of the Network Society', *British Journal of Sociology*, 51 (1), 1–24.

De Angelis (2000) 'Globalisation, New Internationalism and the Zapatistas', *Capital and Class*, 70, Spring, 1–32.

Dobson, Andrew (1998) *Social Justice and the Environment*, Oxford University Press, Oxford.

The Economist, 10 June 2000, London.

Esteva, G. (1999) 'The Zapatistas and People's Power', *Capital and Class*, 68, Summer, 47–59.

Finkler, K. (2000) *Experiencing the New Genetics*, University of Pennsylvania Press, Philadelphia.

Gore, A. (1992) *Earth in the Balance: Ecology and the Human Spirit*, Houghlin Mifflin, Boston.

Habermas, J. (1981) 'New Social Movements', *Telos*, 490, 33–7.

Law, M. and Barnett, C. (2000) 'After Globalisation', *Environment and Planning D*, 18 (1), February, 1–25.

Leach, M. and Fairhead, J. (2000) 'Forest Management Discourses', *Development and Change*, 31 (1), 47–59.

Luke, T.W. (1999) 'Environmentality as Green Governmentality', in E. Darnier (ed.) *Discourses of the Environment*, Basil Blackwell, Oxford, pp. 74–93.

McAfee, K. (1999) 'Selling Nature to Save It? Biodiversity and Green Developmentalism', *Environment and Planning D.*, 17 (2), 58–75.

Miller, D. (1998) 'Social Justice and Environmental Goods', in Dobson, A. (ed.) *Fairness and Futurity: Essays on Sustainability and Justice*, Oxford University Press, Oxford, pp. 87–103.

Redclift, M.R. (1999) *Sustainability: Life Chances and Livelihoods*, Routledge, London.

UNCED (United Nations Conference on Environment and Development) (1992) Agenda 21, Rio de Janeiro.

Vogler, J. (2000) *The Global Commons: Environmental and Technological Governance*, (second edition), John Wiley, Chichester.

Westing, A.H. (1999) 'Towards a Universal Recognition of Environmental Responsibilities', *Environmental Conservation*, 26 (3) September, 235–52.

4. Global environmental change and human security: what do indicators indicate?

Steve Lonergan, Fred Langeweg and Henk Hilderink

1 INTRODUCTION

Environmental activities are closely linked to various development issues. For example, in *Our Common Future* The World Commission on Environment and Development (1987) emphasised the linkages between demography, population growth, social cohesion, economic development, health and environmental activities. Agenda 21 of the UN Conference on Environment and Development contains a practical list of subjects and issues relevant to sustainable development, and includes a call for the identification of appropriate indicators and indicator frameworks. Since this time, there has been a considerable amount of research focused on identifying indicators of sustainable development and, to a lesser extent, human security. The purpose of this chapter is to review some of these indicator frameworks, and to present in detail two of these developed by the authors. The chapter concludes with recommendations for future indicator research.

What is the meaning of terms such as environmental change, human security and sustainable development? Like many concepts, they are constructed according to sets of social, economic and political relations within specific historical and spatial locations. One of the purposes of identifying appropriate indicators is to impart specific meanings to otherwise ambiguous or conditional terms, such as well-being, quality of life, human security or environmental quality. Sustainable development, for example, is usually characterised as a well-balanced development in an economic, social, ecological and institutional sense, with intergenerational equity being an important component. The concept of human security, on the other hand, has a longer history, and is embodied in the Universal Declaration of Human Rights adopted by the United Nations (UN) in 1948. The Declaration states that everyone has the right to life, liberty and personal security. In other words, human security means safety from the constant threats of hunger, disease, crime and repression, and protection from sudden and hurtful disruptions in the patterns of our daily lives – whether in our homes, jobs, communities or environment (UNDP, 1994). According to Lonergan (1999), human security is achieved when and where individuals and communities:

- Have the options necessary to end, mitigate, or adapt to threats to their human, environmental, and social rights;
- have the capacity and freedom to exercise these options; and
- actively participate in attaining these options.

Moreover, human security will be achieved through challenging the structures and processes that contribute to insecurities. Human security basically deals with a secured livelihood and the absence of (armed) conflict within and between societies.

Global environmental change may have a significant influence on human security. Insufficient access to safe water resources and inadequate food supply are detrimental to human security. Recent studies have concluded that development schemes need to address issues such as poverty, global environmental change and security (Rayner and Malone, 1998; Lonergan, 1999a). They also conclude that resources must be directed towards insecure regions to promote adaptation and resilience. Human security thus embodies sustainable communal, economic, ecological, political, gender, health and personal security. The basic requirement for these diverse characteristics of security is good governance at all levels from the global to the local (UNU, 1999).

However, recent empirical work suggests that the direct effect of environmental degradation and resource scarcity per se on the probability of violent conflict is rather weak (Gleditsch, 1998). The type of political system, ethnic fragmentation, population density, power status and the level of economic and human development seem to be far more important factors affecting the likelihood of violent conflict. Stable democracies with a high level of development also seem to experience a lower rate of violent conflict.

Nevertheless, it is clear that sustainable development and *human* security – as opposed to only violent conflict – are closely related. This connection will be further demonstrated by drawing examples of indicator frameworks for policy assessment. Relevant indicators can be derived from theoretical concepts of the linkages between economic, social, ecological and institutional systems (Langeweg, 1998).

2 AN OVERVIEW OF CURRENT EFFORTS IN INDICATOR DEVELOPMENT

The UN Conference on Environment and Development and its Agenda 21 document generated an overwhelming number of initiatives for indicator development. One such initiative was The UN Commission on Sustainable Development (CSD), which started a programme to assist countries by identifying indicators to monitor each country's path toward sustainability. The World Bank took a similar approach by developing a methodology based on indicators to facilitate the measurement of sustainable development. However, this was from a largely economic perspective. Others used the World Bank's approach as a starting point to broaden the scope to social, ecological and institutional domains. Even prior to this, the UN Development Programme (UNDP) began combining simple indicators to develop an index of human development and, eventually, human poverty. This was followed by attempts to develop indicators for human and environmental security. The most important of these initiatives will be described briefly below in an effort to provide an overview of the current state of affairs in indicator and index development. Are there indicators that can help to better understand and measure sustainability and human security? Can these be applied on a global scale? These are key questions that are addressed in the next few sections.

2.1 The World Bank Approach

The World Bank developed a theoretical framework in which sustainable development and human security can be expressed and, conceivably, measured. It connects economic, social, ecological and institutional aspects into one indicator system. The World Bank elaborated this concept into monetised values of mainly economic, natural and human resources (Serageldin, 1996; World Bank, 1995). One of the promising indicators, from an economic perspective, is the genuine savings rate.

The World Bank states that concern about environmental sustainability requires attention to the maintenance and creation of wealth. This requires the generation of genuine saving; that is, the residual of production less consumption, depreciation of produced assets and drawing down of natural resources. So genuine savings might also serve as an indicator for long-term human security. When it becomes negative, the resource base of a community will be eroded, resulting in a decrease in the access to vital economic, social and natural resources essential to human livelihood.

Genuine savings are calculated using standard national aggregates for the gross national product, domestic consumption, payments on foreign debts and depreciation of produced assets. In addition, natural resources are accounted for at a price of 50 per cent of the market price once extracted or harvested. Carbon-dioxide emissions are used as a proxy (at a price of 20 dollars (US) per metric ton of carbon) for all damage caused by the use of fossil fuel. The actual measure of genuine savings is less important than how the index changes over time, and the relative magnitude of the index among regions in the world.

Future steps in the development of this indicator are expected to incorporate savings through education and health investments, and the production costs for primary material to be included in resource rents.

This methodological approach has been elaborated in non-monetary terms by some other institutes. The Balaton Group, a Club of Rome affiliate, uses a framework known as the 'Daly triangle' as a starting point. It relates natural wealth to ultimate human purpose through economy, technology, politics and ethics. At the base of the triangle are the fundamental means out of which all life and economic transactions are built and sustained. These are commonly referred to as natural capital. The top of the triangle is the ultimate end: desires of all humankind, such as happiness, harmony, identity, fulfilment and self-respect. Intermediate means and the intermediate ends are in the middle of the triangle. The intermediate means are tools, machines, labour, infrastructure, materials and energy (economic and human capital according to the World Bank). The intermediate ends are the achievements governments promise and the economy is supposed to deliver. These include aspects of human and social capital, such as health, leisure, mobility and consumer goods.

The Wuppertal Institute (Spangenberg and Bonniot, 1998) adapted the genuine savings rate concept to develop an indicator framework that demonstrates the dynamic linkages between the economic, social and ecological systems, in contrast to the basically linear approach of the Balaton group. The dynamic approach highlights the difference between stocks and flows in these systems. Spangenberg and Bonniot (1998) argue that concrete, policy-relevant indicators need to be selected to facilitate societal debate. Economic production factors and competitiveness, human development as advocated by the UNDP (see below), and the use of natural resources are relevant indicators for that reason. The Wuppertal Institute also proposes to use different indicators at different societal levels varying from individuals to nations to international organisations.

A further development of the genuine savings rate concept is the index of sustainable economic welfare (ISEW), introduced by Daly and Cobb (1989, 1994) as an alternative measure for economic welfare or well-being. Daly and Cobb thought that such a measure would be able to reflect true economic welfare and guide appropriate policy better than the commonly used GNP. The ISEW stems initially from a concept of Hicksian income, in which GNP is corrected by deducting business capita depreciation, defensive expenditures and natural capital depreciation. The ISEW takes further into account the costs of personal pollution control (air and water filter expenditures) and the cost of ozone depletion. The index has currently been developed for the United States and British Columbia, Canada (Lonergan and Gustavson, 1996).

2.2 The UNCSD Approach to Indicators

The CSD has developed a more extensive framework to analyse sustainable development as requested in Agenda 21. An initial list of simple indicators is presented in *Indicators of Sustainable Development: Framework and Methodologies* (UN, 1996). This publication groups the indicators according to the chapters of Agenda 21; hence, they are organized within social, economic, environmental and institutional domains (see Table 4.1). This framework is now being tested for a variety of countries.

In the report, a comparison of indicators and methodologies is made in a comprehensive study carried out in close cooperation between Bhutan, Costa

Table 4.1   Issues covered by indicators as proposed in the UNCSD framework (UN, 1998)

Environmental	Social/Culture	Economic	Institutional
Land use/soil quality	Poverty	Health of the economy	Institutional capacity
Climate change	Demographic dynamics	Openness	Science
Biodiversity	Time management	Labour/ employment	International agreements
Water resources	Health	Economic opportunities	
Forest management	Education	Confidence in economy	Governance
Waste	Shelter/housing	Government budget and expenditures	Actor participation
Energy/material flows	Cultural values		Public information and communication
Urban stress Natural hazards	Crime rates		

Source: UN (1996).

Rica, Benin and The Netherlands. The study emphasized a limited number of issues and related indicators:

- Environmental: land use, biodiversity, forest management, energy and urban stress
- Social/culture: poverty, demographic dynamics, health and education
- Institutional: institutional capacity, actor participation, public information

2.3   The GECHS Indicators of Human Security

The science plan of the Global Environmental Change and Human Security project (GECHS) of the International Human Dimensions Programme (Lonergan, 1999b) suggests that a system of indicators, which express the environmental contribution to human security, should be developed. Lonergan proposes a set of 16 indicators combined to form an index of human insecurity (IHI) to address these issues (see Lonergan et al., 2000). The IHI is scaled from one to ten and assigns equal weight to each individual indicator within its composition. The indicators represent environmental, economic, social and institutional issues as shown in Table 4.2.

The index of human insecurity attempts to link human insecurity and conflict with global environmental change. Preliminary analysis suggests that the IHI may be used as a predictive tool to determine regions that are vulnerable to insecurities. Statistical analysis suggests that a relationship between the incidence of conflict and the level of human development and human insecurity does exist. However it can be argued that the zones of turmoil and insecurity are mainly located in the poorest regions in the developing world,

Table 4.2   *Indicators building the index of human insecurity as proposed by Lonergan et al. (2000)*

Domains	Functional relationships	Structural relationships
Environmental	Net energy imports	Safe water
	Industrial CO_2	Arable land
Economic	Real GDP per capita	Adult illiteracy rate
	Real GDP per capita growth	GDP per capita growth
Social	Population < 15 years (%)	Maternal mortality ratio
	Urban population growth	Child mortality
Institutional	Public expenditures on defence relative to education	Degree of democratisation; Index of human freedoms

such as Sub-Saharan Africa and parts of Asia. Poor environmental conditions and inadequate access to natural resources are associated with these situations of poverty. Poverty in turn predicts the risk of civil unrest most strongly. Thus, environmental change or stress may only be a secondary reason for conflict and the displacement of people.

The index of human insecurity also indicates the *vulnerability* of societies to insecurities, and to changes in sector specific indicators (for example, population displacement may have a strong link to environmental change) and the IHI reflects this since the top ranking countries of origin of refugees also show a relatively high IHI (see Lonergan, 1998). Additional work on the IHI has isolated human insecurity in seven distinct regions.

2.4 The UNDP Indicators of Development and Poverty

The UNDP has chosen a limited number of indicators to comprise its human development index (HDI) and human poverty index (HPI). The *Human Development Report 1990* introduced the HDI. Since then the index has been refined several times. The HDI contains three components: life expectancy at birth, educational attainment, and real gross domestic product (GDP, in purchasing power parity dollars) (UNDP, 1994). In order to normalise these components, minimum and maximum values have been established for the three indicators:

HDI_1 Life expectancy at birth ranging from 25 to 85 years;
HDI_2 Adult literacy and enrolment ratio both ranging from 0 per cent and 100 per cent; and
HDI_3 Real income per capita expressed in 1990 US dollars in PPP ($100 and $40 000).

The HDI is obtained by taking the arithmetic mean of these components, yielding a number between 0 and 1. Later versions of the HDI have added a slight weighting system to the index. The HPI is introduced in the *Human Development Report 1997* (UNDP, 1997). The HPI draws attention to three essential elements of poverty: longevity, knowledge and standard of living. While the HDI measures progress in a community as a whole, the HPI is supposed to measure the proportion of the population left out of such progress. The HPI is calculated as the exponentially weighted proportion of the population having insufficient access to education, health services, safe drinking water, adequate food supply and the proportion that may not expect to exceed the age of 40.

The original HPI shows little differentiation between rich countries. Thus, the *Human Development Report 1999* proposes to use a modified HPI (HPI-

II) for these types of countries. For the HPI-II, higher cut-off points for poverty are used in the case of longevity and education. It also adds additional indicators related to income and unemployment.

Most of the work done so far on the HDI and HPI has been of an empirical nature. The high rate of dynamic interdependencies between the selected indicators appears to be ignored. This is a serious setback in the interpretation of the phenomena the indicators are supposed to represent. Moreover, the HPI does not cover all aspects of deprivation or insecurity. Lack of political freedom, insufficient personal security and inability to participate freely in the life of the community are important indicators missing from the HPI. The development of the HDI and HPI seems to lack a sound theoretical basis. The IHI noted above provides a better theoretical base, but suffers from the same malady as the HDI; strong correlations exist among the specific indicators that comprise the index. There is an urgent need for indices and indicators to embody, in a scientifically sound representation, the systems they are purporting to describe and measure.

3   EXAMPLE OF HUMAN INSECURITY: POPULATION DISPLACEMENT, CONFLICT AND WARFARE

Displacement of people and conflict and warfare are important issues in the field of human security that are often the cause – or outcome – of situations of insecurity. There is no simple relationship between environment and population movement. A number of causes of displacement are mentioned by several authors. The first research report in the IHDP-GECHS series distinguishes five main causes (Lonergan, 1999a):

- natural disasters (for example, floods, volcanoes and earthquakes);
- gradual accumulative change of the environment (for example, soil degradation, deforestation, drought and climate change, partially due to natural processes);
- accidents (for example, nuclear power plan failures (Chernobyl) and industrial accidents (Bhopal));
- construction of infrastructure (for example, dams and irrigation systems); and
- conflict and warfare (both as a cause and as an effect in an environmental sense).

Theories on migration and displacement fall into two broad categories. A neoclassical economic equilibrium approach claims that people's movements are mainly driven by their own utility maximisation. The other – structuralist approach – assumes that power structure and institutional organisation are the governing mechanisms. The theories resemble the modelling approaches of social institutions and are mainly of a descriptive nature.

Theories for the occurrence of conflict and warfare are in an early stage of development (Soysa and Gleditsch, 1999). The oldest, modernisation theory, states that conflict first increases and subsequently decreases during stages of development to mature, democratic and peaceful nations. Conflict follows an inverted U-curve resembling the environmental Kutznets curve for the relation between economic growth and environmental pollution. Other theories however argue that other mechanisms are far more important, including:

- the role of the capitalist system creating inequity as a source of violence (dependency theory);
- the inadequate response of states to disaffected groups causing rebellion (resource mobilization theory); and
- agrarian uprising against, among others, market forces (peasant revolution theory).

Current theory can only cover some factors related to human security in a quantitative, predictive manner. Therefore, empirical research still has an important role to play. The US State Failure Task Force has made a major effort in carrying out this type of research in analysing the mechanisms creating state failures in terms of major political crisis (Esty et al., 1998). State failures are defined as: revolutionary war, ethnic war, adverse or disruptive regime transitions, and genocides and politicides

The US State Failure Task Force has developed a simple statistical model to simulate the likelihood of the types of failures mentioned. This model is based on the analysis of about 130 case histories covering the period 1955 to 1996. It offers a representation of the four domains relevant to sustainable development and human security: the economic, social, environmental and institutional domains. The model was tested against a variety of variables belonging to those domains as to their relevance in explaining state failures. The second phase of this study indicated that only a limited number of variables were relevant:

- material well-being – expressed by infant mortality (social domain);
- the openness of the economy – expressed as the total share of imports and exports in GDP (economic domain); and
- the level of democratisation – expressed as the democracy minus autocracy combined score from the POLITY III global data set covering a scale from +10, representing full democracy, to –10 representing full autocracy (institutional domain).

The model suggests that there are mainly indirect links between environmental change and state failures. Food production and land-related issues such as deforestation, intensity of land use (land burden) and soil degradation seem to be relevant factors influencing the quality of life. This model needs further elaboration from the environmental perspective; mainly by improving the environmental data set and generating new data by means of remote sensing. The environmental impact on state failures can then be defined as a function of environmental change, vulnerability and capacity to react where: environmental change is a change in environmental resources, vulnerability is the magnitude of the potential impact per unit of change of the resource, and capacity is the ratio of actual and potential impact.

The global version of the model estimates the relative risk of failure as 3.4 each for material standard of living and level of democracy and 1.9 for trade openness. A separate analysis at the regional level was done for Sub-Saharan Africa. This model needed three additional variables to arrive at an acceptable explanatory level. These variables are: the level of urbanisation combined with GDP per capita, colonial heritage, and ethnic discrimination. The relative risk factors vary between 2 and 5, with the exception of the level of democracy, which had highest relative risk of 11 attached to it.

The simulation of the level of democracy as one of the most prominent determining factors requires special attention. The Task Force developed a simple statistical model representing transitions to and from democracy and autocracy. Transitions from partial or full democracy to autocracy are best described statistically by the material standard of living (infant mortality or GDP per capita) and the regime durability. The adverse transition to democracy is reasonably well described by regime duration and land burden. The stability of a transition to democracy seems to be characterised by higher trade openness, higher agricultural development, higher urbanisation and a more democratic political situation.

4   INDICATORS AND MODELLING APPROACHES

The overview of efforts in indicator development as given in the previous sections, seems to indicate that four types of systems or domains can be distinguished in looking at sustainability and human security: (1) the economic system; (2) the social and cultural system; (3) the ecological system; and (4) the institutional system.

The main components of human security related to sustainable development are access to economic resources (income), access to natural resources (energy, food and water), access to social resources (education, health care) and the availability of adequate institutional arrangements (self-determination, democracy). These components can also be analysed through modelling exercises. Although some models are available for economic and ecological issues, little progress has been made in the social and institutional domains. In the following sections, examples of modelling approaches are given, which can be used to cover the four domains.

4.1 Modelling Economic Systems

Economic theory can be subdivided into three schools, each representing a specific management style and view on how society functions. The Austrian school (Schumpeter) assumes that development is an evolutionary process. Growth is stimulated by technological innovations. Government has to create the conditions for growth in particular with respect to R&D, education and infrastructure. The Keynesian school attaches high value to government coordination and regulation. Demand policies are used to generate growth and social equity. The neoclassical school advocates market mechanisms to move towards improved economic efficiency. Growth is stimulated via savings and subsequent investments. Most of the economic modelling is associated with this school.

Economic models can be used to analyse long-term developments represented by scenarios. General equilibrium models, built upon neoclassical theory, are used in various shapes and forms to carry out this type of analysis. WorldScan fits into the tradition of applied general equilibrium (AGE) models and was originally built for the long-run scenario study 'Scanning the Future' (CPB, 1992). Later on it was used in other scenario studies, like 'The World in 2020' (OECD, 1997). WorldScan has strong micro-foundations and explicitly determines simultaneous equilibrium on a large number of markets. The model is calibrated on data in a base year (both levels and growth rates). WorldScan is a dynamic model, but does not pretend to describe realistic short-run dynamics. The focus is long run, but the way in which the model focuses on the long run differs from the approach in many other AGE models. Traditionally, AGE models use comparative statistics or comparative dynamics to analyse the long-run impact of current policy shocks (for example, see Francois et al., 1997). In contrast, WorldScan is not designed merely to study steady-state growth paths. Its objective is to analyse structural change over several decades. It includes key issues such as the rise and decline of regions; demographic dynamics; shifts in patterns of consumption, production, trade and capital flows; and the changing distribution of income. The model should be able to describe unbalanced growth, where growth rates differ among regions and sectors and are not necessarily constant (Figure 4.1 presents a schematic overview of the model).

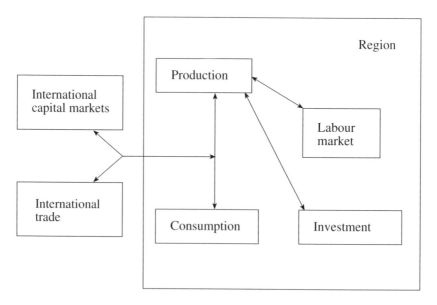

Figure 4.1   Schematic overview of the WorldScan model

4.2   Modelling Ecological Systems (Nature and Environment)

The size and quality of natural resources appear to be of crucial importance
to sustainable development and human security. Environmental pollution and
the disturbance of bio-geochemical cycles (water, carbon, nitrogen and sulphur) pose a major threat to these resources. The quality of natural systems
can be described by means of their size, the rate of disturbance and the
remaining biodiversity. At the global level, land use, climate change, fertilisation (nitrogen deposition) and increasing CO_2 concentrations in the atmosphere
are the major threats to biodiversity (Leemans, 1999).

   Land use shifts involve processes such as changing forest cover to crop
and range lands; loss and degradation of productive crop and range lands
through overgrazing, droughts and other (natural and anthropogenic) factors; conversion of wetlands, urbanisation and so on. Land use shifts are
also caused by natural processes like vegetation dynamics, responses to
environmental change, and disturbances, such as storms and flooding. The
past 10 years have witnessed the rapid development of a new approach
called 'integrated assessment modelling' for describing these anthropogenic and natural impacts on the environment and the earth system. Among
this new category of models is IMAGE (Integrated Model to Assess the
Greenhouse Effect). IMAGE provides an interdisciplinary and geographic

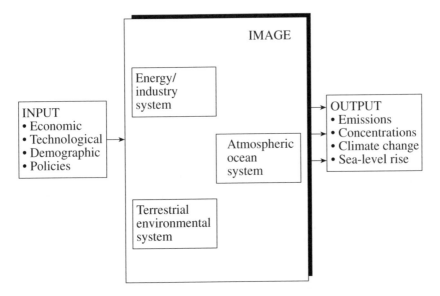

Figure 4.2   Overview of the IMAGE model

overview of the society-biosphere-climate system (see Figure 4.2). There are three components distinguished in IMAGE:

- The energy–industry models are used to compute the effect of economic and population scenarios on industrial production and regional and global energy use/fuel mix. Based on these calculations, the emissions of all important greenhouse gases, and near-term costs of CO_2 reduction are then computed.
- The terrestrial environment models compute land use/cover changes on a grid scale as affected by changes in food, timber, and biomass production, and as influenced by climate change. This set of models produces scenarios relevant to biodiversity and similar land cover issues. Data from these models are then used to compute the land-related emissions of greenhouse gases, and the flux of CO_2.
- The atmosphere–ocean models are used to estimate large-scale changes in the atmosphere and ocean, with a spatial resolution ranging from tropospheric average for chemical calculations to zonal average for temperature and precipitation calculations

Most of the environmental integrated assessment model (AIMs) focus on climate change. Gradually other features are added to these models to cover the broader perspective of global change. The IMAGE model for one will be expanded to include issues like water management, land degradation and the sulphur and nitrogen cycle.

4.3   Modelling Social Systems: Population and Health

Population size and growth are seen as the most important driving forces modifying the physical environment. Population change must be considered in the context of global change. The theory of demographic transition – consisting of both the epidemiological and fertility transition – can be used for a better understanding of historical and future demographic characteristics of a population. A limited number of demography and human health modelling approaches are available, which include an integrated approach of both fertility and mortality processes in relation to socio-economic and environmental conditions. One of these models is the RIVM population and health model (PHOENIX) (see Figure 4.3).

PHOENIX consists of three interwoven components. First, a fertility sub model computing the number of births. The main purpose of the fertility model is the description of the fertility transition. Age at marriage, use of contraceptives, abortion and the period of breastfeeding are considered as the four most important determinants of the fertility transition. These determi-

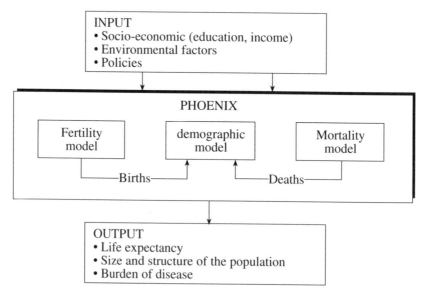

*Figure 4.3   Overview of the population and health model developed by the
               RIVM and the University of Groningen*

nants are strongly influenced by socio-economic factors (child mortality levels, female education and income) representing the process of modernisation. The HDI, which is the composite of these three factors, has a prominent position in the fertility model.

Second, a mortality model simulating the number of deaths. The mortality model describes the epidemiological transition, which shows a shift from infectious causes of death to chronic causes of death. Therefore, the most important determinants of health are distinguished. The major health determinant is socio-economic status, which is a combination of education and income. Further, malnutrition, access to safe drinking water and living in a malaria area are included as environmental risk factors and smoking and blood pressure as life style-related risk factors. In addition, the level of health services determines the mortality risk attached to these health risks.

Third, a demographic model combining fertility and mortality outcomes in a cohort model consisting of 100 age groups and the two sexes. Net migration is only taken into account exogenously.

The model is global by nature distinguishing 17 world regions (Hilderink, 2000). It can also be applied at the national level as shown by several case studies.

4.4 Modelling Institutional Systems

Modelling social institutions is in its early stages of development. The IHDP Science Plan of the Institutional Dimensions of Global Environmental Change (IDGEC) project states that the social sciences may not yield simple and powerful generalisations dealing with the roles of institutions in causing and confronting large-scale environmental changes (Young, 1999). According to the IDGEC project two types of conceptual frameworks or models can be distinguished that emphasise collective action or social practice (see Table 4.3). Collective action models rest on utilitarian premises. Actors are assumed to maximise payoffs to themselves through a process of weighting benefits and costs. In these models, institutions are regulatory arrangements created to solve or manage social dilemmas.

Social practice models look at institutions as arrangements to articulate normative discourses, to engage with informal communities and to encourage social learning. Institutions are assumed to influence the way in which actors perceive their interests. This may lead to routinised or institutionalised behaviour.

The IDGEC Science Plan articulates the challenge to develop descriptive, diagnostic, explanatory or predictive models. In the current phase of development, the emphasis needs to be placed on constructing descriptive models of specific institutions. In addition, research may lead to diagnostic models

Table 4.3   Collective action vs. social practice models of social institutions according to the IDGEC Scientific Planning Committee

	Approaches	
Characteristics	Collective Action	Social Practice
Behavioural assumptions	Actors are primarily utility maximisers	Actors are guided by cultural norms, values and beliefs
Agent/structure relationship	Privileges agents over structure	Privileges structure over agents
Mechanisms of impact	Rules are constraints on individual behaviour	Rules are internalized and shape identity
Institutional development and design	Engineering approach; institutions as instruments	Biological approach; institutions as systems that grow and evolve organically

Source: Young (1999).

describing institutional mismatches, conflicts and the creation of unintended side effects and possibly to an explanation of institutional dynamics. Harmonising quantitative and qualitative knowledge in these models will be one of the major challenges to meet.

The Wuppertal Institute is paying special attention to institutional indicators in its recent work on sustainable development. The Institute assumes that all institutions contain a set of rules for authoritative conflict solution. Three basic systems may be distinguished: (1) the system of institutional orientations (norms, targets); (2) the system of institutional mechanisms (procedures, standards); and (3) the system of organizations (structural, permanent entities with internal rules). These systems are embedded in behaviour, guiding expectations of society.

5   CONCLUSIONS AND RECOMMENDATIONS

Current development of indices and indicators for human security needs to be placed within a sound theoretical framework. Parts of this framework are of a descriptive nature and parts can be used for predictive purposes through modelling exercises. The current state of affairs can broadly be characterized as follows:

- Sustainable development and human security are closely interlinked and have a variety of indicators in common.
- The main indicators for human security are related to access to economic, social and natural resources including the presence of appropriate institutions.
- The indices developed by UNDP (the HDI and the HPI) and the World Bank (genuine savings) are well suited to cover both sustainable development and human security issues. These indices can be used in both a descriptive and predictive manner.
- Failures of social institutions, armed conflict and displacement of people can only be included in a system of indicators in a descriptive empirical manner because of the lack of sound validated predictive theories.

Additional research should mainly focus on shifting theories about the role of social institutions, and the determinants of population displacement and conflict from a descriptive to a predictive mode, as well as a better integration of the index systems and modelling approaches noted above.

REFERENCES

CPB (1992), *Scanning the Future: A Long-term Scenario Study of the World Economy, 1990–2015*, Sdu Publishers, The Hague.

Daly, H.E. and J.B. Cobb Jr. (1989, 1994), *For the Common Good: Redirecting the Economy toward Community, Environment, and a Sustainable Future*, Boston: Beacon Press.

Esty, D.C., J.A. Goldstone, T.R. Gurr, B. Harff, M. Levy, G.D. Dabelko, P.T. Surko and A.N. Unger (1998), *State Failure Task Force Report: Phase II Findings*, McLean, VA: Science Applications International Corporation.

Francois, J.F., B.J. McDonald and H. Nordström (1997), 'Capital Accumulation in Applied Trade Models', in J.F. Francois and K.A. Reinert (eds), *Applied Methods for Trade Policy Analysis*, New York: Cambridge University Press, pp. 45–60.

Gleditsch, N.P. (1998), 'Armed Conflict and the Environment: A Critique of the Literature', *Journal of Peace Research*, 35 (3), 381–400.

Hilderink, H.B.M. (2000), 'World Population in Transition: An Integrated Regional Modelling Framework', Faculty of Spatial Sciences, University of Groningen.

Langeweg, F. (1998), 'The Implementation of Agenda 21 "Our common failure"', *Science of the Total Environment*, 218, 227–38.

Leemans, R. (1999), 'Modelling for Species and Habitats: New Opportunities for Problem Solving', *Science of the Total Environment*, 240, 51–73.

Lonergan, S.C. (1999a), 'The Role of Environmental Degradation in Population Displacement', Research Report No. 1, Global Environmental Change and Human Security Project, University of Victoria, Victoria, BC.

Lonergan, S.C. (1999b), 'Global Environmental Change and Human Security', International Human Dimensions Program on Global Environmental Change, Bonn, 60 pp.

Lonergan, S.C. and K. Gustavson (1996), 'Estimating an Index of Sustainable Economic Welfare for British Columbia', Research Report No. 3, Centre for Sustainable Regional Development, University of Victoria, Victoria, BC.

Lonergan, S.C., K. Gustavson and B. Carter (2000), 'The Index of Human Insecurity', Aviso No. 6, Global Environmental Change and Human Security Project, University of Victoria.

OECD (1997) , *The World in 2020: Towards a New Global Age*, OECD, Paris.

Rayner, S. and E.L. Malone (1998), *Human Choice and Climate Change*, Batelle Press, Columbus, OH, pp. 129–42.

Serageldin, I. (1996), 'Sustainability and the Wealth of Nations: First Steps in an Ongoing Journey', World Bank Discussion Draft, Second Edition, 3 March.

Soysa, Indra de and Nils Petter Gleditsch (1999), 'To Cultivate Peace – Agriculture in a World of Conflict', PRIO Report1/99, Oslo.

Spangenberg, J.H. and O. Bonniot (1998), 'Sustainability Indicators – A Compass on the Road towards Sustainability', Wuppertal papers No. 81, February.

United Nations (1996), *Indicators of Sustainable Development: Framework and Methodologies*, United Nations: New York.

United Nations (1998), *World Population Prospects: 1998*, United Nations, Department for Economic and Social information and Policy Analysis, New York.

United Nations Development Programme (UNDP) (1994), *The Human Development Report, 1994*, Oxford University Press, Oxford.

United Nations Development Programme (UNDP) (1997), *The Human Development Report, 1997*, Oxford University Press, Oxford.

United Nations Development Programme (UNDP) (1999), *Human Development Report 1999*, Oxford University Press, Oxford.

UNU (1999), Work in progress, 15 (3), summer 1999, Public affairs section, United Nations University.

World Bank (1995), 'Monitoring Environmental Progress; A Report on Work in Progress', ESD series, Washington DC.

World Commission on Environment and Development (WCED) (1987), *Our Common Future*, Oxford University Press, Oxford.

Young, O. (1999), 'Institutional Dimensions of Global Environmental Change', International Human Dimensions Program on Global Environmental Change, Bonn.

PART II

Challenges

5. Climate change as a security issue

Johannes Stripple

1 INTRODUCTION

Climate change has been an issue on the scientific agenda for over 100 years, but has only quite recently become a part of international environmental politics. The implications of global climate change for patterns of international order and disorder have, therefore, yet to be revealed. Scholars have in general regarded climate change as both a source of cooperation and as a source of insecurity.

So far, the combination of global climate change and its societal response has not produced any major transition in the patterns of international politics. Instead, the dominant mode of climate cooperation has emerged within the established practices of sovereign states diplomacy and international economic structures. However, there do seem to be signs suggesting that some patterns of world politics are changing as a consequence of international environmental processes. From a scholarly point of view, established building blocks of international relations are currently being reconsidered in the light of global environmental issues. Examples of these 'green reconsiderations' are, for example, that international authority is becoming less state-centred and that established institutions, such as sovereignty and territory and their roles as organising principles in the international system, are being rethought (Litfin, 2000; Lipschutz and Conca, 1993; Wapner, 1997; Kuehls, 1996).

The concept of international security is another building block that has been rethought in the last decade. The end of the Cold War is often regarded to be the major impetus for the new conceptualisation of security. This new conceptualisation has questioned the primacy of the military element and the centrality of the state (security from military threats towards the state). Environmental issues have provided an angle from where the rethinking of security has proceeded. Elliott (1998, p. 219) argues that there exist two major accounts of environmental security. The environment has been regarded both as a cause of human and international insecurity and as a value to be secured (securing the environment). The purpose of this chapter is to advance a constructivist interpretation of climate change as a security issue on both of the above accounts.

I will, after a review of the burgeoning literature on environment and security, establish a constructivist perspective on security. I argue that the treatment of security as a question of fact that can be determined outside politics is problematic. Since security is a concept supplied by the political arena, it has an inter-subjective ontology. The constructivist position implies that neither the threats that count as security threats, nor the entities that need to be secured (such as the territorial integrity of a state or the cultural identity of an ethnic group), should be determined prior to the empirical analysis. Instead, questions can be asked about these issues, for example, which are the reference objects of climate security? Reference objects are defined as an answer to the questions 'what should be secured?' or 'whose security is threatened?'[1]

With the constructivist perspective on security established I turn to the analysis of climate change. I proceed to look into who or what is considered to be threatened by climate change. In order to balance the rather superficial treatment of climate change in the literature on environment and security, I present a quite detailed summary of the climate change issue, how it may be approached together with an overview of the natural and human systems that are perceived to be sensitive and/or vulnerable to climate change.

Climate change is often seen as a threat to humanity as such (global security) and has only in some instances been established as a threat to limited human collectives such as states and nations. I argue that the spatial (global) resolution of climate modelling is partly responsible for this. The global security discourse might be hiding the fact that although many people will suffer severely under a changing climate, the impacts are neither randomly nor evenly distributed. The climate impact literature, and especially the critical edge of the literature on adaptation, points at underlying social structural inequalities as important features of present and future climate insecurity. The constructivist approach in this chapter implies that it is not (only) the actual severity of these impacts that decides whether or not they become security issues. The political discourse also has to frame these issues as security issues.

In the climate change issue, climate stability as an environmental service is perceived to be the 'scarce resource' in need of protection. In this chapter I argue specifically that climate stability has not received the status of a reference object, that is, that climate stability is not regarded as a specifically important value worth securing. The International Climate Convention, which was signed at the Earth Summit in Rio 1992, accepts that humanity contributes to changes in climate, but also states that dangerous changes should be prevented. To comply with this formulation will require substantive reductions in emissions of greenhouse gases. However, according to the convention, reductions below the dangerous level should be achieved within a timeframe sufficient to enable economic development to proceed in a sustainable manner. Hence, it is not the environment that is supposed to be secured but current liberal economic practices and the ensuing implicit belief that growth can be sustained indefinitely. The language of the convention does not express climate security as a universal value, instead it is specific types of human-centred concerns that are in the foreground

Although the concept of security is open for redefinition, the practice of security remains a field embedded in international political structures. The collaboration between small island-states is an interesting example. These island-states are clearly identified as a specific threatened entity of climate change-induced sea-level rise and increased intensity and frequency of storms. I argue that these states, at the same time, represent a new type of (climate) security collaboration, and a (re)confirmation of the state-centric bias of the security discourse.

Future research will probably reduce some of the scientific uncertainties that surround the climate issue. However, even reduced scientific uncertainties would not provide a measure for 'real security'. Scientific information is clearly of great importance but it does not provide an objective factual basis upon which environmental security policy can be formulated.

2   ENVIRONMENTAL ISSUES AND SECURITY ANALYSIS

Following the end of the Cold War, the field of security studies has been subject to considerable debate. A great deal of controversy is present in both academic and policy-making circles over what is (and what should be) the focus and content of security policy and analysis (Baldwin, 1995; Lipschutz, 1995; ECSP, 1998). Military threats toward the security of the state are no longer predetermined as answers to the questions of 'what should be secured?' and 'what phenomena should the security discourse view as potentially security threatening?'. The traditionalist position in security studies has been defined by Walt as dealing with 'the study of the threat, use and control of military force' (Walt, 1991, p. 212). The traditionalist position, with its military primacy and state-centred view of international relations, has however been questioned. According to Krause and Williams the new thinking on security can be classified along the axes of *broadening* and *deepening*. Attempts to broaden the neo-realist conception of security include analyses of a wider range of threats stemming from non-military realms such as the economy, society or the environment. Deepening refers to referent objects of security (what is to be secured?) located on different analytical levels ranging from the individual (human security) to the entire system (global security) (Krause and Williams, 1996, p. 230). The environment has been treated as both a new type of threat and as a value to be secured (security of the environment).

A pervasive theme (along the broadening axis) in environment/security analyses has been the focus on environmental scarcity as a contributor to (violent) conflict. For example, Thomas Homer-Dixon has put forward several hypotheses on the probable linkages between environmental change and acute conflict. Homer-Dixon emphasises the role of scarcity of renewable resources that places stress on socio-political systems and, which given other variables (conditions), will erupt into sub-national violence and strife (Homer-Dixon, 1991; 1994). A salient theme in this 'scarcity' tradition is the focus on water scarcity (Gleick, 1993; Lowi, 1993). There have also been security/environment analyses along the deepening axis. Attempts to locate the security analyses at the individual level (security defined as human well-being) have been made by, for example, Myers (1993), Lonergan (1999) and Mathews (1989). Further, the environment has been proposed to be a referent object located at the system level. Pirages and Rogers have launched the idea of ecological security (the security of critical ecosystems) as a system level referent (Pirages, 1997; Rogers, 1997).

In response to the attempts to juxtapose environment and security two very different lines of criticism have emerged, according to Stern (1995, p. 219). The first is the *orthodox* view, which advocates a narrow definition of national or international security delimited to the concern with threats originating from the military capabilities of other states. Stern cites Walt who criticises the widening of the security agenda by arguing: 'Defining the field in this way would destroy its intellectual coherence and make it more difficult to devise solutions to any of these important problems' (Walt, 1991, p. 213). The second line of criticism is the *radical* view. Deudney, for example, argues that it is analytically misleading to think of environmental degradation as a national security threat, because the traditional focus of national security has little in common with either environmental problems or their solutions. Deudney is especially sceptical towards the different values, connotations and mindsets that are inherent in environmentalism vis-à-vis security institutions: 'For environmentalism to dress their programmes in the blood-soaked garments of the war system betrays their core values and creates confusion about the real tasks at hand' (Deudney, 1990, p. 461).

3   CONSTRUCTIVISM AND ENVIRONMENTAL SECURITY

As seen above, a consensus on how to approach a wider security agenda, or whether the security agenda should be restricted to military threats to the state, has not emerged. In spite of this disagreement, most of the attempts to redefine security, as well as the defence of the traditional approach, have something in common: an objectivist account of security. Hence, security is in essence about threats, and the analyst decides if and for whom the threat really constitutes a security problem. However, since Arnold Wolfers' security analysis in the early 1960s it has been clear that security can be approached both objectively (there is a real threat) and subjectively (there is a perceived threat). Nothing ensures that these approaches make the same assessment (Buzan et al., 1998, p. 30).[2] The inter-subjective dimension of the security concept that Wolfers noted has recently been brought back into security analysis as part of the constructivist turn in international relations.

In recent attempts to outline the constructivist IR landscape, Ruggie (1998, p. 35) differentiates between two main constructivist categories. Ruggie calls the first category 'neoclassical' constructivism to indicate the linkage back to Weber and Durkheim. In this category he puts himself, as well as scholars such as Kratochwil, Onuf, Finnemore, Adler and Katzenstein. He calls his second category 'postmodernist' constructivism as this group makes a more decisive break with the precepts and practices of modernity. Ruggie notes that the intellectual roots of this category go back to Nietzsche, as well as to Foucault and Derrida. Ruggie's 'neoclassical' correlates to what Waever (1997, p. 24) describes as the 'mainstream' constructivist group. However, Waever pictures this group as more explanatorily oriented and he opposes placing Ruggie and Kratochwil among them. Instead he argues that they might be called 'non-mainstream interpretative' constructivists. Other authors, such as Adler (1997) demarcate constructivism as both 'rationalist' approaches as well as 'interpretative' approaches, and Rengger (1999, p. 82) does not want to link constructivism with 'other accounts critical of the mainstream' either.

In relation to the 'broadening/deepening' discussion, Ruggie's neoclassical approach to security is concerned with security issues almost in line with the traditional agenda: military threats towards the security of the state, albeit with a constructivist turn. 'Critical security studies' is a variation of 'postmodern' constructivism (Krause and Williams, 1996; 1997). This tradition combines constructivism with critical theory and post-structuralism. Buzan et al. (1998, p. 203) note that in security studies the 'constructivist–objectivist' axis is used twice: both in regard to security (how socially constituted is the nature of the issue?) and to social relations in general. Critical security studies is constructivist in regard to social relations, but more objectivist in regard to security. Buzan et al. (1998, p. 203) argues for a constructivist approach to threats as well as to social relations. This is similar to the approach outlined by Ed Page in Chapter 1 in this volume; neither the subjects of the security discourse nor the phenomena that are potentially security threatening are predetermined. Before looking more closely into the climate change and security discourse we will need a more detailed picture of estimated causes and effects of climate change.

4   THE CHARACTER OF THE CLIMATE CHANGE THREAT

Climate change is usually seen as a serious threat, and by some even as a security threat. But what is the nature of the threat and what are its character-istics? For those not familiar with the greenhouse theory and its ecological and societal consequences, the following is a brief attempt to summarise the scientific consensus on the greenhouse theory as an explanation of human induced climate change. The greenhouse theory holds that a large number of human activities, such as the burning of fossil fuels, increase atmospheric concentrations of greenhouse gases (GHGs)[3] which, in turn, affect the escape of heat from the earth.

The Intergovernmental Panel on Climate Change (IPCC)[4] predicts in its Second Assessment Report (SAR) that the changes in GHG concentrations will have led to a 1°C–3.5°C rise (in relation to 1990 levels) in global mean surface temperature by 2100 (IPCC WG I, 1995). According to the Third Assessment Report (TAR), the warming is projected to increase by 1.4°C to 5.8°C over the period 1990 to 2100 (IPCC WG I, 2001; Kerr, 2000).[5] Warm-ing is predicted to lead to regional and global changes in climate and climate-related parameters such as temperature, precipitation, soil moisture and sea level (15–95 cm rise by 2100) (IPCC WG II, 1995, p. 3). Both the regional-scale predictions and the estimations of climate variability are un-certain. The IPCC has identified potentially serious changes, including an increase in the incidence of extreme high-temperature events, floods and droughts in some regions. The indirect impacts are, for example, effects on the spatial occurrence, distribution and activity of parasites, altered food productivity, and the likely disturbance of complex ecological systems like tropical forests.

The climate change phenomenon can be captured by measuring different variables such as the concentration of greenhouse gases in the atmosphere, regional and planetary energy balances or global surface mean air tempera-tures, but the existence and comprehension of natural processes of the above kind do not automatically imply a societal relevance (Storch and Stehr, 1997,

p. 66). In reference to the acidification issue: it is one thing to study atmospheric dispersion processes and processes in soil solutions, but to make the natural science part societally relevant a clear link between these processes and their influence on society has to be established. In the acidification issue this link is made via direct effects on infrastructure, food and health, or via indirect effects like reduced productivity in forestry, agriculture, aquaculture, fisheries, energy-crop plantations and so on (see for example, Odén, 1968; Amann, 1999). The same goes for the stratospheric ozone issue. Depletion of the stratospheric ozone layer does not 'mean' anything (it will not mobilise people outside the atmospheric physicist and chemist community) until it is proven, or until it is made sufficiently likely that, the phenomenon is affecting (or will affect) society in terms of health, agriculture and so on. In climate change, societal relevance has to be explored through climate impact research.

Within the IPCC, working group II (WGII) assesses the scientific, technical, environmental, economic and social aspects of vulnerability (seen as a combination of sensitivity and adaptability) to climate change and the climate change impacts on ecological systems, socio-economic sectors and human health.[6] This is analogous to the critical loads concept for acidic deposition, where soil and ecosystem sensitivity to acid compounds in combination with magnitude of deposition determines whether or not a situation is critical. It is not until the climate sensitivity of a range of systems (ecological, technological, institutional, societal) is known and combined with knowledge on the magnitude of climate change, that science and policy can interact and form a platform where climate change dangers can be assessed.

In the IPCC's SAR the impacts of climate on nine natural ecosystems and ten managed systems that provide water, food, fibre, and other goods and services to humans were projected. In a review of the IPCC SAR, Robert W. Kates (1997, p. 30) claims that, in spite of all uncertainties, although most natural and socio-economic systems are sensitive to climate change, there are four areas in which vulnerability to climate change is significant: forests, coastal zones and small islands, human health, and agriculture. Why forests? The answer is that all populations (as parts of ecosystems) are dependent on water and temperature varying within a specific range. New populations will replace existing populations if this range is exceeded. For some species (as for trees) this replacement is slow and for others it is fast. The IPCC predicts that climate change will occur rapidly relative to the speed at which forest species grow, reproduce and re-establish themselves. However, the IPCC forest assessment represents a methodology of greater common interest. It is based on the 1990 assessment by The Stockholm Environment Institute (SEI) (Rijsberman and Swart, 1990). The methodology elaborated on in the SEI assessment was innovative in that it contrasted (and still contrasts) to cost-benefit approaches to climate change targets (Nordhaus, 1991). The SEI methodology resembles the critical loads approach in acid rain discussions. In contrast to cost-benefit approaches (which compare the benefits and costs of abatement strategies) in setting climate change targets, the SEI approach (or sustainability approach) bases its judgement of climate change targets on the most sensitive part of the system. It is the most vulnerable group of people or the most vulnerable ecosystem that defines what constitutes 'overall' dangerous climate change (Azar, 2000, pp. 81–2). The logic of the sustainability assessment is similar to the logic of security as expressed by Waever (1995, p. 55). It focuses on the necessary survival of a specific unit, survival in the face of an existential threat. The use of the sustainability approach is also conducive to the linking of climate change and security since it directs the climate impacts analysis towards vulnerable groups.

Coastal areas are vulnerable to a rise in sea level which will imply increased salinity of fresh water aquifers and estuaries, changes in sediment and nutrient transport and increased coastal flooding. The IPCC estimates put about 45 million people per year at risk of flooding due to storm surges. In the absence of adaptation measures, a 50 cm rise in sea level would increase this number to about 92 million. Population growth and demographic changes will increase this estimate substantially (IPCC WGII, 1995, p. 36). Health effects are directly induced due to an anticipated increase in the intensity and duration of heat waves and indirectly induced due to extensions of the geographical range and season for vector organisms increasing the risk for vector-borne diseases such as malaria, dengue, yellow fever, and some viral encephalitis (Lindgren, 2000). Infectious diseases are currently the world's leading cause of death, killing about 17 million people each year (Burman et al., 1997, p. 66). Albeit with a state-centric bias, NATO noted that increases in health related problems, especially if epidemic, might become security issues (Lietzmann and Vest, 1999).

Turning to the impacts on agriculture, two major effects can be distinguished: first, the carbon dioxide fertilisation effect and, second, the effect of climate change on growth and yield. Many of the changes affecting agriculture are related to temperature and precipitation. Not all such changes will result in damage and some may aid crop growth (Drake, 2000, p. 204). Fischer et al. (1994) predict that climate changes resulting from a doubling of CO_2 would have only a small impact on overall global agricultural productivity. IPCC predicts that climate change does not necessarily affect the total global supply, but rather the access to, and availability of, food for specific local and regional populations. The poorest people in the world live in subtropical and tropical climate areas. These areas show negative consequences more often than do temperate areas. People dependent on isolated agricultural systems in semi-arid and arid regions face the greatest risk of increased hunger due to climate change (IPCC WGII, 1995, p. 33).

One central issue at stake is whether or not the observed changes in the global climate have a natural or a human origin. This is, in the realm of climate research, called attribution. Attribution means that the cause of a statistically significant change (in climate parameters) has been identified. Uncertainty regarding the role of human activities seems to be decreasing over the years. In the IPCC SAR (IPCC WGI 1995, p. 5) the conclusion was that 'the balance of evidence suggests that there is a discernible human influence on global climate'. In April 2000 Kerr (2000) commented on an early draft of the IPCC TAR (Third Assessment Report). Kerr's provisional statement was that TAR concluded that 'there has been a discernible human influence on global climate' (Kerr, 2000, p. 59). Similarly, according to the WGI 'Summary for Policymakers', 'most of the warming observed over the last 50 years is attributable to human activities' (IPCC WGI, 2001, p. 10). In terms of security, it now becomes increasingly clear that climate change is not an issue in the same category as meteors or volcanoes. Climate change has a human root cause, but all humans do not contribute equally to climate change.

5   CLIMATE CHANGE: TWO APPROACHES

How can climate change be approached? Generally, as in the IPCC work, climate change is analysed over long time scales, that is, the IPCC impact analysis 'horizon' is 50–100 years. This approach tends to bias the understanding of when to expect potentially serious consequences to a distant future. Even though the changes in mean temperature over long time periods have historically been the focus of climate change discussions, a new emphasis is currently being placed on anticipated changes in weather variability, such as windstorms, hurricanes, floods and droughts (MacDonald, 1999). Although much has been written on the relationship between climate change and extreme weather events, the IPCC has not been able to come to any firm conclusions on the subject. According to MacDonald, the reason for this 'failure' is that changes in averages have received far more attention than changes in the variability of the weather. MacDonald states that 'the spatial scale of many extreme events is too small to be captured in current climate models' (MacDonald, 1999, p. 2). But there are reasons to believe that this is not only a question of modelling design; a more fundamental scientific difficulty might be present.

Broadly speaking, two traditions emerge from historical discussions of environmental change (Wiman, 1991). The first goes back to Aristotle, Linneaus and Eugene P. Odum and is well represented in classical ecology. It holds that natural systems change very gradually and continuously towards stability and diversity. This continuity tradition holds that, as natural systems mature into more complex systems they become less sensitive to anthropogenic disturbances. When natural systems are put under stress, for instance when the climate becomes subject to increasing emissions, they will, according to this line of thought, respond in a linear and predictable way. The other tradition, in contrast, revolves around discontinuity and while it also has ancient roots, its main influences lie in the science of fluid mechanics and chaos theory (Mason et al., 1986). In short, within the science of fluid mechanics it has been found that beyond a certain point in time the behaviour of a fluid cannot be predicted. Complexity in a natural system will not act as a safeguard against external stress but will rather hide the system's response until a flip-flop threshold zone is entered. At that point, feedback loops in the system might be restructured, releasing a counter-intuitive and unexpected systemic response. The discontinuity tradition focuses on non-linear responses and acknowledges that 'surprises' constitute a normal feature of a natural system's response to perturbations (Wiman, 1991). An understanding of climate change in line with this tradition is more prone to arrive at the conclusion that climate change should be included in the climate security agenda. Security is about urgency, distant threats are not likely to be regarded as security threats (Buzan et al., 1998, p. 29).

Social scientists writing about environmental security have approached these issues. Dalby (1998) for example, argues that recent ecological research leads away from the reductionist and mechanistic thinking that has long been the dominant stance in the environmental security literature.[7] Litfin (1999a, p. 372) outlines two different scenarios of future global environmental change. In the first scenario, environmental change continues at a gradual pace, whereas in the second, environmental change occurs rapidly or even catastrophically. Litfin's diagnosis is that the impacts on the social and political order will be much greater under the second scenario. Enhanced cooperation at all levels of social organisation is the most likely trend for the coming century but if the second scenario comes true, a crisis could provoke an 'us-versus-them' response in which certain states or classes attempt to defend their interests against those of others.

Litfin's argument builds on the idea that collective action will develop more easily if change happens gradually and predictably. Although Litfin's argument seems plausible, we should note that it would be possible to argue that gradual change would instead allow more room (and money) for political manoeuvring and conflict. Also, scholars writing on innovation usually stress that crisis periods generate technological and institutional innovation; 'necessity is the mother of invention' (Boserup, 1965).

6   CLIMATE CHANGE AS A SECURITY ISSUE

In this chapter, security is not viewed as something that can objectively be established but as a social category that arises out of, and is constituted in, political practice. This enables us to explore in what ways climate change has been involved in the security discourse. Buzan et al. (1998, p. 38) note that, in general, individuals or small groups can seldom establish wider security legitimacy in their own right. Also large-scale system referents have problems with establishing security legitimacy. Limited collectives (states, nations, and possibly civilisations) are historically regarded to be the most durable referent objects. The ability to form an interpretative community (a reference to a 'we') is a prerequisite of successfully being recognised as something worth securing (Buzan et al., 1998, p. 38). With the emergence of the environment in the security discourse, arguments for the environment receiving the status of a system-level reference object have become more common (compare Pirages, 1997; Rowlands, 1992).

6.1   Securing the Climate? On Dangerous Anthropogenic Interference

In the case of climate change, what is the reference object for climate security? If we, for example, look at the climate regime that has been developing during the 1990s – what does it aim to protect/secure? The 1992 United Nations Framework Convention on Climate Change (UNFCCC)[8] was negotiated as a response to the public and scientific concern that arose in the 1980s. The follow-up negotiations, the so-called COP meetings,[9] are intended to fulfil the objectives of the convention. Climate change is approached as a 'rate of change in nature' that can be captured by various parameters, for example temperature, precipitation, frequency and intensity of extreme weather events and so on. Whether or not this change will be dangerous depends on the ability to adapt to the changes. Hence, the question is really: what rates of change in climate can ecosystems and societal activities cope with before the situation becomes dangerous? The climate convention states that the 'objective' of the convention is to answer this question. In Article 2, it is, *inter alia*, stated that:

> The objective is to achieve a stabilisation of greenhouse gas concentrations in the atmosphere on a level that would *prevent dangerous anthropogenic interference* with the climate system. Such a level should be achieved within a time frame sufficient to allow ecosystems to adapt naturally to climatic change; to ensure that food production not be threatened; and to enable economic development to proceed in a sustainable manner. (UNFCCC, Art. 2, emphasis added).

We can therefore understand Article 2 as an argument for securing a stable climate or maintaining a rate of change below the dangerous levels for human and ecological systems. In the language of international relations, climate stability is perceived as a collective good that needs to be protected through collective action. However, the convention does not secure a stable climate. The convention accepts that the climate is changing but states that the changes should not be allowed to become 'dangerous'. The threat of climate change is perceived as a threat that arises in the intersection between human and ecological systems and certain levels of atmospheric concentrations of GHGs. This means that the climate has not yet in itself achieved the status of a referent object. This type of environmental security reference object (threats to nature as such) is not common in the climate debate. Although some Greens might argue the human threat to the global climate to be a threat to 'Mother Earth', this is a problematic claim. From an ecologist's point of view, life on earth is not threatened. Human activities, such as the combustion of fossil fuels, can probably alter the conditions of life on earth, but not threaten life on earth as such (Ågren, 2000, p. 105). Therefore, climate change, at least in the language of the convention, is understood as a (relatively) human-centred issue and therefore not likely to be included on the environmental security agenda in the same way as an endangered species or specific ecosystem.

6.2   Global to Local Insecurity

It is often suggested that the concepts 'global warming' and 'climate change' are misleading since they do not convey the scale on which the impacts will be felt: patterns and manifestations of climate change will be of relevance to local and regional scales (Wiman, 2000). However, we know very little about the spatial distribution of climate change on these scales. Who or what is at risk is far from clear. The climate research community is trying to reduce the scale of the GCMs (General Circulation Models) used in climate modelling. This will provide more credible forecasts of sub-national and regional climate changes and impacts (Wilbanks and Kates, 1999, p. 618). As noted above, size or scale is a crucial variable in determining what becomes an established reference object of security. The global scale resolution of climate models has been an instrumental factor in giving environmental change a global meaning by generating images of an insecure earth, that is, humanity at risk.

Many scholars have noted the importance of this. Lipschutz and Conca (1993, pp. 1–18) argue that just the idea of a global environment has been crucial for the debates, dialogues, and disputes by which people recreate or transform the social institutions that give form to the future. Another development is the emergence of a *global* civil society that is becoming a central part of global environmental governance (Lipschutz, 1996). Deudney (1998) predicts that we might experience the emergence of a new planetary identity that might even set the stage for environmental security evolving into a universal value (Dyer, 1997). Litfin (1998, p. 370) argues that a strengthened perception of the earth as ecologically interdependent might have important implications for the creation of innovative North–South partnerships which are necessary in the management of rising GHG emissions.

It is possible that the global scale resolution in climate modelling has prevented the development of middle scale security reference objects. The Alliance of Small Island States which will be discussed later might be one of the few exceptions. The global image notwithstanding, some strands of the emergent adaptation literature draw another picture of climate and society linkages. As noted earlier, one source of uncertainty regarding the impacts of climate change stems from the climate itself, for example from the uncertain spatial distribution of changing meteorological conditions. Even though this uncertainty will eventually be reduced, we still know very little about societal vulnerabilities to climate risks.

In general, responses to climate change have been thought about along two broad types of strategies; mitigation and adaptation. Mitigation refers to the reduction of climate change and its impacts mainly through the limitation of greenhouse gas emissions. Adaptation refers to adjustments in individual, group, and institutional behaviour that aim at reducing society's vulnerability to climate change (Pielke, 1998, p. 159).

Mitigation has, and for good reasons, been the central focus of discussion in the climate change debate, but the past few years show an increasing literature on adaptation (Smithers and Smith, 1997; Tol et al., 1998; Smith, 1997; Pielke, 1998). The critical part of the climate impact literature bears much resemblance to the literature associated with 'critical security studies' (compare Krause and Williams, 1997; Booth, 1991; Macsweeney, 1999). The focus is on questions such as 'whose security?', 'for what purpose?', and 'for what kind of threat?' The bias of the economic method used in the traditional adaptation literature has been criticised. First, economic measures are often inappropriate when individuals suffer harm in areas that cannot be monetised. Second, they generally support aggregate estimates that miss the potential for widely uneven distributions of benefits and costs. They are not useful when looking at very poor countries and/or groups of disadvantaged people within countries (Waterstone, 2000). There has been a tendency in the literature on adaptation to treat societies as homogeneous and monolithic and little attention has been paid to the diverging interpretations of climate events. The extent to which weather is 'extreme' or not depends not so much on the overall 'societal vulnerability' but to a greater extent on where in society one is positioned (Waterstone, 2000).

Poverty is generally recognised as one of the most important correlates of vulnerability. Other correlates include differences in health, gender, ethnicity, and education (Dow, 1992; Liverman, 1990; Liverman quoted in Meyer et al., 1998, p. 240). On a global scale this is exemplified by far higher losses of life due to similar extreme events in the developing world than in the developed world (Meyer et al., 1998). Kates (2000) argues that poor people around the globe can cope with climate change, but only with great difficulty and pain. For example, the social costs of agricultural adaptation to twentieth-century population growth have been enormous: in the lives lost or diminished, the direct costs of adaptation, the costs of adapting to adaptations, and the costs of failing to adapt.[10] It is worth reiterating that continuing structural inequalities are as important in deciding the extent of present and future climate security risks as the climate parameters in themselves (Chong, 2000). As Lipschutz (1998, p. 113) reminds us, we have to be careful that the invocation of the security label does not naturalise what are essentially social, political and economic problems.

6.3   Climate Security Complexes

The possibility of sea level rise as an effect of climate change was recognised in the mid-1970s. Projections of sea level rise have changed (declined) over the years from 5 metres in the 1970s to 50 cm, according to IPCC's latest projections for the year 2100. The variation is due to another assessment – that of the behaviour (disintegration and melting) of the West Antarctica Ice Sheet (WAIS). Mercer regarded even moderate warming as causing catastrophic WAIS integration, but from the late 1980s and onwards WAIS has generally been excluded from impact assessments (Mercer, 1978; Long and Iles, 1997, p. 17). Low-lying coastal areas are vulnerable to sea level rise impacts such as inundation, greater risk of flooding and storm surges, and salinity contamination of fresh water. Recent research has also focused on the vulnerability to extreme weather events as equally important.

The Alliance of Small Island States (AOSIS) has been a key actor in the process of moving the impacts of sea level rise on to the political agenda. AOSIS is an ad hoc coalition of low-lying states and island states that are particularly vulnerable to sea level rise and extreme weather events. The vulnerability stems from obvious geographical factors and a lack of resources for adaptation measures (Soroos, 1998, p. 195; Salinger, 2000). The AOSIS was formed at the second world climate conference in 1990. Later on, the members of the AOSIS held common positions in the negotiations under the UNFCCC. In these the AOSIS has used scientific findings to legitimate proposals for more radical cuts in greenhouse gas emissions than have been suggested by other countries. At the 1997 negotiations in Kyoto, Japan, where a protocol for binding targets of emission reductions was negotiated, AOSIS put forward a proposal targeting a 20 per cent reduction of the 1990 CO_2 levels for 2010. This is to be compared with the 'signed' protocol in which developed countries agree to reduce their emissions by a total of 5.2 per cent on 1990 levels between 2008 and 2010. At the negotiations under the UNFCCC in Buenos Aires, 1998, the AOSIS held a press conference, once again highlighting climate change as an urgent and existential threat to their countries. For example, the Prime Minister of Towalu, Bikenibeu Paeniu, stated that: 'The size of impact observed in our countries has turned the discussion on climate changes into a matter of life or death' (BuenosAyres, 1998, p. 3).

AOSIS is an example of what might be called 'a security independence aggregate'. Buzan et al. (1998, p. 89) argue that 'if actors become interconnected in a political constellation over these security issues they represent a security complex'. The AOSIS in this sense qualifies as a formation of (climate) security interdependencies. Climate change is staged as an existential threat towards the very physical existence (including culture, identity and so on) of these countries, and their increased interdependence pertains to these security issues – they have nothing more in common than a shared vulnerability to climate change. The AOSIS case also points to an interesting theoretical feature. AOSIS is a subset, located at the subsystem level, but it is not a region. This might be conceptualised as more general phenomena: 'relations in the environmental sector in particular are much less mediated by distance, which opens more possibility for nonregional security formations' (Buzan et al., 1998, p. 202).

The AOSIS case also sheds light on the strength and weaknesses of the security concept. One strength of the concept is that it might highlight 'the climate risk landscape' and show how 'climate signals' in certain contexts can become (and be framed as) very serious. The weakness is that the security concept might 'mask' impacts that do not have resonance in the dominating security discourse. One might for example compare the (high) amount of attention that is given to the climate change impacts on 'island states' to the (low) amount of attention that is given to the impacts on other 'coastal regions' (Wiman et al., 2000, p. 134). The AOSIS case also signifies the state-centric bias of the security discourse. From a more theoretical point of view, it might be argued that these states, at the same time, represent a new type of (climate) security collaboration, and a (re)confirmation of the state-centric bias of the traditional security discourse. The green turn in international relations includes patterns of both of continuity and transformation.

7 CONCLUDING REMARKS

Climate change might ultimately be one of the issues that fall into the category that Alvin Weinberg has conceptualised as 'trans-scientific' (Waterstone,

2000, p. 213). Trans-scientific issues are largely political and cannot be re-solved by scientific inputs only. For example, how dangerous climate change is, or to put the question slightly differently, for whom – or what – climate change is to be considered dangerous, is ultimately a value issue. Similarly, the security discourse is also a question of choice, a question of value alloca-tion.

The departure of this chapter was a review of the literature on environment and security. I noted that there is no consensus on how to approach a wider security agenda or on whether the security agenda should be restricted to military threats to the state. I argued that, in spite of this disagreement, most of the attempts to 'redefine' security, and the defence of the traditional ap-proach, have something in common: an objectivist account of security (security is in essence about threats, and the analyst decides if and for whom the threat really constitutes a security problem). In contrast to this, I advanced a constructivist interpretation of climate change as a security issue. The constructivist position has important ontological implications. Whether or not climate change is (or is not) a security issue cannot be resolved outside the world of politics. Hence, I regarded a good place to look for the rhetorical logic of security to be the climate convention. I argued that the convention does not elevate the relative stability of climate into an issue of absolute priority. Instead of securing climate stability the convention secures that current economic practices should not be threatened by activities towards mitigation of climate change. Therefore, climate stability has not received the status of a security reference object.

In the years to come, it is likely that many uncertainties regarding potential impacts of climate change will be reduced. Advances in climate modelling might increase our knowledge about impacts on regional scales and on spe-cific human activities. I argued that the global-scale image of humanity at risk of suffering from climate change might mask social and political founda-tions of climate-induced insecurity. I used the critical edge of the literature on adaptation to argue that vulnerability to climate change is not only dependent on where one is situated geographically, but also on position in economic and political structures. If the scientific estimations hold, many people will surely suffer under a changing climate. Kates (2000) has argued that 'In developing countries, coping with the climate extremes of drought, flood, and storm is the moral equivalent of war – requiring the equivalent effort in percentage of GNP that most countries expend on national defence.' The constructivist approach in this chapter implies that it is not (only) the actual severity of these impacts that decides whether or not they become security issues, but rather if they are treated as such within a political discourse.

For many years, the security discourse was about military threats to the state. Now, in the so-called late Westphalian order, conceptualisations of security are in a state of flux. There is no room in this chapter to further elaborate on the Westphalian state-centric and 'monosectoral' conceptualisation of security. However, the basic constructivist approach, used in this chapter, enables us to view the Westphalian meaning of security not as a law of nature but as socially constructed and, at least potentially, open for restructuring. Waever (1995) has argued that the present organising of political space in a set of overlapping authorities (in contrast to sovereign territorial states) enables new actors and new referent objects to shape the security discourse. Who has the position to make security claims, on what issues, for whom, and with what effects may fluctuate, but the answers are not 'free floating'. The security discourse is embedded in international political structures. Historically this has promoted certain power political structures, but there might be signs of this changing.

Scientists, whose authority is based on knowledge, might emerge as actors with the capability of interfering in the environmental security discourse. However, I would argue that prudence might be in order here. It is a political choice to phrase things in terms of security and security is a powerful discourse. Historically it has legitimised the use of force; it is a mobilising concept that sets priorities among various issues. I will end this chapter with a recent example that might illustrate an 'environmental security dilemma'.

China has over the past few years been hit by severe flooding that has had disastrous effects. The Chinese government has clearly phrased flooding in terms of security, that is, flooding is staged as an issue of absolute urgent priority for China. Flooding is the enemy and the army is called in to 'fight the floods'. An enormous amount of people work (unpaid) as 'flooding heroes'. However, research has shown that this way of 'managing' floods is 'inefficient'. It is a management 'style' that is difficult to combine with land use (in this case people changing the soil structure on the riverbanks and in the catchment basins) and population issues (in this case people moving into flood-prone areas). Since natural disasters don't just happen – but rather arise in the intersection between human and natural systems (societal changes create 'natural' disasters) – applying the logic of security might in this case contribute to even more insecurity (more flooding).

NOTES

1. These 'reference objects' correspond to Edward Page's notion of the 'subjects of the security discourse'. See Chapter 1 of this volume.
2. We also recognise this line of argument from the field of risk analysis where there is a distinction between objective risk, perceptions of risk and risk as a construct. In brief, risk perceptions can be studied with either an objectivist or a relativist ontology. Starting from an objectivist ontology, theories about risk perceptions take for granted that there is a

difference between objective risk and perceived risk and, hence, attempt to explain why risk is 'misperceived'. However, this distinction between objective and perceived risk has in recent years been criticised for precisely its objectivist ontology. With a relativist ontology, risk is equated with perceptions of risk, that is, risk arises from the perceptions of it, and the study of risk will therefore be synonymous with the study of the construction of the risk (Renn, 1992; Wynne, 1996). Recent constructivist approaches to security have many similarities with the 1990s developments (social and cultural approaches) in the field of risk analysis.

3. Greenhouse gases (GHGs) include carbon dioxide, but also rarer gases such as methane, nitrous oxide, and chlorofluorocarbons (CFCs).

4. The Intergovernmental Panel on Climate Change is a specialised inter-governmental body established by the United Nations Environmental Programme (UNEP) and World Meteorological Organisation (WMO) in 1988 to provide assessments of the results of climate change research for policymakers. The IPCC, which consists of over 2000 scientists from around the world, has compiled three 'Assessment Reports' (in 1990, 1995 and 2001) which provide comprehensive analyses of climate change. The third assessment report was published in 2001 by Cambridge University Press (http://uk.cambridge.org/earthsciences/climatechange/).

5. This is because of the 'cooling' effect of sulphur aerosols. The new IPCC report writes that 'the higher projected temperatures and the wider range range are due primarily to the lower projected sulphur dioxide emissions in the SRES scenarios relative to the IS92 scenarios' (IPCC WGI 2001, p. 13).

6. The concepts of sensitivity and adaptability may not be clear to every reader. IPCC defines sensitivity as the degree to which a system will respond to a change in climatic conditions while adaptability refers to the degree to which adjustments to projected or actual changes in climate are possible in practices, processes, or in the structures of different types of systems.

7. I am not sure of the accuracy of Dalby's statement. As far as I know, ecology as a scientific discipline is, today, far more driven by a 'competition paradigm' and, therefore, reductionist rather than holistic.

8. The climate convention, UNFCCC, was signed at the 'Earth Summit'; the United Nations Conference on Environment and Development (UNCED), in Rio, 1992, and entered into force in 1994.

9. Conference of the Parties (COP), the states that signed the protocol. The Kyoto protocol was signed at the COP3 meeting in Japanese Kyoto in 1997. The protocol is the last major agreement within UNFCCC and mandates reductions in overall greenhouse gas emissions by 39 industrialised countries by 5.2 per cent of 1990 levels by 2008–2012. The last COP meeting (COP6) was held in Hague in December 2000 but did not produce an agreement.

10. For the centrality of agriculture in the security discourse, see Soysa and Gleditsch (1999).

BIBLIOGRAPHY

Adler, E. (1997), 'Seizing the Middle Ground. Constructivism in World Politics', *European Journal of International Relations*, **3**(3), 319–63.

Ågren, G.I. (2000), 'Dangerous Anthropogenic Interference with Climate: An Ecosystem Ecologist's View', in B. Wiman, J. Stripple and S.M. Chong (eds), *From Climate Risk to Climate Security*, Kalmar: Kalmar University, Sweden and Swedish Environmental Protection Agency.

Amann, M., I. Bertok, J. Cofala, F. Gyarfas, C. Heyes, Z. Klimont, M. Makowski, W. Schöpp and S. Syri (1999), 'Sensitivity Analyses for Central Scenario to Control Acidification, Eutrophication and Ground-level Ozone in Europe', report for the

23rd meeting of the UN/ECE Task Force on Integrated Assessment Modelling Laxemburg: IIASA (http://www.iiasa.ac.at/~rains/reports/tfiam23.pdf).

Azar, C. (2000), 'Climate Risk Reduction Costs: Tools for Setting Climate Change Targets', in B. Wiman, J. Stripple and S.M. Chong (eds), *From Climate Risk to Climate Security*, Kalmar: Kalmar University, Sweden and Swedish Environmental Protection Agency.

Azar, C. and H. Rodhe (1997), 'Targets for Stabilisation of Atmospheric CO_2', *Science*, **276**, 1818–19.

Baldwin, D.A. (1995), 'The Concept of Security', *Review of International Studies*, **23**(1), 5–26.

Booth, K. (1991), 'Security and Emancipation', *Review of International Studies*, **17**(4), 313–27.

Boserup, E. (1965), *The Conditions of Agricultural Growth*, London: George Allen and Unwin (reprinted in 1993 by Earthscan, London).

BuenosAyres (1998), 'Claiming Sensitivity from the World' *BuenosAyres: Daily Journal at the UNFCCC/COP4*.

Burman, R., K. Kirschner and E. McCarter (1997), 'Infectious Disease as a Global Security Threat', in G.D. Dabelko (ed.), *Environmental Change and Security Project Report 3*, Washington: Woodrow Wilson International Center for Scholars.

Buzan, B., O. Waever and J. de Wilde (1998), *Security: A New Framework for Analysis*, Boulder, CO: Lynne Rienner.

Carlsson, S. and J. Stripple (1999), 'Alla talar om vädret' (Everyone is talking about the weather), *Svenska Dagbladet 1999-06-05*, Stockholm.

Chong, S.M. (2000), 'The Insecurity of Inequality in a Changing Climate', in B. Wiman, J. Stripple and S.M. Chong (eds), *From Climate Risk to Climate Security*, Kalmar: Kalmar University, Sweden and Swedish Environmental Protection Agency.

Conca, K. (1993), 'Environmental Change and the Deep Structure of World Politics', in R.D. Lipschutz and K. Conca (eds), *State and the Social Power in Global Environmental Politics*, New York: Columbia University Press.

Dalby, S. (1998), 'Ecological Metaphors of Security: World Politics in the Biosphere', *Alternatives: Social Transformations and Humane Governance*, **23**(3), 291-319.

de Soysa, I. and N.P. Gleditsch (1999), 'To Cultivate Peace: Agriculture in a World of Conflict', in G.D. Dabelko (ed.), *Environmental Change and Security Project Report 4*, Washington: Woodrow Wilson International Center for Scholars.

Deudney, D. (1990), 'The Case against Linking Environmental Degradation and National Security', *Millenium: Journal of International Studies*, **19**(3), 461–76.

Deudney, D. (1998), 'Global Village Sovereignty: Intergenerational Sovereign Publics, Federal-Republican Earth Constitutions, and Planetary Identities', in K. Litfin (ed.), *The Greening of Sovereignty in World Politics*, Cambridge, MA: MIT Press.

Dow, K. (1992), 'Exploring Differences in our Common Future(s): The Meaning of Vulnerability to Global Environmental Change', *Geoforum*, **23**, 417-36.

Drake, F. (2000), *Global Warming: The Science of Climate Change*, London and New York: Arnold.

Dyer, H. (1997), 'Environmental Security as a Universal Value', in J. Vogler and M. Imber (eds), *The Environment and International Relations*, London and New York: Routledge.

Dyer, H. (1998), 'International Theory and International Security', *Environment and Security*, **1**(3), 133–53.

Ecologists' Statement on the Consequences of Rapid Climate Change. Letter to

President Clinton, dated 21 May 1997. *Global Change*, electronic edition (http://www.globalchange.org/).

ECSP (1998), *Environmental Change and Security Project Report 4*, Washington: Woodrow Wilson International Center for Scholars.

Elliot, L. (1998), *The Global Politics of the Environment*, London: Macmillan Press.

Fischer, G., K. Frohberg, M.L. Parry and C. Rosenzweig (1994), 'Climate Change and World Food Supply, Demand and Trade: Who Benefits, Who Loses?', *Global Environmental Change*, **4**(1), 7–23.

Gleick, P.H. (1993), 'Water, War and Peace in the Middle East', *International Security*, **18**(1), 79–112.

Homer-Dixon, T.F. (1991), 'On the Threshold: Environmental Changes as Causes of Acute Conflict', *International Security*, **16**(2), 76–116.

Homer-Dixon, T.F. (1994), 'Environmental Scarcities and Violent Conflict', *International Security*, **19**(1), 5–40.

IPCC WGI (1995), *Climate Change 1995: The Science of Climate Change: Contribution of Working Group 1 to the Second Assessment Report of the Intergovernmental Panel of Climate Change*, Cambridge: Cambridge University Press.

IPCC WGI (2001), *Climate Change 2001: The Scientific Basis*, Summary for Policymakers: A Report of Working Group 1 of the International Panel of Climate Change, Cambridge: Cambridge University Press (http://www.ipcc.ch/).

IPCC WGII (1995), *Climate Change 1995: Impacts, Adaptations and Mitigations of Climate Change: Scientific-Technical Analyses, Contribution of Working Group II to the Second Assessment Report of the Intergovernmental Panel of Climate Change*, Cambridge: Cambridge University Press.

IPCC WGII (2001), *Climate Change 2001: Impacts, Adaptation, and Vulnerability*, Summary for Policymakers, Cambridge: Cambridge University Press (http:www.ipcc.ch/).

IPCC WGIII (1995), *Climate Change 1995: Mitigation*, Summary for Policymakers of the WGIII Contribution to IPCC Third Assessment Report, Cambridge: Cambridge University Press.

IPCC WGIII (2001), *Climate Change 2001: Mitigation*, Summary for Policymakers of the WGIII Contribution to IPCC Third Assessment Report, Cambridge: Cambridge University Press (http://www.ipcc-ch/).

Johannesson, M. (1998), 'Risk Management under Uncertainty', Doctoral thesis, Stockholm University.

Kane, S. and G. Yohe (2000), 'Societal Adaptation to Climate Variability and Change: An Introduction', *Climatic Change*, **45**, 1–4.

Kates, R.W. (1997), 'Climate Change 1995: Impacts, Adaptations, and Mitigation', *Environment*, **39**(9), 29–33.

Kates, R.W. (2000), 'Cautionary Tales: Adaptation and the Global Poor', *Climatic Change*, (45), 5–17.

Keller, K., K. Tan, F.M.M. Morel and D.F. Bradford (2000), 'Preserving the Ocean Circulation: Implications for Climate Policy', *Climatic Change*, **47**, 17–43.

Kerr, R.A. (2000), 'Draft Report Affirms Human Influence', *Science*, **288**, 58–9.

Krause, K. and M.C. Williams (1996), 'Broadening the Agenda of Security Studies: Politics and Methods', *Mershon International Studies Review*, **40**, 229–54.

Krause, K. and M.C. Williams (1997), 'From Strategy to Security: Foundations of Critical Security Studies', in K. Krause and M.C. Williams (eds), *Critical Security Studies*, Minneapolis: University of Minnesota Press.

Kuehls, T. (1996), *Beyond Sovereign Territory*, Minneapolis and London: University of Minnesota Press.

Lietzmann, K.M. and G.D. Vest (eds) (1999), 'Environment and Security in an International Context', report 232, Bonn and Bruxelles: NATO, Federal Ministry for the Environment, Nature Conservation and Nuclear Safety and Committee on the Challenges of Modern Society.

Lindgren, E. (2000), 'The New Environmental Context for Disease Transmission', PhD Thesis, Department of Systems Ecology, Stockholm University.

Lipschutz, R.D. (1995), *On Security*, New York: Columbia University Press.

Lipschutz, R.D. (1996), *Global Civil Society and Global Environmental Governance. The Politics of Nature from Place to Planet*, New York: State University of New York Press.

Lipschutz, R.D. (1998), 'The Nature of Sovereignty and the Sovereignty of Nature: Problematizing the Boundaries between Self, Society, State, and System', in K. Litfin (ed.), *The Greening of Sovereignty in World Politics*, Cambridge, MA: MIT Press.

Lipschutz, R.D. and K. Conca (1993), *The State and Social Power in Global Environmental Politics*, New York: Columbia University Press.

Litfin, K.T. (1998), *The Greening of Sovereignty in World Politics*, Cambridge, MA: MIT Press.

Litfin, K. (1999a), 'Constructing Environmental Security and Ecological Interdependence', *Global Governance*, **5**, 359–77.

Litfin, K. (1999b), 'Environmental Security in the Coming Century', in T.V. Paul and J.H. Hall (eds), *International Order and the Future of World Politics*, Cambridge: Cambridge University Press.

Litfin, K. (2000), 'Environment, Wealth, and Authority: Global Climate Change and Emerging Modes of Legitimation', *International Studies Review*, **2**(2), 119–48.

Liverman, D.M. (1990), 'Vulnerability to Global Environmental Change', in R.E. Kasperson, K. Dow, J.X. Golding and J.X. Kasperson (eds), *Understanding Global Environmental Change: The Contributions of Risk Analysis and Management*, Worcester: ET Program, Clark University, Worcester, Massachusetts.

Lonergan, S. (1999), 'GECHS Science Plan', http://www.uni-bonn.de/ihdp/gechssp.htm.

Long, M. and A. Iles (1997), 'Assessing Climate Change Impacts: Co-evolution of Knowledge, Communities, and Methodologies', ENRP Discussion Paper E-97-09, Kennedy School of Government, Harvard University.

Lowi, M.R. (1993), *Water and Power: The Politics of a Scarce Resource in the Jordan River*, New York: Cambridge University Press.

MacDonald, G.J. (1999), 'Climate and Catastrophic Weather Events', International Institute for Applied Systems Analysis (IIASA), IR-99-034.

Mason, P.J., P. Mathias and J.H. Westcott. (1986), *Predictability in Science and Society*, London: The Royal Society and the British Academy.

Mathews, J.T. (1989), 'Redefining Security', *Foreign Affairs*, **68**(2), 162–77.

Macsweeney, B. (1999), *Security, Identity and Interests: A Sociology of International Relations*, Cambridge: Cambridge University Press.

Mercer, J.H. (1978), 'West Antarctic Ice Sheet and CO_2 Greenhouse Effect: A Threat of Disaster', *Nature*, **271**, 321–5.

Meyer, W.B., K.W. Butzer, T.E., Downing, B.L. Turner II, G.W. Wenzel and J.L. Wescoat (1998), 'Reasoning by Analogy', in S. Rayner and E. Malone (eds), *Human Choice and Climate Change*, Columbus, OH: Battelle Press.

Myers, N. (1993), *Ultimate Security: The Environmental Basis of Political Stability*, New York: W.W. Norton.

Nordhaus, W.D. (1991), 'To Slow or Not to Slow: The Economics of the Greenhouse Effect', *Economic Journal*, **101**, 920–37.

Odén, S. (1968), 'The Acidification of Air and Precipitation and its Consequences in the Natural Environment', *Ecology Bulletin*, (1).

Paterson, M. (1999), 'Interpreting Trends in Global Environmental Governance', *International Affairs*, **75**(4), 793-802.

Pielke, R.A.J. (1998), 'Rethinking the Role of Adaptation in Climate Policy', *Global Environmental Change*, **8**(2), 159–70.

Pirages, D. (1997), 'Demographic Change and Ecological Security', in G.D. Dabelko (ed.), *The Environmental Change and Human Security Project Report 3*, Washington: Woodrow Wilson International Center for Scholars.

Rengger, N.J. (1999), *International Relations, Political Theory and the Problem of Order: Beyond International Relations Theory?*, London and New York: Routledge.

Renn, O. (1992), 'Concepts of Risk: A Classification', in S. Krimsky and D. Golding (eds), *The Social Theories of Risk*, Westport, CT: Praeger.

Rijsberman, F.R. and R.J. Swart (eds) (1990), *Targets and Indicators of Climatic Change*, Sweden: Stockholm Environment Institute.

Rogers, K. (1997), 'Ecological Security and Multinational Corporations', in G.D. Dabelko (ed.), *The Environmental Change and Human Security Project 3*, Washington: Woodrow Wilson International Center for Scholars.

Rowlands, I.H. (1992), 'Environmental Issues in World Politics', in N.J. Rengger and J. Baylis (eds), *Dilemmas of World Politics: International Issues in a Changing World*, Oxford: Oxford University Press.

Ruggie, J.G. (1998), *Constructing the World Polity*, London and New York: Routledge.

Salinger, J. (2000), 'Book Review: T.W. Giambelluca and A. Henderson-Sellers (eds): *1996 Climate Change: Developing Southern Hemisphere Perspectives*', *Climatic Change*, **45**, 383–6.

Smith, J.B. (1997), 'Setting Priorities for Adapting to Climate Change', *Global Environmental Change*, **7**(3), 251–64.

Smithers, J. and B. Smith (1997), 'Human Adaptation to Climatic Variability and Change', *Global Environmental Change*, **7**(2), 129–46.

Soroos, M.S. (1998), *The Endangered Atmosphere: Preserving a Global Commons*, Columbia: University of South Carolina Press.

Soysa, I. de, N.P. Gleditsch, M. Gibson, M.Sollenberg and A.H. Westing (eds) (1999), *To Cultivate Peace – Agriculture in a World of Conflict*, report 1/99, OSIA: PRIO/Future Harvest.

Stern, E. (1995), 'Bring the Environment in: The Case for Comprehensive Security', *Cooperation and Conflict*, **30**(3), 211–37.

Storch, H.v. and N. Stehr (1997), 'Climate Research: The Case for the Social Sciences', *Ambio*, **XXVI**(1), 66–71.

Tol, R.S.J., S. Fankhauser and J.B. Smith (1998), 'The Scope for Adaptation to Climate Change: What Can We Learn from the Impacts Literature', *Global Environmental Change*, **8**(2), 109–23.

Waever, O. (1995), 'Securitization and Desecuritization', in R.D. Lipschutz (ed.), *On Security*, New York: Columbia University Press.

Waever, O. (1997), 'Figures of International Thought: Introducing Persons Instead of Paradigms', in O. Waever and I.B. Neuman (eds), *The Future of International Relations: Masters in the Making?*, London and New York: Routledge.

Waever, O. and I.B. Neuman (1997), *The Future of International Relations: Masters in the Making?*, London and New York: Routledge.

Walt, S. (1991), 'The Renaissance of Security Studies', *International Studies Quarterly*, **35**(2), 211–39.

Wapner, P. (1997), 'Governance in Global Civil Society', in O. Young (ed.), *Global Governance*, Cambridge, MA and London: MIT Press.

Waterstone, M. (2000), 'Book Review: T. E. Downing, A. A. Olsthoorn, and R. S. J. Tol (eds): *1996, Climate Change and Extreme Events: Altered Risk, Socio-Economic Impacts and Policy Responses*', *Climatic Change*, **44**, 209–13.

Wilbanks, T.J. and R.W. Kates (1999), 'Global Change in Local Places', *Climatic Change*, **43**, 601–28.

Wiman, B. (1991), 'Implications of Environmental Complexity for Science and Policy', *Global Environmental Change*, **1**, 235–47.

Wiman, B. (2000), 'Effects of Global Warming on Environmental Pollution', Encyclopedia of Life Support Systems (EOLSS), 1.4.2.11, draft 000530, http://www.eolss.co.uk.

Wiman, B., J. Stripple and S.M. Chong (2000), *From Climate Risk To Climate Security*, Kalmar: Kalmar University, Sweden and Swedish Environmental Protection Agency.

Wynne, B. (1996), 'May the Sheep Safely Graze? A Reflexive View of the Expert–Lay Knowledge Divide', in S. Lash, B. Szerszynski and B. Wynne (eds), *Risk, Environment and Modernity*, London: Sage Publications.

6. Food security

Colin Sage

1 INTRODUCTION

The 1994 Human Development Report lists seven main threats to human security: economic, health, environmental, personal, community, political and food security (UNDP, 1994). Food security touches on all the dimensions of human security: economics, social relations, health, community development and structures of political power and the environment. Consequently, food security has to be approached in a holistic way that recognises the complexity of intersecting multidimensional processes operating at all spatial scales (from the global to the individual), and in ways that are temporally discontinuous.

Almost 800 million people in the developing world do not have enough to eat, and a further 34 million people in the industrialised countries and economies in transition also suffer from chronic food insecurity (FAO, 1999). Food insecurity is used here to mean a dietary intake of insufficient and appropriate food to meet the needs of growth, activity and the maintenance of good health. In addition to those suffering from chronic hunger many millions more experience food insecurity on a seasonal or transitory basis. Prolonged protein energy malnutrition results in undernourishment with loss of body weight, reduced capacity to work and susceptibility to infectious, nutrient-depleting illnesses, such as gastro-intestinal infections, measles and malaria (Kates, 1996). Even mild undernourishment in children can lead to delayed or permanently stunted growth (DeRose and Millman, 1998). There are almost 200 million children in the world displaying low height-for-age with almost half of the children of South Asia failing to reach the weights and heights considered to represent healthy growth (FAO, 1999).

Although we should keep in mind the victims of food insecurity, the purpose of this chapter is not to map the extent and regional incidence of hunger and malnutrition, or to describe the occurrence, structural causes of and humanitarian response to episodes of starvation. There is an extensive literature devoted to the study of famine and other extreme events and there is no reason to review it here.[1] Rather, the purpose is more conceptual and seeks to trace the development of the term 'food security', to understand the way it is used at different geographical scales, and to explore points of intersection with other dimensions of human security. The chapter draws to a close with a critical evaluation of the way in which food security has come to serve as a label for a variety of rural development interventions by bilateral and non-governmental agencies.

2   THE CHANGING NOTION OF FOOD SECURITY

Food security is a concept that has evolved considerably over time, according to Hoddinott (1999, p. 2), and there are 'approximately 200 definitions and 450 indicators of food security'. In some ways its diversification and evolution mirrors the growth and proliferation of meanings attached to the term sustainable development which, as Redclift observed, has been invoked in support of numerous political and social agendas (Redclift, 1994).

In part, the multiplicity of meanings attached to food security can be attributed to the boundary nature of the concept (Clay, 1997). First, it has not only served as an object of study for various social science disciplines (most especially development economics, geography and sociology), but it has also been a touchstone for more applied work in the agricultural, environmental and health sciences. Second, in terms of national policy and planning, food security overlaps a number of sectors concerned with agricultural production, the environment, food marketing, nutrition, public health and social welfare. Third, food security has been increasingly used by the aid community to label a variety of development interventions including relief efforts, food aid support, agricultural development, environmental rehabilitation, health and social development programmes as well as support of general economic policy (Clay, 1997). We shall return to examine this third aspect in some detail later in the chapter.

Food security first appeared as a policy concept at the 1974 World Food Conference and its definition reflected the supply-side concerns and uncertain international conditions of the time. Food security was defined in the Proceedings of the Conference as the 'availability at all times of adequate world food supplies of basic foodstuffs ... to sustain a steady expansion of food consumption ... and to offset fluctuations in production and prices' (Clay, 1997, p. 9). A prevailing air of neo-Malthusianism in many food policy circles was heightened by the world food crisis of the early to mid-1970s. A conjunction of circumstances, partly triggered by the occurrence of a drought across many major grain-producing regions of the world, led to heavy demand on international grain markets, including secret purchases by the Soviet Union to offset its own domestic harvest failures. The unfolding humanitarian disasters in South Asia, the Horn of Africa and across the Sahel put increased pressure on emergency grain stocks that had been reduced in antici-pation of the promise offered by the Green Revolution. These disasters, resulting in the deaths of more than two million people (Dyson, 1996) did, however, stimulate detailed analyses of the intersection of hunger, famine, environmental causes (drought, flood, land degradation) and the coping strat-egies of those affected.

Probably the single most important contribution to shifting the prevailing view of food security – though it was a term he eschewed himself – was the publication of Amartya Sen's *Poverty and Famines* (Sen, 1981). In this semi-nal work, Sen demonstrates that hunger and starvation are not conditions that must inevitably require a decline in food availability; rather they reflect the circumstances of people not being able to secure access to food. This can be explained, argues Sen, by understanding people's entitlement relations. On the basis of their initial endowments in land, other assets and labour power, a person has entitlements to his own production, the sale of labour for wages or the exchange of products for other goods (for example, food). Under 'normal' conditions these entitlements provide the basis for survival, but new circum-stances may unfavourably impact upon them. Thus a drought-induced collapse of the local labour market severely impacts those whose main entitlement to food is drawn from the sale of their labour. Furthermore, a rise in grain prices affects all those who purchase their food needs and who may simultaneously experience a collapse in the production or price of their own commodities. While Sen acknowledges the strict legal and market framework that governs the operation of entitlement relations, he later develops the notion of ex-tended entitlements that encompass non-legal, cultural and intra-household conventions (Dreze and Sen, 1989).

While this highly condensed summary does no justice to the sophistication of Sen's corpus of work on entitlement relations – nor, indeed, to the wider debate that ensued following publication of *Poverty and Famines* – the pur-pose is simply to highlight how this helped to change the nature of food security analysis by the early to mid-1980s. Sen's intention – to replace preoccupation with the arithmetic of food supply with concern for the iden-tity and capacity of the food insecure – converged with an upswelling of rural, community-based, household-level studies. Important research themes of this period included analysis of the strengths of local farming systems and the environmental and technical knowledge that underpinned them; gender relations and intra-household divisions; and the complex of activities collec-tively subsumed by the notion of 'livelihood strategies'. Efforts to understand people's access to food inevitably involved analysis of those factors mediat-ing or constraining their ability to fulfil needs. As a series of food crises unfolded in Africa during the 1980s, researchers sought to identify the role of drought (the Sahel and Southern Africa), conflict (Ethiopia, Somalia, Sudan, Mozambique) and economic collapse. While the period marked a tendency to draw an overly deterministic causal relationship, it is now well recognised that such events can act as 'triggers' that tip already stretched and vulnerable local societies into acute distress. In this respect making the distinction between transitory and chronic food insecurity highlights the significance of periods of intensified pressure rather than focusing on long-term structural poverty, hunger and malnutrition (Clay, 1997).

Thus the 1980s witnessed a growing interest in household-level food security using livelihood and gender analysis to understand how vulnerable individuals and households cope with environmental, economic and political uncertainty, whether chronic or on seasonal, periodic or irregular time scales. Moreover, recognising the influence of external factors (such as economic shocks) on local food provisioning systems underlined the importance of appreciating the interconnections between the individual, local, regional, national and international levels. This has effectively meant that food security analysis can be applied at a variety of scales from the global to the household levels, with each requiring its appropriate policy measures to ensure it is achieved. We will return to this aspect below.

Throughout the 1970s and 1980s food security was concerned with basic foodstuffs, principally high calorie staples such as cereals and tubers, to resolve problems of protein energy malnutrition. By the late 1980s, however, health and nutrition research had begun substantially to redefine the relationship between food intake and nutritional well-being such that the latter could not simply be inferred from calorie consumption. A better understanding of human physiological capacity to utilise food intake revealed the crucial role played by disease, especially gastrointestinal infections, which impair the body's ability to absorb both micronutrients and calories. The relationship between malnutrition and infection has been described as reciprocal and synergistic where 'disease leads to a deterioration in nutritional status at the same time that malnutrition increases susceptibility to disease' (DeRose and Millman, 1998, p. 8).

The earlier view that increases in calories should effectively translate into better nutrition was further undermined by the increasing recognition of the importance of micronutrients. Deficiencies of iron, iodine and vitamin A, in particular, were seen as not only affecting large numbers of people, but to have severe consequences. Iron deficiency, for example, which may affect up to two billion people worldwide (*The Economist*, 1996), is associated with a lack of physical energy and difficulties in concentration. Iodine deficiency is thought to be responsible for an estimated 655 million cases of goitre and six million people suffering from cretinism. Meanwhile a deficiency in vitamin A was estimated to affect some 231 million children in 1994, being a major cause of childhood blindness and causing increased susceptibility to respiratory and diarrhoeal diseases (DeRose and Millman, 1998).[2]

Given these developments, it is hardly surprising that the term 'food security' has undergone a substantial reconstruction in order to create a singular, universally relevant, definition of the type so beloved of the international policy community. Moreover, social and cultural influences over food preferences have rightly made notions of food security more context specific and, therefore, increasingly complex. Consequently, at the 1996 World Food Summit the Plan of Action adopted a suitably extended definition that states that

> Food security, at the individual, household, national, regional and global levels is achieved when all people, at all times, have physical and economic access to sufficient, safe and nutritious food to meet their dietary needs and food preferences for an active and healthy life. (FAO, 1997)

In this process of definitional refinement and specificity, food security has come to be seen as part of a wider concern for human welfare and social security – and not only in the poorest countries of the world. Indeed, there is growing recognition that food insecurity can affect significant numbers of people in the technologically-advanced industrial societies with long-established welfare states, underlining that hunger, here as elsewhere, is a function of inequality, poverty and the failure of entitlements (Riches, 1997; Köhler et al., 1997). Yet there has been surprisingly little cross-fertilisation of knowledge between policy analysts and community activitists concerned with food poverty in developed welfare states and those concerned with food security in the developing world. It is apparent that there is a much more politically-engaged, empowerment-driven, approach from the first camp. Consider, for example, this definition offered by the Community Food Security Coalition based in the United States:

> Food security can be defined as the state in which all persons obtain a nutritionally adequate, culturally acceptable diet at all times through local non-emergency sources. Food security broadens the traditional conception of hunger, embracing a systemic view of the causes of hunger and poor nutrition within a community while identifying the changes necessary to prevent their occurrence. Food security programs confront hunger and poverty. (Community Food Security Coalition, 2000)

This more empowerment-oriented definition demonstrates that food security engages directly with questions of social justice, health, nutrition and local development. Food policy analysts have, for example, highlighted the difficulties faced by low-income urban communities marked by limited mobility in getting access to fresh, healthy food. Confronted by the policy of supermarkets to relocate to edge-of-town sites, the term 'food deserts' has been used to describe those urban areas of social exclusion deprived of suitable food retail outlets (Lang and Caraher, 1998; Furey et al., 1999). This combines with a range of other barriers faced by those on low incomes in accessing healthy foods (Caraher et al., 1998).

The recognition that food poverty forms part of a wider framework of human insecurity and social injustice is part of a more general restructuring of priorities. This, according to Clay, reflects a paradigmatic shift from the modernist agenda and its preoccupations with growth and development, to broader public policy concerns with risk, insecurity and uncertainty (Clay, 1997). The evolution of food security within public policy debates continues to develop such that a strong and concerted case is being made by which the right to adequate food should be clearly established as a human right under international law (Kent, 2000). Article 11 of the International Covenant on Economic, Social and Cultural Rights affirms 'the right of everyone to an adequate standard of living for himself and his family, including adequate food, clothing and housing'. Indeed, Objective 7.4 of the Plan of Action issued by the World Food Summit calls upon the UN High Commissioner for Human Rights 'to better define the rights related to food in Article 11 of the Covenant and to propose ways to implement and realize these rights ... taking into account the possibility of formulating voluntary guidelines for food security for all' (FAO, 1997, pp. 122–3).

However, as Kent observes, there is currently no mechanism or commitment to ensure the fulfilment of food security. International human rights instruments are concerned primarily with the responsibilities of states to their own people, not to people elsewhere. Yet there needs to be put in place an institutional framework that would act to support national governments in dealing with malnutrition among their people. This would be established by a clear international obligation to provide assistance underpinned by the creation of a regime of hard international nutrition rights. Such a course of action may be idealistic but is vital if a genuine commitment to universal food security is to be achieved (Kent, 2000).[3]

3   THE MULTIPLE SCALES OF FOOD SECURITY

The preceding discussion has demonstrated that food security has both spatial and temporal dimensions, and has come to possess ever more complex and context-specific definitions. This section schematically outlines some of the issues surrounding food security at different spatial scales, with particular reference to human security and environment.

3.1 Global Food Security

As we have seen, much of the early debate around food security was concerned with the broad global picture concerning aggregate food supply, rates of population growth and world trade issues. There remains a strong interest in monitoring developments at this level, usually as medium-term prospective scenario-building exercises (see Box 6.1). However, the range of variables that exercise some bearing on global food security have arguably grown in number and complexity. There is little reason to speculate here on food supply constraints and demographic matters, but I do wish to draw out two areas that will have some bearing on global food security: the world economy and global environmental change.

In the first case, it is apparent that the language of the 1970s with its reference to 'world trade issues' can no longer convey the diversity of forces that influence the international supply and demand of food in a highly integrated global economy. Indeed, the past 25 years have witnessed enormous change to the political and economic landscape. For example, just a quarter of a century ago perhaps up to 1.5 billion people laboured under various forms of rural collectivisation. These stretched geographically and institutionally from the market-induced incentives in parts of Eastern Europe, through the large state farms based on wage labour of the Soviet Union to the people's communes of China (Bideleux, 1985). The failures of centralised state economic planning to deliver adequate supplies of food and other consumer goods ultimately brought about the 'collapse of communism' and led to the dissolution of the Soviet Union. It has also encouraged a move toward more market-based agricultural systems in China, Vietnam and Cuba. Yet whereas Bideleux was able to highlight Soviet Central Asia's striking success with rural collectivisation in providing food security for the region during the 1970s, the situation faced by the Central Asian Republics today is grave, with up to one-third of Tajikistan's population (around two million people) apparently in the grip of acute food insecurity (Babu and Pinstrup-Andersen, 2000; Jackson, pers. comm.).

Meanwhile, for much of the 'long-standing' developing world this intervening period has seen the onset of the debt crisis and the imposition of structural adjustment programmes, economic stabilisation measures and trade liberalisation regimes. Under the world trade agreement countries are expected to remove import controls, eliminate subsidies to domestic producers and maximise efforts to produce for world markets. On the basis of available evidence it is apparent that while there are some winners, the poorest countries remain vulnerable to the volatility of market prices set on trading floors in London, New York and elsewhere, and to the dominance of transnational corporations (McMichael, 1999; Watkins, 1996). The relocation of certain

BOX 6.1   WORLD FOOD PROSPECTS: CRITICAL ISSUES FOR THE EARLY TWENTY-FIRST CENTURY

A recent study (Pinstrup-Andersen et al., 1999) by the International Food Policy Research Institute, which is a member of the Consultative Group on International Agricultural Research (CGIAR) projects the following by 2020:

- A global population of 7.5 billion with the world's urban population doubling to 3.4 billion.
- Per capita incomes are expected to increase in all major developing regions. As a result, meeting the food needs of a growing and urbanising population with rising incomes will have profound implications for the world's agricultural production and trading systems.
- Developing countries will account for 85 per cent of the increase in global demand for cereals and meat to 2020, although per capita consumption of cereals in the South will be less than one-half that of someone in the North, and around one-third for meat products.
- A demand driven 'livestock revolution' is underway in the South with demand projected to double between 1995 and 2020. This will cause a strong demand for cereals for livestock feed, in particular maize, which will overtake demand for wheat and rice by 2020. This is projected to require a 40 per cent increase in grain production over 1995 levels by 2020.
- Food insecurity and malnutrition will persist in 2020 and beyond with 135 million children under five years of age malnourished (down 15 per cent from 160 million in 1995). However, 40 million of these children will live in Sub-Saharan Africa, an increase of 30 per cent over 1995 levels.

The authors of the study observe that the world food situation is mixed but could be significantly worse with a 'deterioration of key variables such as water availability, land quality, human resource development, and technological innovations' (p. 18). They also discuss six emerging issues that could significantly influence the world food situation during the early part of this century. These issues are: new evidence on nutrition and policy (including micronutrients); low food prices; world trade negotiations; the potential of agroecological approaches; the potential of modern biotechnology; and IT and precision farming.

Source: Pinstrup-Andersen et al. (1999).

types of agro-food production to areas where the factors of production, particularly labour, cost less is leading to a new international division of labour (Goodman and Watts, 1997). We return to this in the next section.

If food security is linked to economic prosperity as a result of sufficient income providing adequate exchange entitlements, then a time of economic crisis can lead to widespread food insecurity, particularly for those groups without access to their own production. This became apparent in South-East Asia in 1997 with the onset of the currency crisis that brought to an end the rapid economic growth which had been sustained since the 1980s (Burch and Goss, 1999). While financial analysts were largely caught unawares by the South-East Asian crisis, demonstrating that economic forecasting has arguably become a hazardous business, there are some underlying factors which will exert enormous influence over the global economy, and therefore, over the state of food security.

Probably, the single most strategic influence, other than a global war, is the price of oil. There is surprisingly little appreciation of the degree to which past economic prosperity can be attributed to the plentiful supply of cheap energy. Moreover, the industrial refraction of oil and gas has underpinned the productivity achievements of industrialised agriculture that has long been dependent upon synthetic fertilisers. The present global food system involves the continuing expansion in the volume of international trade in agricultural products and increasing use of air freight to transport them to countries of consumption. The energy intensity of air freight is 37 times greater than shipping for every tonne-kilometre (SAFE Alliance, 1994). Yet market prices will soon reflect the fact that the current decade not only marks the midpoint in the consumption of total global conventional oil reserves, but that the Middle East share of the global oil business is close to the level that it was during the oil-price shocks of the 1970s (Campbell, 1997; Campbell and Laherrere, 1998). The medium-term consequences of a sharp rise in oil prices for global food security have yet to be widely debated.

A second major area that further complicates forecasts about world food prospects is presented by both systemic and cumulative aspects of global environmental change. Climate change and stratospheric ozone depletion are examples of systemic global change, while the depletion and contamination of freshwater resources, deforestation, desertification and dessication of semi-arid environments, soil depletion and biodiversity losses are examples of discrete environmental changes that exert a cumulative effect at the global scale. The connections with food security are manifold, although the precise nature of interrelationships are likely to be complex and uncertain. For example, the concern of atmospheric scientists with the thinning of the stratospheric ozone layer is that this will be translated into increased penetration of ultra-violet radiation to the earth's surface. It is understood that increased UV radiation can weaken the human immune system leaving people more susceptible to infectious disease, while the effect on agricultural crops may be to lower yields (Mintzer and Miller, 1992).

The consequences of climate change for global food security remain uncertain, although increasingly sophisticated scientific models are being used in scenario building exercises. The balance of evidence points to a discernible human influence on the world's climate resulting from the rising atmospheric concentrations of anthropogenically-derived carbon dioxide and other greenhouse gases (Houghton, 1997). As a result climate change is likely to have very different effects on crop yields from region to region around the globe.

Employing a range of models (including Hadley Centre global climate scenarios, crop simulation and world food trade) Parry and colleagues have sought to assess the consequences for world food security. They identify increased levels of atmospheric carbon dioxide as having generally positive effects on crop growth, however, there are a range of other effects that will result in considerable latitudinal variations in crop yields. Generally, the rise in ground level temperatures will lengthen the growing season at mid to high latitudes and should increase yields. On the other hand, increased evapotranspiration and soil moisture losses due to warming will be exacerbated in many regions by a projected fall in precipitation levels that will threaten crop yields. For the developing regions of the low latitudes climate change brings not only warming, which is a concern where crops may already be close to their limits for heat and water stress, but greater variability. This will present an enormous challenge in regions where there is already considerable vulnerability and more limited adaptive capacity. As a consequence, their study projects a marked increase in the numbers of people at risk from hunger in Africa where declining production as a result of climate change will by the 2080s result in between 55 and 70 million hungry people (Parry et al., 1999).

The complexity and uncertainty inherent in such scenario-building models have stimulated others to focus more upon improving our understanding of present vulnerability to hunger to infer lessons for coping with future climate change (Bohle et al., 1994). A vulnerability approach has the further advantage of understanding the consequences of cumulative global environmental change, that is, how particular regional populations are affected by and coping with the depletion of fresh water, land degradation, loss of biodiversity and so on. In some respects it might be useful to speak of a co-evolution of vulnerability with these broader processes of global environmental change that makes it a multidimensional and multilayered condition. Bohle et al. draw from Robert Chambers' work to highlight three basic coordinates of vulnerability: the risk of exposure to crises, stress and shocks; the risk of inadequate coping capacity; and the risk of limited potential of recovery from crises and shocks. As they explain:

> From this vantage point, the most vulnerable individuals, groups, classes and regions are those most exposed to perturbations, who possess the most limited coping capacity and suffer the most from the impact of a crisis or environmental perturbations (such as climate change), and who are endowed with circumscribed potential for recovery. Vulnerability can be, in other words, defined in terms of exposure, capacity and potentiality. Accordingly, the prescriptive and normative response to vulnerability is to reduce exposure, enhance coping capacity, strengthen recovery potentiality and bolster damage control (ie minimize destructive consequences) via private and public means. (Bohle et al., 1994, p. 38)

We shall return to the issue of vulnerability in the discussion of food security at the local level that would seem the most appropriate place to address ways of reducing exposure and enhancing resilience. Yet, it is important to note the effort and resources expended in mapping vulnerability at the global scale and to ask how these constructively contribute to the elimination of hunger. For example, the World Food Summit of 1996 mandated the establishment of a Food Insecurity and Vulnerability Information and Mapping Systems (FIVIMS) programme which brings together a wide range of global and national information systems for use by multilateral and bilateral development agencies. It draws on existing systems such as vulnerability assessment mapping, a GIS-based tool that has been used by agencies such as the World Food Programme in identifying particular sub-national spaces (regions, provinces, districts) characterised by poor nutritional status or vulnerable to food shortages arising from regular crop failure (WFP, 1999).

The FIVIMS online report provides a broad-brushed picture of global hunger, together with national-level profiles of vulnerability that reveal the diversity of circumstances underpinning food insecurity. However, it is difficult to comprehend the added value that the costly FIVIMS project is expected to deliver as its list of vulnerable groups amounts to a roll-call of the usual suspects: victims of conflict (refugees, war widows and orphans and so on), marginal populations in urban areas (unemployed, beggars, orphans and so on), and people belonging to at-risk social groups (ethnic minorities and so on) (FAO, 1999). It arguably provides further evidence for some critics that such high-cost exercises do little to address the fundamental causes of hunger and simply reinforce the accusations that the agencies supporting such work are entirely out of touch with reality on the ground (Hancock, 1989; De Waal, 1997).

This is not to deny that remotely-sensed data might have some value in detecting long-term and widespread environmental degradation or annual changes in vegetation growth conditions which have a direct bearing on crop and range land productivity. Such data provide a useful tool in monitoring trigger events in famine early warning systems, however they offer no insight into social and economic deprivation that underpins vulnerability (Walker, 1989).

Nevertheless, a good example of a global study using remotely-sensed data is the recent mapping work conducted by the International Food Policy Research Institute (IFPRI) which has highlighted the extent of soil degradation on the world's agricultural lands. The unprecedented scale of agricultural expansion during the twentieth century and intensification over the past three decades has, in the IFPRI's view, undermined the productive capacity of many agroecosystems with soil fertility declining and water for irrigation becoming scarcer. Using satellite imagery, the global assessment estimates that up to 40 per cent of agricultural lands worldwide are seriously affected by soil degradation, and in Central America almost 75 per cent of cropland is seriously degraded (IFPRI, 2000).

3.2 National Food Security

It is at the national level where the notion of a secure food system can be best grasped, and Barraclough (reproduced in FAO, 1996, p. 266) has outlined the essential features of such a system:

- The capacity to produce, store and import sufficient food to meet the basic needs of all the population;
- Maximum autonomy and self-determination (without implying self-sufficiency) in order to minimise international market fluctuations and political pressures;
- Reliability, so that seasonal, cyclical and other variations in access to food are minimal;
- Sustainability, so that the ecological system is protected and improved over time;
- Equity, so that all social groups have access to adequate food.

While these features would appear to offer a consensual basis for building national food security, it is apparent that under the current liberalised world trade environment, countries are under pressure to pursue measures that do not enhance their 'autonomy and self-determination'. The imposition of structural adjustment programmes, for example, were designed to ensure that indebted countries met their international financial obligations and reformed their state sectors rather than strengthened national food security. Yet it has been shown that the process of structural adjustment changes national food availability, as currency devaluation increases the price of imported food and changes the price of food relative to the price of labour. This has important implications for the ability of households to secure access to food, especially under rapidly changing social and economic conditions, as well as reducing their capacity to invest in agriculture through the increased costs of imported chemical inputs (DeRose, 1998).

World Bank, IMF and WTO directives to engage with the principles of comparative advantage by promoting exports and lifting restrictions on foreign competition in domestic markets have, moreover, raised questions about the benefits for national food security. Dorosh, for example, argues that trade liberalisation has made a positive contribution to food security in Bangladesh in recent years, by augmenting domestic supplies and stabilising prices (Dorosh, 2001). Yet the trade entitlements of many agricultural commodity exporters remain vulnerable to the declining and fluctuating fortunes of commodity values. Elsewhere, some countries have sought to diversify into new agro-export lines, such as fresh horticultural produce. One such example is Kenya where exports of high-value horticultural crops, including cut flowers, increased by 58 per cent in the five years to 1996, accounting for 10 per cent of total national export earnings (Barrett et al., 1999).

Yet, although export-oriented agricultural production may yield foreign exchange earnings that can be used to import large volumes of food from elsewhere, there are at least two caveats. First, export agriculture diverts resources (land and water), labour and capital from production for local consumption; and, second, export earnings may not be used to buy food for the poor, but used on high prestige development projects. Of course, proponents of liberalisation argue that the problem is not one of trade, but of government policy. A range of government interventions are consequently needed to promote domestic food production alongside export agriculture; ensure the free and effective operation of markets; enhance the availability and value of labour; and, above all, ensure the availability of welfare safety nets for the poor. The question remains to what degree governments have either financial provision or room for manoeuvre for such policies especially under current multilateral trade regimes.

Of course, the way in which the state utilises foreign exchange earnings (as well as domestic revenues) may not reflect the key principles of food security. This has been observed especially in the case of those oil-rich economies where the bonanza from hydro-carbon exports has been accompanied by the stagnation or decline of the agricultural sector. Andrae and Beckman's (1986) study of oil-induced economic growth in Nigeria and its increasing dependence upon large-scale imports of American wheat revealed the complex interplay of internal and external forces which caused food insecurity to develop alongside the conspicuous prosperity from oil revenues. More recently, attention has been drawn to the high incidences of rural malnutrition in some regions of Venezuela, a long-standing, high-volume oil exporter (FAO, 1999).

Food security is most at threat, of course, under conditions of chronic political instability, civil conflict and war. Messer reports that in 1994 there were at least 32 countries in which people suffered malnutrition and acute food shortages as a result of armed conflict, and there were at least 10 more countries where hunger persisted in the aftermath of war, civil disorder, or conflict-related sanctions (Messer, 1998). War triggers displacement of civilian populations, dispossessing them of their means of livelihood and effectively resulting in a collapse of their entitlement relations. Besides the deliberate use of hunger as a weapon of war, the 'scorched earth' strategy of military combatants may turn the communities through which they have passed into highly vulnerable and dependent societies. The appropriation of food stocks, the slaughter and destruction of livestock and other productive assets, and the placing of land-mines in fields all serve to reduce the capacity of local communities to feed themselves for many years to come. The role of appropriate humanitarian aid in situations of chronic political instability and conflict has become a topic of considerable debate (Anderson, 1999; Macrae and Zwi, 1994).

The relationship between conflict and food insecurity is complex, but an examination of those countries in Africa which have suffered drastic famines in recent years – Ethiopia, Sudan, Somalia, Mozambique – reveals that conflict is a common cause which dwarfs all others in its impact. Although these civil conflicts originate from within the political realm, they are pursued by recourse to military hardware rather than through negotiation. In this regard, these societies have been severely harmed by militarisation. In Sub-Saharan Africa this is a debt-incurring mechanism since none of the countries produces its own military hardware. Countries where military expenditure exceeded 20 per cent of the total government budget in 1980 were headed by Ethiopia (43 per cent), Chad and Mozambique (29 per cent) and Zimbabwe (26 per cent) (Raikes, 1988). Although political regimes in these countries have changed since this data, the principle of militarisation still holds in much of Africa, to the extent that de Waal speaks of the development of political economies based upon militarised asset-stripping (de Waal, 1993). It is hardly surprising that such structures impose enormous difficulties for local societies to build a more food secure future.

3.3 Local Food Security: Toward Sustainable Livelihood Security

It is at the local and, most especially, the household and individual levels where the notion of food security is best operationalised. Based on the preceding discussion it should be understood that food security means adequate access to food that is culturally and nutritionally appropriate through-out the year and from year to year. Adequate access does not, of course, imply self-sufficiency in food production but depends upon sufficiently ro-bust entitlement relations that can meet food needs through trade of products or labour, inheritance, transfer or production. However, even assured access to food at the household level does not mean food security for individuals. This will depend upon the intra-household allocation of food between its members as well as the biological utilisation of that food for nutritional well-being.

In the first case it has long been recognised that some individuals go hungry in households enjoying aggregate food security, while some individu-als are well nourished even in households which are food insecure overall (Millman and DeRose, 1998). In very general terms these differentials may follow divisions based on gender and age, with males and wage earners being favoured over girls and children being weaned (Kates, 1996). Second, the biological utilisation of food for conversion into capacity for work and physi-ological maintenance requires not only an adequate diet, but also a healthy physical environment that does not place individuals at risk of contracting disease (Hoddinott, 1999).

Consequently, adequacy at the aggregate level (for example, the commu-nity or the household) does not necessarily guarantee food security at the lower level (the household or the individual). Understanding the specific factors that constrain its achievement can only be understood through de-tailed empirical analysis at local level. As we shall see in the next section, however, there is a tendency for many outside agencies to introduce food security projects into communities without a sufficiently thorough under-standing of the dynamics of undernourishment at local level. Clearly, the prospects for food security at local level are 'framed' by a number of important external factors. Principal among these are the institutional struc-tures and policies of government, business and the market. There is also the cohesion and stability of civil society, including relationships of trust and cooperation, and the existence of welfare safety nets amongst the poor. Finally, the physical environment plays a large role in determining the types of activities that can be pursued by rural households (Hoddinott, 1999).

As the prospects for food security at household level will depend upon household endowments in land, labour and other assets, and because we cannot project aggregate food sufficiency to individual security, it becomes less useful to focus only upon the achievement of this objective at this level. Indeed, some households may not prioritise increased quantity or quality of their food consumption, but place more store on sending their children to school. Just as there has been some appreciation of 'insider definitions' of famine which more accurately reflects the experience of the victims (de Waal, 1989), so there needs to be greater sensitivity toward alternative interpretations of food security based on local understandings and priorities. For these and other reasons, a concern with food security at household level has increasingly given way to a focus on livelihoods, livelihood security and sustainable livelihoods.

The concept of sustainable livelihoods has proved an especially useful and increasingly popular one, with the capacity to integrate a range of important variables at the household level (Sage, 1996). Chambers and Conway (1992, pp. 7–8) have defined sustainable livelihoods as follows:

> A livelihood comprises the capabilities, assets (stores, resources, claims and access) and activities required for a means of living; a livelihood is sustainable which can cope with and recover from stress and shocks, maintain or enhance its capabilities and assets, and provide sustainable livelihood opportunities for the next generation.

It is the number of core principles embodied within the sustainable livelihoods concept which has made it such a popular and robust idea among researchers and analysts as well as development practitioners. For example, it can be said to be poverty-oriented and people-centred, in that it starts with an appreciation of the capabilities, resources and constraints of the poor and seeks to build upon existing strengths. Second, it is holistic and understands the importance of complexity and diversity in the construction of more secure livelihood outcomes. Third, it starts from the need to recognise and understand the context of vulnerability in which the rural poor exist. Sources of vulnerability (DFID, 2000) comprise:

- Seasonality – which is largely determined by the prevailing rainfall pattern that distinguishes periods of intense agricultural activity from prolonged dry spells of relative underemployment;
- Shocks – the occurrence of natural hazards, such as drought, unseasonal rainfall, pest infestation, conflict, epidemics and so on, which can destroy assets directly or force people to abandon their homes or dispose of assets (livestock, land) as a short-term survival measure;
- Trends – include high population growth rates, increasing landlessness and conflict over resources, and other trends (economic, political) which can have long-term consequences for livelihoods.

The need to reduce people's vulnerability to these diverse sources of risk might involve various forms of action. For example, policy initiatives that include efforts to reduce conflict, provide social safety nets at times of stress, or generally improve institutional responsiveness. On the other hand helping people to become more resilient and better able to withstand shocks and stress is a central objective of the sustainable livelihoods approach. This would involve building up the assets of rural households making them more robust and enabling them to diversify their portfolio of livelihood strategies. Increasingly, assets are being viewed as comprising more than tangible stocks such as stores of food, cash savings, or items that can be converted into food (for example, jewellery); or resources such as land, livestock, trees and so on. Rather (DFID, 2000), assets include:

- human capital – the skills, knowledge and capacity to pursue different livelihood options;
- social capital – the relationships of trust and cooperation that provide the basis for safety nets amongst the poor; and
- natural capital – that provides for resource flows and services that support local livelihoods, in addition to the financial and physical capitals representing tangible stocks of savings, income and equipment needed to support livelihoods.

Naturally, each household will have different asset endowments and will combine these assets in different ways to generate positive livelihood outcomes. Assets can be created through supportive policies (investment in basic infrastructure, health and education, reform of property rights) and appropriate development interventions (skills training, environmental rehabilitation, credit schemes). They can also be destroyed by the different sources of vulnerability (trends, shocks and seasonality). Generally speaking, the greater and more diverse the asset endowment of a household, the more options are available to develop multiple livelihood strategies, and the greater is the chance of achieving food security. Consequently, building sustainable livelihood security is a way of ensuring human security in all its manifold dimensions. Yet, as we shall see in the next section, this cannot be done by blueprint design.

4   FOOD SECURITY INTERVENTIONS: CASE STUDIES

The international arrangements to underpin food security are in disarray. (ODI, 2000, p. 1)

This is the opening sentence of a briefing paper that outlines the failure of food aid to combat poverty, improve food consumption and raise the nutritional and health status of poor and vulnerable people. While emergency relief plays a vital role in limiting nutritional stress in acute crises caused by conflict or natural disaster, food aid is otherwise a very clumsy instrument in contributing to food security. Yet food aid and food security have gone hand in hand insofar as many food security programmes have been underpinned by the disbursement of food commodities. While there has been a welcome loosening of arrangements for funding food security projects, with increased use of finance rather than commodities, many projects remain subject to the short-term thinking implicit in the disbursement of food aid. Moreover, food security is increasingly being used as a label to cover a variety of rural development interventions, some of which have marginal or questionable impacts on the nutritional status of target populations. The tendency for projects to specify a number of non-complementary objectives under the label 'food security' diminishes the vital importance of ensuring access to food by all people, especially the poorest, at all times. Combining this with the failure of such projects to engage in nutritional assessment or to use other measures of food security involving the monitoring of food availability, seasonal coping strategies or other indicators of stress, justifies the assertion that food security is indeed in disarray.

This does, of course, demonstrate the significant disparity between food security researchers and development practitioners, particularly Northern non-governmental organizations (NGOs) which engage in food security projects as a means to access donor resources and which take a rather more pragmatic line. Many of these NGOs have experience of disbursing food aid through emergency relief programmes and this partly colours their perceptions of food security interventions. However, donors themselves are culpable as they support food security programmes often with only short-term commitments (of one or two years duration), usually accompanied by the current conditionalities of development aid that demonstrate best practice (addressing the needs of women, environmental sustainability, equity and participation, poverty-targeting and so on). The whole package might then be tied into one of the prevailing fads of the development industry, such as microfinance. Unsurprisingly, such projects emerge as blueprint designs where the coherence of a local food security intervention strategy is lost within a package of non-complementary objectives that are to be attained within an unrealistic time frame and evaluated with reference to a range of inappropriate indicators of achievement. Thus there is a tendency towards spurious quantification (numbers of 'beneficiaries', length of terracing constructed, trees planted) rather than with better identification of the poor, and tracking qualitative changes in their access to, and consumption of, food. Some of these shortcomings are discussed within two case studies below.[4]

4.1   The Pakistan Food Security Project

The overall objectives of the Pakistan Food Security Project (FSP) can be summarised as:

- Increase agricultural production of traditional food crops as well as new and diversified, market-oriented crops.
- Create and strengthen the capacity of farmer-managed revolving funds within the framework of community-based organisations.
- Provision of food aid through school and supplementary feeding programmes to education, training and welfare organisations.

The agricultural component is ostensibly designed to improve the food security of poor farmers through the provision of agricultural inputs on credit. The objective is to increase productivity of food crops and to diversify into more market-oriented agricultural production. Improvements in food security would thus result from higher yields obtaining from existing crops, and from increased flows of food and/or cash arising from involvement in new crops and livestock production. The project has provided the following inputs: wheat, vegetables, potato and maize/fodder seeds; chemical fertilisers; hand tools; pesticides; goats and heifers. The value of these inputs has then served to capitalise revolving funds which are, eventually, to be managed by the community based organisation (CBO).

There are no explicit objectives to establish more sustainable farming practices through low external input systems or through improved resource management. Rather, the concern is with strengthening existing systems of agricultural production with the expectation that these will yield greater food security. However, many of the farmers are heavily involved in the production of non-food cash crops, such as sugar cane, cotton and tobacco, and indicate more enthusiasm for maintaining or increasing their involvement with these crops rather than with wheat, potatoes or vegetables.

Consequently, there is something of a paradox in a food security project working with farmers producing non-food crops in areas of high agricultural potential. The project

- is not engaged in the food-deficit (and rain-fed) areas of the mountainous north, or of the variously semi-arid, drought-prone or desert areas of the country where agriculture is more risk-prone and rural households more vulnerable to food insecurity.
- supports, and effectively subsidises, high external-input farming systems engaged in the production of agro-industrial crops rather than low-input cropping systems of food for local consumption.

- has not commissioned a thorough analysis of the marketing implications of its efforts to increase and diversify production, leaving farmers vulnerable to the power of intermediaries in regulating market prices so that they fail to benefit from their efforts.
- has not established whether benefits are reaching the poorest. Indeed in the project localities there appears to be a high degree of differentiation with a few small land owners, but many more securing access to land through renting or sharecropping. The assumption that food security will be improved through the distribution of seeds and fertilisers effectively excludes the landless and sharecroppers who work with providers of inputs and primarily benefits those who own land.

The capital stock of the revolving fund represents the value of the agricultural inputs supplied to the project. The objective of the fund is to create a line of credit for small producers in order to increase food production and to diversify sources of household income. However, there is a risk to the capital stock from loans being concentrated in high cost, high risk but occasionally lucrative activities such as cotton production. Over the preceding three years there have been two major crop failures, while in the third year merchants refused to buy from farmers at prices set by the state. Safer returns have led to lending moving away from agriculture and towards economically diversified activities, such as small shops, tailoring, dressmaking, and food preparation for sale. There is a need to ensure a diversified portfolio of lending, so that the revolving fund of a CBO is not 'exposed' to unnecessarily high risk, yet the funds are to help strengthen food security rather than being tied up in more speculative – and riskier – agro-industrial commodities.

Another area of concern is that of data gathering, monitoring and evaluation. It is disturbing to conduct a project evaluation and to find a lack of basic socio-economic data that would help to establish answers to such questions as: who are the poorest? Are they benefiting from the project through access to credit? Is this being translated into nutritional improvements for household members? Are there other poverty alleviation and food security interventions that might be appropriate? The need for better local-level data is apparent in many projects, and it is partner NGOs, in collaboration with local people, that are best placed to perform baseline and end of project evaluations in order to measure project achievements. Importantly, there needs to be a much better understanding of the dynamics of poverty at village level in order to avoid projects being hijacked by the better-off. Appropriate monitoring systems also need to be put in place that look at seasonal stress and other dimensions of vulnerability.

4.2   Central America

This project is located in a region of marked seasonality of rainfall such that for almost half the year crop production is limited by the lack of available moisture. The goal of this project is to improve food security for 3000 resource-poor households by reducing their vulnerability to production losses and by diversifying sources of income. The project objectives can be summarised as:

- Developing more sustainable systems of agricultural production and improving post-harvest management;
- Strengthening the capacity of community-based and counterpart organisations and the participation of women;
- Contributing to income generation through the provision of credit.

Since inception, the project has experienced significant disruption and delay due to the effects of El Niño and, most especially, Hurricane Mitch which, in October 1998, hit Central America leaving 9000 dead and 3 million homeless. The first phase of the project was tied to a number of specific credit instruments including vegetative material for use in soil conservation. About 90 per cent of the fruit trees, plants and saplings distributed died under the prolonged dry season caused by El Niño. The greater part of the project's activities are concerned with introducing soil conservation measures and with supporting agricultural diversification. Despite the marked seasonality of rainfall which imposes such a constraint on agricultural production, there has been limited support for the installation of measures to capture water for small-scale irrigation systems during the dry season.

The provision and management of credit forms a very significant part of the project, with the capital fund for loans constituting slightly more than half of total EU funding. Counterpart funding covers the further cost of salaries for credit specialists, and other administrative personnel. The credit element of the project is developing in quite different ways across the three countries. In El Salvador savings and loans cooperatives have been created and they appear to be moving swiftly away from lending to agriculture in favour of more secure loans for micro-enterprise and commercial activities. In Nicaragua and Honduras solidarity groups of up to 10 people are responsible for borrowing, distributing amongst themselves and repaying the loan. Preliminary observations seem to suggest that many borrowers are absorbing credit to bolster consumption, then repaying loans through temporary wage labour migration.

The project is consequently heavily influenced by the current orthodoxy that small-scale agriculture would be so much more productive if it could benefit from a strategic injection of funding. While there are undoubtedly examples where this would be true, as a generality it is a fallacy. If a line of credit was linked to on-farm experimentation, such that groups of producers themselves developed new techniques or cropping systems that would benefit from a small strategic investment, it would be clear that they had full responsibility for, and ownership over, the exercise. Yet the credit element of the project is tied to the transfer of technologies designed elsewhere. The distribution of large amounts of trees and plants without careful preparation created indebtedness at a stroke. It is not apparent that the credit is contributing to food security. Indeed, in their need to ensure the capital stock is not diminished, cooperatives in El Salvador are seeking out more secure borrowers than small farming households.

It is undoubtedly the case that rural people in the region have insecure livelihoods and are vulnerable to a range of uncertainties: economic, sociopolitical and, it appears above all, natural hazards such as flood, drought and seismic events. Despite the devastation wrought by Hurricane Mitch, rural people have developed strategies and capabilities to adapt and survive the many difficulties that they face. One of these difficulties is the strongly seasonal nature of the annual agricultural cycle when, in the absence of rains, rural people are left with few economic options other than to migrate in search of work. However, the tried and trusted strategies of seasonal employment in the sugar cane or coffee harvests, or as casual labour in the towns and cities, are becoming more difficult. This makes the task of finding new ways to overcome the marked seasonality of the region and to lessen dependence upon temporary migration ever more urgent. This surely is the principal task facing food security interventions.

5 CONCLUSION

The case studies demonstrate a tendency for food security interventions to manifest many of the worst characteristics of a blueprint project with a top-down imposition of priorities uninformed by local understandings, and driven by the need to reach unrealistic targets. The projects appear to foster dependency by rural people on introduced technologies and bury their capacity to learn, adapt and innovate. There appears to be too little discussion of what might constitute local understandings of food security and to develop, through participatory means, more locally appropriate production strategies and technology portfolios. There is also too little understanding of the nutritional dimension of food security at individual and household level and a failure to track changes in people's access to food.

I have been suggesting that food security is in danger of losing its value through being used as a general label to cover a variety of rural development interventions. Recent events have illustrated the vulnerability of people in Central America to climatic hazards. It is likely to be the case that, under the processes of anthropogenically-induced global climate change, major perturbances to pre-existing cycles will take place. In other words, the appearance of El Niño may become more frequent and its consequences possibly more far-reaching. Hurricanes in the region may also increase in severity as ocean temperatures rise. Existing rainfall patterns may change. These are all circumstances that point to a deepening of poverty, an increase in vulnerability and an intensification of food insecurity unless project interventions are designed, from the outset, with enhancing people's capacity to cope. This means making agricultural and livelihood systems more resilient and better able to withstand stress and shock. It cannot be for projects to impose the elements of such systems on rural people, but to work with them in genuinely collaborative ways to design more robust systems capable of providing sustainable livelihoods and food security even in the face of environmental uncertainty.

NOTES

1. See inter alia, Devereux (1993), de Waal (1989 and 1997), Sen (1981), Dreze and Sen (1989), Walker (1989), Field (1993).
2. We should note here the efforts currently underway by biotechnologists to genetically engineer increased levels of vitamin A in rice. Swiss scientists developed the modified grain by inserting genes from a daffodil and a bacterium into rice plants that then have sufficient beta-carotene to meet total vitamin A requirements in a typical Asian diet. Work is now underway at the International Rice Research Institute in the Philippines to breed this genetic modification into suitable Asian varieties of rice (World Bank Development News, 18–21 January 2000). The degree to which genetic engineering will improve food security for the poor remains a contested area.
3. The interested reader is encouraged to consult George Kent's superb tutorial on Nutrition Rights: The human right to adequate food and nutrition located at: http://www2.hawaii.edu/~kent/tutorial2000/titlepage.htm.
4. The case studies presented here draw on recent project evaluation work conducted for a European NGO working in collaboration with a US partner on a food security programme funded by the European Union. The observations made here have been echoed by recent publications (Hoddinott, 1999; Hoddinott and Morris, 1999; Clay et al., 1998).

REFERENCES

Anderson, M. (1999) 'Do No Harm: How Aid Can Support Peace – Or War', Boulder, CO: Lynne Rienner.

Andrae, G. and Beckman, B. (1986) *The Wheat Trap: Bread and Underdevelopment in Africa*, London: Zed Press.

Babu, S. and Pinstrup-Andersen, P. (2000) 'Achieving Food Security in Central Asia – Current Challenges and Policy Research Needs', *Food Policy*, 25: 629–35.

Barrett, H., Ilberry, B., Browne, A. and Binns, T. (1999) 'Globalization and the Changing Networks of Food Supply: The Importation of Fresh Horticultural Produce From Kenya into the UK', Trans. Inst. Br. Geog. NS 24, 159–74.

Bideleux, R. (1985) *Communism and Development*, London: Methuen.

Bohle, H.G., Downing, T.E. and Watts, M.J. (1994) 'Climate Change and Social Vulnerability: Towards a Sociology and Geography of Food Insecurity', *Global Environmental Change*, 4, 1: 37–48.

Burch, D. and Goss, J. (1999) 'An End to Fordist Food? Economic Crisis and the Fast Food Sector in Southeast Asia', in D. Burch, J. Goss and G. Lawrence (eds), *Restructuring Global and Regional Agricultures: Transformations in Australasian Agri-Food Economies and Spaces*, Aldershot: Ashgate, pp. 87–110.

Campbell, C. and Laherrere, J. (1998) 'The End of Cheap Oil', *Scientific American*, 278, 3: 60–65.

Campbell, C. (1997) *The Coming Oil Crisis*, Brentwood, Essex: Multi-Science Publishing Company and Petroconsultants.

Caraher, M., Dixon, P., Lang, T. and Carr-Hill, R. (1998) 'Access to Healthy Foods: Part 1. Barriers to Accessing Healthy Foods: Differentials by Gender, Social Class, Income and Mode of Transport', *Health Education Journal*, 57: 191–201.

Chambers, R. (1989) 'Vulnerability, Coping and Policy', *IDS Bulletin*, 20, 2: 2–7.

Chambers, R. and Conway, G. (1992) 'Sustainable Rural Livelihoods: Practical Concepts for the 21st Century', Discussion Paper 296, Institute of Development Studies, University of Sussex.

Chen, R. and Kates, R. (1994) 'Climate Change and World Food Security: Editorial', *Global Environmental Change*, 4, 1: 3–6.

Clay, E. (1997) 'Food Security: A Status Review of the Literature', ODI Research Report, London: Overseas Development Institute.

Clay, E., Pillai, N. and Benson, C. (1998), 'The Future of Food Aid: A Policy Review', London: Overseas Development Institute

Community Food Security Coalition (2000), (http://www.foodsecurity.org) (21/11/00).

de Waal, A. (1989) *Famine That Kills: Darfur, Sudan 1984–1985*, Oxford: Clarendon Press.

de Waal, A. (1993) 'War and Famine in Africa', *IDS Bulletin*, 24, 4: 33–40.

de Waal, A. (1997) *Famine Crimes: Politics and the Disaster Relief Industry in Africa*, London: African Rights and the International African Institute in association with James Currey.

DeRose, L. (1998) 'Food Poverty', in L. DeRose, E. Messer and S. Millman, *Who's Hungry? And How Do We Know? Food Shortage, Poverty and Deprivation*, Tokyo: United Nations University Press.

DeRose, L. and Millman, S. (1998) 'Introduction', in L. DeRose, E. Messer and S. Millman, *Who's Hungry? And How Do We Know? Food Shortage, Poverty and Deprivation*, Tokyo: United Nations University Press.

Devereux, S. (1993) *Theories of Famine*, London: Harvester Wheatsheaf.

DFID (Department for International Development) (2000) *Sustainable Livelihoods Guidance Sheets*, London: DFID.

Dorosh, P. (2001) 'Trade Liberalization and National Food Security: Rice Trade between Bangladesh and India', *World Development*, 29, 4: 673–89.

Dreze, J. and Sen, A. (1989), *Hunger and Public Action*, Oxford: Clarendon Press.

Dyson, T. (1996) *Population and Food: Global Trends and Future Prospects*, London: Routledge.

Economist, The (1996) '1996 Feeding Frenzy', 23 November, pp. 145–6.

FAO (Food and Agriculture Organization of the United Nations) (1997) 'Report of the World Food Summit', 13–17 November 1996, Part One. Rome: FAO.

FAO (Food and Agriculture Organization of the United Nations) (1999) 'The State of Food Insecurity in the World 1999', Rome: FAO.

Field, J.O. (1993) *The Challenge of Famine: Recent Experience, Lessons Learned*, West Hartford, Conn.: Kumarian Press.

Furey, S., McIlveen, H. and Strugnell, C. (1999) 'Food Deserts: An Issue of Social Justice', *M/C: A Journal of Media and Culture*, 2, 7. (http://www.uq.edu.au/mc/9910/deserts.html) (01/03/00).

Goodman, D. and Watts, M. (eds) (1997) *Globalizing Food: Agrarian Questions and Global Restructuring*, London: Routledge.

Hancock, G. (1989) *Lords of Poverty*, London: Macmillan.

Hoddinott, J. (1999) 'Operationalizing Household Food Security in Development Projects: An Introduction', International Food Policy Research Institute Technical Guide No.1, Washington, DC.

Hoddinott, J. and Morris, S. (1999) *Designing Institutional Arrangements to Maximise Household Food Security, Technical Guide 11*, Washington, DC: International Food Policy Research Institute.

Houghton, J. (1997) *Global Warming: The Complete Briefing*, Cambridge: Cambridge University Press.

IFPRI (International Food Policy Research Institute) (2000) 'Global Study Reveals New Warning Signals: Degraded Agricultural Lands Threaten World's Food Production Capacity', (http://www.cgiar.org/ifpri/pressrel/052500.htm) (27/07/00).

Jackson, Stephen (2001) Personal Communication.

Kates, R. (1996) 'Ending Hunger: Current Status and Future Prospects', *Consequences*, 2, 2: 3–11.

Kent, G. (2000) 'Nutrition Rights: The Human Right to Adequate Food and Nutrition', (http://www2.hawaii.edu/~kent/tutorial2000/titlepage.htm).

Köhler, B.M., Feichtinger, E., Barlosius, E. and Dowler, E. (eds) (1997) *Poverty and Food in Welfare Societies*, Berlin: Edition Sigma.

Lang, T. and Caraher, M. (1998) 'Access to Healthy Foods: Part II. Food Poverty and Shopping Deserts: What Are the Implications for Health Promotion Policy and Practice?', *Health Education Journal*, 57: 202–11.

Lipton, M. (1977) *Why Poor People Stay Poor: A Study of Urban Bias in World Development*, London: Temple Smith.

Macrae, J. and Zwi, A (eds) (1994) *War and Hunger: Rethinking International Responses to Complex Emergencies*, London: Zed Press.

McMichael, P. (1999) 'Virtual Capitalism and Agri-Food Restructuring', in D. Burch, J. Goss and G. Lawrence (eds), *Restructuring Global and Regional Agricultures: Transformations in Australasian Agri-Food Economies and Spaces*, Aldershot: Ashgate, pp. 3–22.

Messer, E. (1998) 'Conflict as a Cause of Hunger', in L. DeRose, E. Messer and S. Millman, *Who's Hungry? And How Do We Know? Food Shortage, Poverty and Deprivation*, Tokyo: United Nations University Press.

Millman, S. and DeRose, L. (1998) 'Measuring Hunger', in L. DeRose, E. Messer and S. Millman, *Who's Hungry? And How Do We Know? Food Shortage, Poverty and Deprivation*, Tokyo: United Nations University Press.

Mintzer, I. and Miller, A. (1992) 'Stratospheric Ozone Depletion: Can We Save the

Sky?', in Bergesen, H. (ed.), *Green Globe Yearbook of International Cooperation on Environment and Development 1992*, Oxford: Oxford University Press.

ODI (Overseas Development Institute) (2000) Briefing Paper 1, January 2000.

Parry, M., Rosenzweig, C., Iglesias, A., Fischer, G. and Livermore, M. (1999) 'Climate Change and World Food Security: A New Assessment', *Global Environmental Change*, 9, S51–S67

Pinstrup-Andersen, P., Pandya-Lorch, R. and Rosegrant, M. (1999) 'World Food Prospects: Critical Issues for the Early Twenty-First Century', Food Policy Report 2020 Vision. International Food Policy Research Institute, Washington, DC.

Raikes, P. (1988) *Modernising Hunger: Famine, Food Surplus and Farm Policy in the EEC and Africa*, London: James Currey.

Redclift, M. (1994) 'Sustainable Development: Economics and the Environment', in M. Redclift and C. Sage (eds), *Strategies for Sustainable Development: Local Agendas for the South*, Chichester: John Wiley, pp. 17–34.

Riches, G. (1997) 'Hunger and the Welfare State: Comparative Perspectives', in Riches, G. (ed.), *First World Hunger: Food Security and Welfare Politics*, Basingstoke: Macmillan Press, pp. 1–13.

SAFE Alliance (1994) *The Food Miles Report*, London: Sustainable Agriculture, Food and Environment (SAFE).

Sage, C. (1996) 'The Search for Sustainable Livelihoods in Indonesian Transmigration Settlements', in M. Parnwell and R. Bryant (eds), *Environmental Change in South-East Asia: People, Politics, and Sustainable Development*, London: Routledge, pp. 97–122.

Sen, A. (1981) *Poverty and Famines: An Essay on Entitlement and Deprivation*, Oxford: Clarendon Press.

UNDP (United Nations Development Programme) (1994) *Human Development Report 1994*, Oxford: Oxford University Press.

Walker, P. (1989) *Famine Early Warning Systems: Victims and Destitution*, London: Earthscan.

Watkins, K. (1996) 'Free Trade and Farm Fallacies: From the Uruguay Round to the World Food Summit', *The Ecologist*, 26, 6: 244–55.

WFP (World Food Programme of the United Nations) (1999) 'Food Security Zones of Pakistan. Vulnerability Analysis and Mapping Unit', WFP Regional Office, Islamabad, Pakistan.

7. Water and 'cultural security'

Chris Cocklin

1 INTRODUCTION

> The idea that nature has had something to do with the shaping of cultures and history is an idea that is both obviously true and persistently neglected. (Donald Worster, 1985, p. 22)

In discussions of the possible links between environment and security, we often find reference to water (Cooley, 1984; Falkenmark, 1986; Starr, 1991; Gleick, 1993; Lonergan and Brooks, 1994; Postel, 1996; Wolf, 1999). This is not surprising, given that there are widespread scarcities of supply, it is essential to human survival, has value in economic terms, and that some water bodies are of strategic significance as, for example, in the Middle East (Lonergan and Brooks, 1994; see also Wolf, 1999). The extent and intensity of social, environmental, economic and strategic problems associated with water are bound to increase in the future. In the *Global Environmental Outlook 2000* (UNEP, 1999), it was reported that 20 per cent of the world's population already lacks access to safe drinking water and that 50 per cent of the population do not have access to adequate sanitation. In the context of an increasing world population and the seemingly inexorable processes of industrialisation and urbanisation, many are predicting a global water crisis. According to the UNEP report, 'Water security, like food security, will become a major national and regional priority in many areas of the world in the years to come' (p. xxii). Postel (1996, p. 47) similarly predicted threats to human security as a result of increased competition for water, observing that: 'Neither governments nor the international community is prepared for the internal social disruption and external conflict that could result as water scarcity deepens and spreads.'

Analyses of water scarcity issues typically emphasise the implications for human health and survival, the potential for economic disruption, and the extent of water and related environmental degradation. Some authors have suggested that the threats posed by these various dislocations are potentially significant enough to bring about violent conflict (for example, Cooley, 1984; Starr, 1991; Postel, 1996), though others are sceptical about such claims

(Wolf, 1999). The fact that water degradation and scarcity disproportionately affect the world's poor and underprivileged has rightly been a recurrent theme as well. At a conference of seven of the world's poorest nations in June 2000 (the so-called P7 Summit), delegates called for water to be treated as a fundamental human right, not as a market commodity (Harding, 2000).

In the environmental security literature there has been less attention to the implications for cultural values that arise from the development, use and degradation of water. However, cultural values can be undermined by what some people regard as inappropriate uses of water, the environmental degradation of water bodies, and through competition-induced scarcity that limits the ability of groups and individuals to realise opportunities to sustain their livelihoods, for example in terms of food supply or economic activities. An interest in what we might call 'cultural security' arises out of a well-established literature on the cultural significance of nature and the environment (for example, Glacken, 1967; Hutterer et al., 1985; Callicot and Ames, 1989; Croll and Parkins 1992; Ellen and Fukui, 1996) and the more recent debates about the social construction of 'nature' and 'environment' (for example, Proctor, 1998).

My objective in this chapter is to argue that decisions taken about the use and development of water resources can have the effect of undermining cultural security. This argument rests on claims about the social construction of nature and the inseparability of nature/culture. Whereas some environmentalists have denounced post-structuralist discourses about 'nature' and 'environment', on the grounds that they undermine the potential for action to protect the environment, the position is taken here that a social constructionist view does not in fact preclude a nature-affirming ethic. Indeed, the entanglement of nature/culture, and the derived notion of 'cultural security', is a possible foundation for an ethic that promotes environmental protection. This argument is developed here with reference to examples of the nature/culture relation among the Maori of Aotearoa/New Zealand and the Aborigines of Australia.

2   ENVIRONMENT AND HUMAN SECURITY

The relationships between environment and security have been the subject of extensive debate within both academic and policy communities, but since many of the important elements of this debate and the associated literature are reviewed in Part I of this book, only a cursory review is presented here. Linking environment and security has been an outgrowth of a broadening of the concept of national security (Griffiths, 1997; Lonergan, 1999). Although extended concepts of national security date back several decades, it was not until the 1980s that people began explicitly to link environment with security, and papers by Ullman (1983), Myers (1986), Westing (1989) and Mathews (1989) were among the first to make this association. Noting that during the 1970s concepts of national security had been broadened to encapsulate international economics, Mathews (1989, p. 162) asserted that: 'Global developments now suggest the need for another analogous, broadening definition of national security to include resource, environmental and demographic issues.'

As a result of this work the linkages between environment and security were becoming clearer conceptually, but the need remained to verify and substantiate the arguments put forward by Ullman, Myers, Mathews, Westing and others. A number of studies aimed at establishing the nature of the relations between environment and security with greater conceptual and empirical clarity followed. Probably the best known examples are the studies on the role of environmental change and resource degradation in causing violent conflict, carried out by the Peace and Conflict Studies Programme at the University of Toronto (Homer-Dixon, 1991; 1994; Homer-Dixon et al., 1993). The central issue for this group was the question of whether and how environmental scarcities, caused by environmental change, population growth and the unequal social distribution of resources, might lead to violent conflict (Homer-Dixon, 1991; 1994).

Other programmes are now exploring how human security can be achieved in the face of changing environments and human living conditions. The International Human Dimensions Programme on Global Environmental Change (IHDP) has recently established a project on environment and security, namely the Global Environmental Change and Human Security project (GECHS). The GECHS project of the IHDP is focused explicitly on *human security* and how options and social capacity can be developed in the face of global change.

The GECHS interpretation of human security and its achievement refers to the active engagement of people in responding to threats and reducing vulnerabilities (Lonergan, 1999). Human security is achieved when and where individuals and communities:

- have the options necessary to end, mitigate, or adapt to threats to their human, environmental, and social rights;
- have the capacity and freedom to exercise these options; and
- actively participate in attaining these options (Lonergan, 1999).

According to Lonergan (1999), three premises underlie this definition: (1) human perceptions and use of environments are socially, economically, and politically constructed; (2) environmental problems must be addressed from a perspective that encompasses both world poverty and issues of equity, and;

(3) the appropriate spatial level in which to deal with both environmental and security concerns is not necessarily the nation-state, but the level at which the knowledge base is the greatest, which is often the local level.

The concept of cultural security is interpreted here in terms of this definition. Accordingly, cultural security is taken to be an element of human security. Human security will be undermined by circumstances that threaten nature/culture or, conversely, will be promoted in circumstances in which people have a sense that their cultural heritage and well-being will not be compromised by threats of environmental degradation (for example, because they have the options to mediate these threats).

3   CULTURE AND HUMAN SECURITY

An interesting feature of recent literature on the relations between society and nature has been the, occasionally acrimonious, debate between environmentalists and post-structuralists (for recent reviews, see Proctor, 1998; Quigley, 1999). Whereas the latter seek to establish the relativistic and socially constructed character of 'nature' and 'environment' (for example, Bird, 1987; Bennett and Chaloupka, 1993; Cronon, 1995; Gandy, 1996), their environmentalist critics decry what they perceive to be the effect of these discourses in distracting attention from the urgency of environmental problems (Evernden, 1992; Gare, 1995; Sessions, 1995; Soule and Lease, 1995).

The literature on the social construction of nature provides an essential theoretical window on the relationships between society and 'environment', though. Moreover, recent reflections on the debate between the environmentalists and the post-structuralists reveal that there could possibly be a common goal of environmental protection. This is implied in Proctor's (1998) attempt to establish a complementarity between critical realism and pragmatism, philosophical perspectives that he suggests are both founded in notions of relativism, yet also have the potential to reveal truths about nature. In recent essays, Darier (1999), Levy (1999) and Quigley (1999) find spaces in Foucault's thinking to develop a nature-affirming ethic. Quigley (1999, p. 198), for example, suggests: 'If nature could be seen as a force that disrupts, overwhelms, undermines, explodes or otherwise "makes strange" our ideological consensus, our anthropocentricism, then it is possible to see it as an agent of criticism and deconstruction, as well as of reconstruction.' In a similar vein, Wynne (1994) argued that an understanding of the cultural and social construction of knowledge should not render scientific understandings impotent. Instead, this recognition would permit us to expose the indeterminacies and the inherent value judgements. These directions in the debate are important, since as Ellen and Fukui (1996, p. 29) commented 'we must be careful not to get caught up in a web of reflexiveness which will ultimately prevent us from explaining anything. Recognition of infinite relativity (even if we can surmount the problem of solipsism) is no basis for scientific comparison, intellectual communication or practical action.' Cronon (1995) has referred to this as 'soft' social constructionism, an acceptance that the natural world does in fact exist, but that human relations with it are created and structured by values, perceptions and assumptions (see also Matless, 1992).

In concert with these authors, I suggest it is correct to acknowledge the relativistic, socially constructed character of 'nature' and 'environment', but that this need not obviate an environmental ethic. Indeed, the ethic is based in the reflexivity of nature/culture; in the words of Ellen and Fukui (1996, p. 31) 'culture gives meaning to nature, nature gives meaning to culture'. Worster (1985, p. 22) stated: 'A more credible strategy would be to regard nature as participating in an unending dialectic with human history, seeing the two, that is, as intertwined in an ongoing spiral of challenge-response-challenge, where neither nature nor humanity ever achieves absolute sovereignty, but both continue to make and remake each other.' The ethic, as Levy (1999) suggests, might be described as shallow and anthropocentric, and as such would not appeal to the deep ecologists. It is perhaps better described as a sustainability ethic rather than an environmental ethic, because it assigns values simultaneously (and inseparably) to both the social (cultural) and the environmental. The entanglement of nature and culture is fundamental to the arguments that are developed in this chapter about 'cultural security', interrogated here with reference to water, and the interpretation of nature/culture is central to my subsequent suggestions about resistance (in the Foucauldian sense; see also Darier, 1999).

Through time and across societies, water has assumed special significance in terms of nature/culture (McCully, 1996). In the collection of essays *Water, Culture and Power* (Donahue and Johnston, 1998), various authors write about the importance of water in nature/culture among indigenous societies. In their paper on the Hopi Indians, for example, Whiteley and Masayesva (1998) suggest that the phrase 'Hopi environmentalism' is a redundancy, because the very identity of these people is inextricably linked to an environmental ethic. Within this world view, water is central:

> It is hard to imagine anything more sacred – as substance or as symbol – than water in Hopi religious thought and practice … Springs, water, and rain are focal themes in ritual costume, kiva iconography, mythological narratives, personal names, and many, many songs that call the cloud chiefs from the varicolored directions to bear their fructifying essence back into the cycle of human, animal, and vegetal life. That essence – as clouds, rain, and other water forms – manifests the spirits of the dead. When people die, in part they become clouds; songs call to

the clouds as ascendant relatives. Arriving clouds are returning ancestors, their rain both communion with and blessing of the living. The waters of the earth (where kachina spirits live) are, then, transubstantiated human life. (Whiteley and Masayesva, 1998, p. 15)

Cultural survival, identity and the very existence of indigenous societies depend to a considerable degree on the maintenance of environmental quality. The degradation of the environment is therefore inseparable from a loss of culture and hence identity.

The affirmation of the nature/culture nexus does not lead automatically to claims about a ubiquitously benign relationship between indigenous people and the environment, however. Both the Maori and the Aborigines, for example, extensively transformed the landscapes of Aotearoa/New Zealand and Australia, through forest clearance, the introduction of species, and cultivation (see, for example, Kohen, 1995). While some radical environmentalists have championed interpretations of the relationships between indigenous people and the environment as models for the future (for example, Devall and Sessions, 1985; Tokar, 1987), they have overlooked evidence of disharmony within many of these societies and between people and the environment. A rebuttal of these radical green visions is presented in Lewis's book *Green Delusions* (Lewis, 1994), while Stevens (1997) cautioned that we should not over-romanticise the environmental values and practices of indigenous peoples. By way of further qualification, we should not assume that nature and, more specifically water, is constructed culturally in the same way among all indigenous groups, or indeed even among the various tribal groups of the same indigenous people. In Aotearoa/New Zealand, for example, important differences between tribal groups in their attitudes and beliefs about nature and the environment have been revealed in recent contests over the development and use of resources.

These comments do not disrupt my arguments about the centrality of the nature/culture relation, though, and it remains that environmental degradation and resource use that lies outside the socio-cultural norms of a society will diminish cultural security. Traditions of nature/culture establish patterns of behaviour and social norms that regulate and define human–environment relationships and when these norms are violated, the nature/culture relation will be destabilised; that is, cultural security will be diminished. The potential for this to happen is revealed in Worster's (1985) engrossing account of water in modern American society, which tells of a nature/culture relation that contrasts starkly with those outlined above:

Here then is the true West which we see reflected in the waters of the modern irrigation ditch. It is, first and most basically, a culture and society built on, and absolutely dependant on, a sharply alienating, intensely managerial relationship with nature ... Quite simply, the modern canal, unlike a river, is not an ecosystem. It is simplified, abstracted Water, rigidly separated from the earth and firmly directed to raise food, fill pipes, and make money. (Worster, 1985, p. 5)

Worster's comments point explicitly to important differences between the attitudes to and philosophies of nature among modern Western societies and those of many indigenous people.[1] It is the potential for conflict between this world view and that of indigenous societies, specifically the Maori and Aborigines, that frames the subsequent discussion of water and cultural security.

To this point, there are three main elements to my argument. One is that culture and nature are inextricably intertwined, such that threats to nature (for example, environmental degradation) can also constitute a threat to culture and identity. The second is that in many indigenous societies, water constitutes a fundamental element of the nature/culture nexus. Third, human security can be interpreted in terms of vulnerability to threats posed by environmental change. Cultural security is a component of human security and so threats to nature/culture are also threats to human security. These themes are now developed with reference to water and the indigenous people of Australia and Aotearoa/New Zealand.

4   WATER AND CULTURAL SECURITY IN AUSTRALIA AND AOTEAROA/NEW ZEALAND

When it comes to water, Australia and Aotearoa/New Zealand are in many respects very different countries. Australia is the driest inhabited continent, while Aotearoa/New Zealand benefits from abundant rainfall. The two countries are similar though in that water is central to the cosmologies of both the Aborigines and the Maori.[2] Consider, for example, the account of water in Maori society and cosmology presented below (Box 7.1).

For Aboriginal people, water is just as significant. Langton (1998, p. 4) observed that:

> For coastal groups and those who live in the semi-arid regions where there are saline water sources, the distinction between freshwater and saltwater is critical in the cultural construction of social and economic ideas about institutions. Freshwater and saltwater domains are distinct and separate rules applying to the use of resources in each emphasise the distinctness in daily life. This distinction is not merely economic or biogeographic, but social and spiritual as well.

While distinct, the domains are not separate, though: 'Aboriginal dreaming tracks flow out over the seas, embracing tidal areas, offshore reefs and islands, forming an indissoluble link with the land' (Allen, 1994, p. 40).

BOX 7.1 WATER AND MAORI

Water has a very special significance for Tangatawhenua (literally, 'people of the land'). Water harbours food species (fish, shellfish) which has sustained our people for centuries.

Water or wai, is of two basic kinds, Waimori – freshwater, and Waitai – saltwater. The former falls under the aegis of Tane Mahuta (essentially, the god of the forests). Tane had the role of dealing with the pain and grief of the separation of the primal parents Ranginui-o-te-ra (translated as the sky father) and Papatu-a-nuku (earth mother). It is the tears of Rangi, his embracing mists, his adorning cloak of snow which form the substance of wai Maori. All such water orginates from pain, separation and anxiety and thus attracts a mauri, or life force of its own. Wai tai, or saltwater, rests under the authority of Tangaroa, elder brother of Tane Mahuta.

Natural waters are especially revered in Maori tradition and custom. Water is perceived as being here at the very beginning of time, to be an integral part of the creation story, to comprise one of the major components from which Io, the supreme being, fashioned the world in which we live.

Our belief goes well beyond the mere preservation of water quality to ascribe to water life itself (mauri). Water is not to be mis-treated in any way, but to be nurtured like a living thing.

Water is an essential part of the tohi rights at birth concerning the separation of the umbilical cord and in the removal of tapu at death.

Source: Huakina Development Trust (1990, p. 20).

Langton (2001) suggests that in Aboriginal society, cultural identity is associated with localised water bodies:

For the clan-based group, riverscapes are constructed as complexes of places, each a localised spiritual source of an ancestral being of local groups. The estates of these groups are located along river systems and are linked to each other by 'dreaming tracks', or the pathways of ancestral beings, and thence by economic and social exchange links.

As in Maori society, and rather like that of the Hopi Indians referred to earlier, there is a sense in which water links, at a spiritual level, the unborn, the living and the dead. 'People believe that at conception the spirit enters women from the sacred clan billabong. After death, if the proper ceremonies take place, that spirit returns to the billabong. The ancestors and the unborn are together' (P. Cooke cited in Langton, 2001, p. 4).

So, in common with many traditional societies, water is fundamental to the nature/culture relation among Maori and Aboriginal people. It has social significance because of its spiritual associations and the fact that water links the phenomenal world with the spiritual world, and because certain social traditions (for example, institutional systems, such as those of exchange) are configured in relation to water. In what ways, then, has the 'cultural security' of the Aborigines and the Maori been undermined in relation to water?

It is important to acknowledge first that the institutional frameworks that structure the relationships between Aborigines and wider Australian society are different to those in which the Maori operate relative to Aotearoa/New Zealand's contemporary society. With regard to Australia, three features stand out. One is that there is no treaty between the Aborigines and the European settlers. A second is that until the 1992 *Mabo* High Court judgement, there had been a presumption that European settlement had extinguished indigenous land rights. This was based on the belief that Australia was *terra nullius*, or unoccupied and unowned land. According to Mercer (1997), the *Mabo* decision overturned this long-standing belief, establishing that native title could be claimed where:

- There had been an uninterrupted connection with the land by Aborigines throughout the period of European settlement;
- Title had not been extinguished by legislation enacted by the Commonwealth or state government; and
- Rights to native title were evident in the traditional customs and laws of the people concerned.

The implications of *Mabo*, and of concerted efforts since then by the incumbent Commonwealth government to curtail Aboriginal land and resource rights, for their entitlements to water resources are still largely unknown, however (Langton, 1998).

Relative to Aotearoa/New Zealand, a third feature of the Australian institutional context of note is that it is federal system, in which both the Commonwealth and the states have the power to enact legislation that has direct implications for Aboriginal people, whereas in Aotearoa/New Zealand, a unitary state, legislation can be enacted only by the national government. The significance of this is that Aboriginal people have to deal with policies of the Commonwealth and the respective state government that might reflect quite different attitudes towards the rights and responsibilities to them. Also, much of the legislation relating to environmental management is administered at the state level and there are significant differences across the states and territories in their approaches to policy.

As far as Aotearoa/New Zealand is concerned, there is a treaty – Te Tiriti O Waitangi/Treaty of Waitangi. For a long time it was considered not to have legal standing, but in 1987 the New Zealand Court of Appeal ruled that it does. In making this ruling to uphold the principles of the Treaty, the door was opened for Maori to pursue their rights and duties in respect of the environment and natural resources with much greater authority than had been the case previously. Of further significance in the Aotearoa/New Zealand context was the implementation in 1991 of the Resource Management Act (RMA), an omnibus statute that governs almost all aspects of resources and the environment (Furuseth and Cocklin, 1995). Interestingly, the RMA includes within it several Maori words and phrases. The Act specifies, for example, that in its implementation, there must be 'particular regard' to *kaitiakitanga*, defined in the legislation as 'the exercise of guardianship'. The inclusion of Maori terms has important implications, since as Burton and Cocklin (1996a) observed, it is unclear whether their use is a simple gesture of respect or whether it is intended to open the way for the inclusion of distinctly Maori principles governing human–environment relationships into the practice of resource management. The distinction is important because, if it is the former, decisions over the allocation and use of resources will be made in the context of Western concepts of private property and an ethic of individual wealth accumulation. In contrast, the alternative interpretation would need to account for concepts of collective (tribal) decision-making in terms of resources, and notions of ancestral authority and cultural tradition (Burton and Cocklin, 1996a). The difference becomes particularly poignant in the context of water, since Maori are likely to assume a collective responsibility as *kaitiaki* (guardians), whereas the Crown's decisions about resource use are likely to lead to privatised entitlements to use. The significance of this difference of interpretation was highlighted in a case involving decisions over water allocation that I refer to below.

There can be no doubt that Maori people are in a much more favourable position than the Aborigines when it comes to their rights to resources, and more generally. While the record in terms of Aotearoa/New Zealand's treatment of its indigenous people is far from perfect, Australia's is poorer in all respects. Indeed, Australia stands out as being among the worst in the Western world when it comes to the treatment of its indigenous people.[3] That said, the cultural security of Maori people is under threat in many places as a result of the development and use of water resources, as is the cultural security of the Aborigines.

The character of such threats is evident in a case involving proposals for the abstraction of water from a river for the purpose of irrigating dairy pastures in the northern part of Aotearoa/New Zealand. The case has been described in detail elsewhere (Burton and Cocklin, 1996a, b; Cocklin and Blunden, 1998), but, in short, it involved a request from a group of farmers to dam tributaries and extract water from the Mangakahia River in the northern reaches of Aotearoa/New Zealand in order to irrigate their dairy pastures. The case was an important one, because the Resource Management Act, referred to earlier, had only recently been enacted and this was looked to as a landmark decision in terms of what importance would be assigned to Maori cultural values in the determination over the farmers' application.

When the proposals were first put to the Northland Regional Council (the consent authority) in late 1993 and public submissions were called for, the local Maori (the *tangata whenua*, meaning literally 'people of the land') lodged objections on the basis that, inter alia, the abstraction of water would be in direct conflict with their spiritual and cultural values. At the time, the Council was inclined to agree, stating in its first report on the proposals that:

> It is considered that taking into account the Northland Regional Council's commitment to recognize and provide for the relationship of Maori and their culture and traditions with water, the perceived benefits of granting the consents for a use of water which has not been fully proven in the Northland situation does not outweigh a known adverse effect on the cultural and spiritual value of the Mangakahia River as *taonga* (treasure) to the *tangata whenua*. (Northland Regional Council, 1993, p. 31)

The case subsequently stretched out over another two years, culminating in a court hearing in 1995 before what is known in Aotearoa/New Zealand as the Planning Tribunal.[4] Throughout the various hearings and negotiations, the *tangata whenua* maintained their objections to the irrigation proposals, principally on the grounds that the abstraction of water would undermine the cultural and spiritual significance of the river. In particular, they claimed that:

- The river is a *taonga* of great cultural and spiritual significance;
- Diversion and abstraction of water from the river system for the purposes of irrigating pasture would be an inappropriate use of this *taonga*; and
- To fulfil their role of guardianship (*kaitiaki*), the *tangata whenua* would have to be included in the formulation of any management plans and decisions pertaining to the river.

Writing about the case after the final decision, a Maori woman who had played an instrumental role in orchestrating the case for the *tangata whenua* wrote:

> Rivers have their place in the physical needs of humanity but deeper than that is the pulse of what life means to us, therefore the degradation of Papatuanuku means the non-existence of humankind ... Therefore in Maori terms, taking of water is more than is obvious to the outside observer. It is not only the physical and economic taking of water, so that others are deprived of it, but also that use the water is going to. In terms of Maori understanding of the correct uses of it, inappropriate uses will pollute that river and degrade the life force of the river. To allow them to do this is not upholding our responsibility as *Kaitiaki* as it would be allowing people to violate our ultimate mother. (Kaipo, 1997, p. 1)

The presiding judges acknowledged the depth of the cultural significance of the river to the *tangata whenua* but approved the consents nonetheless. There are two assumptions underlying this decision that deserve mention here. One was that Maori cultural values should not be accorded any greater significance than those of Aotearoa/New Zealand's non-Maori peoples. This view allowed for the entry of wider social and economic concerns, particularly the right of private landowners to extract resources for their individual economic benefit. The other assumption was that by imposing limits on the resource consents, in terms of quantity of water that could be taken and the time over which the rights to the water would extend, a suitable compromise would be achieved. This amounts to a belief amongst the judges that there is a measure of divisibility of the cultural value of the resource, such that taking less water would not have as much impact than if more was taken. It is an assumption that most Maori would not agree with, since any disturbance of natural waters is considered to be a culturally anathematic.

There are numerous other examples in the Aotearoa/New Zealand context of contests over the use of water that have at their foundation the significance of the nature/culture relation to Maori. While each and all of these examples cast their own important light on the complexities of resource allocation and use, the issues are essentially the same. As implied earlier, there is also a basic similarity with contests over water in the Australian context.

A claim for rights over land and water in the north-central part of the state of Victoria provides one example. The Yorta Yorta people have occupied what is now known as the Murray-Goulburn region for all known time (Atkinson, 1995). European settlement had an immediate and devastating impact on the Yorta Yorta, reducing their population by about 85 per cent within the first few decades. Atkinson (1995) suggested that the demands of the Yorta Yorta for compensation for their dispossession of resources date back to the 1860s. More recently, in 1984, claims were put to the Victoria State Government for the reinstatement of rights to land and other resources. The *Mabo* decision in 1992 established a stronger legal foundation for the claims of the Yorta Yorta, which became one of the first to be considered in the post-*Mabo* period and which was significant also in that the claim included water. As noted earlier, under the *Mabo* decision Aboriginal people have to establish a continuous and interrupted link with the land. Atkinson (1995, p. 6) was convinced that this was the case:

> The Yorta Yorta people have continued to exercise their natural rights as the indigenous occupants and owners of the forest. Furthermore, the Yorta Yorta have shown through oral, documentary and material evidence that their social, spiritual, economic and cultural links with the area have never been broken. In other words they can clearly demonstrate that their relationship with the area has continued since time immemorial.

This conviction was not shared by those deciding on the claim, however, which has been denied (Spindler, 1998). This decision is still under appeal to a higher court.

Other cases in which the cultural security of Aboriginal people has been undermined in the context of decisions over the use of water are reviewed in Langton (1998). One of the cases she refers to is a proposal to dam the Fitzroy River in the Kimberley region of the State of Western Australia. Like the Aotearoa/New Zealand case discussed previously, the dam proposals are based on perceived opportunities for economic gain. More specifically, the proposals involve the construction of as many as three dams, primarily to provide water for the irrigation of cotton plantations. The population of the region is primarily Aboriginal, yet all indications are that their values and opinions will be overlooked in the decisions over the development of the water resources. Langton (1998, p. 12) reports that several of the Aboriginal language groups (that is, clans or tribes) are collaborating under the name of the Bandaralngarri Committee to contest the proposed developments on the basis of 'native title, the protection of cultural sites and values, and concerns about health, social impacts, and the environment'. Langton (1998, p. 14) is not optimistic however. 'The amended NTA (Native Title Act 1994) and the dam development plan specifically exclude the rights of Aboriginal people. Moreover, the traditional owners of the area are prevented from the outset from having any interest in the water rights despite their knowledge and cultural ties to water sources.'

The pattern in both countries, then, is one of development of water re-sources that disturbs the nature/culture relation of the indigenous peoples. It seems not to matter much whether there are legal overtures to cultural values, as in Aotearoa/New Zealand's Resource Management Act, or not, as in Aus-tralia. The outcomes of decisions do not in general favour the cultural values of either the Maori or the Aborigines. Implicitly at least, the underlying assumption is that the values (economic rather than cultural) of the European settlers take precedence. One result of this is a diminution of the cultural security of the respective indigenous people.

5 POWER/KNOWLEDGE, RESISTANCE AND CULTURAL SECURITY

In *Western Times and Water Wars*, Walton (1992) writes about the resistance and ultimate conquest over the Native Americans through the development of the Owens Valley, California. He proposes that the modern state achieves legitimation through rational-legal principles which themselves are based in cultural traditions. In other words, the authority and domination of the state rests on its ability to demonstrate consistency with the cultural constructions of ascendant social groups. He suggests also, though, that culture can work in a reflexive or reciprocal way. 'On the other hand, challenges to the state, whether as resistance or redefinition of the public realm, also claim legitimacy from tradition, law, the conflicting tenets of the state itself, or some combination of all these' (Walton, 1992, p. 307).

In a paper that analyses the Mangakahia River case referred to earlier, Greg Blunden and I drew on the work of Foucault to explain the implications of power/knowledge in determining the outcome of the decisions over the allocation of the river's water (Cocklin and Blunden, 1998) and there are some important similarities between our analysis and Walton's. Our arguments hinged on the following statement by Foucault:

> Each society has its regime of truth, its 'general politics' of truth: that is, the type of discourse which it accepts and makes function as true; the mechanisms and instances which enable one to distinguish false and true statements, the means by which each is sanctioned; the techniques and procedures accorded value in the acquisition of truth; the status of those who are charged with saying what counts as true. (Foucault, 1980, p. 131)

Thus, regimes or systems of truth establish what is true and what is false, or more accurately, what is accepted and what is not accepted as truth or falsity. These truth systems are sustained by their discourses and, naturally, different truth systems are characterised by their own discourses. The discourses of dominant groups within society will hold sway, and they are firmly inscribed in the regulatory structures, representational space and ethical systems of society (Cocklin and Blunden, 1998; see also Darier, 1999). A related point is that knowledge is a source of power: truth systems, sustained by discourses, are themselves founded on specific knowledge, and discourses are therefore part of the tactics of power relations (see, for example, Quigley, 1999). According to Harvey (1996, p. 174) 'dominant systems of power can advance and protect a hegemonic discourse of efficient and rational environmental management and resource allocation for capital accumulation (and to some degree even construct policies, institutions, and material processes that draw upon such discourses)'. Peet and Watts (1996) have used the term 'environmental imaginary' to capture essentially similar ideas, namely that hegemonic discourses establish 'truths' about thought and behaviour in respect of nature and environment. The environmental imaginary refers to accepted social norms that define and structure human–environment relations within specific societies.

In the Mangakahia case, the *tangata whenua* faced the imposing challenge of contesting a discourse of sustainability in relation to water resources founded in the dominant power/knowledge systems of Western science and economics. It was a contest that they lost. In essence, what the local Maori people had to establish in the minds of the court judges was an understanding and empathy for a world view through which nature itself is constructed differently, in which environmental change is not measured by instruments and models, and in which culture and nature are inseparably entwined. Stacked against them was the hegemonic discourse of Western science and the deeply ingrained Lockeian social ethic that commands accumulation of material wealth by individuals. Not only was this a significant challenge in its own right, but the local Maori in this case, and in the numerous others that have or will be played out around the country, must tackle it with modest financial resources, limited time, and in most cases little or no formal training and experience in the conventions and mechanisms of European law. The circumstances of the Australian Aborigines are much the same. According to Langton (1998, p. 29): 'The national imaginary is being redefined by these struggles and yet there is little assurance of environmental security for those indigenous peoples who seek to sustain their own traditional governance of resources, which are being re-regulated and re-defined in institutions far away from their homelands.'

How does this relate to the concepts of human security that I outlined earlier? The definition suggests that human security will be achieved when groups have the options to end or mitigate threats to their human, environmental and social rights, the capacity and freedom to exercise these options, and when they can actively participate in attaining these options. It is fair to question whether this definition is met in relation to the Maori and Aboriginal people when it comes to contests over the allocation and use of water resources and, indeed, all other resources. They are at once frustrated by hegemonic discourses that accord little or no weight to their perspectives on nature/culture. Additionally, there is limited access to resources – financial, professional, and intellectual – and this also thwarts attempts to challenge development proposals. In both countries, petitions for the allocation of water resources have persistently favoured the Western ethic of economic development, to the exclusion of the cultural and environmental values of the indigenous peoples. There is doubt, therefore, as to whether the Aborigines or the Maori really have the options or the capacity to end or mitigate threats to their cultural, social and environmental values. Their cultural security is consequently in a tenuous state.

There is a source of optimism, however. In the statement quoted above from Walton there is a suggestion that the prevailing power/knowledge regime is subject to resistance, challenge and reinterpretation. According to Foucault (1980, p. 142) 'there are no relations of power without resistances; the latter are the more real and effective because they are formed right at the point where relations of power are exercised'.

Foucault's thoughts on power and resistance are enlisted in essays by Quigley (1999) and Levy (1999) to outline prospects for the emergence of an influential environmental ethic; their arguments have direct relevance to the struggles of indigenous people to maintain cultural security. Quigley suggests that power is susceptible to challenge and that its existence should not lead to apathy but to activism. Quigley draws on Foucault's concept of heterotopia to define a nature-based site of resistance to prevailing regimes of power/knowledge. In doing so, he upholds the constructivist character of 'nature' leading to the conclusion that: 'Nature may be a place to escape to, but it is not a world elsewhere, another realm, or a place containing sacred ideas or lessons. It is a place to gather strength against the forces of domination, but also a place we have created, and a place to remember that nature has frequently been a weapon of oppression' (Quigley, 1999, p. 201).

Darier (1999) also outlines a strategy for the pursuit of a 'green' ethic through self and social reflection and widespread resistance. Hence: 'Green ethics based on resistance must be understood as an aesthetic of human existence rooted in a permanent, radical questioning and re-questioning of the broader conditions which result in humans seeing the world as they see it, so as to think differently from the way they now think' (p. 234). There are potential risks in this for a post-structuralist, however; how do we avoid the pitfall of this 'green' ethic becoming a foundationalist and normalising ethic? Darier suggests that this can be achieved by ensuring that the ethic itself must be based on constant reflection, criticism and resistance, a hyper-activity that strives towards persistent reinvention.

Thus, persistent action and resistance should be directed towards de-stabilising regimes of power/knowledge that threaten cultural values and the respective nature/culture relation. It is a project of importance not only to the indigenes, but of much wider social significance as well, since it would promote a 'green' ethics of the sort that Darier refers to. Sustained resistance by indigenous groups might have the effect of redefining human–environment relations in ways that are not only consistent with their own constructions of nature/culture, but in a way that supports a more broadly-based environmental ethic.

From a post-structuralist perspective there might be a concern as to whether this might ultimately lead to one normalising ethic supplanting another, along the lines that Darier (1999) anticipates. Avoidance of this would demand of indigenous people the kinds of self and social reflection on culture/nature that Darier talks about – a perpetual reconsideration of the nature/culture nexus. In other words, the relation must be an eternally dynamic one, shaped for example by its opposition and resistance to the dominant regime of Western ideas about nature, which themselves are in a constant state of reinvention. Such a dynamic is nothing new to indigenous societies. As Kohen (1995) pointed out with reference to the Aborigines, they have adapted culturally and practically to environmental change, which in some cases they have caused themselves (for example, through the extensive use of fire), over the many thousands of years they have occupied the continent of Australia.

6   IN PURSUIT OF CULTURAL SECURITY

Nature and environment are relativistic and socially constructed identities. Thus, the meaning of nature/culture for Aborigines and Maori is quite different from that of the more recent European settlers. The insistence of post-structuralists that 'nature' is socially and culturally contingent has unsettled many environmentalists, who fear the relativism inherent in this view will undermine efforts to protect and conserve nature. This suspicion is not entirely without foundation, but there are also those among the post-structuralists who have argued that it is at once possible to acknowledge the social contingency of nature while at the same time upholding an environmental or 'green' ethic.

One of the essential characteristics of Aboriginal and Maori world views is that nature and culture are inseparable. For them sense of place – socially, spiritually, as well as geographically – is profoundly inscribed, based on deeply-set relationships between geographic location, physical identity, personal, family and community relations, spirituality, and day-to-day livelihood. It is a view of nature and environment that contrasts with that of Australia's and Aotearoa/New Zealand's more recent settlers, for most of whom the nature/culture relation is a far more utilitarian one.

The associations for Aborigines and Maori between place, personal and communal identity, and the significance of water in their respective cosmologies are fundamental to an understanding of their resistance to proposals for water use and development. Not only do such proposals often have implications for their own livelihood and material well-being but, more significantly, development in many cases threatens their cultural security. It has been argued here that a circumstance of *in*security persists, because the Aborigines and Maori confront on unequal terms a hegemonic regime of power/knowledge that is inconsistent with their own constructions of nature/ culture. Moreover, in practical terms, the transaction costs of participating in contests over the allocation and use of resources impose immense burdens on communities that often have limited resources.

There is a view, though, that power inevitably engenders resistance. This has been argued from various philosophical and disciplinary perspectives. Foucault, for example, makes such claims and interpretations of his work (for example, Darier, 1999; Levy, 1999; Quigley, 1999) build on these ideas to show how resistance might lead to the emergence of an environmental ethic. I have suggested here that the power/knowledge regimes that threaten the cultural security of Aborigines and Maori through the development of natural resources similarly engender resistance and that this might ultimately reconstruct human–environment relations in ways that are more in sympathy with their nature/culture relation. Indeed, there are clear signs that this is already so. In Aotearoa/New Zealand, for example, in the Resource Management Act Maori terms are used to define the principles of sustainable management. While the Mangakahia and other cases suggest this does not yet mean that Maori concepts have been internalised in decision-making, it is an important step all the same. Similarly, in Australia there are examples of co-management of resources (Ross et al., 1994).

An implication of this argument is that I am privileging a particular interpretation of nature/culture within Maori and Aboriginal societies over the prevailing environmental imaginaries, to use Peet and Watts' (1996) term, within the wider societies of Aotearoa/New Zealand and Australia. This can be justified on two grounds. One is an argument based on my perception of injustice being done to the first settlers of Australia and Aotearoa/New Zealand, because inadequate regard is afforded to their attitudes and values about nature. A second justification lies in the belief that current practices in regard to the management and use of water resources are unsustainable and that support must be given to sources of resistance to the prevailing ethic of relatively unconstrained exploitation. There is ample evidence that contestation of water resource developments by Maori and Aboriginal groups is underpinned by a nature-affirming ethic and their resistance has the potential to limit some of the excesses that will arise out of the development ideology.

Ongoing resistance to resource policy and management that undermines the cultural security of Aboriginal and Maori people will tax their resources heavily. Their challenges to the dominant discourses of Western science and economic rationalism already impose significant burdens upon their limited administrative, professional and financial capabilities. Progressively perhaps, through legal precedents and a gradual and continuous reconstruction of values and discourses, the task might become easier. However, as both Quigley and Darier suggest, there must be constant reflection and questioning. Certainly, for the Aborigines and Maoris, whatever progress has been made so far has been modest, while at the same time the threats to cultural security have tended to increase in number and extent. There is no sign that the pursuit of cultural security in the face of development of water and other resources can be anything other than relentless.

In closing, it is appropriate to address the question of what this discussion adds to the literatures on culture, environment and security. What, for example, does the notion of human security add to our understanding of culture–nature relationships? There is the related question of what the literatures on nature/culture contribute to the understanding of human security. In answer to the first, the definition of human security that I have employed here casts a somewhat new, though not radically so, light on the analysis of culture and nature. The substantial literatures in cultural anthropology and cultural geography, for example, already tell us a great deal about the interconnections between culture and nature and there is a good deal in this literature that explores how the nature/culture relationship can be disturbed by development, particularly in relation to indigenous societies. Even so, the concept of human (including cultural) security adds something to this, particularly in the emphasis that the definition used here gives to options to ameliorate threats.

The literature on environment and security stands to benefit more substantively through an engagement with the concept of nature/culture, however. The concepts of human security are under-theorised and there is a noticeable shortage of attention to the cultural dimensions. While there are acknowledgements within this literature that concepts of both environment and security are socially constructed (see, for example, the definition presented earlier in this chapter) there has been little in the way of substantive analysis of human security that works explicitly from this premise. Moreover, the concept of cultural security, as a specific dimension of human security, has not been considered to any great extent. The literatures on culture and nature, including the relatively recent post-structuralist interpretations that emphasise the contingent and relativistic character of nature/culture, have the potential to contribute to a more elaborate social theory of human security. There is no better context with which to begin than with the threats to the cultural security of indigenous people such as the Aborigines and the Maori.

NOTES

1. For detailed explorations of Western environmental thought, see Hargrove (1989), Hayward (1994) or Pepper (1996)
2. Note that reference to 'Aborigines' and 'Maoris' is a European construction of race and identity. What we are referring to in each case are numerous tribal or clan groups, who respectively share common historical origins, but which differ to varying degrees in their patterns of behaviour, belief systems, languages, and aspects of social organisation. It is misleading to suggest therefore, as the terms Aborigine and Maori implicitly lead us to do, that there is homogeneity amongst them. Even so, it is possible to establish certain commonalities within Maori and Aboriginal societies in respect of nature/culture and indeed there are some similarities to other indigenous societies.
3. This is evident in the fact that the life expectancy of Aborigines is about 20 years less than non-Aboriginal Australians, the number classified as living in poverty is about 2.5 times higher, and that the unemployment rate for Aborigines is about 3 times higher (State of the Environment Advisory Council, 1996). In 2000 Australia has been under scrutiny by the United Nations Human Rights Committee for alleged discrimination and abuses, centred on laws that permit mandatory jail sentencing without trial, laws that impact predominantly upon Aboriginal people.
4. The Planning Tribunal was later renamed the Environment Court.

REFERENCES

Allen, D., 1994, 'Salt-water Dreaming', in P. Jull, M. Mulrennan, M. Sullivan, G. Crough and D. Lea (eds), *Surviving Columbus: Indigenous Peoples, Political Reform and Environmental Management in North Australia*, Casuarina, Northern Territory: North Australia Research Unit, Australian National University, pp. 39–46.

Atkinson, W., 1995, 'Yorta Yorta Struggle for Justice Continues', http://users.mcmedia.com.au/~yorta/wayne.htm.

Bennett, J. and Chaloupka, W. (eds), 1993, *In the Nature of Things: Language, Politics, and the Environment*, Minneapolis: University of Minneapolis Press.

Bird, E., 1987, 'The Social Construction of Nature: Theoretical Approaches to the History of Environmental Problems', *Environmental Review*, **11**, pp. 255–64.

Burton, L. and Cocklin, C., 1996a, 'Water Resource Management and Environmental Policy Reform in New Zealand: Regionalism, Allocation and Indigenous Relations', *Colorado Journal of International Environmental Law and Policy*, **7**(1), pp. 75–106.

Burton, L. and Cocklin, C., 1996b, 'Water Resource Management and Environmental Policy Reform in New Zealand: Regionalism, Allocation and Indigenous Relations II', *Colorado Journal of International Environmental Law and Policy*, **7**(2), pp. 331–72.

Callicott, J. and Ames, R. (eds), 1989, *Environmental Philosophy: The Nature of Nature in Asian Traditions of Thought*, Albany: State University of New York Press.

Cocklin, C. and Blunden, G., 1998, 'Sustainability, Water Resources and Regulation', *Geoforum*, **29**(1), pp. 51–68.

Cooley, J., 1984, 'The War over Water', *Foreign Policy*, **54**, pp. 3–26.

Croll, E. and Parkins, D. (eds), 1992, *Bush Base, Forest Farm: Culture, Environment and Development*. London: Routledge.

Cronon, W (ed.), 1995, *Uncommon Ground: Toward Reinventing Nature*, New York: W.W. Norton.

Darier, E., 1999, 'Foucault against Environmental Ethics', in E. Darier (ed.), *Discourses of the Environment*, Oxford: Blackwell Publishers, pp. 217–40.

Devall, B. and Sessions, G., 1985, *Deep Ecology*, Salt Lake City: Peregrine Smith.

Donahue, J. and Johnston, B. (eds), 1998, *Water, Culture and Power: Local Struggles in a Global Context*, Washington: Island Press.

Ellen, R. and Fukui, K. (eds), 1996, *Redefining Nature: Ecology, Culture and Domestication*, Oxford: Berg.

Evernden, N., 1992, *The Social Creation of Nature*, Baltimore: Johns Hopkins University Press.

Falkenmark, M., 1986, 'Fresh Waters as a Factor in Strategic Policy and Action', in A.H. Westing (ed.), *Global Resources and International Conflict: Environmental Factors in Strategic Policy and Action*, New York: Oxford University Press, pp. 85–113.

Foucault, M., 1980, *Power/Knowledge: Selected Interviews and Other Writings 1972–1977 – Michel Foucault*, ed. Colin Gordon, Brighton, Sussex: The Harvester Press.

Furuseth, O. and Cocklin, C., 1995, 'An Institutional Framework for Sustainable Resource Management: The New Zealand Model, *Natural Resources Journal*, **35**(2), pp. 243–73.

Gandy, M., 1996, 'Crumbling Land: The Postmodernity Debate and the Analysis of Environmental Problems', *Progress in Human Geography*, **20**, pp. 23–40.

Gare, A., 1995, *Postmodernism and the Environmental Crisis*, London: Routledge.

Glacken, C, 1967, *Traces on the Rhodian Shore*, California: University of California Press.

Gleick, P., 1993, 'Water and Conflict: Fresh Water Resources and International Security', *International Security*, **18**(1), pp. 79–112.

Griffiths, F. 1997, 'Environment in the U.S. Security Debate', *The Woodrow Wilson Centre Environmental Change and Security Project Report*, **3**, pp. 15–28.

Harding, G., 2000, A Global Right to Water, *Sustainability Review*, 26, 26 June 2000 (http://www.eeeee.net/).

Hargrove, E., 1989, *Foundations of Environmental Ethics*, New Jersey: Prentice Hall.

Harvey, D., 1996, *Justice, Nature and the Geography of Difference*, Oxford: Blackwell Publishers.

Hayward, T., 1994, *Ecological Thought: An Introduction*, Cambridge: Polity Press.

Homer-Dixon, T., 1991, 'On the Threshold: Environmental Changes as Causes of Acute Conflict', *International Security*, **16**, pp. 76–116.

Homer-Dixon, T., 1994, 'Environmental Scarcities and Violent Conflict: Evidence from Cases', *International Security*, **19**, pp. 5–40.

Homer-Dixon, T., Boutwell, J. and Rathjens, G., 1993, 'Environmental Change and Violent Conflict', *Scientific American,* **268**, pp. 38–45.

Huakina Development Trust, 1990, 'A Report Documenting for the Waikato Regional Council from the Viewpoint of the Tangatawhenua Maori Issues and Cultural Values Associated with the Waiuku/Pukekohe and Pukekawa/Onewhero Catchment', Pukekohe, New Zealand: Huakina Development Trust.

Hutterer, K., Rambo, T. and Lovelace, G. (eds), 1985, *Cultural Values and Human Ecology in Southeast Asia*, Michigan: Center for South and Southeast Asian Studies, University of Michigan.

Kaipo, S., 1997, 'Te Tangi a te Iwi/Why Our People Cried: Mangakahia Irrigation from a Tangata Whenua Perspective', Auckland: Occasional Publication 35, Department of Geography, University of Auckland.

Kohen, J., 1995, *Aboriginal Environmental Impacts*, Sydney: University of New South Wales Press.

Langton, M., 1998, 'Freshwater: Water Rights and the New Frontier in Northern Australia', paper presented to the Water and Human Security in Southeast Asia and Oceania Workshop, Canberra, Australia, November.

Levy, N., 1999, 'Foucault's Unnatural Ecology', in E. Darier (ed.), *Discourses of the Environment*, Oxford: Blackwell Publishers, pp. 203–16.

Lewis, M., 1994, *Green Delusions*, Durham, NC: Duke University Press.

Lonergan, S. 1999, 'Global Environmental Change and Human Security – Science Plan', IHDP Report 11, Bonn: International Human Dimensions Programme on Global Environmental Change.

Lonergan, S. and Brooks, D., 1994, *Watershed: The Role of Fresh Water in the Israeli-Palestinian Conflict*, Ottawa: International Development Research Centre.

Mathews, J., 1989, 'Redefining Security', *Foreign Affairs*, **68**, Spring, pp. 162–77.

Matless, D., 1992, 'An Occasion for Geography: Landscape, Representation, and Foucault's Corpus', *Environment and Planning D*, **10**, pp. 41–56.

McCully, P., 1996, *Silenced Rivers: The Ecology and Politics of Large Dams*, London: Zed Books.

Mercer, D., 1997, 'Aboriginal Self-determination and Indigenous Land Title in Post-*Mabo* Australia', *Political Geography*, **16**(3), pp. 189–212.

Myers, N., 1986, 'The Environmental Dimension to Security Issues', *The Environmentalist*, **6**(4), pp. 252–7.

Northland Regional Council, 1993, Order paper for Hearings Committee Meeting – Applicant: Mangakahia Farm Irrigation 30–99, Whangarei, NZ: Northland Regional Council.

Peet, R. and Watts, M. (eds), 1996, *Liberation Ecologies: Environment, Development, Social Movements*, London: Routledge.

Pepper, D., 1996, *Modern Environmentalism: An Introduction*, London: Routledge.

Postel, S., 1996, 'Forging a Sustainable Water Strategy', in L. Brown (ed.), *State of the World, 1996*, London: Earthscan and New York: Norton, pp. 40–59.

Proctor, J., 1998, 'The Social Construction of Nature: Relativist Accusations, Pragmatist and Critical Realist Responses', *Annals of the Association of American Geographers*, **88**(3), pp. 352–76.

Quigley, P., 1999, 'Nature as Dangerous Space', in E. Darier (ed.), *Discourses of the Environment*, Oxford: Blackwell Publishers, pp. 181–202.

Ross, H., Young, E. and Liddle, L., 1994, 'Mabo: An Inspiration for Australian Land Management', *Australian Journal of Environmental Management*, **1**(1), pp. 24–41.

Sessions, G., 1995, 'Reinventing Nature: The End of Wilderness?', *The Wild Duck: Literature and Letters of Northern California*, November.

Soule, M. and Lease, G., 1995, 'Preface', in M. Soule and G. Lease, *Reinventing Nature? Responses to Postmodern Deconstruction*, Washington, DC: Island Press, pp. xv–xvii.

Spindler, S., 1998, 'The Yorta Yorta Decision: Raising the Barriers', *Australian Rationalist*, **48**, pp. 17–18.

Starr, J., 1991, 'Water Wars', *Foreign Policy*, **82**, pp. 17–36.

State of the Environment Advisory Council, 1996, *State of the Environment – Australia, 1996*, Collingwood: CSIRO Publishing.

Stevens, S. (ed.), 1997, *Conservation through Cultural Survival: Indigenous Peoples and Protected Areas*, Washington, DC: Island Press.

Tokar, B., 1987, *The Green Alternative: Creating an Ecological Future*, San Pedro, California: R. & E. Miles.

Ullman, R., 1983, 'Redefining Security', *International Security*, **8**(1), pp. 129–53.

UNEP (United Nations Environment Program), 1999, *Global Environmental Outlook, 2000*, London: Earthscan.

Walton, J., 1992, *Western Times and Water Wars*, Berkeley, CA: University of California Press.

Westing, A., 1989, 'The Environmental Component of Comprehensive Security', *Bulletin of Peace Proposals*, **20**(2), pp. 129–34.

Whiteley, I. and Masayesva, V., 1998, 'The Use and Abuse of Aquifers: Can the Hopi Indians Survive Multicultural Mining?', in J. Donahue and B. Johnston (eds), *Water, Culture and Power: Local Struggles in a Global Context*, Washington, DC: Island Press, pp. 9–34.

Wolf, A., 1999, '"Water Wars" and Water Reality: Conflict and Cooperation along International Waterways', in S. Lonergan (ed.), *Environmental Change, Adaptation and Security*, Dordrecht: Kluwer Academic Publishers, pp. 251–65.

Worster, D., 1985, *Rivers of Empire*, New York: Pantheon Books.

Wynne, B., 1994, 'Scientific Knowledge and the Global Environment', in M. Redclift and T. Benton (eds), *Social Theory and the Global Environment*, London: Routledge, pp. 169–89.

PART III

International cases

8. The European Union and the 'securitisation' of the environment

John Vogler

1 INTRODUCTION

> Environmental degradation, resource scarcity and the subsequent socio-political impact are a potential threat to security as they may give rise to or exacerbate civil conflicts and conflicts between states. We therefore welcome that the international institutions are attaching increasing importance to the relationship between environmental stress and security. We will examine how to further the issue of preventing and reducing conflicts of environmental origin. (Communique, G8 Environment Ministers Meeting, Schwerin 26–28 March 1999)

The ending of the Cold War in Europe destroyed many of the old certainties about the character of threats, the meaning of security and the identity of the providers of security. It also coincided with the upsurge of public and political interest in global environmental change in the late 1980s and early 1990s. One result was an ongoing academic debate on the redefinition or extension of existing security concepts with particular reference to environmental threats.

Much of the argument was conducted in North America (Deudney and Matthew, 1999) but there were also significant European contributions. Some commentators explored the prospects for a radical redefinition of the core concept of security. In international relations the term had long been interpreted to mean the absence of military threat to the territorial integrity, independence and core values of the state. Lack of such security in an anarchic world of armed nations represented the basic problematic for generations of scholars and statesmen. In the aftermath of the Cold War and in an increasingly interdependent world where environmental degradation and climate change appeared to have replaced nuclear war as the pre-eminent threat to human survival, the logic of redefining security appeared to be compelling (Mathews, 1989; Ullmann, 1983). In this reading a focus on defending the state against armed attack would be replaced by a commitment to the survival of the species through sustainable development.

However, most academic work shied away from such a radical redefinition and opted instead to extend existing security concerns with armed conflict to encompass the consequences of environmental change. Thus there have been a range of studies investigating the links between environmental degradation and the outbreak of violence. Homer-Dixon's (1991, 1994) work is well known in this respect as is the Environmental Change and Security Project of the US Woodrow Wilson Center.[1] There have also been significant European contributions, notably in modelling the relationships between physical and socio-economic change and conflict behaviour (IMAGE, waterGAP, GLASS, ECOMAN).[2] Such work has revealed, what many had already guessed, that there are hardly any conflicts in which a simple causal connection can be traced from environmental stress to warlike human behaviour. Instead there are long and complicated chains of consequence in which environmental stress constitutes one among many variables, the effects of which are mediated by political, social and cultural variables. This work is of evident interest to governments and continues to receive substantial funding. It also brings together academic researchers and policy-makers.

An important example is the study funded by NATO's Committee on the Challenges of Modern Society (CCMS) 'Environment and Security in an International Context' (Lietzmann and Vest, 1999). It set out in 1996 to 'summarise the existing knowledge on the links between environment and security and to develop appropriate policy approaches for preventive action' (ibid., p. 4). Using an explicitly orthodox and state-centred definition of security it identified fifteen syndromes where environmental degradation might be associated with violent conflict. The end result of the NATO-sponsored project is not of purely academic interest, because it seeks to move towards usable forms of threat assessment and decision support based upon recognition of the patterns depicted in the syndromes. The relevant policy responses identified in the NATO study are interesting because they relate only marginally to the capabilities of a military alliance. Instead, as will be argued at the end of this chapter, the relevant environmental, development and foreign policies are exactly in those areas where the EU has generated substantial capabilities, even before it became formally concerned with security issues.

A similar but smaller scale study has also been produced for the EU in the form of the Ecologic[3] report on 'The Use of Global Monitoring in Support of Environment and Security' (JRC, 2000). This relates to the NATO CCMS and summarises European work on environment–conflict linkages. Its main thrust, however, is to stress the importance of building a dedicated European satellite-based observation system as a key instrument in the development of the Union's environmental security policy. There is in this an implicit ambition to emulate the United States and to generate the kind of intelligence that is in part disseminated through NATO channels. 'Whereas the US administration and selected UN institutions started to react to environmenal conflicts in developing countries in the early 1990s, the question of appropriate political responses to environmental conflicts is only just emerging at the European level' (ibid., p. 36).

Both these reports constitute tiny, but perhaps significant, parts of the reconstruction of European security institutions in the post-Cold War era. While NATO has attempted since the elaboration of its 1991 New Strategic Concept to categorise environmentally-induced conflicts as one among a number of 'new' risks justifying the continuance of the alliance, the European Union has also become involved in explicit considerations of security. Marked by the formal creation of a Common Foreign and Security Policy (CFSP) at Maastricht in 1992 this represented a major departure. Following the collapse of the ill-fated plan for a European Defence Community in 1954, questions of military security were strictly beyond the remit of the European Community. Thus there was throughout the remainder of the Cold War a clear division of labour with NATO. While the EC became a very significant actor in its own right in terms of trade, development and, increasingly, in the field of environmental diplomacy its 'political' and foreign policy activities were limited to attempts to coordinate the policy positions of the Member States through European Political Cooperation (EPC). Meanwhile the majority of EC Member States ensured their security in the face of what seemed to be an overwhelming military threat from the USSR through an institutionalised alliance with the United States–NATO.

The ending of the Cold War disrupted this long-established division of responsibilities. On the one hand, the historic rationale for the Atlantic alliance, the ever present military threat upon which it had been predicated, disappeared at a stroke. On the other, doubts about the continued European commitment of the United States and the new possibilities that opened up for giving the EC a military and political role that might match and draw strength from its existing economic role, led to the inauguration of the CFSP. Since then progress has been slow and faltering, A succession of disappointments in the Balkans only served to emphasise the renewed vitality and effectiveness of NATO at the expense of the manifest incapacity of the CFSP. A renewed effort to give substance to the CFSP was provided by procedures established under the Treaty of Amsterdam and developed through the appointment of the High Representative, former NATO Secretary General Xavier Solana, and of Chris Patten as Commissioner to take charge of the, all too often discordant, external activities of the Commission. The experience of the Kosovo operation in the spring and summer of 1999, which starkly revealed the extent of European dependence upon US national assets deployed within NATO, spurred on the quest for an indigenous European defence capability. The agreements at the Helsinki (1999) and Nice (2000) European Councils to set up a European Rapid Reaction Force suggest that at some time during the first decades of the twenty-first century, the EU will become a fully-fledged security actor in the more traditional sense of the word. Whether or not this will be at the expense of NATO or in some form of combination with the American-led alliance has yet to be determined.

This, then, was the political context into which ideas about environmental security were introduced. The remainder of this chapter seeks to understand how the EU has framed the question of environmental security and to consider the extent to which it could, or indeed should, become involved in environmental security politics. To do this the concept of 'securitisation', developed in the next section, is employed.

The 'securitisation' of the environment in Europe is very much a question of the kind of new, and potentially rival, actors that are under construction in the post-Cold War situation and how they have utilised the emerging perceptions of the environment/security nexus. One central difference between the two principal contenders is evident at the outset. NATO is an organisation which has defined itself in terms of narrow conceptions of military security, but has found it necessary to expand its concept to include environmental considerations. While having access to unmatched military, logistic and communications and surveillance capabilities, the alliance is almost entirely deficient in the tools and capabilities required to ameliorate environmental problems and disasters. An exception would be its (largely American owned) monitoring capabilities, if they were to be targeted towards environmental conflict indicators. Also, there is the possibility of redirecting the mission and training of military formations assigned to NATO commmand towards some kind of environmental 'fire fighting' role .

By contrast the EU possesses very substantial capabilities in areas normally regarded as highly relevant to the solution of environmental problems: the control of trade instruments, aid and technical assistance, scientific cooperation. Such areas of policy generally lie within 'community competence' by contrast with the emergent CFSP which remains the paradigm expression of Member state competence. Above all the Union has become an actor of global significance both in terms of the implications of its internal environmental policies and its external involvement in environmental diplomacy and international cooperation. The EU did not until very recently make any explicit connection between its extensive environmental activities and security problems in Europe, still less the emergent CFSP. The watchword was not environmental security but the pursuit of sustainable development – an objective which post Amsterdam has Treaty status (Art. 6). There is really no equivalent to NATO's new strategic concept to be found in the core CFSP documents and a dedicated EU defence capability as outlined at Helsinki and Nice is still in its embryonic phase. In early 1999 the European Parliament (Own Initiative Report on Environment and Security) invited the Commission, as well as Member States, to establish a common strategy linking the

CFSP with trade, aid, development and environmental policies between 2000 and 2010. Significantly, the Parliament also urges the creation of the kind of capabilities for the EU, 'military satellite imaging and tracking technology' and military 'environmental emergency assistance brigades' already available or potentially available to NATO.

2 SECURITISING THE ENVIRONMENT

One way to understand how the EU (and indeed NATO) have approached the question of environmental security is to follow a path pioneered by a distinctive European contribution to the academic debate from the 'Copenhagen School'. Its members, Buzan, Waever and de Wilde proceed from the assumption that security is not an objective 'given' in international politics but is socially constructed. The politics of securitisation is the politics of identifying existential threats in order to give them, and a whole range of associated interests, a greater salience and higher priority.

> 'Security' is the move that takes politics beyond the established rules of the game and frames the issue either as a special kind of politics or as above politics. Securitisation can thus be seen as a more extreme version of politicisation. (Buzan et al., 1998, p. 23)

The emergence of environmental issues on to the agenda of international politics, a process that could readily be observed between the UN conferences at Stockholm in 1972 and Rio in 1992 testifies to politicisation (Vogler, 1997). What appears to have been occurring since the end of the Cold War is an attempt at what Buzan et al. (1998) describe as 'securitisation'. There is a seductive logic in the argument that runs: 'if security involves existential threats to societies then after the Cold War the pre-eminent threats derive from the human-induced collapse of vital ecosystems rather than the receding possibility of major inter-state war and nuclear conflagration'. The old security paradigm addressed the latter but a new paradigm would have to contend with the former. As Myers (1989, p. 41) put it, 'could the time be coming when as much lasting security can be purchased through trees as through tanks?' For its advocates, securitisation and its widespread acceptance would open the prospect of extraordinary measures and state resources – on a par with those lavished on defence – being devoted to the solution of environmental problems.

Securitisation inevitably represents an intensely political process. At stake are access to resources and, very much to the point, the future prospects of organisations. As Buzan et al. (1998) point out, a real and demonstrable threat may not be required. 'Security' is thus a self-referential practice, because it is in this practice that the issue becomes a security issue – not necessarily because a real existential threat exists but because the issue is presented as such a threat (ibid., p. 24). The social constructivist orientation of the Copenhagen School is in some ways complementary to that adopted by the present author and his collaborator in a study of the European Union as an actor in international politics (Bretherton and Vogler, 1999). Both share the fundamental idea that actors and roles in the international system do not have an observer-independent existence. Instead they are continuously constructed. In the present instance the interesting conjunction is the way in which self-referential processes of securitisation of the environment interact with very substantial changes in the character of NATO and the EU as actors, necessitated by the ending of the Cold War. (It is, however, worth noting that the EU as global actor study relies heavily not upon the 'self-referential' elements of the development of the EU as an actor in its own right, but upon the ascription of 'actorness' by outsiders.)

For the members of the Copenhagen School securitisation is a 'speech' act in which a 'referent object' is declared to be under existential threat. In orthodox discussions of security the referent object is normally the state and the threats usually derive from the military activities of other members of an 'anarchic' international system. However, international history has many examples of threats which, while not possessing a strictly military character, were regarded as such significant sources of state insecurity that military remedies were justified. The most obvious examples involve economic changes imperilling sources of vital raw materials or the interruption of communications. Strictly speaking, in such instances the national economy was securitised but this would have been regarded as the foundation of the state. The first and most prevalent way in which the environment has been drawn into post-Cold War debates about security essentially relates environmental change to classic resource and population threats. In the academic literature this can be seen most clearly in the work of Homer-Dixon (1991, 1994) who specifies three types of environmentally-related conflict: resource scarcity, migration and relative deprivation. A key departure from older views of the security problem (for example those of Morgenthau, 1948) is that the environment is no longer regarded as a constant but is subject to human induced change and degradation. As Macsweeney (1999, p. 89) writes, this can transform some environmental phenomenon from natural to social threats:

> When they arise from natural causes, environmental threats would not normally be categorised as security questions. But an accident at a nuclear reactor, or a volcanic explosion, or global warming, may be given a security dimension depending upon how the danger is confronted. This would most notably be the case if environmental changes were seen to be associated with violent social change.

This form of securitisation is readily understandable from a conventional perspective. It continues to use the state or states as a referent object and may be regarded as an extension rather than a redefinition of security. As we shall see most, but not all, of the securitising discourse in European organisations involves an extension of existing conceptions in order to enclose environmental change.

A redefinition of security in relation to the environment has much wider implications. The Copenhagen School, for example, has proposed the notion of 'societal security' involving 'the sustainability, within acceptable conditions for evolution, of traditional patterns of language culture, association, and religious and national identity and custom' (Waever et al., 1993, p. 23). Booth (1991) has argued for the rejection of an oppressive concern with the security of the state in favour of a new conception founded upon the emancipation of individuals. Macsweeney (1999, p. 209) provides a complex redefinition inspired by recent sociological theory in which 'The security of the social order is inseparably linked to the identity of the collectivity which is its subject.' Under this conception it is confidence in the social order and identity which is securitised. Threats to identity and resulting security problems can occur at different systems levels 'reproducing at the collective level the same logic inherent in social action at the level of the individual' (ibid.). In all these instances the environment itself is not the referent object. Yet, given the complex interdependence of individuals and societies with their ecosystems it should be a relatively easy matter to make the appropriate connections. In fact much of the sustainable development literature does exactly that, usually without resort to security concepts. In Buzan et al. (1998) the environment itself is considered as one of four 'sectors' that are to a varying degree securitised (the others are military, economic and societal). The environment itself rarely becomes a referent object although it is possible to argue that it is so fundamental to all human purposes that 'other issues will lose their meaning' in which case 'sustainability might be the environmentalists equivalent to state sovereignty' (ibid., p. 38). In keeping with the understandable anthropocentric bias of most writers it is in fact civilisation dependent upon the environment that is the referent object to be securitised.

The next section of this chapter proceeds to consider the ways in which the EU has moved to securitise the environment. This is significant because it represents one aspect of the process of reconstruction attendant on the passing of the old certainties of the Cold War era. However, securitisation is a political act intended to redirect policy and resources and although there is little evidence that this has yet occurred in relation to the environment it is worth considering the actual and potential capabilities and roles of the EU this respect. Such a review takes up the penultimate part of this chapter.

3   THE EU SECURITISES THE ENVIRONMENT

The EU has only lately come to consider explicitly the connections between environment and security. This is despite the fact that since the late
1970s it has carved out for itself a very substantial role as one of the pre-
eminent actors in international environmental diplomacy (Vogler, 1999). In
fact it initiated this role in 1979 through participation in the Long Range
Transboundary Air Pollution negotiations. Involving the old Soviet bloc the
negotiation of the LRTAP Convention under the auspices of the United
Nations Economic Commission for Europe were evidently connected to the
broader East–West strategic situation. However, a consideration of the environmental dimensions of security did not figure in the initial development
of the CFSP.

From 1995 the European Parliament placed environment and security on
its agenda with reference to the 'potential use of military-related resources
for environmental strategies' (EP, 1999, p.3). A report from the Committee on
Foreign Affairs, Security and Defence Policy was drafted during 1998 and
presented in January 1999 (EP, 1999) with the Parliament adopting a Resolution on Environment, Security and Foreign Affairs (A4-0005/1999) in the
same month. The Parliament's primary interest was clearly in exploiting the
'peace dividend' for environmental purposes. The threat had changed and as
noted by the Parliament's Resolution 'preventive environmental measures are
an important instrument of security policy'. Accordingly Member States
were urged 'to define environmental and health objectives as part of their
long-term defence and security assessments, military research and action
plans'. While the Foreign Affairs committee proposed wholesale redirection
of the efforts of the armed forces along the lines pioneered in Sweden,[4] the
opinion of the Environment Committee differed in calling for a switch of
military resources away from the military sector. The 'securitising' logic is
very clear here, but it is worth noting that the EP's proposals are no more than
recommendations. The European Community has, at present, no influence
over the training and disposition of its members' national forces. EU Member
States which are also in NATO are, however, involved in a continuous force
planning exercise carried out by the alliance.

The EP Resolution contained a long list of other security-related issues,
but most significantly it called for an integration of the Union's security-
related policies in:

> a common strategy, as foreseen by the Amsterdam Treaty, which brings together
> the CFSP aspects of EU policy with its trade, aid, development and international
> environmental policies between 2000 and 2010 so as to tackle the following
> individual issues and the relationships between them;

a) agricultural and food production and environmental degradation;

b) water shortages and transfrontier water supply;

c) deforestation and restoring carbon sinks;

d) unemployment, underemployment and absolute poverty;

e) sustainable development and climate change;

f) deforestation, desertification and population growth;

g) the link between all of the above and global warming and the humanitarian and environmental impact of increasingly severe weather events.

Faced with this Herculean labour, the Commission responded that it had already been investigating a number of security problems and their economic consequences in a broader context. It had been taking a 'closer look' at the risks associated with climate change and the Environment Directorate General would be focusing on issues related to water resources and shortages (EP Debates, 27.1.99, No. 4-532/19).

An OSCE (Organisation for Security and Cooperation in Europe) meeting later in 1999 (7th Economic Forum, Prague 25–28 May), which was to discuss 'security aspects in the field of the environment', provided a catalyst. In its approach to this meeting the Commission attempted a 'working definition' of security with respect to EU external relations:

> With respect to the relationship between environment and security, the EU has to be able to guarantee continuity in imports and raw materials, well-managed, shared ecosystems (e.g. the Mediterranean) and a stable global climate system, in ways that provide for stability and minimise civil, commercial and military tensions and ultimately avoid violent conflict. Four areas of major concern for the EU can be distinguished:- challenges to the EU ability to secure access to external resources;- conflict generated by environmental scarcity and/or degradation its borders;- physical threats resulting from environmental damage to surrounding areas;- the impact of global environmental change. (European Commission, 1999, pp. 36–7)

In the first of the 'areas of major concern' involving challenges to the EU ability to secure access to external resources, the referent object of securitisation is the single market itself. It is not surprising that this should top the Commission's list, but it is entirely consistent with the classical precepts of state security policy since the days of the mercantilists and before. Clearly, however, the source of the potential interruption of commerce is different. Whereas in the past boycotts and blockades could be challenged by the exercise of military power, ecological threats to supply require different measures. Wedded as it is to participation in the world trade regime, the Commission regards trade liberalisation as 'only sustainable if it is seen as accommodating environmental and development concerns as well'. Otherwise there is a growing risk of 'trade wars as countries opt for different environmental strategies and use trade measures to implement them ("eco dumping" and "green protectionism")' (EC, 1999, p. 38). The tools of security policy faced with environmentally-driven threats to commerce are not the navies of old but development assistance, trade measures to support sustainable production and an insistence on bringing environmental concerns into WTO rule-making.

The second 'major concern' is 'conflict generated by environmental scarcity and/or degradation on its borders'. Here the territories and interests of the EU are securitised in an essentially orthodox way and the analysis is similar to that found in the NATO CCMS study. Environmental degradation, in the context of the fragile economies of the old USSR and Eastern bloc, may threaten EU investments and commerce and might even contribute to armed hostilities. Environmental stress will tend to generate movements of population which provides one of the most evident causal links to the outbreak of war. But there is more than this. For some years the EU and its Member States have felt the rising pressure of economic immigration and political asylum seeking. The securitisation of EU societies and their maintenance in the face of a threat which is now extensively perceived (to put it politely) by European publics is a subtext never far from the surface. The EP report notes 'An estimated 25 million people are refugees from drought, soil erosion, and other environmental problems, which may be compared with 22 million "traditional" refugees' (EP, 1999, p. 14). It notes the possible consequences in terms of conflicts and violence and calls for the official recognition of environmental refugees and further international cooperation and grant of aid to affected areas. While the Parliament stops short of characterising the flow of immigrants into the Union as a 'security threat' its Resolution speaks of 'direct pressure on EU immigration and justice policies'. The security problems are elsewhere 'in the form of regional instability in other parts of the world'. It is likely that many Member State governments would afford the direct impact of immigration higher priority than this. Most attention has been focused on the East, where economic collapse has been the primary impetus to migration. The need to tighten the eastern borders of the CEECs has been a persistent theme of the accession negotiations. Yet, it should never be forgotten that four of the Union's members have Mediterranean coastlines. The creeping desertification of North Africa allied to chronic economic underdevelopment is already setting up substantial migratory pressure upon the Union's southern borders which has been a major security concern in Paris, Madrid and Rome.

Beyond its immediate borders the EU and its Member States share a wider concern for the maintenance of stability as manifested in the objectives of OSCE. An example is to be found in the outcome of the Prague conference which led to an initiative on shared watercourses in Central Asia – seen as the environmental problem which, if left unresolved, would be most likely to lead to armed hostilities.[5]

The third major concern highlights physical threats resulting from environmental damage in surrounding areas. Here it is the EU environment and by extension the health of its population that is securitised. The Chernobyl disaster of 1986 demonstrated the reality of the threat posed by nuclear installations and stockpiles, a threat which was accentuated by the break-up of the Soviet Union. From the beginning of its post-Cold War relationship with the newly independent states, the importance accorded by the EU to the need to contain and remove transboundary nuclear threats was demonstrated by the level of funding devoted to this end within the Union's technical assistance programme for the successor states of the USSR (TACIS) programme. Despite this, the view expressed in the EP report is that the problems have not been solved and 'one of the potentially most serious threats that exist on the EU's doorstep lies in the inadequate monitoring of waste from nuclear arms processing and of biological and chemical weapons stores and in the need for decontamination following military activity' (EP, 1999, p. 9). There is a parallel concern with the transboundary pollution threats posed by other parts of the decaying Soviet era industrial infrastructure.

According to the Commission (1999, p. 50) 'scarcity of freshwater resources is arguably the most prominent and serious threat to the EU environmental security'. The conflict potential of water shortages elsewhere in the OSCE area (the Aral Sea and the Central Asian republics) has already been mentioned. There are also potential direct threats to existing and potential EU members where watercourses are shared (Danube basin).

Any review of current environmental security threats would be incomplete without reference to climate change and the EP and Commission are no exception to this rule. However, the analysis of the exact ways in which climate change might be presented as a security threat tends to be lacking. The EP report proceeds from the assumption that on IPCC estimates 'a rise in sea level would submerge large ares of land and several million people would be affected by famine owing to the loss of extensive areas of agriculture'. The actual threat identified has already been mentioned – the destabilising effect of the environmental refugees fleeing inundation or desertification (EP, 1999, p. 14). The Commission does not attempt to consider the security implications. As de Wilde (Buzan, Waever and de Wilde, 1998) asserts it might be possible to securitise the global ecosystem itself, but in practice securitisation takes as its referent object human civilisation. Interestingly EU statements to date, while going into some detail on the leadership role of the Union at the FCCC and the importance of climate change, only attempt securitisation in a very limited and conventional way. There is not even a reference to the obvious point about the need to preserve the territory of Member States with low-lying coastal regions.

The problem with global warming is that although it potentially represents the ultimate existential threat, on a par with the terrifying prospect of a nuclear winter resulting from a strategic exchange between the two old superpowers, the effects are seen (probably mistakenly) to be too uncertain and remote for serious securitisation. In the end the EU will have to rank and make trade-offs between its objectives and be involved in the kind of debate to be found in the classic discussions of foreign policy decision-making. For example it may be a question of whether in Wolfers' (1962) terminology the mitigation of climate change is represented in terms of *possession* or *milieu* goals. The old fashioned discussions using these concepts highlighted the dilemma of pursuing security through increases of national power and wealth or through improvement in the international milieu (in the traditional debate the latter might include support for a collective security system). While it is easy to make declaratory statements about the global environmental predicament it is very difficult to securitise climate change in such a way as to give it precedence over the pursuit of short-term economic advantage. By definition security interests will take precedence over others, but the extraordinary range of environmentally-related issues currently securitised could well complicate the process. While the Parliament provides a catalogue of environmental security threats, the Commission is alive to the need to produce risk assessment criteria to determine whether an issue qualifies 'as a security risk in any meaningful sense, and in order to prioritize amongst environmental security threats' (EC, 1999, p. 37). Suggested criteria include 'geographic proximity of the risk to EU territory, the immediacy in time and the magnitude of the problem' all to be based on sound scientific advice (ibid.).

4   CAPABILITIES

Securitisation may amount to little more than a word game if capabilities are absent. In the end there will be a reality test. The EU's declaration of its own role in the Balkans provides a salutary example. An important function of securitisation is indeed to generate capability. A good example is provided by the report on environmental security and monitoring (JRC, 2000) mentioned at the beginning of the chapter. Prepared for the Joint Research Centre of the Commission it was the outcome of lobbying by the European space industry for a satellite monitoring capability to rival that possessed by the United States.[6]

Capability implies a capacity for purposive action – something that is still subject to considerable debate in the case of the Union's overall role in the international system but is especially problematical in relation to security politics. One approach to the analysis of the nature and impact of the Union is to draw a distinction between 'presence' and 'actorness' (Bretherton and Vogler, 1999). Presence denotes the effects of the mere existence of the EU as a single market and as the largest trading bloc in the international economy. In the most profound sense the EU has, since its inception in the Coal and Steel Community, been involved with security. The collapse of the attempts to create a European Defence Community meant that it would not become an actor in Cold War security politics, but the very existence of the Common Market had enormous security implications. In terms of the relations between the original six members this had been the express intention of the founding fathers and with US support the presence of the EC became a key factor in establishing the Western position in the Cold War and in providing the economic growth and prosperity which undercut the appeal of the Soviet model.

In terms of the environment/security nexus, there are both positive and negative elements of the presence of the contemporary EU in the global system. On the negative side, the sheer scale of economic activity and energy use (matched only by the US) casts a substantial and damaging footprint. In the politics of global climate change this is readily acknowledged by EU representatives but there is less willingness to consider, for example, the depredations of the long-range fishing activities of EU fleets operating in acordance with the Common Fisheries Policy. In more positive ways the EU with its battery of environmental legislation serves as an example of sound environmental practice. It must also cope with the fact that it not only represents a magnet to outsiders but for the CEECs is regarded as the solution to their environmental and security problems.

Presence provides a basis for actorness but is not synonymous with it. In the orthodox study of international relations and indeed in international law, states are regarded as the only legitimate actors (with some post-1945 allowances for international organisations). Actors must display volition and independent decision-making capability and they must also be recognised as such by other actors. The extent to which the European Union may be regarded as an actor distinct from its Member States has long been a source of controversy. It is certainly not equivalent to a nation-state.

The extent to which the EU may be regarded as an independent actor varies by policy sector and is significantly determined by competence. The weakest area in external relations is represented by the CFSP which despite reforms at Amsterdam retains an essentially embryonic and intergovernmental character. The strongest area of exclusive competence is trade, while environmental policy exhibits mixed competence. Despite this, the EU has become a very substantial player in its own right in international environmental politics (Vogler, 1999). The EU and its Member States also represent the largest aid giver in the international system, however tardy and incompetent the delivery of such assistance may prove to be. Finally, the accession process in which applicants are continuously monitored and schooled in taking on the policy 'acquis'[7] of the community provides it with enormous influence in east-central Europe.

For the Union the policy instruments to address environmental security issues are already at hand. Arguably the Union is already a very significant actor in this field – even if its actions may represent 'security by stealth' (Macsweeney, 1999). Although the European Union is never mentioned in the NATO CCMS study there is in fact a very close match between the policy desiderata set out in the study and the principles and capabilities of the Union. In contrast NATO capabilities, which are almost exclusively military and political, appear irrelevant to much of what is being proposed.

The findings of the NATO CCMS report emphasise the complexity of the linkages between environmental stress and conflict and the necessarily inter-sectoral character of policy responses. Conflict is seen as a dynamic process with 'different threshold levels of intensity along a continuum' (Lietzmann and Vest, 1999, p. 149). Early and preventive action is required at a point at which environmental stress is still a matter of dispute rather than overt violence. 'At this stage, environmental and development policy mechanisms can be applied in order to tackle the environmental and socio-economic sources of the conflict' (ibid.). It is only later, when much of the damage has been done, that the foreign and security policy mechanisms in which the EU is, at present, relatively deficient will predominate. The three types of policy response, environmental, developmental and foreign and security should all 'follow shared principles'. 'These include the principles of sustainable development, precaution, integration and co-operation' (ibid.). For students of the development of the EU and most particularly of the incorporation of environmental concerns into the treaties at Maastricht and Amsterdam, these principles and the attempt to enshrine them across policy sectors will have a familiar ring to them.

The CCMS report proposes a raft of environmental policy responses to enhance security in the face of disruptive environmental change. Most of them involve functions which are, in Western Europe, already being performed by the Union and many fall directly within the ambit of Community competence (6.2.2.1 Integration and Coordination; 2.2 Enhance Common Knowledge Base; 2.3 Comprehensive Assessment Mechanisms; 2.4 Institutional Reform; 2.5 Integration of Social Forces; 2.6 Dialogue and Cooperation).

Because 'environmental stress tends to be transboundary in nature' international and regional environmental agreements are seen to have particular significance (ibid., p. 153). Here the participation of the Union is unavoidable. Over the last 20 years it has established itself as a major actor in international environmental diplomacy (the European Community is a signatory of over 50 Multilateral Environmental Agreements) although the exact form of participation is variable and sometimes difficult because competence is shared between Member States and the Community (Vogler, 1999). The development of regional regimes for the management of shared resources has immediate relevance to conflict potential but may also serve as a wider confidence building mechanism (Lietzmann and Vest, 1999, 6.2.35, 154–5). Examples of active EU involvement in such regime-building activities abound. Member States and the Commission have, for example, been involved in the development of regional seas regimes for the Baltic and North Sea. In the Baltic the Helsinki Commission has since 1974 involved the EU with first the old Eastern bloc countries and then Russia and the CEECs in joint action to control pollution. For the Mediterranean there is now the Short and Medium Term Priority Environmental Action Programme (SMAP) – a component of the 'Barcelona Process'. This EU policy aims to involve the Mediterranean 'partners' in a variety of environmental projects to reduce stress on the Mediterranean and its coastal zones and to combat desertification. It is, however, only a minor part of the wider Barcelona Process which relies heavily on the development of trade and aid agreements between the Union and the twelve littoral states of the South Mediterranean. The genesis of the process is to be found in the Barcelona Declaration of 1995 which in a situation fundamentally altered by the recession of Cold War politics in the Mediterranean, sought to establish 'a zone of shared stability, prosperity and peace'. It is well described by Joffe (2000, p. 3) as a 'soft security' arrangement in contradistinction to the 'hard security' provided by NATO and as a set of agreements that 'exist primarily to exclude migration' to the EU.

Another well-established post-Cold War exercise in regional environmental cooperation which directly addresses the Union's security needs involves nuclear protection. Stimulated by the Chernobyl disaster 20 per cent of EU TACIS funding directed towards the newly independent states of Eastern Europe and the territories of the old Soviet Union has been earmarked to safeguarding nuclear power facilities. TACIS funding is also being deployed to fund transboundary watercourse management projects between Russia and Ukraine, Russia and Kazakhstan, Belarus and Ukraine and the Caucasus republics. Problems arising from shared watercourses are, as already indicated, one of the most frequently mentioned potential sources of environmentally-related insecurity. EU member states and institutions possess extensive experience in water management and are significant donors of expertise and funding. This provides a basis for future intervention in the politics of water security as evidenced by recent OSCE related initiatives towards Central Asia.

As far as the aspirant members of the EU are concerned, they are involved in a client relationship with the Union that goes well beyond regional cooperation and reaches to the very essence of their national economies and societies. Preparation for membership involves adoption of the 'acquis' including full approximation of all existing 240 pieces of binding EU environmental legislation. Taking a longer view, the EU–CEEC relationship is also driven by security concerns on both sides. Interestingly, polling evidence from the early 1990s indicated that CEEC publics perceived environmental degradation as a security threat second only to that posed by a revanchist Russian neighbour (Bretherton, 1999).

The Union also has policies to 'enhance non-governmental input' (Lietzmann and Vest, 1999, p. 155) in its efforts to build up civil networks in the CEECs via Regional Environmental Centres, through its own openness to public participation and support for the Aarhus Convention on access to information to which the Community and Member States are signatories. The Union is also an exemplar in that Aarhus draws heavily on its internal directives on rights to environmental information. It is also worth mentioning in this respect that while the NATO report calls for the extension of majority decision-making in international environmental policy (Lietzmann and Vest, 1999, 6.2.4.1, 155), the EU itself has, since the Single European Act, applied qualified majority voting in the Council to its own environmental legislation.

Many of the potential conflict scenarios envisaged in the NATO CCMS report relate directly to underdevelopment and degradation in the South. Thus it is not surprising that the report highlighted development policy alongside environmental policy in its repertoire of potential responses. These involve not only bilateral and multilateral development aid but also a concern with population policy, democratisation and human rights (Lietzmann and Vest, 1999, 6.3.1.4–1.7, 158–63). The EU lays claim to being the largest aid donor in the world. It has also been proactive in the pursuit of democratisation and human rights in the development of the Lome and now Cotonou conventions. As one of the two dominant trading blocs in the global system it rivals the United States in its influence over the shaping of the WTO regime and may potentially play the same role in the international monetary order. Previous Union policies, protective of the single market and high cost European agriculture, have probably served to exacerbate economic conditions conducive to environmental degradation and conflict. There are many contradictions and difficulties evident in the way in which the Union has handled the trade/environment relationship (tuna–dolphin or leghold traps cases for example). However, in the recent past it is possible to make out a case that the Union has become more receptive to Southern concerns and above all to the environmental consequences of economic liberalisation. Instances would include sponsorship of the Basel Convention ban on North–South trade in hazardous waste and opposition to the US and its allies over transboundary movement of GMOs (the Cartagena Protocol, 2000) .

In summary the EU is capable of acting in ways which the NATO CCMS report defines as critically relevant to environmental security. What has been characterised as the 'presence' of the Union has also exerted a long-term and benign influence. The comparison to the very limited and militarily focused activities of NATO within its 'partnership for peace' (PFP) is particularly striking, especially in relation to the CEECs. NATO of course possesses in full measure the infrastructural and military capabilities that are at present unavailable to the Union, but these are only relevant to the narrow and traditional conception of security and have very limited relevance to the avoidance of environmental conflict scenarios outlined in the CCMS report. In the future the EU might, through the development of the CFSP and truly European defence identity, come to acquire a full range of capabilities and what is just as significant a unified and extensive view of security policy that encompasses an environmental dimension. At present the EU system fails to make effective links between 'security policy' proper in the CFSP and the wide range of external economic, aid and environmental policies that have made it in certain respects a formidable international actor. These are, of course, exactly the policies that have been mentioned above in relation to environmental security. In EU terminology this is a 'coherence' rather than a 'coordination' problem (the latter refers to differences between Member States). There are a number of reasons for this, including rivalries and duplication within the RELEX Directorates General in the Commission charged with making and implementing external policy. Above all, however, there is the 'cross pillar' relationship between CFSP and the other policy areas. While the latter generally are matters of Community competence (Pillar I) or at least mixed competence – allowing the Commission a major initiating and spokesman role the CFSP remains, despite the reforms agreed at Amsterdam, very much an intergovernmental activity in which exclusive Member State competence pertains (Pillar II).

5   CONCLUSION

In the aftermath of the Cold War both NATO and to a lesser extent the EU have moved to securitise the environment. NATO thinking includes environmental change as one source of the new threats that justify the continued existence of the alliance. Although the environment is thus 'securitised' the focus remains resolutely upon armed conflict and the referent object remains the nation-state. The alliance's CCMS report provides an authoritative view of the possible linkages between environmental change and conflict and the most developed analysis of what would be involved in a security policy designed not only to provide early warning of threats but also to alleviate them at source.

Key elements of such a security policy, in all but name, are already present in the external relations of the EU. A re-framing of the European Union's role is clearly under way as it adopts a new role as a traditional security actor complete with a military headquarters and a 60 000-strong Rapid Reaction Force on call. The securitisation of the environment is a political act that must be seen within this wider context. Securitisation emphasises the policy assets of the EU in the environmental field and serves as one means of generating support for new capabilities (in this case a satellite monitoring system) to rival those of the United States and NATO.

All this is understandable in terms of the construction of Europe as, to use Tony Blair's words, a 'super power rather than a superstate'. However, from the perspective of protecting the environment rather than the referents of EU security policy it may not be desirable. Deudney (1990) has warned convincingly of the dangers of mixing the discourses of environmental sustainability and security. As the conclusions of the NATO CCMS report may illustrate in an unintended way, security thinking and security establishments are in many ways antithetical to effective environmental policy. It is difficult to conceive of military formations reinventing themselves as protectors rather than despoilers of the natural world. Securitising the environment in an EU context may in fact obscure the rather positive role that the Union already plays and its special capabilities as a new type: of actor and purveyor of 'soft security'. This involves:

> the character of the EU as a 'civil power', with its roots mainly in trade and economic policies and with only limited experience in security matters, could prove to be a distinct advantage in tackling the environment and security agenda as, unlike superpowers and security organisations, it would be free to take a fresh look at matters and might be less prone to be influenced by pre-conceived ideas. (EC, 1999, p. 37)

NOTES

1. See the annual reports of the Center: The Woodrow Wilson Center '*Environmental Change and Security Project Report*', or the Web site: http://ecsp.si.edu.
2. These research projects are usefully summarised in JCR, 2000.
3. The abbreviated name for the Centre for International and European Environmental Research, Berlin.
4. The Swedish Parliament agreed in 1996 to make environmental protection part of its defence policy but as noted in the EP Report (1999, pp. 24–5) the proposals to train 10 000 conscripts a year has not yet been implemented.
5. Although this was a British initiative the Commission was necessarily involved and participated in an exploratory visit to Central Asian capitals in February 2000.
6. Interviews with officials in Brussels indicate that a deliberate act of securitisation was undertaken to give extra salience to the development of European environmental monitoring capability (see European Space Advisory Group 99, 3). Previously, the defenders of the US military satellite reconnaissance system had used environmental security arguments to defend it in the aftermath of the Cold War. For the US system see Debarred, R.J. 'Military Monitoring of the Environment' in Woodrow Wilson Center 1996 *ECSP Report*, pp. 28–32.

7. The concept of the 'acquis communitaire' defies translation into English. It denotes the rights and obligations attaching to the Community system and its insitutional framework. This includes the entire content of the Treaties plus legislation and case law following them. Additionally the 'acquis' compromise statements and resolutions adopted by the Community and all its external agreements and obligations. The 'acquis' were first defined and formally communicated to applicant states (Austria, Sweden, Finland and Norway) in 1993.

REFERENCES

Booth, K., 1991, 'Security and Emancipation', *Review of International Studies*, **17**(4), pp. 313–26.

Bretherton, C., 1999, 'Security Issues in the the Wider Europe: The Role of EU-CEEC Relations', in Mannin, M. (ed.) *Pushing Back the Boundaries*, Manchester, Manchester University Press, pp. 183–213.

Bretherton, C. and Vogler, J., 1999, *The European Union as a Global Actor*, London, Routledge.

Buzan, B., Waever, O. and de Wilde, J., 1998, *Security: A New Framework for Analysis*, Boulder, CO, Lynne Rienner.

Deudney, D., 1990, 'The Case against Linking Environmental Degradation and National Security', *Millennium*, **19**(3), pp. 461–76.

Deudney, D.H. and Matthews, R.A. (eds), 1999, *Contested Grounds: Security and Conflict in the New Environmental Politics*, New York, State University of New York Press.

EC (European Commission), 1999, 'Seventh Meeting of the OSCE Economic Forum, Prague, 25–28 May 1999, Implementation Review of Commitments in the Economic Dimension: Security Aspects in the Field of the Environment', Working document of the Commission Services.

EP (European Parliament), Committee on Foreign Affairs, Security and Defence Policy, 1999, 'Report on the Environment, Security and Foreign Policy', Rapporteur: Mrs Maj Britt Theorin, 14 January, A4-0005/99.

Homer-Dixon, T.F., 1991, 'On the Threshold: Environmental Changes as Causes of Acute Conflict', *International Security*, **16**, pp. 43–83.

Homer-Dixon, T.F., 1994, 'Environmental Scarcities and Violent Conflict. Evidence from Cases', *International Security*, **19**(1), pp. 5–40.

Joffe, G., 2000, 'Europe and the Mediterranean: The Barcelona Process Five Years On', London: RIIA Briefing Paper New Series No.16.

JRC (Joint Research Centre of the European Commission), 2000, 'The Use of Global Monitoring in Support of Environment and Security', Brussels.

Lietzmann, K.M. and Vest, G.D. (eds), 1999, 'Environment and Security in an International Context', NATO CCMS Report No. 232.

Macsweeney, B., 1999, *Security, Identity and Interests*, Cambridge, Cambridge University Press.

Mathews, J.T., 1989, 'Redefining Security', *Foreign Affairs*, **68**(2), pp. 162–77.

Morgenthau, H.J., 1948, *Politics Among Nations: The Struggle for Power and Peace*, New York: Knopf.

Myers, N., 1989, 'Environment and Security', *Foreign Policy*, **74**, Spring, pp. 23–41.

Ullman, R.H., 1983, 'Redefining Security', *International Security*, **8**(1), pp. 129–53.

Vogler, J. 1997, 'Environment and Natural Resources', in B.White, R. Little and M.Smith (eds) *Issues in World Politics*, London, Macmillan, pp. 222–45.

Vogler, J. 1999, 'The EU as an Actor in International Environmental Politics', *Environmental Politics*, **8**(3), Autumn, pp. 24–48.

Waever, O., Buzan, B., Kelstrup, M.and Lemaitre, J., 1993, *Identity, Migration and the New Security Agenda in Europe*, London, Pinter.

Wolfers, A., 1962, *Discord and Collaboration*, Baltimore: Johns Hopkins University Press.

9. Human security and the environment: the North American perspective

Richard Matthew

1 INTRODUCTION

For over two decades, researchers and policymakers in North America have been interested in the linkages between environmental change, conflict and security (for example, Falk, 1971; Brown, 1977; Ullman, 1983; Lipschutz, 1989; Mathews, 1989; Deudney, 1990; Gleick 1991; Homer-Dixon, 1991, 1994, 1999; Christopher, 1997, 1998; and Environmental Protection Agency, 1999). This interest grew rapidly after 1989, partially in response to research and policy opportunities created by the end of the Cold War.[1] In the past ten years several of the most influential and widely-cited studies of these link-ages have been carried out in the United States and Canada; numerous conferences and workshops held in North America have generated far-reaching and lively debate; academic and policy journals have been established dedicated to this topic; and a range of government agencies and non-govern-mental organisations (NGOs) have integrated this perspective into their activities, often with a substantial investment of financial and human re-sources.

According to a number of pundits and scholars, such as Jessica Tuchman Mathews (1989) and Thomas Homer-Dixon (1999), the remarkable activities of the 1990s have a sound intellectual and practical basis: growing environ-mental scarcities – especially of water, cropland, forests and fisheries – are undermining social systems by aggravating existing tensions and introducing new sources of insecurity and violent conflict. More and more people are being forced to eke out an existence on barren lands. Many of these poor, desperate individuals contribute to regional instability by crossing interna-tional borders as they search for viable livelihoods. Drought, soil erosion, deforestation and pollution are among the environmental problems that ad-versely affect economic performance while creating conditions ripe for disease epidemics and other costly disasters, compelling governments – many of which are unstable at the best of times – to respond to greater and greater needs with fewer and fewer resources. All too often, scarce funds are used to manage crises rather than develop human capital and build infrastructure, propelling nations into a vicious circle that is extremely hard to escape.

These are pervasive, dynamic, interactive phenomena – clearly evident in large swathes of Africa, Asia and the former Soviet bloc – that may well become the pre-eminent challenges to societies such as China and India, and hence to the majority of people on the planet (Feshbach, 1995; Homer-Dixon and Blitt, 1998; Goldstone, 1999). Indeed, the journalist Robert Kaplan, not one to mince words, describes environmental change as 'the national security issue of the twenty-first century' (Kaplan, 1994, p. 61). Throughout the world, insecurity and conflict have environmental dimensions. As social systems tax ecological systems, this relationship intensifies. It is important, and perhaps essential, insist the advocates of this argument, to focus resources and attention on this vexing issue.

Other academics, however, have expressed varying degrees of scepticism about the alleged linkages between environment, conflict and security. They have criticized the findings of researchers such as Homer-Dixon as well as the bold claims and policy recommendations of commentators like Mathews and Kaplan. These critics suggest that 'environment', 'conflict', and 'security' are remarkably vague, user-friendly terms. They are easy to link in abstract and conceptual ways; on this basis bleak scenarios of the present and future can be readily elaborated; but the critics are not convinced that we know enough about these relationships to justify the fears that have been expressed and the policy dollars that have been spent. In fact sceptics such as Marc Levy (1995), Nils Petter Gleditsch (1997) and Gleditsch and de Soysa (1999) have bludgeoned North American research initiatives for being methodologically tenuous and conceptually flimsy. According to the methodologist David Dessler, the most influential work in the field has not progressed beyond identifying some possibly interesting associations (2000).[2] It is premature, the sceptics contend, to write about causality or fret about the future; and without considerable highly detailed fieldwork it is unlikely that we will ever be in a position to do so (see Dabelko and Matthew, 2000).

These critical concerns strike other observers as pedantic and petulant. They are much persuaded by the common-sense empiricism of thinkers such as Norman Myers (1989, 1993). After all, like Myers, we can observe expanding deserts and shrinking forests. We can see hundreds of millions of people suffering from water-borne diseases that are preventable, and from the bone-deep impacts of starvation and malnutrition; there is no question that from Chisec to Chitral, armies of people are living in squalor and fear, without adequate access to food, fuel and fresh water, without sufficient livelihoods or opportunities. We can see the violence they experience daily, the diffuse pervasive context of conflict and tension in which they are hard-pressed to survive, and we 'know' that environmental stress is one of the factors behind these bleak outcomes. The point is not to prove causality beyond a shadow of a doubt; which, in any case, is inevitably a failed venture in the social sciences. Rather, it is to act to improve the human condition on the basis of knowledge that must always be incomplete, susceptible to manipulation, and open to rearrangement.

But before one finds the common-sense resolve to act forcefully in a world of competing values, imperfect information and causal complexity, yet another group of thinkers has approached the issue from a rather different perspective that also merits consideration. Scholars such as Daniel Deudney (1990; 1999b), Ken Conca (1998) and Simon Dalby (1999) have raised the age-old question (that is, the question asked 2500 years ago by Thrasymachus to Socrates in Plato's *Republic*): whose interests are being served by this concept or discourse? Who stands to gain – and who stands to lose? Given that a disproportionate amount of global research and policy activity in this area has been undertaken by the defence establishment of the world's only superpower, this concern has at least a prima facie validity.

One of the concerns expressed by this group is that the language of environmental security and the emphasis on conflict invite military participation into – and potentially military control over – an area that ought to be addressed in an open, transnational, non-military manner (for example, Deudney, 1990, 1999b; Deibert, 1996). Another concern is that a paradigm for environmental rescue is being elaborated that emphasises the inherently conservative value of 'security' and hence, in some significant way, is liable to privilege the status quo and the interests of the North over substantive change and the interests of the South (for example, Dalby, 1999; see also Connolly and Kennedy, 1994).

Clearly environmental security is a topic that has captured the imagination and attention of North Americans from many backgrounds. Why this has happened, what it means for the United States and for the rest of the world, and what lies ahead, are questions that have elicited strong views and considerable disagreement. In this chapter I will provide: (a) a brief overview of environmental security research and policy activities in North America, (b) a review and assessment of principal areas of controversy and critique, and (c) a somewhat unconventional perspective on the issue that situates it in the context of the singular – and historically unprecedented – status of both the US and environmentalism in contemporary world affairs. The chapter also includes an extensive list of North American references.

2 ENVIRONMENT AND SECURITY IN NORTH AMERICA

A brief history of environment, conflict and security in North America must include some discussion of both the research and scholarly debates that have taken place and the policy statements and initiatives that have emerged over the past 20 years. It is generally acknowledged that links between the natural environment and some conception of security can be identified throughout human history (for example, Ponting, 1991; Diamond, 1997). Climate and geography have been vital forces shaping and disrupting social systems over the millennia, conferring capacity here and imposing vulnerability there (for example, Deudney, 1999a). An earthquake or a flood has often achieved what massed armies could not (Fagan, 1999). But it was only in the latter part of the twentieth century, in an age unsettled by the environmental consequences of much human behaviour, that these links began to be isolated and given the sustained and explicit attention of researchers and practitioners.

In this regard, one might note that a cluster of ideas linking environmental change to new understandings of security originated in North American environmental and academic communities in the late 1970s and early 1980s (for example, Ophuls, 1977; Brown, 1977; Ullman, 1983). Richard Ullman, for example, argued that the concept of national security ought to be broadened to include anything that could reduce a state's options or the quality of its citizens' lives, and suggested that environmental degradation might thus qualify as a security problem. As the Soviet threat declined and environmental degradation increased, the wisdom of this suggestion garnered support. In 1989, Jessica Mathews and Norman Myers took full advantage of the openings provided by the end of the Cold War to make compelling cases for environmental security in the United States's flagship foreign policy journals. Their views were taken especially seriously by post-Cold War students of international affairs working to develop new analytical frameworks for a world undergoing rapid and unprecedented change.

A series of projects directed by the Canadian scholar Thomas Homer-Dixon became the intellectual backbone of this continental initiative.[3] In 1991 Homer-Dixon published a seminal article entitled 'On the threshold: environmental changes as causes of acute conflict'. On the eve of the Rio Conference and at the dawn of the New World Order, this article found a highly receptive audience in the United States. Indeed, three years later Homer-Dixon's work was the subject of an *Atlantic Monthly* cover story, 'The coming anarchy', by Robert Kaplan. According to Kaplan, Homer-Dixon's research was generating the analytical framework that would allow us to understand environmental change and conflict, and hence respond to what was becoming a fundamental foreign policy challenge for the United States, and for the rest of the world.

With considerable support and encouragement from the United States, Homer-Dixon directed three major research projects throughout the 1990s. His findings remained remarkably constant during this period. They are well-summarized in the concluding chapter of his 1999 monograph:

> what I call environmental scarcity ... can contribute to civil violence, including insurgencies and ethnic clashes ... [T]he incidence of such violence will probably increase as scarcities of cropland, freshwater, and forests worsen in many parts of the developing world. Scarcity's role in such violence, however, is often obscure and indirect. It interacts with political, economic, and other factors to generate harsh social effects that in turn help to produce violence. (1999, p. 177)

The argument that leads to these conclusions is straightforward. Resource scarcity is the product of insufficient supply, too much demand, or the unequal distribution of a good that forces some sector of a society into a condition of deprivation. These three sources of scarcity are in turn caused by variables such as population growth, economic development and pollution. They interact in various ways – for example, declining supply due to pollution can prompt one group to seize control of what remains of a resource, simultaneously forcing another group onto an ecologically marginal landscape, thereby exaggerating its experience of deprivation.

Faced with growing scarcity, societies may experience health problems, social segmentation and declines in agricultural and economic productivity. People then may be compelled to move in order to survive, often intensifying group identity tensions. Demands on government may increase while tax bases are being eroded. Ultimately, violence may ensue or, if already present, worsen.

It is in this volatile, interactive context that environmental scarcity can be described as a cause of conflict. Scarcity is not, Homer-Dixon stresses, likely to be a sufficient or necessary cause, but its growing presence in the causal chains that generate violence is, he believes, clear and growing clearer. Where is this the case? It is likely, Homer-Dixon contends, that developing countries with small supplies of social and technical ingenuity will prove most vulnerable to the negative effects of environmental scarcity. Unless we find ways to increase their amount of ingenuity – 'ideas for new technologies and new and reformed institutions' (Homer-Dixon, 1999, p. 180) – we can expect more of this type of violence in the years ahead.

Already alerted to the potential value of linking environment and security by Mathews and Myers, senior policymakers in Washington reacted strongly to Homer-Dixon's bold, predictive arguments. Their attention built upon a number of small but significant measures undertaken in the 1970s and 1980s.[4]

For example, in 1973 the Department of Defense issued Directive 5100.50, 'Protection and enhancement of environmental quality', in response to concerns about pollution that had escalated in the US following the publication of Rachel Carson's *Silent Spring* in 1962, the first Earth Day in 1970, and the Stockholm Conference in 1972. Four years later, the military experienced at first-hand the emerging network of environmental constraints through the 'Convention on the prohibition of military or any other hostile use of environmental modification techniques (1977)', a measure prompted by the use of Agent Orange and other chemical defoliants in Southeast Asia during the Vietnam War. The Chernobyl disaster in 1986 and the grim warnings scattered throughout the World Commission on Environment and Development's 1987 report, *Our Common Future*, also contributed to creating a context receptive to the concept of environmental security. In 1991 President George Bush established a secure basis for policy development in this area by adding threats posed by environmental change to the National Security Strategy of the United States.

Events of the early 1990s added urgency to this matter. These included Homer-Dixon's early articles (1991 and 1994); the bleak environmental assessments disseminated at the Rio Conference in 1992; Kaplan's 'coming anarchy' thesis (Kaplan, 1994); a flood of evidence about the dire environmental conditions of the former Soviet Union (Feshbach, 1995); and a string of crises such as those in Haiti and Rwanda, where human misery and oppression appeared to be due to an interlocking mix of grinding poverty, political violence, social injustice and environmental collapse. Moreover, the new US administration included Vice-President Al Gore, who over the years had focused considerable personal effort on gaining expertise and recognition in two issue areas: technology and the environment. With a supportive President Clinton, free of Cold War calculations and committed – at least in the pragmatic way American politicians are committed – to growing the economy while saving the environment, conditions were conducive to advancing the environmental security agenda.

Through two administrations, Gore spearheaded a series of measures that entrenched environmental security into major federal departments such as State and Defense, as well as key agencies including the Central Intelligence Agency (CIA), the Environmental Protection Agency (EPA) and the US Agency for International Development (USAID). For example, Gore promoted the Medea Project which paired intelligence analysts with civilian scientists to assess the environmental value of archived and current satellite imagery. He established the Task Force on State Failure, and, after its initial findings were released in 1995, he pushed for a second phase of research aimed at assessing the environmental dimensions of crisis, disaster and war. He urged the intelligence community to strengthen its expertise in this area, leading to the founding of the Environmental Security Center. He worked with Russian leaders to address the problem of free-range radioactive materials, and he oversaw the creation of a number of high-level bilateral commissions and common agendas on environmental cooperation and security. Very quickly agreements were negotiated with Australia, Brazil, Canada, China, Egypt, the European Union, India, Japan, Kazakhstan, Mexico, Russia, and South Africa – major powers representing more than half of the world's people.

Other elements of the US government – responding to pressure from the Gore camp, persuaded by the Homer-Dixon argument, or finding the issue compatible with advancing their particular interests – joined in the policy efforts. For example, in 1996, a year of bold promises in Washington:

- Secretary of State Warren Christopher made a landmark speech at Stanford University that promised to integrate environmental concerns into the mainstream of American foreign policy, largely because 'environmental forces transcend borders and oceans to threaten directly the health, prosperity and jobs of American citizens' (1997, p. 81).[5]
- John Deutch, Director of the Central Intelligence Agency, argued, in a speech delivered to the World Affairs Council, that the intelligence community was well-situated to produce environmental intelligence, and was committed to expanding public and international access to its resources in this area.
- Sherri Goodman, Under Secretary of Defense for Environmental Security, described in a speech at the National Defense University her office's plan to study 'where and under what circumstances environmental degradation and scarcity contribute to instability and conflict, and to address those conditions early enough to make a difference'.

Official statements such as these triggered a flood of meetings and reports, the most important of which have been faithfully summarised in the Woodrow Wilson Center's *Environmental Change and Security Project Report*. Sifting through this mass of documents, one can identify at least seven distinct themes that have been developed by American policymakers:

- Identifying, tracking and responding to environmental problems linked to conflict and instability in areas of strategic, economic or humanitarian interest to the United States or its allies. This concern, for example, has prompted the Department of Defense and the CIA to work on developing early warning systems that include environmental indicators.
- Addressing threats to US access to extra-territorial environmental goods. An obvious recent example of this was the Gulf War in which access to

Middle Eastern oil figured prominently among the motivations for American involvement.

- Combating environmental terrorism. Throughout the 1990s American vulnerability to terrorism – and especially terrorism using biological or chemical weapons that might affect ecological systems or be transmitted through environmental media – was the subject of significant discussion and policy action. Deutch, Clinton and others argued that the US is vulnerable to this sort of attack, and ill-prepared to deal with a large-scale terrorist act (Matthew and Shambaugh, 1998).

- Greening the military. Attention also focused on the extent to which the US military was involved in degrading the natural environment at home and abroad, and what could be done to make its training, testing and war fighting activities less harmful. According to some reports, the US military has responded to this concern and made significant strides in reducing toxic emissions and other forms of waste. It has increasingly agreed to respect local, state and federal environmental regulations rather than bargain for exemption on the basis of security imperatives. It also has made some progress in the area of base clean-up (Butts, 1994).

- Using security assets for environmental purposes. There has been considerable – and heated – discussion on the pros and cons of applying American military and intelligence expertise and manpower to a range of non-conventional missions, from reforestation to the development of more efficient technologies.

- Promoting dialogue and transferring skills abroad through military-to-military contact programmes. The environment has proved a useful anchor for international meetings and dialogue about common security problems. A number of analysts regard this as an unexpected and extremely valuable benefit of this approach to exploring and discussing security (Butts, 1994).

- Providing disaster and humanitarian relief. The devastation caused by Hurricane Mitch is a good example of how the effects of natural disasters might be amplified by human activities that have rendered some groups of people highly vulnerable to natural events like flooding. In cases such as this, the US is expected – by both Americans and non-Americans – to provide assistance. Many would like to see increased attention given to pre-emptive measures.

Many of these policy initiatives can be linked to research and debates in academic and environmental circles. Canadian scholars have played a significant role in these areas. For example, in addition to the work of Homer-Dixon, an international project on Global Environmental Change and Human Security (GECHS) was established in the mid-1990s by Stephen Lonergan at the University of Victoria in British Columbia. This project seeks to shift the focus away from environmental change as a national security concern towards environmental change as a human security issue. Additionally, the journal *Environment and Security* was founded in Canada by Simon Dalby and Paul Painchaud.

As one might expect, research initiatives in the United States during this period have also been considerable.[6] Many major universities, including California at Irvine, Cornell, Maryland, Michigan and Yale have established research and teaching programmes that include or focus on environmental change, conflict and security. Foundations including W. Alton Jones, Rockefeller and MacArthur have supported research in this area. Prominent think tanks and NGOs have become involved, including the Consortium for International Earth Science Network (CIESIN), Evidence Based Research and the Nautilus Institute, whose director, Peter Hayes, received a MacArthur genius award for his work on energy, security and the environment.

One phenomenon of some significance has been the widespread attempt to design projects and organise meetings that bring together university, think tank, NGO, business and government experts. At the forefront of this activity has been the Woodrow Wilson Center's Environmental Change and Security Project. Established in 1994, it has played a major role in encouraging and reporting on research; promoting cross-community dialogue; educating diverse government and non-government entities; and advising policymakers about environment, population, conflict and security linkages.

In the brief period of about ten years an enormous amount of research, dialogue and policy development has been carried out in Canada and the United States due to the pervasive interest in possible links between environment and security. Beneath this interest lies the common-sense notion that some forms of environmental stress have significant effects on social systems – effects that, under certain conditions, are likely to be highly negative. In its extreme, worst-case formulations, environmental stress can trigger, generate or amplify violent conflict. At the very least, it can compel people to migrate, subject them to levels of disease and starvation they might not otherwise experience, reduce their personal freedom and livelihood options, and generally make their lives difficult and miserable. Moreover, these relationships are becoming more prominent in societies worldwide as larger numbers of people place greater stresses on ecological systems: extracting at rates that nature cannot tolerate; polluting and disposing of waste at rates that nature cannot assimilate or neutralise; and modifying land and water systems in ways that render nature dysfunctional or to which its living systems cannot adapt. This widespread and prolific sub-field of international relations has, however, raised a number of concerns that must also be discussed.

3   CONTROVERSIES, CRITIQUE AND COUNTER-VIEWS

Critical responses to the mainstream activities described above can be organised into two relatively independent groups. The first group focuses on analytical issues pertaining to research design and theory development; the second group focuses on political issues related to language, power, knowledge and justice. In both cases the theoretical arguments associated with the research directed by Homer-Dixon serve as a logical starting point for this discussion, given the undeniable extent of their influence in North America.

To anyone who has seen families in West Africa seeking refuge from the heat or rain in packing cases with corroded, corrugated metal roofs; or leading desperate lives in the rough, crowded, toxic streets of Karachi and Peshawar; or struggling to draw sustenance from a patch of pallid, parched land in Guatemala, the arguments advanced by Homer-Dixon and others may seem quite plausible. At the very least, it is surely reasonable to suggest that environmental scarcity may have some sort of 'obscure and indirect' but nonetheless positive relationship to conflict and violence in countries with scant technical and social capacity, especially if they are already driven by ethnic or other tensions and cleavages.

Plausible, reasonable, but nonetheless disputed for at least three reasons, having to do – respectively – with the research question Homer-Dixon addresses, the research design he employs to answer this question, and the explanatory power of the theory that both shapes and emerges from his research. First, some writers (for example, Levy, 1995) have criticised Homer-Dixon's work for expending considerable resources to demonstrate very little: that is, it is not very intriguing to learn from a decade of research that, under conditions that are difficult to specify, environmental scarcity may be linked in an obscure way to some forms of social strife and violence. A typical complaint is that his arguments are largely uninteresting, or at least of little consequence, because he focuses on the wrong question. 'Can the sources and nature of the conflict, I ask, be adequately understood without including environmental scarcity as part of its causal story?' (Homer-Dixon, 1999, p. 7). Homer-Dixon focuses on this question 'to avoid entangling myself in the metaphysical debate about the relative importance of causes' (1999, p. 7). What scholars and policymakers tend to want, however, is a theory, supported by empirical evidence, that explicitly addresses the relative importance of causes. The question many people care about is not, *does the environment matter – at least in some 'obscure and indirect' fashion*, which Homer-Dixon answers convincingly, but *just how much does the environment matter, and when*, which he avoids.

Second, Homer-Dixon's work has been attacked for using a methodology that stacks the deck in favour of the outcomes he desires. Specifically, his research focuses on cases selected because they exhibit both high levels of environmental scarcity and violent conflict. To then determine that the prominent features of these cases may be linked in some 'obscure and indirect' manner is wholly unremarkable; more importantly, the value of this finding is impossible to assess until placed in a broad comparative context. Is it a rare or commonplace relationship? How do explanations of conflict that draw on indirect environmental factors compare to explanations that focus on factors such as ethnic rivalry, greed or fear? What is the value added of this research? In his writings, Homer-Dixon spends a considerable amount of time defending his case selection on the grounds that, armed with a generally persuasive theory, it makes sense to begin research by selecting cases that appear to fit. This strategy allows Homer-Dixon to develop a series of theory-driven stories about the causes of conflict in different parts of the world, and provides a foundation for later waves of research that can – and should – cast a broader net, one that encompasses cases in which one or the other condition is absent. In spite of this spirited methodological defence, however, critics such as Levy (1995) continue to wonder how much can be learned from this approach (see also Dabelko and Matthew, 2000).

To this concern about case selection, one might add a related criticism that will be familiar to all social scientists: the terms of distinction, the selection criteria, are themselves quite vague. For example, it is not very clear what 'environmental scarcity' means. No doubt it would be difficult to set rigorous standards – to say, for example, that scarcity occurs when the per capita supply of resource X is 30 per cent less than in comparable countries or than it was ten years earlier, and the deficit cannot be made up through trade or substitution. But without something approaching this form of definition, one worries about the extent to which the dependent variable may be shaping the definition of the independent variable. It seems rather too easy to link scarcity to conflict when the concept of scarcity is left undefined. Or, put another way, if the meaning of scarcity is and must be context-dependent, then how valuable is this type of theory? And how tenuous are its predictive aspirations?

Finally, a range of critics are not convinced that the theory itself is generally persuasive. It is, of course, central to the work of Homer-Dixon and many others who have followed the same research path that the theory be perceived as compelling: in its simplest formulation, environmental stress contributes to conflict. For decades, however, the generally foreboding tenor of environmental thought in North America has been called into question by a perspective most closely associated with the demographer Julian Simon: the alarming statements about environmental degradation and its consequences are naive and misinformed, flying in the face of significant historical and empirical evidence (for example, Simon and Kahn, 1984; Simon, 1989). The gist of this familiar argument is that environmental stress triggers human innovation leading to the development of new and more efficient technologies that then create the conditions for a growing number of people to live comfortably and safely on this planet. Long historical trends in population growth, per capita income, literacy, health and energy efficiency are among those used to support this position. In this light Homer-Dixon's concern that environmental stress will overwhelm developing countries because they lack sufficient ingenuity to cope seems at once patronising and historically ungrounded. Could it not be that, rather than slip irrevocably into violence and despair, countries in Africa, Asia and elsewhere, under the great pressure of a cascade of environmental woes, will in fact begin to innovate and change? If countries like the United States step into this process too early and with too little historical sensibility, might they distort and even undermine a trajectory that has characterised and elevated human systems for hundreds of thousands of years? (See, for example, Fagan, 1990; Ponting, 1991; Diamond, 1997; and Matthew, 1999b).

Of course, the two perspectives are not mutually exclusive. It may be that environmental stress contributes to conflict and insecurity which then become the more proximate causes of innovation and progress. If this is true, then policy development aimed at acting early to neutralise conflict outcomes might be misguided, at least in some cases. If one gives any credence to the views of Simon, then it becomes vitally important to move well beyond the simple theory of Homer-Dixon if one wants to provide a sound basis for aggressive, interventionist policies. Ideally, one needs a theory that makes some distinction between those cases in which environmental stress is likely to produce conflict that will mobilise positive social responses, and those cases in which it is not. This may prove to be a very ambitious undertaking, but it would be foolish to act on the basis of claims made by Homer-Dixon, Kaplan and others without seriously considering the possible links between environmental stress, conflict and progress.

Critics also have challenged the Homer-Dixon thesis on the grounds that it might, in fact, describe a relatively rare occurrence. There is a considerable body of evidence that suggests (a) that environmental stress, including scarcity, often leads to cooperation rather than conflict (for example, Deudney, 1990, 1999b; Wolf, 1998), and (b) that conflict is generally better understood as the product of other factors (for example, Gleditsch, 1997; Gleditsch and de Soysa, 1999). The message in both cases is that, as suggestive as Homer-Dixon's arguments are, a great deal of further research is required before policymakers should feel confident in acting on them.

A different body of criticism focuses on the political implications of the environment, conflict and security paradigm as it is emerging in the United States and elsewhere in the Northern hemisphere. As Simon Dalby notes, 'there is much more than an academic research agenda involved in these discussions. The debate about environmental security is about how politics will be rethought and policy reoriented after the Cold War' (Dalby, 1999, p. 157). Later Dalby writes that 'universal political claims often have a nasty habit of turning out to be parochial concerns dressed up in universalist garb to justify much narrower political interests' (Dalby, 1999, p. 157). Dalby proceeds to draw links between the concept of environmental security taking shape in North America, and policies aimed at preserving the status quo, even to the point of 'limiting the use of resources, slowing population growth, and curtailing specific economic activities in the South' (1999, p. 160).

This is part of a common dissident theme in the field of international relations. Critics of mainstream thought frequently point out that much international relations theory has been developed in the North (and especially in the United States and Great Britain), represented to the world as objective, used as the basis of foreign policy, and embedded in international organisations such as the United Nations. On closer inspection, they argue, these Western theories of development, security, the state, international law, ethics and so on disclose political qualities that can be described as hegemonic or imperialistic. They create standards and legitimise practices that tend inevitably to justify and affirm the values, beliefs and institutions prevalent in Western nations. They sustain hierarchies of power; they justify interventions in the – allegedly – disorganised, corrupt and dangerous quasi-politics of the Third World; they validate the status quo; and they act to undermine and discredit forces of substantive change that focus on redistributing wealth and power, valorising cultural differences, or experimenting with alternative ways of organising economic and social life.

Arguments about environmental security do provide the West with material that might be mobilised in support of intervening in the developing world. They also provide some support to a battery of arguments suggesting that population growth and freewheeling development strategies in the South might damage the shared environment and threaten a wide range of present and future interests. One must also ask, however, if these arguments provide any benefits to the developing world. Certainly a number of analysts – like Homer-Dixon, Mathews and Kaplan – have suggested that they do. At this point in time, it is extremely difficult to measure and assess the real-world costs and benefits of the complex of ideas that has been articulated in the context of thinking about environment, conflict and security linkages. Nonetheless, the anxieties expressed by Dalby and others ought to be taken seriously, especially by those searching for theories to support efforts to make the world a better place for the poor and disadvantaged people in the South.

Ironically, another group of critics have argued that the emerging discourse of environmental security is a threat to environmentalism and the long-term interests of the North, as well as to the prospects for reform and transformation advocated by the South and its supporters. Daniel Deudney considers 'environmental security' an ill-conceived 'motivational strategy' (Deudney, 1999b, p. 194). 'Advocates of environmental security reason that if people reacted as urgently and effectively to environmental problems as to the national-security-from-violence problem, then much effort and resources would be directed to environmental problems' (p. 195). Such a strategy, he contends, is liable to backfire because of a series of unintended consequences, including 'the expansion of state capabilities to regulate and manage the environment', creating conditions amenable to coercion while putting 'individual freedom at risk' (p. 197). Moreover, because arguments about security tend to become arguments about national security, such a strategy risks strengthening the position of advocates of state sovereignty, making it more difficult to address many environmental problems because effective solutions often require 'arrangements that divide and pool authority, and thus run against the normal practices of state sovereignty' (p. 198).

A third concern raised by Deudney is that, in general, the concept of security favours a zero-sum mentality, a militaristic world view in which we are irrevocably in competition with others for scarce resources and in which there must ultimately be winners and losers. Hence, it is a way of thinking about our environmental problems that Deudney regards as at odds with the way we ought to be thinking about them. The sad state of the environment should be instilling us with a sense of global community and purpose, creating the foundations of a cosmopolitian identity, rather than reinforcing the particular, territorially-defined, nation-based identities which, arguably, have played an important role in creating conditions conducive to many forms of environmental degradation, and which are not especially compatible with the multilateral, open, participatory practices the world needs today and will continue to need in the future (p. 199).

4   CONCLUSION

Much has been written about the methodological and theoretical shortcomings of environmental security research, and about the political motivations and risks linked to environmental security discourse. Little has been written about why the writings of Homer-Dixon, Mathews, Myers, Kaplan and others have received so much attention in the United States. Meetings and conferences have been held, journals have been founded, speeches have been written, funds have been allocated, and programmes have been established, all inspired by some notion of environmental security. Why has this concept been moved into such a central position in the American policy arena, earning extended commentary from the most senior government personnel including the President, the Vice-President, the Secretary of State, and the Secretary of Defense – especially given that it is a vague and disputed concept? Was Robert Kaplan prescient – and correct – in describing this as the 'the national security issue of the twenty-first century' (Kaplan, 1994, p. 61)? Or is this an example of the random character of contemporary politics, of the unpredictable processes through which some knowledge claims become social practices while others simply disappear? Or, again, as Simon Dalby and others imply, is this an idea receiving support because of the particular interests it currently serves?

Perhaps the most straightforward explanation is that this is an idea with enough merit to warrant serious consideration that, after spending a few years on the margins of public discourse, was able to take advantage of the opportunity to attract attention provided by the end of the Cold War. On its own the idea lacked broad appeal. Moreover, during the Cold War, few security specialists were interested in the environmental dimensions of security. The demise of the Soviet threat, however, created a space that this rather weak and marginal idea was able to fill, with the speed and fanfare characteristic of the high-tech information age.

There is probably some truth in each of these perspectives; deciding among them may ultimately be a matter of personal judgement and interest. Rather than proceed along this pathway, I propose to add one more perspective that situates the concept of environmental security in the context of (a) several of the diacritical tensions or challenges of contemporary world politics; (b) the unique position of the United States in world politics; and (c) the evolution of contemporary environmentalism.

4.1 Tensions and Challenges of World Politics

Over the past 50 years, much international relations theory and research has focused on the following forms of tension, division and inequality in the world system:

- the economic and political arrangements of the United States and Europe versus the economic and political arrangements of the Soviet bloc;
- the rich countries of the North versus the poor countries of the South;
- states versus nations;
- states versus other non-state actors;
- forces, arguments and ideals validating the status quo and incremental reform versus forces, arguments and ideals promoting more fundamental or revolutionary change;
- processes of integration versus processes of fragmentation; and
- social systems versus ecological systems.

It is perhaps not surprising that a discipline founded to study the problem of war and peace, and soon obsessed with the cataclysmic potential of the rivalry between the United States and the Soviet Union, should continue to expand its purview by identifying new dualisms in need of investigation, assessment and, if possible, resolution. There is something appropriately Machiavellian about approaching politics in this way, and it is convenient as well. Of course it runs the risk of simplifying complex phenomena: for example, does North versus South really capture much more than a crude sense of a world of haves and have-nots – a compelling image, sure, but one that really has very little analytical value? Nonetheless, throughout the latter half of the twentieth century these dualisms, however imprecise and contrived, fiercely divided scholars and practitioners. On some issues, such as the relative status of states and non-state actors or the prospects for fundamental systemic change, entire careers grew from clever arguments. Different positions often have been affirmed or challenged through realist, liberal or Marxist theories, whose proponents claim to have a privileged understanding of the character and behaviour of the international system. For cold war warriors, of course, the dualistic character of world politics was an article of faith, and a virtually permanent condition whose imperatives ought to shape all foreign policy. Dissidents and social critics spent decades attacking this world view as false and dangerous.

It also has been popular in the field, albeit to a lesser extent, to call into question the value of choosing one side of a dualism over the other. For example, an influential study by James Rosenau, *Turbulence in World Politics*, develops at length an image of 'the two worlds of world politics', state and non-state, possibly locked in a condition of 'enduring bifurcation' (Rosenau, 1989, pp. 5 and 447).

4.2   The position of the US in World Politics

With the end of the Cold War, a new dualism has appeared on the scene: the United States versus the rest of the world. This is not simply a handy but misleading image. Events of the 1990s affirmed and reaffirmed a deeply felt sense of exceptionalism and privilege in the United States. For example, acting more or less alone, the US:

- eviscerated the 1992 Rio Conference on Environment and Development by refusing to sign the Biodiversity Convention and stripping the Framework Convention on Climate Change of schedules and targets;
- designed the World Trade Organisation, ending decades of negotiations to update the General Agreement on Tariffs and Trade;
- engineered the war against Iraq;

- engineered the expansion of the North Atlantic Treaty Organisation;
- engineered the bombing of Serb forces in Bosnia and Kosovo;
- severely weakened the United Nations' capacity to respond to a sudden increase in demands by refusing to pay much of its annual dues;
- acted to isolate Cuba from world trade; and
- opposed, albeit unsuccessfully, the International Campaign to Ban Landmines.

This list is not in any way intended to be comprehensive; rather it seeks to demonstrate that the US occupies a very unique and important position in the global system that often pits it against much, if not all, of the rest of the world.

Curiously, according to James Lindsay, 'at the very moment that the United States has more influence than ever on international affairs, Americans have lost much of their interest in the world around them' (Lindsay, 2000, p. 2). Lindsay argues that while Americans have clear positions on many foreign policy issues, positions he characterizes as 'internationalist' and regards as generally desirable, they do not care much about whether the government acts on the basis of their preferences (pp. 4–5). Consequently the small number of Americans who feel passionate about an issue, and are prepared to make a lot of noise, tend to shape foreign policy. This is why the US has elected to isolate Cuba, impoverish the United Nations, demonise Pakistan, and refuse to place troops on the ground in hot spots around the world – even though the general sentiment in the country – and abroad – opposes each of these choices. In some measure the US stands alone on so many issues because extremists are determining where it will stand on these issues.

4.3 The Evolution of Contemporary Environmentalism

Finally, one of the tensions noted above deserves a bit of elaboration, that between social and ecological systems. Deudney expresses a widespread and strongly held belief when he argues that environmental problems are transnational problems whose severity is due, in part, to the fact that power and authority are divided among the world's 200 sovereign states while many ecosystems – such as evolutionary, hydrological and climate systems – are shared (Deudney, 1999b). Garrett Hardin's notion of the 'Tragedy of the Commons' helps to explain the dynamics of much environmental degradation. Often the actions of one party or state provide it with immediate benefits (for example, energy to run plants, wood to build houses, fish to eat) while imposing costs (global warming, biodiversity loss, destruction of fisheries) that are distributed widely over time and space. For a very long time, the full share of benefits may exceed the part share of costs. Moreover, the fear that if

state A does not use resource X, state B will, accelerates the rate of environmental degradation. In light of this, Deudney and others have argued, it
would be advisable to encourage thinking that shifts emphasis away from the
particular and towards the universal. Attitudes in the United States are particularly important because it is a major polluter, it has extensive resources
that might be directed at environmental rescue, and it plays a leadership role
in world affairs.

This commitment to an inclusive perspective, of course, has always been a
significant feature of contemporary environmentalism (McCormick, 1989).
Since the 1960s and perhaps earlier, it has been a self-consciously transnational
movement. Many environmental groups place great value on things like
openness, cross-cultural sensitivity and communication, and cooperation across
borders and disciplines. Moreover, prominent among environmental discourse
are many strands that are sharply critical of the status quo, and especially of
the profligate economies of advanced industrial states such as the US.

We have, then, a world that is deeply divided along many fronts including
wealth, power, territory, culture and ideology. Its sole superpower, the United
States, often behaves in ways that the rest of the world – and many of its own
citizens – oppose. This may be partly because post-Cold War apathy has
made it relatively easy for extremists – like the small groups opposing the
United Nations, Castro, Pakistan, and climate change initiatives – to exert
tremendous influence over American foreign policy. Further complicating
matters, the strained and mutually destructive relations between social and
ecological systems have nourished an environmental movement with deeply
embedded radical and transnational impulses. These various aspects of twenty-
first century planet Earth combine to make the challenge of tackling any
global problem extremely daunting. How easy it is, for example, to subvert
strategies to reduce climate change by linking them to hidden agendas to
constrain economic growth in the South, or to undermine strategies to
strengthen the United Nations Environment Programme or the World Bank
by linking them to hidden agendas to free ride on American largesse – and
who can deny that such linkages always have at least some justification?

It is in this tangled context that the concept of environmental security
seems particularly fortuitous. It has emerged and evolved as an innovative
way of cutting across historically constructed and seemingly unbridgeable
divisions, of bringing together institutionally hostile powerholders and
stakeholders who might otherwise never meet, and of putting the state of the
environment on the table afresh – without all of the baggage environmentalism has acquired over the decades. This observation is not intended to invalidate
the legitimate concerns – both analytical and political – reviewed above.
Rather it is to suggest that in spite of its flaws as a concept and theory, and in
spite of the fact that environmental security could assume policy forms that

privilege some interests over others, it has in many ways breathed new life into the environmental movement. It has done this through a language that is attractive to individuals and groups that have tended to ignore the environment, or to regard it as outside their expertise and mandates. Moreover, this is a language that resonates positively with the anxieties and aspirations of the post-Cold War era. It is a language that pays tribute to the past while looking ahead to a better future.

What is especially valuable, then, is not whether Homer-Dixon has proved that scarcity contributes to conflict or whether the military can support environmentalism in one way or ten ways or not at all. What is important is that environmentalism as an intellectual and political force has continued to evolve by tackling new problems, developing new perspectives, and inviting the participation of new actors – without sacrificing its most fundamental belief: human activities are harming the environment in ways that are not tolerable. Like environmental justice and sustainable development, environmental security should not be regarded as a clear and distinct idea, a simple principle or norm, but rather as an ongoing, multi-perspectival discussion that brings environmental concerns into new areas of human value and activity.

Over the years, a typical complaint from Southern sceptics has been that environmentalism is at root a self-serving, elitist, and Western programme. According to this familiar critique, the West became rich by exploiting its environment; now its wealthy intellectuals seek to use their immense power to direct – and slow – development in the South, thereby preserving both the Western world's privileged position in the international system and its unfettered access to unspoiled nature beyond its borders. From this perspective, sustainable development becomes a code word for Western imperialism; and eco-tourism becomes the paradigm of global environmentalism.

Environmental security has enabled representatives from North and South to meet again to discuss environmental problems without the constraints of an established and suspect paradigm. Indeed, Southern intellectuals and policymakers have recognised the potential value for them of the concept of environmental security, as well as the potential risks. The Association of Small Island States, for example, has made headway in global fora by characterising climate change as an environmental security issue. Specialists in conflict prone countries such as Rwanda and Pakistan have found this approach useful for modelling some of their problems and for gaining internal support for conservation measures. Southern countries have met to discuss regional problems using environmental security as the neutral theme to kick off discussions.[7] Similarly within the United States, environmental security has created interest in the environment in government agencies such as State and Defense; it has stimulated a significant amount of inter-agency dialogue and cooperation; it has led to some measures – such as the greening of the military – that are clearly desirable; and it has provided arguments that gain attention in a generally hostile Congress and a supportive but apathetic public. In a world of multiple divisions, powerful countervailing forces and US exceptionalism, environmental security is serving as a bridge for dialogue and cooperation.

For some people, inevitably, the ultimate question is: has this helped the environment? Unfortunately, the tangible benefits of this discourse cannot be measured easily; indeed, it may be premature even to attempt such an assessment. But there is another way of thinking about the impacts of environmental discourse, including the discourse of environmental security, that provides some basis for optimism. Environmental thinking and activism are generating models for institutional and behavioural change. In Pakistan, for example, the military government that seized power in 1999 committed itself to attacking official corruption and improving the quality of governance and the efficiency of government services.[8] It determined that a combination of strengthening and streamlining federal agencies, reducing the 'middle' or provincial layer of government, and empowering local communities would advance these goals. The activities of Pakistan's remarkably successful environmental movement, spearheaded by the International Union for the Conservation of Nature (IUCN), have been used as models for local empowerment programmes.

In other words, the environmental movement has been a tremendous example of innovation throughout the world. It has spurred the development of new technologies, promoted experiments with sustainable economic arrangements, furthered community-based forms of democracy, and expanded thinking about moral obligation and justice. While it is not alone in pioneering new practices, institutions, values and beliefs, it has certainly been prominent in many areas of reform and transformation – from the most personal and individual to the regional and global. It is difficult to imagine that these changes are not, overall, good for nature.

Now this vibrant, collaborative, forward-looking, morally inclined political movement has turned some of its attention to the problem of security – human, national, global and ecological. There is no doubt that this process of rethinking security and involving security institutions and experts in environmentalism will produce some undesirable outcomes. It is therefore important to follow this process, and to raise concerns about it. But there is great potential here for environmental thinking to infiltrate and reshape traditional conceptions of security. Its democratic and cooperative tendencies could well foster reforms in institutions that have been all too often inaccessible, secretive, and aloof.

At a more general level, environmental security creates opportunities to diminish some of the divisions that plague the international system and make global problem-solving so daunting. It invites North and South, and state and non-state, into the same room to discuss different conceptions of a secure and just world guided by the shared desire to reduce tensions between ecological and social systems. Finally, environmental security is a strategy that might help bring the United States into a more constructive and multilateral relationship with the rest of the world by unsettling its very conventional notion of achieving security by maximising power, especially military power, in an essentially hostile inter-state system.

In conclusion, it may be that the success of environmental security in North America has much to do with the fact that many different groups can see value in this concept, and can use it as a way of gaining access to other groups at home and abroad. In this regard environmental security is a tribute to the innovative character of contemporary environmentalism.

NOTES

1. Other factors include the mounting evidence of human-generated environmental degradation and its diverse social effects; the environmental interests of leading public figures such as Vice-President Al Gore; concerns raised in the Brundtland Report (1987) and at the Rio Conference in 1992; and the influence of journalists and policy analysts such as Robert Kaplan and Jessica Mathews who chose to champion this perspective.
2. Presentation at 'Environment, Population, and Conflict Workshop', University of California Irvine, 19 March 2000.
3. This discussion of Homer-Dixon's work borrows from a review written by the author and published in the *Journal of Political Ecology* in December 1999.
4. It may also be the case that, faced with demands to reduce the defence budget following the collapse of the Soviet Union, senior officials were looking for arguments that might help them protect their assets. It is nonetheless true that this interest can be situated in a history that gradually has linked the environment to the defence establishment in a variety of ways.
5. In this speech, Christopher made four explicit promises: (1) to produce an annual report on US environmental priorities; (2) to host a conference on strengthening compliance with and enforcement of international environmental agreements within two years; (3) to establish twelve environmental opportunity hubs around the world; and (4) to promote public–private partnerships in this area. One innocuous, very general report, 'Environmental Diplomacy', was produced in 1997. The proposal for an annual report, together with items (2) and (4) were dropped due to lack of funding. Twelve opportunity hubs have been established in US embassies around the world; at this time, they are poorly funded and, based on interviews with environmental officials in host countries, they do not appear to be very active or focused yet.
6. So much so that an overview is not feasible. Interested readers are advised to consult volumes 1 to 6 of the *Environmental Change and Security Project Report*, which provide this information. Much of it is also available on line at http://ecsp.si.edu. For similar information from a Canadian source, one might consult http://www.gechs.org.
7. See, for example, Naqvi Nauman (1996).
8. My views on Pakistan are based on fieldwork conducted in the North West Frontier Province during the summer of 1999 and on extensive interviewing that included a wide range of individuals.

REFERENCES

Ayres, Ed (1999), 'New missions for the military', *World Watch*, (January/February), pp. 3–4.

Brown, Lester (1977), 'Redefining national security', *Worldwatch Paper*, **14**.

Brown, Lester (ed.) (1992), 'State of the World', Worldwatch Institute report on progress towards a sustainable society, London: Earthscan.

Butts, Kent (1994) 'Why the military is good for the environment', in Jyrki Kakönen (ed.), *Green Security or Militarized Environment*, Brookfield: Dartmouth Publishing Company, 22–7.

Carius, Alexander and Kurt Lietzmann (eds) (1998), *Environment and Security: Challenges for International Politics*, Berlin: Springer.

Chen, Robert S. (1997), 'Environmental stress: concepts and cases', Paper presented at the Environmental Flashpoints Workshop, Director Central Intelligence – Environmental Center: 45–62, Reston, VA. 12–14 November 1997.

Christopher, Warren (1997), 'American diplomacy and the global environmental challenges of the 21st century', *Environmental Change and Security Project Report*, **3**, 81–5.

Christopher, Warren (1998), 'Diplomacy and the environment', in Warren Christopher, *In the Stream of History: Shaping Foreign Policy for a New Era*, Stanford, CA: Stanford University Press, 412–24.

Conca, Ken (1998), 'The environment-security trap', *Dissent*, **45**(3), 40–45.

Conca, Ken and Ronnie D. Lipschutz (eds), *The State and Social Power in Global Environmental Politics*, New York: Columbia University Press.

Connolly, Matthew and Paul Kennedy (1994), 'Must it be the west against the rest?', *Atlantic Monthly*, **274**, 61–83.

Dabelko, Geoffrey D. and P.J. Simmons (1997), 'Environment and security: core ideas and U.S. government initiatives', *SAIS Review*, **17**(1), 127–46.

Dabelko, Geoffrey D. and Richard A. Matthew (2000), 'Environment, population, and conflict: suggesting a few steps forward', *Environmental Change and Security Project Report*, **6**, 99–103.

Dalby, Simon (1999), 'Threats from the south? Geopolitics, equity, and environmental security', in Daniel H. Deudney and Richard A. Matthew (eds), *Contested Ground: Security and Conflict in the New Environmental Politics*, Albany: SUNY Press, 155–85.

Deibert, Ronald J. (1996), 'Military monitoring of the environment', *Environmental Change and Security Project Report*, **2**, 28–32.

Deudney, Daniel H. (1990), 'The case against linking environmental degradation and national security', *Millennium*, **19**, 461–76.

Deudney, Daniel H. (1999a), 'Bringing nature back in: geopolitical theory from the Greeks to the global era', in Daniel H. Deudney and Richard A. Matthew (eds), *Contested Ground: Security and Conflict in the New Environmental Politics*, Albany: SUNY Press, 25–57.

Deudney, Daniel H. (1999b), 'Environmental security: a critique', in Daniel H. Deudney and Richard A. Matthew (eds), *Contested Ground: Security and Conflict in the New Environmental Politics*, Albany: SUNY Press, 187–219.

Deudney, Daniel H. and Richard A. Matthew (eds) (1999), *Contested Ground: Security and Conflict in the New Environmental Politics*, Albany: SUNY Press.

Diamond, Jared (1997), *Guns, Germs and Steel: The Fates of Human Societies*, New York: W. W. Norton.

Environmental Protection Agency (1999), 'Environmental security: strengthening national security through environmental protection', Washington, DC: Office of International Activities.

Fagan, Brian (1990), *The Journey from Eden: The Peopling of our World*, London: Thames and Hudson.

Fagan, Brian (1999), *Floods, Famines and Emperors: El Niño and the Fate of Civilizations*, New York: Basic Books.

Falk, Richard A. (1971), *This Endangered Planet: Prospects and Proposals for Human Survival*, New York: Random House.

Feshbach, Murray (1995), *Ecological Disaster: Cleaning Up the Hidden Legacy of the Soviet Regime*, New York: Twentieth Century Fund Press.

Gleditsch, Nils Petter (ed.) (1997), *Conflict and the Environment*, Dordrecht: Kluwer Press.

Gleditsch, Nils Petter and Indra de Soysa (1999), 'To cultivate peace: agriculture in a world of conflict', *Environmental Change and Security Project Report*, **5**, 15–25.

Gleick, Peter (1991), 'Environment and security: the clear connections', *Bulletin of the Atomic Scientists*, **47**, 17–21.

Gleick, Peter (1993), 'Water and conflict: fresh water resources and international security', *International Security*, **18**, 79–112.

Goldstone, Jack A. (1999), 'Imminent political conflicts arising from China's population crisis', in Daniel H. Deudney and Richard A. Matthew (eds), *Contested Ground: Security and Conflict in the New Environmental Politics*, Albany: SUNY Press, 247–66.

Gore, Al (1992), *Earth in the Balance: Ecology and the Human Spirit*, Boston: Houghton Mifflin.

Homer-Dixon, Thomas F. (1991), 'On the threshold: environmental changes as causes of acute conflict', *International Security*, **16**, 43–83.

Homer-Dixon, Thomas F. (1994), 'Environmental scarcities and violent conflict: evidence from cases', *International Security*, **19**, 5–40.

Homer-Dixon, Thomas F. (1999), *Environment, Scarcity, and Violence*, Princeton, NJ: Princeton University Press.

Homer-Dixon, Thomas F. and Marc Levy (1995/96), 'Correspondence', *International Security*, **20**(Winter), 189–98.

Homer-Dixon, Thomas F. and Jessica Blitt (1998), *Ecoviolence: Links Among Environment, Population and Security*, New York: Rowman and Littlefield Publishers.

Kaplan, Robert (1994), 'The coming anarchy', *Atlantic Monthly*, **273**, 44–76.

Levy, Marc A. (1995), 'Is the environment a national security issue?', *International Security*, **20**, 35–62.

Lindsay, James M. (2000), 'The new apathy: how an uninterested public is reshaping foreign policy', *Foreign Affairs*, **79**(5), 2–8.

Lipschutz, Ronnie D. (1989), *When Nations Clash: Raw Materials, Ideology and Foreign Policy*, New York: Ballinger.

Lonergan, Steve (ed.) (1999), *Environmental Change, Adaptation, and Security*, Dordrecht: Kluwer.

Lowi, Miriam R. and Brian Shaw (eds) (2000), *Environment and Security: Discourses and Practices*, London: Macmillan Press.

Mathews, Jessica (1989), 'Redefining security', *Foreign Affairs*, **68**, 162–77.

Matthew, Richard A. (1995), 'Environmental security and conflict: an overview of the current debate', *National Security Studies Quarterly*, **1**, 1–10.

Matthew, Richard A. (1996), 'The greening of American foreign policy', *Issues in Science and Technology*, **XII**(1), 39–47.

Matthew, Richard A. (1997), 'Rethinking environmental security', in Nils Petter Gleditsch (ed.), *Conflict and the Environment*, Dordrecht: Kluwer Academic Publishers, 71–90.

Matthew, Richard A. (1998), 'Environment and security: concepts and definitions', *National Security Studies Quarterly*, **4**(4), 63–72.

Matthew, Richard A. (1999a), 'Review essay: recent books on environment and security', *Journal of Political Ecology*, (December), **6**.

Matthew, Richard A. (1999b), 'Social responses to environmental change', in Steve Lonergan (ed.), *Environmental Change, Adaptation, and Security*, Dordrecht: Kluwer, 17–39.

Matthew, Richard A. (1999c), 'Security and scarcity: a common pool resource perspective', in Samuel Barkin and George Shambaugh (eds), *Anarchy and the Environment*, Albany: SUNY Press, 155–75.

Matthew, Richard A. (2000a), 'The environment as a national security issue', *Journal of Policy History*, **12**(1), 101–22.

Matthew, Richard A. (2000b), 'In the balance: the environment and U.S. foreign policy', *Georgetown Journal of International Affairs*, Winter/Spring, 107–14.

Matthew, Richard A. and George E. Shambaugh (1998), 'Sex, drugs and heavy metal: transnational threats and national vulnerabilities', *Security Dialogue*, **29**(2), 163–75.

McCormick, John (1989), *Reclaiming Paradise: The Global Environmental Movement*, Bloomington: Indiana University Press.

Mohammed, Nadir A.L. (1994), 'The development trap: militarization, environmental degradation and poverty and prospects of military conversion', Organization for Social Science Research in Eastern Africa, Occasional Paper, 5.

Mohammed, Nadir A.L. (1997), 'Environmental conflicts in Africa', in Nils Petter Gleditsch (ed.), *Conflict and the Environment*, Dordrecht: Kluwer Academic Publishers, 137–56.

Myers, Norman (1989), 'Environment and security', *Foreign Policy*, **74**, 23–41.

Myers, Norman (1993), *Ultimate Security: The Environmental Basis of Political Stability*, New York: Norton.

Nauman, Naqvi (ed.) (1996), *Rethinking Security, Rethinking Development: An Anthology of Papers from the Third Annual South Asian NGO Summit*, Islamabad: Sustainable Development Policy Institute.

Ophuls, William (1977), *Ecology and the Politics of Scarcity*, San Francisco: W.H. Freeman.

Ponting, Clive (1991), *A Green History of the World: The Environment and the Collapse of Great Civilizations*, New York: St. Martin's Press.

Porter, Gareth (1995), 'Environmental security as a national security issue', *Current History* (May) **94**(591).

Renner, Michael (1989), 'National security: the economic and environmental dimensions', *Worldwatch paper*, **89**.

Rosenau, James N. (1989), *Turbulence in World Politics: A Theory of Change and Continuity*, Princeton: Princeton University Press.

Saad, Somaya (1991), 'For whose benefit? Redefining security', *Eco-Decisions* (September), 59–60.

Simon, Julian (1989), 'Lebensraum: paradoxically, population growth may eventually end wars', *Journal of Conflict Resolution*, **33**, 164–80.

Simon, Julian and Herman Kahn (eds) (1984), *The Resourceful Earth: A Response to Global 2000*, New York: Basil Blackwell.

Springer, Allen L. (1996), 'Unilateral action in defense of environmental interests: an assessment', Paper presented at the International Studies Association Annual Convention, San Diego, CA (16–20 April).

Ullman, Richard (1983), 'Redefining security', *International Security*, **8**, 129–53.

United Nations Development Programme (1994), 'New dimensions of human security', *Human Development Report 1994*, Oxford: Oxford University Press.

United Nations Environment Programme (1997), *Global Environmental Outlook*, Oxford: Oxford University Press.

VanDeveer, Stacy D. and Geoffrey D. Dabelko (1999), 'Redefining security around the Baltic: environmental issues in regional context', *Global Governance*, **5**, 221–49.

Wæver, Ole (1995), 'Securitization and desecuritization', in Ronnie Lipschutz (ed.), *On Security*, New York: Columbia University Press, 46–86.

Westing, Arthur (1989), 'The environmental component of comprehensive security', *Bulletin of Peace Proposals*, **20**, 129–34.

Wilson, Edward O. (1992), *The Diversity of Life*, Cambridge, MA: Harvard University Press.

Wolf, Aaron (1998), 'Conflict and cooperation along international waterways', *Water Policy*, 1(**2**), 251–65.

Woodrow Wilson Center (1995–2000), *Environmental Change and Security Project Report*, Issues 1–6.

World Commission on Environment and Development (1987), *Our Common Future*, Oxford: Oxford University Press.

10. Human security and the environment in Sub-Saharan Africa: the challenge of the new millennium

Kwasi Nsiah-Gyabaah

1 INTRODUCTION

In the developed countries, there has been tremendous socio-economic development and the introduction of new technologies to protect the environment and meet basic human needs. However, in many developing countries, particularly in Africa, the security of livelihoods has been undermined by socio-economic factors such as poverty, overpopulation, human rights abuses and environmental degradation caused by toxic contamination, global warming and ozone layer depletion, soil degradation, pollution and loss of biodiversity. Other natural, and anthropogenic, forces that contribute to insecurity and environmental degradation include drought, soil erosion, volcanic eruption, deforestation, earthquakes, political oppression, armed conflicts and so on. The natural and socio-economic factors that constitute a barrier to sustainable development and human security are the key challenges facing Sub-Saharan Africa (SSA) in the twenty-first century.

Recent media reports from Africa show refugees displaced by fighting, famine and stark images of starving children standing naked pleading for food. The spectre of ethnic conflicts and human rights abuses, widespread poverty, violence and discrimination against women, accelerated environmental degradation and the chaotic socio-cultural, economic and political systems, have created human insecurity and given an image of a continent in poverty and permanent environmental crisis.

Statistics about the scale of the problems cannot be ignored because they result in the fear that Africa is a lost continent because Africans are incapable of reversing their socio-economic and environmental problems. However, in reality, all hope is not lost as a result of globalisation, communication technology, socio-economic and environmental reforms and the democratic governance that is taking place on the continent.

As the world enters the twenty-first century, the complex socio-economic and environmental problems need to be tackled at their roots so that the image of a continent in permanent 'environmental crisis' can be erased. However, to succeed, we must understand what has gone wrong and determine what needs to be done in the new era of contradictions, challenges and opportunities.

2 ENVIRONMENTAL PROBLEMS AND INTERNATIONAL RESPONSES

Since the publication of the State of the World Report in 1992 by Lester Brown and the Brundtland Commission's Report *Our Common Future* (World Commission on Environment and Development (WCED, 1987)), concern for the environment and human security have increased globally. The major findings and conclusions of the two reports created awareness about the radical environmental changes brought about by human activities and their consequences for the earth's capacity to sustain the ever-growing human population (WCED, 1987).

The Global 2000 Report to the President of United States of America by Gerald Barney also noted that widespread loss of species and important life-sustaining capabilities would undermine the foundations of agricultural productivity, threaten human security and increase poverty.

With this background, issues of environmental and ecological sustainability, poverty alleviation and a rethinking of development strategies to support a sustainable society came to the fore. In June 1992, many countries from both North and South and a large number of non-governmental organisations (NGOs) attended the UN Conference on Environment and Development at Rio de Janeiro in Brazil to address the issue of sustainability. They drew up a convention to protect biodiversity and resolved to cut down emissions that cause global warming and ozone layer depletion and ensure sustainable development.

3 MEANING OF SUSTAINABLE DEVELOPMENT

Although the International Union for Conservation of Nature and Natural Resources (IUCN, 1980) created the term 'sustainable development', it was the Brundtland Commission that provided a vague, but meaningful definition. Sustainable development was defined as: 'a process of change in which the exploitation of resources, the direction of investments, the orientation of technological development, and institutional change are all in harmony and enhance both current and future potential to meet human needs and aspirations' (WCED, 1987).

Since the Brundtland report, *sustainable development* or progress that occurs without further damaging the ecosystem has become popular in environmental debate and development literature because it offers a degree of optimism regarding the degradation of the planet (Mannion, 1992). However, definitions and interpretations have sometimes moved away from the original concern with the natural environment, often depending on the writer's background training and interests (Rees, 1990). Redclift (1992) has rightly pointed out that sustainable development expresses different views of development.

Agenda 21, the UN Conference on Environment and Development (UNCED) and the Department for International Development (DFID) also placed the elements of sustainable development in a general context when they called on countries to meet their needs today and those of future generations without sacrificing their resources. They noted that without sustainable development poor countries will not be able to eliminate poverty (United Nations, 1992; WCED, 1987).

In this context, 'sustainable development' involves development that not only generates economic growth but also distributes benefits equitably; that regenerates the environment rather than destroying it and that empowers people rather than marginalising them. Sustainable development gives priority to the poor, enlarging their choices and opportunities and providing their participation in decisions affecting them. It is development that is pro-poor, pro-nature, pro-jobs and pro-women. In sum, sustainable development stresses growth, but growth that is consistent with employment, empowerment, human security, equity and a flourishing environment.

Although sustainable development is a useful 'point of entry' in discussing Africa's socio-economic and environmental problems, putting its tenets into practice has been nothing less than revolutionary. In many countries, the conditions that were enunciated by the Brundtland Commission and Agenda 21 with regard to the poor remain unchanged (Titi and Singh, 1994).

In spite of the lack of consensus on definition, sustainable development has been widely accepted as a development strategy that meets the needs and aspirations of people and many African countries have adopted sustainable development as the goal and a means to poverty alleviation and environmental improvement.

Perhaps the major contribution of the Brundtland Commission and the summits that followed it at the global level is that they have succeeded in getting virtually all the participating countries to agree to work more closely in tackling global environmental problems. This has led to the popularisation of environmental science and an increasing awareness of environmental issues in both the developed and developing countries.

4   WHY IS SUB-SAHARAN AFRICA AN IMPORTANT AND USEFUL CASE STUDY OF HUMAN INSECURITY AND ENVIRONMENTAL PROBLEMS?

Although developing countries in general are vulnerable to environmental change and insecurities associated with environmental degradation, Africa, and especially SSA, is relatively more vulnerable because of its bio-physical, socio-cultural and economic conditions. Consequently, the media has portrayed an unduly gloomy view that the problems of Africa are permanent and beyond solution.

There is a need to understand better the causes and relationships between environmental change and human security in SSA and to find appropriate solutions to the socio-economic and environmental challenges because, in spite of the abundant natural and human resources, research accomplishments and development assistance, Africa has not been able to utilise its rich resources effectively to fulfil the aspirations for equitable development of the people on the continent. Recent reports about Africa show pessimism on the future of the Africa and point to an impending catastrophe.

A cursory look at the continent shows poverty, hunger and malnutrition, unemployment, gender inequality, powerlessness, child abuse, increasing crime and deepening environmental crisis. In the last three decades, the quality of life has declined as a result of rapid population growth, corruption, debt burden, land degradation, food insecurity and HIV/AIDS that have undermined security of livelihoods and sustainable development.

These problems are compounded by ethnic conflicts that have led to insecurity, lack of freedom and dignity and complete disintegration of states and endless lines of refugees in countries such as Liberia, Rwanda, Burundi, Sierra Leone, Angola and so on. In Sierra Leone, for example, about 500 000 people were displaced by fighting. Kaplan, focusing on Africa to explain how scarcity, crime, overpopulation, tribalism and disease are rapidly destroying the fabric of many African countries described what is in store for Africa as 'The coming anarchy' (Kaplan, 1994). The UN Secretary General, Kofi Annan, recently pointed to the challenges facing Africa at the Annual Assembly of Heads of State and Government of the OAU in Harare when he stated that:

> Africa has, in the past five decades, been through a series of momentous challenges. First came decolonization and the struggle against apartheid. Then came a second wave, too often marked by civil wars, the tyranny of military rule, and economic stagnation. Let us make this third wave one of lasting peace, based on democracy, human rights, and sustainable development. (Annan, 1997)

As a result of the socio-economic and environmental problems facing the continent, some people have given up hope of Africa ever solving its many and varied problems. Consequently, some pessimistic observers have noted that recolonisation may be the only plausible solution to the challenges facing the continent.

Yet, to some optimists there are signs of hope, especially at the grassroots level where people are beginning to feel responsible for their livelihoods and environment while exploiting natural resources to meet their pressing needs. The rise of democratic governance in countries such as Ghana and South Africa, the rapid socio-economic and environmental reforms, the empowerment of women and advances in information and biotechnology offer a vision of hope that Africa will be able to overcome the current development quagmire.

The world is becoming increasingly interconnected and whatever happens to Africa either directly or indirectly affects the world at large. There cannot be real solutions to global human security and environmental problems if SSA, where the majority of the world's poor and vulnerable people live, is marginalised and poverty and environmental degradation are not properly addressed. Whereas the long-term solution to environmental degradation and insecurity of livelihoods may be out-migration, most countries in the developed world cannot accommodate movements of large numbers of mostly poor households from the sub-region in the short term. In this sense, the future of SSA eventually will be the problem of the world at large. The developed countries must therefore be interested in Africa's problems and show sensitivity to the factors that undermine efforts by SSA to build sustainable economies.

5   PROFILE OF SUB-SAHARAN AFRICA

SSA is composed of countries that lie to the south of the Sahara desert. It is geographically vast, ecologically, culturally, economically and politically diverse. However, there are some similarities between the countries that make broad generalisations possible.

SSA covers 42 countries on the mainland; plus six island groups and Madagascar located about 160 km off the East African coastline. The subcontinent falls into tropical rainforest or humid forest, savannah, Sahel, desert and Mediterranean ecological zones. The sub-region has a population of over half a billion. The population growth of the region remains the highest in the world and it does not seem to be declining. From 1960 to 1994, population growth averaged 3 per cent per year and is projected to remain so until the year 2000. In mid-1997, the total population was 614 million, representing about 10 per cent of the world's total (Jones, 1998).

There are more than 800 different ethnic groups who speak more than 1000 different languages or dialects. The major languages are English, French and Portuguese. SSA is the poorest area in the world and about 13 per cent of the people live in countries that are extremely poor and whose natural resources hold little promise for sustainable development. Malnutrition is common, especially among children under five.

The region has the highest death rate in the world and this is rising in many countries because of the HIV/AIDS epidemic. Life expectancy is 51 years compared to the world average of 66 years. SSA is the least urbanised but most rapidly urbanising part of the world. It is estimated that about 49 per cent of the region's population would be urban by 2025 compared to 11 per cent in 1950 and 32 per cent in 1996. Horrors of civil wars and dictatorship still persist in some countries.

6   ENVIRONMENT AND HUMAN SECURITY IN THE CONTEXT OF SSA

Many challenges face SSA because people are destroying the very resources on which they depend for their survival. Forests are being degraded, fresh water resources are polluted, biodiversity and soils are declining, soil erosion and desertification are increasing and climate is changing. One of the major challenges facing SSA is how to maintain ecosystem and ecological processes and increase food production to keep pace with rapid population growth without causing irreparable damage to the environment.

The natural and anthropogenic factors that adversely affect the environment also undermine food security and sustainable development. For example, deforestation, apart from precipitating soil erosion, has had tremendous socio-economic and environmental impacts. The major effects of deforestation are soil erosion, fuel wood scarcity, loss of soil fertility and declining production of food and cash crops for millions of small farmers.

Climate variability is another factor affecting the livelihoods of people in SSA. Drought is a chronic problem in SSA but drought risk is not yet well managed. Severe droughts in the 1980s significantly reduced agricultural production, accelerated bush fires and resulted in loss of lives and property. There is a growing concern that drought might become more frequent as a result of global warming.

Food shortages threaten poor households in SSA. Available statistics show that SSA is the only region in the world where food production per capita has declined over the past two decades. Images of famine and drought and suffering people, and protracted socio-economic decline in most countries make the prospects of long-term stability and sustainable development gloomy. In addition, military conflicts that affect about 30 per cent of Africa also represent a major impediment to building political and economic stability.

Since the 1970s, the disparity between SSA and other developing countries has become increasingly noticeable because food production and economic growth have declined and environmental degradation has accelerated. Available information shows that by any indicator, SSA is poorer and more marginal than any other developing region (World Bank, 1997). In the last two decades, SSA has found itself retreating economically while other developing areas of the world are advancing strongly. For example, at independence in 1957, Ghana was more prosperous than the Republic of Korea but by 1993 the Republic of Korea's economy was six times larger than Ghana (World Bank, 1997).

7 HISTORICAL PERSPECTIVE OF ENVIRONMENTAL PROBLEMS IN SSA

Although pre-colonial Africa made significant contributions towards civilisation and its agricultural techniques were outstanding (Davidson, 1992, 1994), in modern times Africa's contribution to science and technology has been negligible because of the complex political, socio-economic and environmental challenges facing the continent.

Today, less than 1 per cent of thousands of scientific discoveries and papers published in internationally recognised journals in the world every year originates from Africa. More than 75 per cent of those that are published by Africans originate from Africans in European or American environments.

During the 1960s when many African countries gained independence, a mood of optimism prevailed over much of the continent. The hope of peace, human security, solidarity and sustainable development in the United States of Africa was the dream of African leaders such as the late Dr. Kwame Nkrumah of Ghana. During this period, African economies were buoyant, and economic and environmental problems were insignificant. Population was low and technological development did not have serious negative impacts on the environment. Under low population, traditional agriculture, based on principles of organic farming, crop rotation and long fallow periods were stable, biologically efficient and sustainable because they did not pose a major lasting threat to the ecosystem and human security (Kang et al., 1989).

However, in the 1970s, the spur of economic growth enjoyed in the early post-independence years declined steadily. Political instability, faulty development policies and mismanagement of natural resources resulted in a host of environmental problems that affected the quality of life of the people. The vision of development, based on the traditional economic growth model with industrialisation, growth in personal income and national wealth as the primary objectives, gave rise to poverty and environmental degradation. Many people blamed Africa's problems on long years of misrule by European colonial powers whose economic policies, especially exportation of raw materials and labour, enriched Europe at the expense of Africa.

In fact, the responsibility for Africa's economic decline and environmental problems cannot be attributed entirely to Africa itself because changes in the international economy that occurred during the 1980s also had negative consequences on the environment. The promotion of primary export industries and undiversified economic policies of the colonial government and over-exploitation of natural resources under inappropriate methods led to resource degradation, hunger and poverty (Jones, 1998).

Increasing poverty and environmental problems led many African countries to enter into severe debt, prompting the debt crisis of the 1980s. In 1960, SSA owed about *US$3 billion* with an average ratio of debt-service to exports of 2 per cent. In contrast, by 1980 the region's debt stood at approximately *US$90 billion*, which represented the value of 96 per cent of all exports from the region at that time (Jones, 1998). Currently, the external debt has increased dramatically, and today, it represents a major constraint on human security and sustainable development in Africa.

The severity of the socio-economic and environmental conditions also forced many countries to adopt the World Bank and International Monetary Fund (IMF) sponsored Structural Adjustment Programmes (SAPs) in an effort to restructure their economies. Certainly, it would be naive to underestimate the economic growth that was achieved in the first years of adjustment. However, some of the policies have worsened the socio-economic and environmental conditions of vulnerable groups in the population. In Ghana, for example, the short-term objectives of SAP not only contributed to economic and gender inequalities, but also exacerbated the trend towards environmental degradation as men and women struggled to survive on an deteriorating resource base.

Moreover, the desire of foreign investors and key local investors to earn foreign exchange led to over-exploitation of natural resources (especially timber, precious stones and metals) with diverse social, political and environmental consequences. For example, in July 1996, the Minister of Environment in Ghana conceded that whereas surface mining was causing the devastation of large areas of land, degrading the soil and polluting water and air, underground mining was causing intrusion and was adversely affecting water quality. These destroyed the soil, undermined security of livelihoods and made development unsustainable in the affected areas.

8 IMPACT OF ENVIRONMENTAL CRISES ON FOOD SUPPLY AND HUMAN SECURITY

Environmental degradation poses a growing threat to food security, physical health and socio-economic development in SSA and underlies the importance of resource conservation and environmental protection at local and national levels. Many African countries suffer from inadequate food supplies because they do not earn sufficient income to purchase enough food on international markets to satisfy their needs. The problem is both food scarcity and scarcity of incomes. In an overview of the urban food situation in SSA, Atkinson (1995, p. 155) suggested that given current trends the question of urban food security may be the 'greatest humanitarian challenge of the next century'.

According to the United Nations Food and Agriculture Organisation (FAO) 'food security' means that food is available at all times, that all persons have access to it; that it is nutritionally adequate in terms of quantity, quality and variety; and that it is acceptable within the given culture. Only when all these conditions are in place can a population be considered 'food secure'.

Although over the years African governments, with support from the FAO and other development agencies, have addressed food security and its related elements in many ways, over 40 per cent of the people in Africa are unable to enjoy food security. Erosion and degradation of soils, loss of fertility, deforestation, drought and desertification have undermined food production and are causing malnutrition and migration. Another critical factor that has undermined food security is nutrient depletion of much of the agricultural soils through erosion.

As a result of rapid population growth, urbanisation and environmental degradation, crop yields have decreased and food shortages have become the worst form of insecurity in the African sub-region. The FAO publication 'Agriculture: towards 2010' (FAO, 1993) and the IFPRI Vision 2020 initiative (IFPRI, 1995) have both predicted global food increases in the near future. However, from the regional perspective, it is predicted that there will be a serious deterioration in food security in SSA.

It is estimated that the African region as a whole experienced a food deficit of 19.6 million tons of cereals in 1995. The famine that struck SSA in the 1980s persisted for many years. In 1997, about 37 countries suffered from food deficits. The most vulnerable to food insecurity are smallholder farmers, pastoralists and female-headed households. A recent FAO report gave a grim picture of the food outlook for 1999 and beyond due to the cumulative effects of adverse weather, long-running civil wars and uncontrolled crop pests and diseases.

9   CAUSES AND RELATIONSHIPS BETWEEN HUMAN SECURITY AND ENVIRONMENTAL DEGRADATION

The relationship that exists between human security and environmental degradation is best illustrated in the agricultural sector. Human insecurity stems from a complexity of cause and effect relationships including politics, population, poverty, environment and food supply. Food insecurity stems from a variety of causes such as unsuitable biophysical conditions, deforestation, soil erosion, drought, loss of fertility, loss of species, desertification and poverty.

9.1   Unsustainable Agricultural Practices

Many subsistence farmers in SSA practice slash-and-burn agriculture that has become unsustainable under rapid population growth. The growth needed in agricultural production to meet the demand for food of the rapidly growing population has led to an increase in the cultivated area at the expense of restorative bush fallow. Continuous cropping on poor soils results in soil fertility decline and low crop yields. In the process of burning debris during land preparation, the resource base is further depleted.

Unlike Asia where famine was averted through the Green Revolution, the biophysical conditions, climate variability and poor fragile soils in many countries in the sub-region make agriculture difficult because the soils quickly lose organic matter if they are exposed or intensively farmed.

9.2   Deforestation

Forests are a source of food, timber, firewood and other goods. They also play an important role in soil and water conservation, maintaining a healthy atmosphere and maintaining biological diversity of plant and animals. However, most of the rainforest that covered tropical Africa at the beginning of the century has been destroyed as a result of unsustainable agricultural practices, timber extraction, fuel wood collection and bush fires. Country and sub-regional statistics from the FAO about the rate of deforestation in Africa are alarming. Annual deforestation is estimated to be about 9 per cent in Insular East Africa, 8 per cent in Tropical Southern Africa and 0.7 per cent in West and East Sahelian Africa (FAO, 1997). It is estimated that more than 75 million people are affected by the impact of deforestation in Africa.

In Ghana alone, it is estimated that about a third of the forest cover was destroyed between 1955 and 1972. Since then, the average annual rate of deforestation has been estimated at 750 sq. km (World Bank, 1997). *The Daily Graphic*, a Ghanaian daily, reported that the Minister of Lands and

Forestry lamented the accelerated destruction of the forests at a forum in Accra when he observed that at the beginning of the twentieth century the country had 8.2 million hectares of forests that represented 41 per cent of the total land area. However, by 1999 only 1.2 million hectares of forests, representing 6 per cent of total land, remained. He concluded that given the annual rate of exploitation of 75 000 hectares, Ghana would soon be importing timber (*Daily Graphic*, July 10 1999).

The causes of accelerated deforestation in SSA include rapid population increase, rapid urbanisation and industrialisation, inadequate technological and managerial capacities and a range of concessions for mining and logging. The latter are granted at the national capital with little information exchange to enable local people to monitor and control the activities of timber companies and illegal chain-saw operators. Policies and regulations to control deforestation still largely remain as regulations, without action and with little impact at the local level (Inkoom, 1997). The effect of accelerated degradation of forests is increased poverty, aridity and desertification and food insecurity.

9.3 Land Degradation

Land degradation is the most important environmental problem affecting extensive areas of both developed and developing countries. Throughout Africa, land degradation is severe and is worsening day by day. Land degradation affects about 65 per cent of cropland area in Africa compared with 51 per cent in Latin America and 38 per cent in Asia. Degradation of pasture is also extensive in Africa, affecting 31 per cent of the land as compared with 20 per cent in Asia and 14 per cent in Latin America (Olderman, 1992; Olderman et al., 1990).

Land degradation is serious because the productivity of large areas is declining just when populations are increasing rapidly (UN, 1992). Land degradation has many causes but deforestation that is occurring throughout the region has reduced the land cover and increased soil erosion, leading to loss of fertility, decline in crop yields and insecurity of livelihoods. One of the major challenges facing SSA is how to maintain ecosystem and ecological processes and increase food production to keep pace with rapid population growth without irreparable damage to the environment.

9.4 Drought, Aridity and Desertification

Since UNCED in 1977, there have been major efforts to combat drought and desertification in Africa. The Lomé III Convention signed in 1984, the Earth Summit and UNCED and its subsequent negotiations on conventions on climate, biodiversity and desertification (UNCED, 1997) took up the issue of combating drought and desertification. In spite of these efforts, drought, defined here as a partial or total lack of water, affects agriculture and food supply in many ways (Campos, 1995).

Since agriculture is mainly rain-fed, the variability in rainfall and long droughts that are characteristics of SSA make agriculture vulnerable and contribute to poverty, famine and accelerated desertification. An estimated 3 million people died in the mid-1980s because of drought in SSA. Almost all of the people living in the dry and semi-arid regions in Africa are either affected by desertification or threatened by it. It is estimated that more than 16 million people are already suffering severe hardships on account of desertification, 7 million are stock raisers.

Desertification is the process of land degradation caused by variations in climate and by human impact. There is now a consensus among scientists that climate change is causing climatic anomalies and that Africa is likely to suffer most from the impacts of climate change (Otieno, 1998). The most obvious impacts of desertification are the degradation of rangelands, decline in food production, poverty and starvation. State decay, furthered by the rapid increases in population that have increased pressure on the limited resources, has had severe consequences in terms of food security and environmental sustainability.

10   POPULATION GROWTH AND POVERTY IN SSA

An important contribution of various approaches to the analysis of environmental degradation and human insecurity is the recognition that rapid population growth accelerates poverty that, in turn, contributes to accelerated environmental degradation. The IUCN and WCED's global enquiry into the state of the world concluded that poverty was one of the inhibiting factors in achieving sustainable development (WCED, 1987; IUCN, 1980). While population growth is often blamed for environmental problems and poverty, the issue is more complex than is generally understood.

However, poverty seen in all dimensions remains the major challenge to development efforts in SSA. Poverty is often associated with rapid population growth, lack of resources, unemployment, malnutrition, illiteracy, inequality, exposure to environmental risks and limited access to social and health services. It is estimated that 20 per cent of Africa's population lives in absolute poverty, defined as an income equivalent of less than a dollar a day. Based on the most recent data available, the number of Africans living on less than a dollar a day increased by almost 40 million between 1987 and 1993 (an increase of 22 per cent) (Amoako, 1999). Women constitute the overwhelming majority of the poor in Africa. In the last decade, the number of women living in poverty has increased compared to men, and the risk of falling into poverty is particularly acute among women in the rural areas.

Dealing with the problem of poverty is a goal in itself as well as a means to protecting the environment. However, in SSA, the rhetoric of poverty alleviation programmes has fallen behind achievable targets and the performance of programmes oriented to the alleviation of rural poverty does not offer much cause for optimism.

11   THREE DIMENSIONS OF POVERTY, HUMAN INSECURITY AND THE ENVIRONMENTAL CRISIS

Human security and sustainable development have also been hampered by political instability, horrific ethnic conflicts, lack of access to basic infrastructure, powerlessness, fall of foreign direct investment and development assistance, and increased external debt burden and sexually transmitted diseases (AIDS/HIV). War, terrorism and other forms of physical coercion are elements of human insecurity. Over-consumption and waste, depletion of natural resources and absence of regulations to protect natural resources can endanger the environment and threaten human security.

In SSA, the decline in social expenditure and basic state services has undermined the states' ability to govern effectively and meet the expectations of the people. In the last decade, many countries have experienced political instability and ethnic clashes that have led to insecurity and general disintegration of societies. Currently, 16 wars and conflicts are raging among 22 countries on the continent culminating in a very serious refugee problem. The ethnic conflicts in Liberia, Sierra Leone, Rwanda and Burundi have left in their wake the disintegration of families, socio-economic and political structures, the total collapse of social values and a trail of massive human rights abuses, including murder, amputations, rape and torture.

In 1994 alone, the genocide and war in Rwanda took more than one million lives. Available statistics show that, in 1995, two million out of six million refugees in Africa were from Rwanda (UNHCR, 1999). This represented 33 per cent of the refugees in Africa. The cumulative effect is poverty, disease and under-development.

Unconstitutional changes of governments still haunt many countries such as Liberia and Sierra Leone. In some countries, strict censorship and harassment of members in opposition have reduced intellectual freedom to insignificance. The culture of silence and fear of betrayal have prevailed in government, academic institutions and industry.

Human security and livelihoods in SSA are also threatened by the AIDS/HIV virus. HIV/AIDS is believed to be killing more Africans than war. It is estimated that SSA is home to more than 70 per cent of the world's 33.4 million people living with HIV. Every day, about 5500 Africans die of AIDS and about 30 million Africans are expected to die of AIDS within the next five years (Hain, 1999). United Nations statistics indicate that in 1998, AIDS killed an estimated 1.4 million people in eastern and southern Africa and left 6 million children orphaned, overtaking armed conflicts as the number one killer in the region. Because of ignorance about prevention, reckless sexual behaviour, cultural taboos and the embarrassment of openly talking about sex, HIV/AIDS and other related diseases are wreaking havoc on Africans worldwide.

AIDS is not just a threat to human security, it is also a threat to the socio-economic development of SSA. While the HIV/AIDS epidemic is depriving Africa of the opportunity to advance socio-economic, political and environmental development, it is snuffing out the lives of the vibrant, the creative, and the invaluably hopeful, without regard to economic status or social standing.

11.1 Urbanisation and the Environment

Throughout Africa, urbanisation is increasing. In 1998, about 35 per cent of the continent's population of 749 million was urban, and it was growing at 8 per cent each year. Rapid urbanisation has brought many social and economic benefits, but the environmental and health risks have been significant. Urban growth has accelerated resource exploitation, increased food insecurity and worsened living conditions in cities.

Water, land and air pollution have become a serious threat to people in the urban and peri-urban areas. As a result of urbanisation, high population growth, social change and industrial development, problems of waste disposal and waste management and pollution from the use of agro-chemicals in urban agriculture have increased. While city authorities lack adequate technical expertise and logistics to cope with heaps of garbage, farmers have been denied the potential benefits of the nutrients that could be recycled from the wastes to increase agricultural production and ensure adequate food supply, improving income and nutrition as well as the environment. The importance of domestic waste in closing the nutrient cycle for urban and peri-urban food security and environmental protection therefore needs to be researched.

11.2   Fall in Official Development Assistance and External Debt Burden

The amount of development aid and investment into SSA has been declining. Political instability and lack of commitment by African leaders has prevented SSA from attracting the much-needed investment and aid for socio-economic and sustainable environmental development.

Much of the limited financial and technical assistance that Africa has received from the developed countries has gone largely on showcase urban infrastructure projects and into interventions aimed at appeasing the more politically advantaged urban population to the neglect of rural people and the environment. The direct environmental effects of the decline in international assistance is often to force the poor countries to exploit their natural resources over-intensively and to eat away their capital stocks.

Africa's debt burden is seen as one of the obstacles to recovery. The tremendous debt burden that stood at 90 per cent of GNP for SSA in 1998 has made it difficult for African governments to finance programmes designed to protect natural resources and improve the environment. Debt relief is therefore one way to free resources for priority spending to promote investment and thus help poor countries in SSA to tackle famine, poverty and environmental degradation.

12   POTENTIAL AND PROSPECTS FOR SUSTAINABLE DEVELOPMENT IN SSA

Although this chapter has reinforced the generally negative coverage that Africa has received in recent years, a number of events and development trends show that the balance is tilted in favour of success rather than disaster. Unfortunately, the media has given little publicity to the positive achievements of countries that have gone through processes of democratisation, good governance and environmental sustainability compared to the publicity given to civil strive, famine and human rights abuses. The negative reporting on Africa has given the impression that the chances of turning back the tide of continental tragedy are remote.

In spite of the political, socio-economic and environmental challenges and the portrayal of SSA as a land of perpetual hunger, there are positive signs that give hope for optimism. Many countries have developed a workable formula to resolve ethnic conflicts and ensure tribal coexistence. Serious efforts have been made by countries in SSA to maintain a comparatively efficient public transport system and establish a network of roads and communications to facilitate the flow of information and movement of people. In reality, some African countries have been performing well in political, macro-economic and environmental terms.

First, the movement toward more democratic forms of government in contemporary Africa has strengthened local pressure groups and provided the poor with greater access to local political processes. Since the dismantling of apartheid, the number of dictatorial regimes has reduced. Many African countries are engaged in bilateral, and multilateral initiatives designed to promote good governance among themselves and with their external partners. The Organisation of African Unity (OAU) has made efforts to prevent and resolve conflicts and has encouraged dictatorial regimes to establish democratically elected governments, release political prisoners and bring about national reconciliation in countries such as Nigeria, Sierra Leone, Ghana and so on.

Second, some countries such as Ghana, Nigeria, Kenya and so on have adopted measures to increase their competitiveness on world markets and are providing incentives that are attractive to investors. Globalisation has provided an opportunity for countries in SSA to improve their records on human rights abuses, ensure good governance, good international relations, transparency and accountability to attract more aid.

Third, there is a new sense of renewal and of hope for the future because African governments have entered into dialogue with the developed countries on debt cancellation for the socio-economic development of Africa. Africans are beginning to look at political, socio-economic and cultural constraints that have often limited opportunities for increased agricultural development, particularly storage, land tenure and processing. This is an opportunity that must not be overlooked. Moreover, Africa, especially SSA, has been moving rapidly towards trade liberalisation. African countries are taking advantage of globalisation and new information technology to heighten awareness and improve the living conditions of the people.

12.1 Promotion of Sustainable Agriculture

In the last decade, there has been an upsurge of interest in the development and promotion of sustainable agriculture to feed the rapidly growing population. Countries such as Ghana, Tanzania, Ivory Coast and so on have achieved excellent growth rates in agriculture ranging from 3.5 to 5 per cent. Many countries have increased the export volume of high-value cash crops such as cocoa, tea and coffee and revenue from the export of agricultural products has sustained agricultural production.

Increased agricultural production and related activities have created more jobs for the unemployed and underemployed. In addition, the development and promotion of renewable energy technologies have contributed to reducing deforestation caused through fuel wood production. The implementation of structural adjustment policies and increased participation of women in resource management have had positive impacts on food production and resource conservation.

12.2　Indigenous Coping and Adaptive Strategies

As regards the environment, a number of measures, based on indigenous knowledge, have been employed by local people to manage natural resources efficiently and minimise environmental degradation resulting from human activities. Many countries have established special institutions and agencies to manage natural resources and the environment at national and local levels. In Ghana, for example, National Environmental Action Plans have been introduced and Environmental Impact Assessment (EIA) has become a necessary requirement in socio-economic development. At the local level, District Environmental Management Committees (DEMCs) have been formed to protect the environment.

12.3　Women in Resource Conservation

Recently, there has been a surge of interest in women's roles in farming and resource management, both at the grassroots and national levels. In Ghana, for example, women are making significant advances and are playing an important role in resource management, politics, and the protection of the environment. Moreover, international dimensions have been built into environmental policies, and environmental education has focused on women with the aim of reducing the continuing pace of resource degradation and its negative effects on global climate, biodiversity, watershed stability, ozone layer depletion and so on.

13　CONCLUSION

Land degradation, deforestation, unequal access to markets, widespread poverty, violent conflicts and other obstacles are challenges that will face the people in SSA in the twenty-first century. Although the overall socio-economic, political and environmental development record has been disappointing, some countries, such as Ghana, Nigeria and Kenya, have made significant progress in transforming their economies and improving the living conditions of the people and the state of the natural environment. It is therefore vital for governments in SSA to be encouraged and assisted in adopting an appropriate mix of policy interventions that have succeeded elsewhere in addressing urgent socio-economic and environmental problems.

Striving to create sound economies in the face of complex problems would require adequate financial and technical support from the developed countries. Merely sending grain during emergencies is not enough. However, building and strengthening of local capacities are necessary to ensure sustainable development. Non-governmental organisations (NGOs) must therefore invest more in poor people and provide incentives to promote active local participation in sustainable management of natural resources.

In addition, ensuring human security and sustainable environmental development will require a good understanding of the causes and effects of the changes that are taking place. Therefore, research efforts must be directed to the analysis of causes of human insecurity, poverty and environmental degradation so that effective measures can be taken to control them.

Africa must transform its economies and erase the image of a continent in persistent stagnation and permanent crisis. This can be achieved through active local participation in resource conservation, environmental planning and development. Effective management of natural resources and good governance would not only contribute to poverty alleviation but also ensure security of livelihoods and environmental sustainability in the region.

Africans must work together to ensure that equal rights of men and women enshrined in the UN Charter become a reality. Africans must work together to implement the goals of global conferences at Rio, Vienna, Cairo and Copenhagen to ensure sustainable development and protection of the environment.

BIBLIOGRAPHY

Amoako, K.Y., 1999, 'African universities, the private sector, and civil society: forging partnerships for development', International Association of University Presidents Africa Regional Council Conference, Economic Commission for Africa, Accra.

Annan, Kofi, 1997, Speech by UN Secretary-General, Kofi Anan, 2/5/97 to the Annual Assembly of Heads of State and Government of the OAU, Harare.

Atkinson, S., 1995, 'Approaches and actors in urban food security in developing countries', *Habitata International*, 19 (2), pp. 151–63.

Barney, G.O. (ed.), 1980, *The global 2000 report to the president of the U.S. entering the 21st century*, Oxford: US Navy.

Brown, L. (ed.), 1992, 'State of the World', Worldwatch Institute report on progress toward a sustainable society, London: Earthscan.

Campos, J.N.B., 1995, 'Vulnerabilidade do Semi-Arido as Secas, Sob o Ponto de Vista dos Recursos Hidricos', Projecto ARIDAS-RH (Brasilia, SEPLAN/PR).

Dadson B.A., 1993, 'The role of science and technology in economic development', Proceedings of Round-Table Meeting on Science, Technology and Culture: Harnessing Science and Technology for Development, Policy Research and Strategic Planning Institute, Accra. P25–44.

Davidson, Basil, 1992, *The Black Man's Burden: Africa and the Curse of the Nation-State*, London: James Currey; New York: Times Books.

Davidson, Basil, 1994, *The Search for Africa: A History in the Making*, London: James Currey; New York: Times Books.

FAO, 1991, 'Issues and perspectives in sustainable agriculture and rural development', Main document No.1. FAO/Netherlands Conference on Agriculture and Environments' Hertogenbosch, Netherlands.

FAO, 1993, 'Agriculture: towards 2010', Conference Paper C 93-24, Rome: FAO, and The Hague: Ministry of Nature Management and Fisheries of the Netherlands.

FAO, 1997, *State of the World's Forests*, Rome: FAO.

Goodland, R. and Ledic, G., 1987, 'Neoclassical economics and principles of sustainable development', *Ecologica Modelling*, 38, 19–46.

Hain, Peter, 1999, Speech by the newly elected Minister of State for Africa, Foreign and Commonwealth Office, UK, at the Wilton Park Conference on September 13, 1999, setting out his strategy for a British partnership with Africa.

Hince, Bernadette, 1999, 'Women at the helm', *Agroforestry Today*, 11 (1–2), pp. 3–4.

Holmberg, J. (ed.) 1992, *Policies for a Small Planet*, London: Earthscan.

IFPRI, 1995, 'A 2020 vision for food, agriculture and the environment', Speeches made at an International Conference, June, pp. 13–15.

Inkoom, D., 1997, 'Forest policy and deforestation in Ghana – what needs to be done', *European Forest Institute Proceedings*, 12.

IUCN, 1980, 'The world conservation strategy: living resource conservation for sustainable development', United Nations Environment Programme, World Wildlife Fund, Geneva.

Jones, Sam, 1998, 'Stolen sovereignty: globalization and the empowerment of Africa', A Special Report from World Vision, Policy and Research.

Kang, B.T., Van der Kruijs, A.C.B.M. and Couper, D.C., 1989, 'Alley cropping for food production in the humid and sub-humid tropics', in Kang B.T. and Reynolds, L. (eds), *Alley Farming in the Humid and Sub-humid Tropics*, Ottawa: IDRC.

Kaplan, Robert D., 1994, 'The coming anarchy', *Atlantic Monthly*, 273, pp. 44–76.

Mannion, A.M., 1992, 'Sustainable development and bio-technology', *Environmental Conservation*, 19, pp. 298–305.

Mathews, J.T., 1989, 'Redefining security', *Foreign Affairs*, 68, pp. 162–77.

Mies, M. and Shiva, V., 1993, *Ecofeminism*, London: Zed Books.

Nkandu, Luo, 1999, 'Looking into the future: setting priorities for HIV/AIDS in Africa', Speech delivered by Zambia Health Minister of Health on the theme at the 11th International Conference on AIDS and Sexually Transmitted Diseases in Africa, Lusaka, Zambia, 12–16 September.

Nsiah-Gyabaah, K., 1994, *Environmental Degradation and Desertification in Ghana*, Chichester: Avebury.

Olderman, L.R., Hakkeling, R.T.A. and Sombroek, W.G., 1990, 'World Map of the Status of Human-induced Soil Degradation: An Explanatory Note', International Soil Reference and Information Centre, Nairobi.

Olderman, L.R., 1992, 'Global extent of soil degradation, biannual report', International Soil Reference and Information Centre, Wageningen.

Otieno, Dorothy, 1998, 'El Niño causes mayhem in Africa', *Impact*, Newsletter of Climate Network Africa, 22, March, pp. 1–3.

Oucho, J.O., 1992, 'Population, resource and sustainable development in Sub-Saharan Africa', Paper Presented at the Conference on Towards Sustainable Environmental and Resource Management Futures for Sub-Saharan Africa, Accra, Ghana, 2–6 November 1992.

Redclift, M., 1987, *Sustainable Development: Exploring the Contradictions*, London: Methuen.

Redclift, M., 1992, 'The meaning of sustainable development', *Geoforum*, pp. 395–403.

Redclift, M., 1994, 'Reflections on the sustainable development debate', *International Journal of Sustainable Development and World Ecology*, 1, pp. 3–21.

Rees, W.E., 1990, 'The ecology of sustainable development', *Ecologist*, 20, pp. 18–23.

Renner, M., 1989, 'National security: the economic and environmental dimensions', Worldwatch Paper 89, Washington DC, Worldwatch Institute.

Shiva, V., 1989, *Staying Alive: Women, Ecology and Development*, London: Zed Books.

Titi, V. and Singh, N.C., 1994, 'Adaptive Strategies of the Poor in Arid and Semi-Arid Lands: In search of Sustainable Livelihoods', Working Paper, IISD, Winnipeg.

United Nations, 1992, 'Agenda 21', United Nations Conference on Environment and Development: The Earth Summit, Rio de Janeiro.

United Nations, 1998, 'Africa promoting good governance', *Co-operation South*, 1, p. 79.

UNCED, 1997, United Nations Conference on Desertification, 29 August–9 September 1977, Round-up, Plan of Action and Resolution, United Nations, New York.

UNESCO, 1992, 'The earth summit', *CONNECT* (UNESCO-UNEP Environmental Education Newsletter) XVII (2), pp. 1–8.

WCED, 1987, *Our Common Future*, Oxford: Oxford University Press.

World Bank, 1997, *Africa South of the Sahara*, Washington DC: World Bank.

World Population Data Sheet, Washington DC: Population reference Bureau, Hediger, W. 1997, 'Towards an ecological economics of sustainable development', In Richard Wilford (ed.), *Sustainable Development*, John Wiley, 5 (3), December, pp. 101–9.

11. The semantics of 'human security' in North-west Amazonia: between indigenous peoples' 'management of the world' and the USA's state security policy for Latin America[1]

Oscar Forero and Graham Woodgate

1 'HUMAN SECURITY': SECURITY FOR WHOM?

Previous chapters in this book have clearly demonstrated that 'security' is a contested concept. A variety of political actors seek to legitimise policy and practice in the name of national or human security. They have found support among a diverse audience of governments and NGOs seeking to defend human and/or environmental rights that, not coincidentally, aim to guarantee some form of security. In response to national and international policy, various social movements and actor networks have developed counter-discourses to support grassroots activists in their struggles to win political reform.

On 1 October 1995, the French government detonated an underground nuclear device at their Mururoa Atoll test site in the Pacific Ocean. The event was justified as a necessary component in the development of the French national security system, which was perceived to be too dependent on NATO capabilities. Environmentalists claimed that the risks associated with nuclear explosions under the Mururoa Atoll were too high and that testing should be abandoned. Greenpeace activists attempting to disrupt the test were arrested and their ships and helicopter confiscated.

As an immediate result of the tests, the Mururoa lagoon turned white as the blast heaved up the ocean floor and loaded the water with sediment. Scientists are divided with respect to the long-term effects, but it is obvious that the powerful nuclear explosions increased the vulnerability of marine ecosystems and human health to environmental risks. The political instability that the action brought was expressed in an international declaration condemning the action of the French government.

The US and British governments claimed that the bombing of Baghdad on 16 February 2001 was necessary to diminish the threat of military attack by Iraqi armed forces. The attack on the Iraqi nation was justified as 'foreign collaboration in the country's process of democratisation'. It was carried out, however, without the consent of the United Nations Security Council and was condemned even by supporters of the 1991 attack on Baghdad. International political tensions ensued: Turkey and France demanded an explanation, while China and Russia rejected and condemned the unilateral action of USA and British forces. The environmental implications of the attack did not, however, receive a mention despite clear evidence of the ecological devastation wrought by the so-called 'Gulf War'.

US foreign policy is aimed at enhancing the security of US citizens and promoting the development of liberal democracy around the world. To these ends, within carefully selected 'friendly' countries, official US support may even be provided for military expansion, justified for example as an authentic effort to control international drug trafficking. The third case we shall mention, and the one upon which this chapter will focus, provides an example.

As we shall demonstrate, the pursuance of human security in Colombia involves a complex and contradictory mixture of local, national and international initiatives, all of which seek to promote various aspects of human and environmental security. The actions specified under 'Plan Colombia'[2] include eradication of coca plantations (Plan Colombia, 1999, ch. 5). This is being achieved by the aerial application of herbicides, leading to the degradation of large swathes of the Amazonian environment – an action that has been repeatedly denounced and rejected by farmers and environmentalists in Colombia and abroad (Vargas-Meza, 1999). Plan Colombia also sanctions military action within drug producing areas, where indigenous forest people are caught up in growing coca for the illicit cocaine processing and trafficking industry. This case deserves particular attention, as Amazonia and its people are both highly symbolic icons employed by industrialised countries and institutions of global governance in developing international policies aimed at promoting environmental security.

Images of 'rainforest' vulnerability have long been used to promote western environmental policy (Stott, 1999), while forest people have been seen as guarantors of its conservation (Hemming, 1995). Ethnoscientists have corroborated these ideas (Reichel-Dolmatoff, 1996; 1997) and their translations of indigenous ecological classifications systems have contributed to dialogue between indigenous and Western knowledge, promoting partnerships between scientists and indigenous peoples for environmental management and sustainable development (Schultes, 1992; 1994).

If the implementation of security strategies in South America (Plan Colombia being one of the most notable) is placing the conservation of Amazonian biological and cultural diversity at risk, why is the USA involved? Is it that there are strong vested interests in promoting such outcomes? Some researchers (such as Mairovich, ex-secretary on anti-drug policy to the Brazilian Government) have stated that the most direct beneficiaries of Plan Colombia will be the weapons and drugs traffickers themselves and the associated criminal economy (CBN News release, 9 April 2000).

It is likely that drug prices will increase with the implementation of Plan Colombia, and this is already occurring in Bolivia (DRCNet, 2000) and drug production is also being pushed into other parts of Amazonia, notably Ecuador and Peru (Jones, 2001; Lama, 2001). It is unlikely that military action in Amazonia will do anything to stop money laundering activities in US and European financial markets, nor that it will affect the export of chemicals employed in the processing of coca leaves into narcotics from the European Union (EU) and USA (Colombian Ambassador's speech at Cunning House, 27 November 2000).

The European Parliament voted 474 to 1 against Plan Colombia: 'Stepping up military involvement in the fight against drugs involves the risk of sparking off an escalation of the conflict in the region' (European Parliament, 2001). If, despite objections based on the observed outcomes of Plan Colombia and similar initiatives, the militarist policy continues successfully to be justified on the basis of 'security' gains, there must be some strong ideological grounds that render this official discourse acceptable to a significant proportion of civil society. In this chapter we seek to tease out these ideological underpinnings and also to explore the grounds upon which counter-discourses are constructed. To do this we will attempt to answer two questions. First, what does security – human and environmental – mean for the indigenous people of North-west Amazonia, and how are they responding to international policies and official discourses? Second, what are the ideological grounds that allow significant elements of civil society to accept international policy and official discourse?

2   THE NATION-STATE AND HUMAN SECURITY

There are good reasons for citing national governments as the main instigators of human security policy in North-west Amazonia, and we shall explore these in the context of the Colombian Amazon. Before we do this, however, a word must be said about the role of national governments in human and environmental security in general.

Governments in the twenty-first century are highly dependent on international finance capital and the private sector. Their economic policies are tied to the development of international markets and they do not have the same degree of autonomy in national security policymaking as they did prior to the Second World War. In this sense, the sovereignty of nation-states is called into question. Private finance capital seeks out opportunities in locations with limited risks and fewer environmental constraints; national policies respond accordingly. The welfare of the labour force, natural environment and public health – all customary concerns of nation-states – have to be developed in ways that are not perceived as threats to free markets or foreign investment (Beck, 1998; Castells, 1999).

In less industrialised countries this dependency is even greater. Often reliant on the financial support of global institutions such as the IBRD, IMF and WTO, any attempts at independent development planning or monetary management are restricted by international economic imperatives. Many Latin American countries find themselves caught on the horns of a dilemma; on the one side pressured to comply with structural adjustment policies, on the other, struggling to cope with the social unrest prompted by the economic liberalisation and reductions in government spending, which such policies demand. This has been the case in the Bolivian insurrection (April 2000) against privatisation of water services, the two-year conflict for the exploitation of oil in the Uwas lands of Colombia and in the indigenous rebellions of Ecuador (January 2000).

> The National Government, conscious of the existence of historical conflicts not resulting in [good] relations between the State and the Indigenous People, and that the process of structural adjustment impacts the indigenous people and poor sectors of the country, ... aims to generate state policies to overcome the historical exclusion of the people and the inequalities created by the [economic] adjustment. (Extract from the Agreement between the National Government and the Native, Social, and Farmer Organizations of Ecuador, signed by the President Gustavo Novoa, 9 February 2001)

This is to say that local governments are located at the centre of divergent perspectives about environmental and human security. National policies, if successful, legitimise government action. But, nation-states find achieving the right balance between local/indigenous people's aspirations and global corporate demands ever more taxing. To make things worse, less industrialised nation-states are now experiencing pressure to confront drug trafficking. In the case of nations with territories in North-west Amazonia, stopping the illicit trade in narcotics has been an impossible task, largely due to the close, yet clandestine, links between the global criminal economy and legal financial markets.

Having said something about the context in which national governments must define and deliver human and environmental security policy, we shall now turn to our first question, which concerns the meanings of 'human' or 'environmental' security for indigenous people in North-west Amazonia.

3   EXPLORING THE LOCAL PERSPECTIVE IN NORTH-WEST AMAZONIA: INDIGENOUS PEOPLE'S 'MANAGEMENT OF THE WORLD'

Colombia occupies the north-western corner of the Amazon Basin, where it shares international borders with Venezuela, Brazil, Perú and Ecuador. The Colombian Department[3] of Amazonas is situated in the south-east of the Country. In the north-east of the Department, the Royeyaká or Taraira River marks the international border with Brazil for 150 kilometers. The Royeyaká is a tributary of the Apaporis, which delineates the international frontier for a further 43 kilometers until it reaches the Caquetá[4]/Japurá[5] River at the Brazilian border town of Villa Betancourt. In turn, the Caquetá/Japurá is a tributary of the Amazon.

In this north-western corner of Amazonia there are three main linguistic groups: Arawack, Eastern Tukano and Makú-Puinave. At the beginning of the twentieth century (1903–5), Koch-Grunberg made the first detailed study of these ethnic groups. In fact he was the first to attempt a classification of languages. Those people pertaining to the Eastern Tukano linguistic group are divided among Tukano, Makuna, Tanimuka, Yahuna, Letuama, Barasano, Itana, Desana and other ethnic groups.

The indigenous peoples of North-west Amazonia have been establishing and modifying their territories for centuries. Reichel-Dolmatoff (1996) suggested that the Tukano have social memories of their historic journey along the Rio Negro as they moved north from present day Brazil into what is now Colombia. When they entered the Department of Vaupés (to the north of Amazonas) they intermarried with the Arawack. The Tukano and Arawack shared their different experiences of what we might call agroforestry. Apparently, the cultivation of manioc and a more sedentary pattern of life were acquired by the Tukano from the Arawack. This encounter also prompted social transformation among the Tukano: from matrilocal residency and matrilineal affiliation to virilocal residence and patrilineal affiliation.

At the beginning of the twentieth century, the Tukanoan Makuna were living principally along the Pirá-Paraná River, but oscillated between there and the Apaporis. As they journeyed along the Apaporis they entered the territories of Yahunas and Letuama. Tukanoans also interacted with the Yujup-Makú that were moving around throughout the area between the Pirá-Paraná and Ugá Rivers, and further east into Brazil.

The Yujup were said to be people of the forest, while the Tukano were said to be river people. While Tukanoans have been described as sedentary agriculturists, the Yujup had been described as nomadic (Reichel-Dolmatoff, 1996). However, we now know that the Yujup were used to the manipulation of plants and did not rely exclusively on gathering and hunting. The Yujup share with the river people (Tukano and Arawack) a form of territorialisation that maintains the 'environment within'. The management of society and environment is integrated in what they call the 'management of the world'. According to them, the well-being and health of indigenous people depend on taking care of their 'trade' with other beings, for example, 'fish-people', 'game-people' and 'plant-people'. This trade is understood in terms of vital energy sharing and is accomplished through shamanism (Reichel-Dolmatoff, 1996; Arhem, 1990; Rodriguez and Van der Hammen, 1996; Von Hildebrand, 1983; Forero et al., 1998).

We know quite a bit about indigenous management of Amazonian environments. Arawack and Tukano have developed sophisticated management systems for *chagras* (gardens planted with diverse crops), *rastrojos* (old gardens where particular species are preserved as elements of secondary and tertiary forest) and *trochas* (linear gardens along the footpaths that connect different habitats and indigenous settlements). Management is carried out in accordance with multiple agroecological factors (Van der Hammen, 1992; Forero, 1999a). Similar patterns have been found in Brazilian Amazonia where Kayapó have been found to have knowledge of micro-climate and habitat, and refined systems of management to improve the productivity of local ecosystems (Posey, 1985, pp. 139–58). The same was shown for the Ka'apor speakers of Tupí-Guaraní (Balée and Gély, 1989).

Indigenous management does not simply relate to subsistence production or the material growing of crops; spiritual and aesthetic dimensions are also involved. All these spaces (*chagras, rastrojos* and *trochas*) are 'humanised' and, from an indigenous perspective, plants and animals are treated as 'types of people'. The distribution of plants is therefore managed and controlled, river ecosystems are carefully observed and there are open and closed seasons for certain fish and game species. The agricultural practices are linked to shamanism: the system that deals with the trade of energy between forest beings.

Rapids and waterfalls have special sacred importance for indigenous people; this comes as no surprise as these places are also ecologically important. Rapids and waterfalls prevent some fish species from spreading up stream and therefore affect species distribution. The changes in humidity produced by the water vapour that surrounds waterfalls affect vegetation composition. When these changes combine with differences in soils the changes are even more marked: this is the case at Yuisi. Tukanoan mythology refers to this waterfall as the place where the river was born. The myth says this was the place where the *Imarimakana*, 'the four sons of time', felled the tree whose trunk and branches, once on the ground, formed the Apaporis and its tributaries. The place is of sacred importance to all indigenous groups in the vicinity of the Apaporis, Pirá-Paraná and Mirití Rivers.

Iañakopea waterfall, on the Apaporis near the Tanimuka community of La Playa, is another important place within Tukanoan mythology and shamanistic tradition. Iañakopea, not surprisingly, is also of significant relevance to ecological structure. It demarcates boundaries in terms of fish species distribution, and the height of the vegetation reduces up river from the waterfall. There are numerous rapids, islands and undulations up stream of Iañakopea until the river encounters Jiri-Jirimo waterfall. If ecosystem changes are marked at Yuisi and Iañakopea, they are outstanding at Jiri-Jirimo. The site surrounding the waterfall is full of orchids and epiphytic plants. The mixture of vegetation provides a special niche, which is found nowhere else along the Apaporis.

The complexity and refinement of the growth, distribution and use of plants, and the management of the forests, mark these indigenous peoples out as accomplished agroecologists. However, they go beyond what we might consider agroecology when we take account of the spiritual and aesthetic dimensions of management (Forero, 1999b).

Our description of indigenous 'management of the world' here is brief,[6] but when studied in greater detail it reveals a way of living through which North-west Amazonian indigenous peoples have created a form of territorialisation in which individual well-being relies on a close integration within both the social group and the environment. The integration of environmental, aesthetic and spiritual dimensions within the lives of Amazonian indigenous people has been referred to as 'ecosophy' (Arhem, 1990) and has led ethnoscientists to write about the 'humanised rainforest' (Correa, 1990). In this context, it does not make sense to attempt to distinguish between human and environmental security. The reluctance of indigenous people to separate nature from society may explain why, after years of continuous contact with Western society, there continue to be numerous specialised roles associated with the health and well-being of communities and providing instruction on how to follow an indigenous way of life: shamans, healers, singers and so on.

4   THE 'MANAGEMENT OF THE WORLD' AND THE CHALLENGE OF EXTRACTIVE ECONOMIES

Extractive economies have affected the lives of hundreds of different indigenous groups throughout the Amazon. Throughout the twentieth century, there were several intrusions by white people into the Apaporis region. There were the infamous rubber camps, prospectors looking for gold and traders who attempted to build cold stores for the fishing industry. The forms of territorial expansion and territorialisation used by the white people working in extractive economies were very different to those of indigenous people and these differences have resulted in conflict.

The rubber camps that were built in the area around the Caquetá, Apaporis and Mirití Rivers, and the Catholic internee schools, enforced the treatment of indigenous peoples as a generic class of people – 'Indians' – who were denied some of the fundamental rights that white people enjoyed. Their shamanism was considered superstition, they were forbidden to speak their languages and they were considered minors under civil law. The objective of the Colombian Republic was to assimilate them by eliminating their identities (Correa, 1992). Indigenous peoples were driven to make new alliances in order to preserve their territories and their ways of living. Indigenous groups offered different forms of resistance. In this area of North-west Amazonia they have always demonstrated their intention of maintaining socio-political practices, especially shamanism, which they see as fundamental to their security. Today, the peoples of the Yaigojé Reserve continue to believe that without their 'management of the world' they will be driven into extinction.

The twentieth century has witnessed the development of indigenous rights. In the case of the indigenous peoples of Colombia, the law now recognises their languages, their territories and their right to govern them. All citizens are equal under the law and have the right to exercise their religious and cultural traditions. However, advances in legislation do not imply that the territorial conflicts have ceased. In the Yaigojé Reserve, conflicts still arise and need to be resolved among indigenous groups and, as a generic group, indigenous people have conflicts to resolve with the 'white people'.

In 1905, Grunberg reported the presence of a camp made by Colombians ('white people') in the Apaporis. He took a photograph of this camp called 'Libertad', which was located close by the Yuisi waterfall. Today this camp has developed into the Colombian town of La Libertad. In 1997, indigenous people from the Yaigojé Reserve received the support of the Colombian judicial system, when a tribunal endorsed their entitlement to protect their cultural and religious rights. The tribunal ruled that buildings, which had been constructed by the local government of La Libertad at Yuisi, constituted a violation of the cultural and religious rights of the indigenous people. The tribunal ordered the government to rectify this. Later on, the same tribunal supported the indigenous people's territorial rights, by forcing a governmental institution to correct failures in administrative procedures and proceed with the enlargement of the Yaigojé Reserve. Yuisi (La Libertad) was to be inside the extended boundaries of the reserve.

5   THE WHITE PEOPLE HAVE LEFT THE RESERVE BUT THEIR WAYS OF LIVING REMAIN

To date, there has not been any marriage between 'white' and indigenous people within the Yaigojé Reserve. There are, however, indigenous people from the Yaigojé that have decided to live among white people in their towns. The older generation perceives this migration as a threat to their group's survival. The youngest generations are willing to grab whatever opportunities may come their way. ACIYA, a local organisation of indigenous authorities, is looking for help from government and NGOs to provide education and employment for new generations as a way of limiting out migration.

The 'white people' with whom indigenous people associate are visitors to their territories. The relationship between them reflects indigenous notions of 'white people's power'. In the past, 'white people' ordered them to work and had the means to enforce such orders. It is through documents written in the language of white people that they are now recognised to have a territory of their own, it was white people's institutions that determined the procedures for recognising indigenous territories. From the perspective of ACIYA, indigenous people do not interfere with the government of white people and they should be accorded the same respect:

> Many times we have been tired of white people's government, a government that has been imposed over our lands and our lives. But we could not go to Bogotá, to demolish the building where the congress and the president work, and start ruling on our own. We could not build a maloca (communal house) there, to start managing white people in our way. How could we manage the industry, markets and other things that belong to white peoples? The white people would not let us manage them. You want to knock down our 'maloca of thought'. How could you take care of the world, so that sickness and evil would not visit us? ... You want to take our land from us; this is like erasing our inherited line of thought, leaving us without means to defend ourselves. It is as if we were attacking you, destroying the congress and the president, the defenses of white people. (Extract of a letter sent by ACIYA to the Administrative Director of Protected Areas – 26 October 1996)

Traders, missionaries, armed groups, doctors and nurses, researchers and occasionally a government functionary visit indigenous peoples in the Yaigojé Reserve. The way these people relate to them varies from violence to paternalism and, from there, to real recognition. It is very difficult for the inhabitants of the Yaigojé to deal with the contradictions of 'white people's rule'. The conservation of indigenous peoples' territories, the autonomy of local authorities within these territories and the right to have an education that would allow them to enjoy the same opportunities as the rest of Colombian society without losing their identity, are the aims of ACIYA.

A great deal of political negotiation has taken place since the formation of ACIYA in the mid-1990s. The complexity and long-windedness of the bureaucratic process that ACIYA has had to follow in trying to secure their territory has dumbfounded indigenous people. They waited years for the Yaigojé Reserve to be legally enlarged and hoped that the enlargement would lead to governmental protection of their fundamental rights, but ACIYA had to fight a separate battle for judicial protection of their rights. Yet, even now they have won it, the management of their territory and their future is not entirely in their hands.

The functioning of trade and extractive economies: wildlife trading, timber, mining and, more recently, the production and trafficking of drugs, usually occurs outside the law. The groups of people directing these activities escape the control of the Colombian state. Indigenous groups, like the Tanimukas from La Playa, have refused to work for narcotics dealers but they have no means to prevent anyone entering the Reserve. They fear the armed groups that cross their territory and know themselves to be vulnerable to any attack. To complicate matters further, some indigenous families are willing to get involved in the business: something that has already happened in the indigenous reserves of the neighboring Department of Vaupés. Young single males are likely to be lured by the money to be earned by growing coca and this seems to be the case in a number of communities in the Yaigojé.

ACIYA perceived a major risk when dealers offered substantial financial inducements in exchange for the clearing of an airstrip in Apaporis. Yet, when appraised of ACIYA's concern in 1994, the Colombian authorities ignored them and their plea for protection of their territories and peoples. Even though ACIYA refused the offer, they know that a single family or small group of people could turn their backs on the organisation and accept the money at their own risk. This has happened in other parts of North-west Amazonia.

6 DIVERGENT DISCOURSES SURROUNDING AMAZONIAN TERRITORY AND INDIGENOUS PEOPLES IN COLOMBIAN SOCIETY

Besides those working in extractive economies, there are other kinds of 'white people' that visit the Yaigojé Reserve. They come from academic institutions, NGOs, Christian churches and, occasionally, the regional government. However, there is little coherence among such groups, except for the fact that they are all considered visitors by indigenous peoples. They have diverse political ideas and different perspectives with respect to cultural and biological diversity.

6.1 Conservationists

Conservation institutions' view of 'rainforest management' is distinct from that of indigenous organisations, and legal and social advisers from NGOs could and have contradicted the prescriptions of conservation bodies.

In respect of environmental management, the State of Colombia has copied legislation from the USA. In order to protect the environment and avoid the perceived danger of communal property, legislation appropriates conservation areas as State property limiting or prohibiting use and management by other parties. This makes it very difficult for any kind of collaboration between park managers and local communities.

The Colombian Special Administrative Unit for the National Natural Parks System (UAESPNN) has, at least at the level of rhetoric, recognised that part of the problem of managing conservation areas has been the preconception that conservation is only possible without people. In Colombia, 42 conservation areas are inhabited and in 16 of them there are extensive processes of colonisation. Only 5 areas are uninhabited. There are 38 areas that need to accommodate human populations, but in 20 of these, UAESPNN is attempting to force people to move elsewhere (MMA, 1998a, p. 146). Even when conscious of the need to accommodate people in parks, the principal measures taken by the UAESPNN have been related to the development of norms and other legal tools (MMA, 1998a, p. 127).

There is ambiguity with respect to indigenous management of rainforest. Extreme preservationists still aim to create and maintain natural reserves without people and undertake enforcement to safeguard 'natural environments'. Some of this radicalism is inspired by criticism of the concept of indigenous peoples as genuine rainforest guardians.

Alvard (1993) has criticised the notion of the 'noble ecological savage'. Through the development of 'foraging theory'[7] he has suggested that indigenous hunters do not conserve prey populations for green ethical reasons, but for gaining long-term hunting efficiency, which is an anathema to radical conservationists. Criticism of ethno-scientific perspectives on indigenous models of rainforest management is usually based upon neo-Darwinist concepts and terminology, which can be linked to the utility function employed by environmental economists. The proposal of foraging theory is that traditional populations must be seen as groups of individuals, in which is each person is trying to maximise their individual fitness or the fitness of very close kin (Milner-Gulland and Mace, 1998).

Some of the results of these researches echo Hardin's 'tragedy of the commons' for indigenous management. Referring to the Machiguenga people of the Peruvian rainforest Johnson (1989, p. 221) says that they: 'appear to regard the world as something like a great supermarket in which one forages for the best bargains. Just as, until recently, we regarded water and air as "free goods" to be exploited at will.'

Conservationists use these constructions to advocate a radical political position, that of protection of nature from human interference. Grzimek campaigning for a Seringeti National Park pushed for the expulsion of Masai people: 'No men, not even native ones, should live inside its borders' (cited in Adams and McShane, 1992).

The experience of excluding indigenous peoples has been tragic for all: governments, local authorities, conservationists, wildlife and indigenous peoples. Resentments have led to violence and political insurgence (Roy and Jackson, 1993; Colchester, 1996). These events have forced conservationists to change their approach and accept cooperation with local peoples. However, partnerships between conservation agencies and indigenous people have not often carried conviction about indigenous management capacity; they reflect the advance of legislation towards indigenous peoples' rights, not an ideological change (Colchester, 1996, p. 36). Conservationists have entered partnerships with indigenous peoples with distrust and this is reflected in the results. In a review carried out by the World Bank in 23 protected areas it was concluded that it was not possible to assure that the projects' aims of reducing pressure on the environment had been achieved. The study showed that the involvement of local people was rhetorical (Wells and Brandon, 1992; West and Brechin, 1991; Colchester, 1996).

New agreements between conservationists and indigenous peoples need to be made. Indigenous peoples' supporters and indigenous peoples themselves are calling the attention of conservationists to the fact that decisions cannot be taken from the top-down anymore. Indigenous people have had a long and painful experience of dealing with political conflict and, usually, are willing to make allies with other groups. Conservationists could gain much from good partnerships with indigenous peoples, but for now there are still huge groups of environmental radicals that prevent a general alliance between the two.

In the declaration of the first Latin-American Congress of National Parks and Other Protected Areas, it was stated that: 'When protected areas are super-imposed on lands or indigenous territories, the fundamental rights of local communities should be recognized, such as territoriality, forms of self-management, use and management of the existing resources'[8] (Proceedings of the Congress, 1998, p. 267). At the workshop on Protected Areas and Indigenous Lands or Territories, an additional declaration stated that governmental and non-governmental organisations could support but not replace communities or indigenous people (COAMA and COICA, 1998, pp. 13–15). Representatives of the Colombian Environment Ministry, the NGO Natura and Colombia Conservation International (CCI) signed both declarations.

Just a few months later, Natura and CCI became involved in a dubious agreement with certain members of ACIYA for the establishment of a conservation area that divided the indigenous authorities of Apaporis and weakened their political institutions (Forero, 1999a, pp. 192–203).

Following this dubious agreement, the FARC[9] guerrillas moved into the indigenous territories. The reasons for the action as stated by the FARC are varied. They have pointed out that the establishment of the conservation area demonstrated indigenous people's inability to manage their territory and that the policies of the indigenous reserves were unfair because they ignored the needs of colonisers for land for development. More recently, the FARC claimed that all institutions receiving international funding represented a risk to Colombian sovereignty (Forero, 2000). Some days later the FARC expelled scientists working at a boiological research station near Lake Mujutupia.[10] These events, however, did not stop Natura or CCI promoting a research project in the new conservation area both nationally and internationally (Forero, 1999a; 2000).

The reason that representatives of such different ideologies present discourses so much alike is explained partially by the fact that both aim to control the territory. Environmental NGOs usually establish links with grassroots organisations under the rhetoric of participation but maintain a top-down managerial approach, facilitating the incursion of global environmental agencies. Our Environmental Sociology group[11] has found similar patterns of action in Cameroon, where the discourse of 'participation' provides a lens through which the environmental state can extend its gaze over natural resources and into the life-worlds of forest margin communities (Ambrose-Oji et al., 1999).

6.2   The Churches

Catholic and evangelical protestant groups often compete for educational or missionary territory in Latin America and this is also the case in Colombian Amazonia.[12] In an attempt to promote individualisation or religious consciousness among indigenous peoples in Amazonia, who are perceived as primitive communists, the US Government has financed religious groups such as the Summer Institute of Linguistics. The FARC have perceived the work of these religious groups in Amazonia as part of an ideological campaign aimed at undermining their own ideological work among peasants and indigenous peoples.

On 9 March 1999 the FARC killed three US citizens belonging to one of these religious groups working with indigenous peoples in Colombia. And recently, a US Government official, Phillip Chicola, who met with the FARC in Costa Rica in 1998, said that US policy is that there will be no further discussions with the FARC until they bring the assassins to justice (*Espectador*, 2001). The relationship between religious groups and the US Government has a strong influence on US security policy, which should not be underestimated.

At the same time, the Catholic Church has been linked to, and financed by, the Colombian Government. Prior to the adoption of the National Constitution of 1991, the Colombian State delegated the administration of the poorest and indigenous peoples of Colombia to the Catholic Church. This agreement is illegal under the new constitution because it violates the principle of equity for all citizens and because the new constitution officially recognizes indigenous languages and aboriginal religious practices. However, the government has not yet revised the covenant and indigenous organisations have not yet asked for its repeal. The desire of indigenous people's organisations to manage their own education services has sometimes been perceived by Catholic educational institutions as a menace and the NGOs that support indigenous initiatives have also been perceived as hostile.

With the reform of the Colombian Constitution, the division between the Catholic Church and the State was clarified, but there are long lasting links between the two institutions and national peace commissions always include representatives of the Catholic Church. There is also an historic and important relationship between the Catholic Church and the conservative party, the party of President Pastrana, stemming from the Church's support for the conservative party during the 'Violence' of the 1950s, which was promoted by leaders of the Colombian liberal and conservative parties.

The origins of the FARC, the biggest guerrilla movement in South America, can also be traced to the 1950s, when the leaders of the conservative and liberal parties signed the 'National Front' Agreement. Under the 1958 Agreement both parties promised that when elected they would divide key posts in the state bureaucracy between one other in order to guarantee the sharing of power. The agreement left out many factions especially those representing rural areas. Feeling betrayed by the political leaders these factions came together and embarked on a revolutionary project.

This should not lead the reader to think that all members of the Catholic Church have identified themselves with the more conservative groups in civil society. Since the 1960s Catholic priests, influenced by liberation theology, have been involved in the conflict on the side of the poor. Yet, the Church is institutionally conservative and its influence among state officials is pervasive, such that it has been very influential in the formulation of security policy in Colombia.

7   IS INDIGENOUS TERRITORIAL POLICY PLAUSIBLE?

The previous sections illustrate the complexity of the political scenario in the Colombian Amazon. In these multifaceted circumstances, indigenous organisation has emerged and continues to operate. It seems, however, that the groups involved, especially indigenous peoples and the NGOs that support their political aims, have yet to understand that, like sustainability, territorial ordering is best conceived of as a continuous process of (re)construction.

It is unclear whether indigenous organisations in Amazonia have realised that obtaining legal protection, based on national and international legislation, does not guarantee in perpetuity indigenous control over their territories. Indigenous peoples' organisations would like, but cannot expect, to have a single interlocutor in pursuing their legitimate interests. Furthermore, the various institutions with which they do interact vary their policies toward, and treatment of, indigenous organisations as a function of their changing perspectives with respect to the rainforest and its indigenous inhabitants.

Images of Amazonia and its indigenous people change depending on the observer and the moment of observation. The Europeans of colonial times and then *mestizos* from American republics modified their legal treatment of indigenous peoples depending on these changes of perspective. The Amazon has been seen as an impenetrable jungle, a storehouse of resources and more recently as a fragile ecosystem in need of protection. Indigenous peoples have been considered sub-human animals, free sources of labour, legal minors, 'ecologically noble savages' and even primitive communists that threaten the security of the world's most powerful nation. Similarly, shamanism has been seen as witchcraft, vernacular medicine or agroforestry practice, depending on the interests of the observer at the moment of observation. Depending on who is referring to indigenous peoples they may be guardians of biodiversity or a menace to the environment and society at large. In summary, indigenous peoples have been what outsiders have made of them.

With respect to national and human security, state policies directed at indigenous peoples often deal with territorial conflicts. These policies reflect the temporary pictures that nations (for example, Colombia and Brazil) have of indigenous peoples and their territories, and regulations and codes are devised to assure the desired policy outcomes. However, in accordance with Agenda 21, the democratic systems of the twenty-first century should take note of the rights and responsibilities of all citizens and thus complex processes of territorial ordering should be subject to continuous political negotiation.

At the time of writing, the Government of Colombia is holding separate peace talks with the FARC and the National Liberation Front (ELN – the second largest insurgent group in Colombia). The FARC, as already mentioned, have made themselves felt in Amazonia and they have clear interests in this important territory. The Government of Colombia has pleaded for foreign help. The United States of America have agreed to support Plan Colombia, as an initiative to combat drug trafficking. For the USA, peace talks and territorial ordering in Amazonia impinge upon their own interests and they are willing to fund an initiative derived from their own security policy in order to resolve the problem. For the European Community, Plan Colombia is excessively militaristic in complexion, and leaves out vital socio-political components. Europe is therefore following a different policy towards Colombia. Colombia's neighbouring states, Ecuador, Peru, Brazil and Venezuela, do not have a common stance towards the Plan. They do not want to get involved in an armed conflict like the one that has plagued Colombia, but it is obvious that the problem of the narcotics trade affects them all and that sooner or later they must reach some agreement if human security in the region is to be achieved and the rule of justice re-established. Without an internationally agreed system of justice with the power to enforce human rights, including environmental and indigenous peoples' rights, it will be very difficult to resolve the even more complex issues related to territorial ordering, namely, those concerned with the functioning of extractive economies that do not comply with national regulations or international agreements.

8   THE USA AND COUNTER-INSURGENCE

Plan Colombia represents one of the most recent phases of a long-running strategy in Latin America. US economic and political interests have been protected for many years. Direct involvement of US troops in a guerrilla war is very difficult to justify to the US public since the Vietnam War, but the training of right wing and mercenary paramilitaries has been common policy. In the 1970s, during the presidency of Richard Nixon, the USA was being encouraged by multinational corporations with interests in Chile to fight against the freely elected government of Salvador Allende. Henry Kissinger created a covert unit within the US Central Intelligence Agency whose subversive mission was to destabilise the Chilean Government. The unit was eventually implicated in the assassination of General Schneider and the military coup led by General Pinochet in 1973 (Hitchens, 2001).

Perhaps the most widely cited example of US security policy in action occurred in Nicaragua in the 1980s. In 1986, Colonel Oliver North, under instruction from high-ranking members in the Reagan administration, arranged for the sales of arms to Iran in direct violation of existing United States laws. Profits from the $30 million arms sales were given to the Nicaraguan, right wing, 'contra' guerrillas to procure arms for their struggle against the democratically elected Sandinista Government of President Daniel Ortega. Although the International Court of Justice determined that this was a direct violation of International Law the USA veto in the United Nations Security Council was used to reject a resolution that compelled all States to obey international law.

Another example was the invasion of Panama and arrest of General Norriega in 1989 under the authority of the Bush administration, after which the newly elected Panamanian Government facilitated the operation of financial markets favouring US banks and investments. The General Assembly of the UN condemned the invasion, but the USA and Britain used their vetoes to block another resolution of the UN Security Council (Chomsky, 1997). By this time, anti-drug rhetoric was already in use. However, despite the indictment and conviction of Norriega in April 1992 on eight counts of cocaine trafficking, racketeering, and money laundering, there was never any serious attempt to control the financial markets implicated in money laundering.

There are many other examples that there is not space to mention here, but what they all indicate in that US security policy is regularly enforced in Latin America through the financing of military coups, paramilitaries and corrupt national leaders that are all portrayed by the US as allies in their fight for 'justice' and the enhancement of human security. Without the assistance of such groups and individuals, the USA would be unable to enforce their policies, which are often prosecuted in direct contravention of their own national and even international law. Recognition of this state of affairs is important to our understanding of the semantics of official security discourses.

In Colombia there are also right-wing paramilitaries. Initially these arose as people who suffered extortion at the hands of left-wing guerillas organised themselves and employed military trainers in order to fight back. Amnesty International and other human rights organisations have denounced the links between the Colombian armed forces and these paramilitary groups. More recently, the Colombian Government and armed forces have pursued a process of reforms to clear their names and, in a very important political gesture, a military court has convicted an army general who permitted the massacre of peasants by paramilitaries in the Department of Vaupes.

Once established, the paramilitaries sold their 'security services' to cattle ranchers and other wealthy groups of people, some of whom were involved in the trafficking of narcotics. However, the mercenaries soon realised that they themselves could take control of drug trafficking and they have since become renowned for employing the most brutal forms of coercion. Fully 80 per cent of all killings associated with the war between the left and right in Colombia are attributed to paramilitaries; however the condemnation of the US Government and media is usually reserved for the left-wing guerrillas.

Yet what would happen in the hypothetical case of the State succeeding in its war against the guerillas? The former peace commissioner, V.G. Ricardo, Colombian Ambassador to the USA, said in a recent speech to the Colombian Society of the London School of Economics that if peace is achieved with the guerrillas, the raison d'être of the paramilitaries will cease to exist. Yet we must question whether an armed force, which has influence over large parts of the national territory, would simply abandon one of the most lucrative enterprises of our time. The political raison d'être might disappear but economic motivation will remain. Not only drug trafficking, but also war itself is a lucrative business, which can pay off in political as well as financial terms. When the leader of the paramilitary AUC (the Colombian Union for Self-defence), Carlos Castaño was interviewed for *television*, Amad, a renowned Colombian television presenter, manipulated Castaño's image to such good effect that subsequent opinion polls reflected growth in the number of para-military sympathisers and political voices started to be heard calling for political talks with the AUC.

Castaño has been implicated in the murder of numerous human rights activists, and he is presently imposing a reign of terror over the Colombian city of Barrancabermeja. The public attorney has claimed that this reign has continued, even after the arrival of government troops in the city. Further-more, Castaño has opposed the setting up of demilitarised zones aimed at encouraging the development of peace talks and has 'warned' President Pastrana that he will not tolerate demilitarisation in the Department of Bolivar, where the government planned to hold peace talks with the ELN. Finally, he has openly stated that he will not support any presidential candidate that is committed to the continuation of the peace process (Molano-Bravo, 2001).

9   CONCLUSION: PLAN COLOMBIA AND THE CLOSING OF THE VICIOUS CIRCLE

While George Bush Senior was enforcing US security policy in Latin America his son became a consultant for the Harken Energy Corporation, a company that benefited greatly from the events and aftermath of the Gulf War. The Bush family still owns a majority share in Harken, whose principal investment is in Colombian oil enterprises. The company is part of the US–Colombian Business Partnership that started lobbying the US Congress for the approval of Plan Colombia. The US Congress is now seeking President George W. Bush's advice on the implications of Plan Colombia for US security policy and North American investments.

The distinction between state security policy and corporate business strat-egy has never been clearly differentiated by US governments, and therefore it is unlikely that the Congress will object to continuing US support for Plan Colombia. Thus the militarist project is likely to expand. But this would not happen if the USA did not enjoy the support of conservative forces inside Colombia or if the 'rhetoric of the fight against drugs' were to be exchanged for real political action towards the regulation of financial markets.

National and international support for environmental NGOs such as Natura, which seek to enhance environmental security by preserving pristine environments and excluding people from parks, threatens Tukano security by undermining their ability to 'manage the world'. The key point we wish to make is that for indigenous peoples such as the Tukano, we cannot distinguish between environmental security and human security. They do not see themselves as distinct from the environment in which they live, they are part of the 'world' and in managing it they instinctively manage themselves. Thus, rather than translating the Cold War discourse on security into scientific, environmental terms for the world at large, we might do better to consider translating the Tukano concept of 'managing the world' in order to inform international discourses on sustainability.

Unfortunately, the future of the rainforest and its inhabitants is not in the hands of indigenous peoples: it has not been for many years. They have influenced our way of seeing and treating the forest but had no power to protest against the international security policies that have been developed so far away from their reserves. To talk of an autonomous indigenous territory, even when assured by international and national laws, is at present an illusion. Wars in Latin America are directly linked to the expansion of profitable businesses, the majority of them illegal, and none of them delivering any real benefits to the peasants or indigenous peoples of North-west Amazonia. So how might indigenous and peasant communities, environmentalists and other social movements mobilise in sufficient strength to prompt transnational corporations, Latin American and foreign governments to engage in processes that would facilitate the formulation and implementation of 'world security' policies that affect traditional territories and the global environment? The answer, many think, is the networking of civil society through information and communication technology: however, in a world where fewer than 1 per cent of people have access to such technology this remains a pipe dream. When they are granted no more than rhetorical 'participation' in the governance of their own territory, the chances of the Tukano's and other indigenous peoples' perspectives influencing a new global semantic of 'security' seem very limited indeed.

NOTES

1. The critique of official discourse and international policy presented in this chapter should not be taken to represent the views of the social actors to whom we refer. We would like to thank many colleagues and friends that work in Amazonia, but have decided not to mention their names in order to preserve anonymity and safeguard their personal security. The local authorities of the Yaigojé Indigenous Reserve (ACIYA) invited the GAIA foundation, a Colombian NGO, to advise and support them in the organisational and legal aspects of the territorial ordering process. Oscar Forero worked with this NGO and remained in North-west Amazonia from 1994 to 1998. The accounts of indigenous people of the Yaigojé to which we refer in this chapter were recorded during that period.
2. 'Plan Colombia' is an anti-drug trafficking strategy. The Colombian Government has claimed that: 'Plan Colombia is made by Colombians for Colombia'. However, the strategy was designed in accordance with the USA State Security and Anti-drug Strategies. Before being ratified by the Governments of Colombia and the USA it was approved by the US Congress. However, the Colombian Congress and public only became aware of the details of the strategy once international agreement between the two countries had been reached.
3. A Colombian political administrative division.
4. Spanish.
5. Portuguese.
6. For more detailed description and analysis see Arhem (1990, 1996), Correa (1990), Forero (1999a), Hugh-Jones (1979, 1999), Reichel-Dolmatoff (1996, 1997), Rodriguez and Van der Hammen (1996), Van der Hammen (1992), Von Hildebrand (1983).
7. A development of the theory of decision making, further explained in Milner-Gulland and Mace (1998) and Cardenas (1998).
8. The Congress took place in Santa Marta, Colombia. 21–27 May 1997.
9. The Revolutionary Armed Forces of Colombia.
10. Tom and Sara Deffler were undertaking their research with the support of the Natura Foundation. Dr Deffler is also a teacher at the National University of Colombia in Amazonas.
11. The Environmental Sociology group at Imperial College at Wye is currently undertaking research in North-west Amazonia, Cameroon, Chile and UK.
12. On the history of this competition in the Departments of Vaupes and Amazonas the interested reader should consult Jackson (1984) and Reichel-Dolmatoff (1972).

BIBLIOGRAPHY

ACIYA, 1996, Letter to Carlos Castaño, Director of the Special Administrative Bureau for National Parks – 26 October 1996. Archive of the X Congress of Captains of the Apaporis, River. Bocas del Pirá. Copied from the archive of the GAIA Foundation – Colombia, Bogotá.

Adams, J.S. and McShane, T., 1992, *The Myth of Wild Africa: Conservation without Illusion*, London: W.W. Norton and Co.

Agreement between the National Government and the Native, Social, and Farmer Organizations of Ecuador, February 2001. Ratified by the President of Ecuador, Gustavo Novoa. Eight more signatures. Complete text in Spanish and English at http://icci.nativeweb.org/levantamiento2001/.

Alvard, M.S., 1993, 'Testing the ecologically noble savage hypothesis – Interspecific prey choice by Piro Hunters of Amazonian Peru', *Human Ecology*, **21**(4), pp. 355–87.

Ambrose-Oji, B., Allmark, T., Buckley, P., Clements, C. and Woodgate, G., 1999,

'The environmental state and the forest; of lookouts, lumberjacks, leopards and losers', RC24 conference, 6–7th August. Chicago

Arhem, K., 1990, 'Ecosofia Makuna', in *La Selva Humanizada. Ecología alternativa en el trópico humedo colombiano*, Ed. Fracais Correa, Bogotá: ICAN, FEN, CEREC.

Arhem, K., 1996, 'The cosmic food web: human-nature relatedness in the Northwest Amazon', in Desola, P. and Pálsson, eds, *Nature and Society. Anthropological Perspectives*, London: Routledge.

Balée, W. and Gély, A., 1989, 'Management forest successions in Amazon: The ka'apor case', *Advances in Economic Botany, New York Botanical Garden*, No.7, pp. 149–73.

Beck, U., 1998, *Que es la globalización? Falacias del globalismo, respuestas a la globalización*, translation to Spanish from German by Moreno, B. and Borras, M.R., Barcelona: Paidós.

Cardenas, J.C., 1998, 'Biodiversidad, Teoría de Juegos y Economía Neo-Institucional: Aplicaciones al Problema de los Recursos Naturales', working paper, programa de uso y valoracion, Institute de Investigaciones Cientificas y Recursos Biológicos Alexander Von Humboldt, Villa de Leyva, Colombia.

Castells, M., 1999, *The Power of Identity. The Information Age. Economy Society and Culture, Vol. 2*, Second edition, London: Blackwell Publishers.

Castells, M., 2000, *End of the Millennium. The Information Age. Economy Society and Culture*, Second edition, London: Blackwell Publishers.

CBN, 2000, 'Plan Colombia Aumentara Tráfico de Armas y Drogas', Transcription of the radio interview to Walter Mairovich. News release, 9 April, 2000.

Chomsky, N., 1997, *El nuevo orden mundial (y el viejo)*. Las letras de Drakonos, Directors: Josep Fontana & Gonzalo Potón, Translation to Spanish of Carme Castells. Grijalbo Mondadori, Barcelona.

COAMA & COICA, 1998, 'Taller 1: Areas protegidas y tierras o territorios indígenas. Simposio IV: Integrando Nuestro Entorno Humano', Primer Congreso Latinoamericano de Parque y otras Areas Protegidas. Documento de Trabajo No. 4.

Colchester, M., 1996, 'Beyond "participation": indigenous peoples, biological diversity conservation and protected area management', *Unasylva, 186*, Vol. 47, pp. 33–9.

Correa, F., 1990, *La Selva Humanizada. Ecología alternativa en el trópico humedo colombiano*, Bogotá: ICAN, FEN, CEREC.

Correa, F., 1992, 'Derechos Etnicos: Derechos Humanos', Symposium Derechos Humanos en la construccion de las Americas. VI Congreso de Antropología en Colombia. Universidad de los Andes, Bogotá.

DCRNet, 2000, 'Effects of Plan Colombia on coca prices', DCRNet Issue No.157 – 10 July 2000. Available at www.drcnet.org.

El Espectador, 2001, Bogota, Colombia, 28 February.

European Parliament, 2001, 'European Parliament voted 474–1 against Plan Colombia', France Press, 1 February 2001.

Forero, O.A., Tanimuka, J. and Laborde, R.E., 1998, 'Colombia: Yaigojé Indigenous Resguardo Natural Reserve', From principles to practice: Indigenous peoples and biodiversity conservation in Latin America, IWGIA Document No. 87, Copenhagen, pp. 108–28.

Forero, O.A., 1999a, 'From pure sciences to ethnosciences, a broad perspective on ecosystem analysis and governance. Examining the environmental management problems of the Yaigojé Resguardo indigenous reserve on the Colombian Amazonia', MSc. Thesis, Ecosystems Analysis and Governance, University of Warwick.

Forero, O.A., 1999b, 'The dance of the dolls or the march of the manikins: an analysis of a Tukanoan ecological management ritual for Northwest Amazonia', Presented at the PILAS annual Conference – 1999, University of Hull. Unpublished.

Forero, O.A., 2000, 'Territoriality and governance in the Colombian Amazon', Presented at SLAS Annual Conference – 2000, University of Hull. Unpublished.

The Guardian, 15 March 2001, 'US u-turn on emissions fuels anger'.

Hemming, J., 1995, *Red Gold*: *The Conquest of the Brazilian Indians*, 1500–1760, revised edition, London: Macmillan.

Héndez, J.E., 2001, 'Apoyo a preferencias arancelarias', *El Espectador*, 28 February 2001.

Hitchens, C., 2001, *The Trial of Henry Kissinger*, London: Verso Books.

Hugh-Jones, S., 1979, *The Palm and the Pleiades: Initiation and Cosmology in Northwest Amazonia*, Cambridge: Cambridge University Press.

Hugh-Jones S., 1997, Éducation et culture. Réflections sur certains développements dans la région colombienne du Pira-Parana', *Cahiers des Amériques Latines*, No. 27, pp. 94–121.

Hugh-Jones, S., 1996, 'Bonnes raisons ou mauvaise conscience. De l'ambivalence de certains Amazoniens envers la consommation de viande', *Terrain*, 26, March, pp. 123–48.

HRW – Human Rights Watch, 2001, *World Report 2000/2001*. Report to the US Department of State. English version available at: www.hrw.org/wr2k/americas-03.htm.

Jackson, J.E., 1984, 'Traducciones competitivas del Evangelio en el Vaupés', *America Indígena*, **44**(1).

Johnson, A., 1989, 'How the Machiguenga manage resources: conservation or exploitation of nature', *Advances in Economic Botany Vol.7. New York Botanical Garden. N.Y.*, pp. 213–22.

Jones, P.M., 2001, 'Colombia's drug war spills into Ecuador', *Chicago Tribune*, 17 February 2001.

Koch-Grunberg, T., 1995, *Dos Años entre los indios. Viajes por el Noroeste Brasileño, 1903–1905*. Bogotá: Editorial Nacional de Colombia.

Koehnlein, B., 2001, David McReynolds on the Iraq bombing, 19 February 2001, text copyright: @Google http://groups.google.com/groups.

Lama, A., 2001, 'Cocaine economy begins its resurrection', Interpress Third World News Agency – IPS, 17 January 2001, Lima.

Milner-Gulland, E.J. and Mace, R., 1998, *Conservation of biological resources*, Oxford: Blackwell Science.

MMA – Ministerio del Medio Ambiente – Colombia, 1998a, *Diagnóstico Regional y estrategias de desarrollo de las áreas protegidas de América Latina*.

MMA – Ministerio del Medio Ambiente – Colombia, 1998b, Memorias del Primer Congreso Latinoamericano de Parques Nacionales y otras Areas Protegidas.

Molano-Bravo, A., 2001, 'Cartas Destapadas', *El Espectador – Colombia*, 11 March 2001.

One World – News Service 1995, 'French nuclear test goes ahead', Photo of Mururoa explosion, copyright: @Greenpeace. Image and text on line: www.oneworld.org/news/world/news_french_test.htm.

Plan Colombia, 1999, Full version of 'Plan Colombia' (English, French and Spanish) at www.PlanColombia.com.

Posey, D.A., 1985, 'Indigenous management of tropical forest ecosystems: the case of the Kayapo indians of the Brazilian Amazon', *Agroforestry Systems*, **3**, pp. 139–58.

Reichel-Dolmatoff, G., 1972, 'El Misionero ante las culturas indígenas', *America Indígena*, **32**(4), pp. 1138–49.

Reichel-Dolmatoff, G., 1996, *The Forest Within. The World-View of the Tukano Amazonian Indians*, Devon: Themis Books.

Reichel-Dolmatoff, G., 1997, *Chamanes de la selva Pluvial. Ensayos sobre los Indios Tukano del Norsoeste Amaznomicaso*, Translation to Spanish by Efraín Sánchez. Devon: Themis Books.

Revista Cambio, 2001, 'Petroleo en Colombia', *Revista Cambio – Colombia*, 12–19 March 2001.

Ricardo, V.G., 2000, Closure speech, Colombian Ambassador at Canning House: Drugs an international dialogue, 27 November 2000, London.

Ricardo, V.G., 2001, 'On the peace process', Talk for the LSE Colombian Society, 27 January 2001, London.

Rodriguez, C. and Van der Hammen, C., 1996, 'Sembrar para nietos y bisnietos. Manejo de la sicesion forestal por los indígenas Yukuna-Matapí de la Amazonia Colombiana', *CESPEDESTA*, **27**(67), Enero/Julio 1996 Primer Congreso Colombiano de Etnobiologia, pp. 256–71.

Roy, S.D. and Jackson, P., 1993, 'Mayhem in Manas: the threats to India's wildlife reserves', in E. Kemf, ed., *Indigenous Peoples and Protected Areas. The Law of Mother Earth*, London: Earthscan, pp. 151–61.

Schultes, R.E., 1991, 'Ethnobotany and technology in the North-west Amazon: example of partnership', *Environmental Conservation*, **18**(3), pp. 264–7.

Schultes, R.E., 1992, 'Ethnobotany, Biological Diversity, and the Amazon Indians', *Environmental Conservation*, **19**(2), pp. 97–100.

Schultes, R.E., 1994, 'The importance of ethnobotany in environmental conservation', *American Journal of Economics and Sociology*, **53**(2), pp. 202–9.

Stott, P., 1999, 'Tropical rain forest: a political ecology of hegemonic mythmaking', *IEA Studies on the Environment*, 15, London: London School of Economics.

Van der Hammen, M.C., 1992, *Nature and Society by the Yukuna of the Colombian Amazonia*, Bogotá: Tropenbos.

Vargas, M., 2001, 'Un fallo histórico', *Revista Cambio – Colombia*, 19–26 February 2001.

Vargas-Meza, R., 1999, *Fumigación y Conflicto. Politicas Antidrogas y deslegitimación del Estado en Colombia*, The Netherlands: TNI.

Von Hildebrand, M., 1983, 'Cosmovisión y el concepto de enfermedad entre los Ufaina', *Medicina, Chamanisma y Bótanica*, Bogotá: Editorial presencia, FUNCOL.

Wells, M. and Brandon, K., 1992, *People and Parks: Linking Protected Area Management with Local Communities*, Washington DC: World Bank/WWF/USAID.

West, P.C. and Brechin, S.R., 1991, 'National parks, protected areas and resident peoples: a comparative assessment and integration', in West, P.C. and Brechin, S.R., eds, *Resident Peoples and National Parks*, Tucson: University of Arizona press, pp. 363–400.

12. Fresh water in Costa Rica: abundant yet constrained

Álvaro Fernández-González and Edgar E. Gutiérrez-Espeleta*

1   INTRODUCTION

Life-support systems for humans and other species are critically dependent on water quality and availability. Among the greatest current challenges to human security are the risks to public and environmental health stemming from the degradation or depletion of water resources. And there are other impacts of water conditions on human security, both in the economic and social realms. The increased cost of making water available and potable (when possible at all) must be borne by public or private agencies and, therefore, to some degree, by the public itself. This has national implications in terms of decreased overall competitiveness, as well as more individual or localised outcomes, such as a loss of real estate value or eventual displacement of populations. Most troubling perhaps is the fact that conflicts between users of the resource, and between different uses of it, can produce escalating costs and disturbances, even with regional and international consequences.

Water resources in Costa Rica, and drinking water in particular, are abundant. Yet they are constrained: there are symptoms that pollution and overexploitation might pose serious dangers for the future, bringing about tensions and contradictions between its uses as a source and sink. Water stress from aquifer overexploitation has become a distinct possibility, as extraction expanded by 400 per cent in the metropolitan area in the 1996–2000 period. In addition, these aquifers show the increasing presence of carcinogenic nitrates, which could have taken 20 years to leach their way underground, when use of nitrogen compounds in fertilisers was much less intense than now (indicating current use of fertilisers will have an even greater impact in the next 20 years). Similarly, the use of surface water for human consumption – which at present accounts for 20 per cent of total consumption, according to some estimates – is threatened in many areas by surface runoff with agrochemicals or intentional discharges of pesticides and

267

organic waste affecting water sources, rivers and streams. This is compounded
by the fact that water sanitation normally requires dosages of chlorine that
entail carcinogenic risks. Recent bottled drinking water imports from Italy,
Spain and Brazil are signalling an alert that must be heeded. Conflicts over
water pollution and overexploitation – reaching Costa Rican courts in growing proportions – sometimes follow unconventional, even violent, courses of
action, given the shortcomings of legal institutions and water management
arrangements in the country.

This chapter presents an overview of the current status of water resources
in Costa Rica, pointing out some of its implications for human security (with
examples of the nature of conflicts arising in this context). The main focus is
on water quality and availability, with reference to three major groups of
factors: population dynamics, activities with an impact on the state of the
resource, and institutional and policy responses.

2   FRESH WATER IN COSTA RICA

As stated above, Costa Rica has abundant water resources. The combination
of a mountainous topography and high rainfall over a small geographic area
(51 100 sq. km) provides water runoffs for surface waters and plentiful recharge of groundwater. Although the quantity of water does not pose a
problem in itself, constraints are imposed by the requirements of distribution
and by pollution at the sources (Reynolds, 1996).

2.1   Availability of Water Resources

Rainfall in Costa Rica ranges between 1300 and 7500 cubic millimetres per
year, and is quite evenly distributed along the watersheds: 47 per cent in the
Pacific watershed and the remaining 53 per cent in the Caribbean watershed,
the latter composed of the northern slope and the eastern Caribbean slope
(CCAD, 1998). Surface water is abundant all year round except in the north-
western part of the country, which has a dry season from December through
April. During such time smaller streams in the area may go dry.

Water availability in the country was estimated in 1994 at 29 800 cubic
meters (m^3) per inhabitant (on a hydrological balance basis), while total extraction per inhabitant was estimated at 779 cubic meters (89 per cent for agriculture,
7 per cent in industry, and 4 per cent consumption) (CCAD, 1998).

Watersheds

Costa Rica has approximately 100 watersheds; 34 of them are regarded as
major basins. The largest watersheds include Grande de Térraba (5077 km²),

Table 12.1   Major watersheds of Costa Rica

Name	Area (Km²)
Grande de Térraba River	5 077
Nicoya Peninsula and Northern Coast	4 202
Tempisque River	3 405
Reventazón – Parismina River	2 950
San Carlos River	2 646
Zapote River and others	2 594
Sixaola River	2 331
Grande de Tárcoles River	2 169
Bebedero River	2 050
Osa Peninsula rivers	1 969
Others	20 409

Source: Costa Rican Water and Sewage Authority (1997); (http://www.netsalud.sa.cr/aya/34cuencs.html).

Nicoya Peninsula and Northern Coast (4202 km²), Tempisque (3405 km²), Reventazón-Parismina (2950 km²), and San Carlos (2646 km²) (see Table 12.1).

Two of these watersheds are strategic in nature in view of their multiple functions as sources of fresh water and other environmental services. The Reventazón River basin provides hydroelectricity (at Río Macho, Cachí, and Birrís power plants), drinking water (with the Orosi pipeline supplying 40 per cent of the drinking water for the greater metropolitan area), flood control and recreation (at the Cachí reservoir and dam). The Arenal reservoir watershed and dam provide around 50 per cent of the country's hydroelectricity in the dry season (at the Arenal, Corobicí, and Sandillal power plants), flood control and irrigation (through the Arenal-Tempisque irrigation district), and flood control and recreation (at the Arenal Reservoir/lake). A third watershed – that of the Grande de Tárcoles River and the Virilla River, one of its tributaries, discussed in more detail below – is of strategic importance to Costa Rica not only because of its functions as a source (its aquifers provide the metropolitan population with 60 per cent of its drinking water), but also as a result of the tensions and contradictions related to its functions as an environmental sink: this watershed receives around 67 per cent of the organic pollution load in the country.

Irrigation
Currently, there are three major irrigation projects in the country, feeding mainly from surface waters. The Arenal-Tempisque district is the largest,

extending over 18 000 hectares that require an annual average flow of 35 m^3 per second. The other two are, one in the southern zone, with 2000 hectares under irrigation and taking water from the Térraba River at a flow of 3.5 m^3 per second, during the first four months of the year; and the Small Irrigations project that includes a cluster of plots in several parts of the country, consuming an average annual flow of 3.5 m^3 per second with water from minor rivers and nearby wells (Coto, 2000). In all cases, water is taken directly from the rivers and made available to irrigation with no treatment process whatsoever. Only some sand settling tanks are in place.

Aquifers and wells

According to the Costa Rican Water and Sewage Authority Web (ICAA, 1997), aquifers provide around 80 per cent of total drinking water in the country and 60 per cent of total consumption in the metropolitan area, the rest coming from surface waters (20 per cent for the country at large and 40 per cent for the greater metropolitan area, GMA). To evaluate the availability[1] of groundwater in Costa Rica, systematic hydrogeological studies have been made in three zones: the GMA, Guanacaste, and Port Limón (Gómez, 1996). These areas take 50 per cent or more of the water from aquifers to provide drinking water. Major aquifers in the country are listed in Table 12.2.

Aquifers with the greatest potential thus far tapped in the country are found in the Tárcoles-Virilla River watershed. A sequence of lava beds and

Table 12.2　Major aquifers under exploitation in Costa Rica

Name	Volume (litres per second)
Caribbean watershed	
La Bomba	30
Moín River	n.d.
Northern watershed	
Santa Clara (San Carlos River)	10
Pacific watershed	
Bagaces – Liberia	380
Tempisque	50–100
Barranca – El Roble	n.d.
Colima – lower	80
Colima – upper	750
Barva	20–100

Sources:　Gómez (1996) and SENARA (2000).

tufa has given origin to three superimposed aquifers, namely (in ascending order) Lower Colima, Upper Colima, and Barva (Gómez, 1996). About 66 per cent of the country's population takes water from these aquifers, with an extraction rate at around 5 m³ per second (Morera, 2000).

Areas adjacent to these aquifers are intensely used in drilling wells for public and industrial supply of water. SENARA (Servicio Nacional de Aguas Subterráneas, Riego y Avenamiento, Costa Rica's national groundwater, irrigation, and drainage authority) is the agency in charge of granting permits for well drilling and concessions for water extraction. As of July 2000, 5711 wells were reported in the Central Valley, accounting for 52.4 per cent of total wells in Costa Rica. Since the late 1980s, the number of wells in this area has grown by 217 per cent (SENARA, 2000). Flows taken from these wells are difficult to estimate because close to 30 per cent of them do not have pumping analyses. Demand for water concessions is growing at an annual rate of 10 per cent, and applications for drilling permits are growing at an annual rate of 30 per cent. Such applications are not only for drinking and irrigation, but also for private hydroelectric power generation. There is no monitoring from SENARA or other agencies to verify that water extraction is consistent with concessions. This is aggravated by the fact that no systematic studies are available about the hydrological potential nationwide; only partial studies exist for given areas. The existence of a large number of unauthorised wells compounds the problem: 11 000 to 15 000 unauthorised wells are estimated to be in use throughout the country. In order to mitigate this problem, efforts have been made to extend the water pipeline and sewage system to remote areas of Costa Rica, thereby reducing well water supply for domestic use, mainly in the Guanacaste Province.

The existence of clandestine wells excludes public monitoring of drinking water quality. Some wells may be experiencing pollution or saltwater intrusion problems if they are located near the seacoast. Another associated problem is the difficulty in preventing overexploitation of aquifers.

Two aquifers recently studied in the northern part of the country are the Liberia and Bagaces formations, the first overlaying the latter. The region where these are located is periodically affected by droughts and the El Niño phenomenon, with severe impacts. Another pressure factor is the fast-growing tourism development in the city of Liberia and its resulting rise in demand for drinking water. The study determined that full protection should be established for mountainous areas where the Bagaces formation crops out, since pollution in these areas may swiftly show up in the aquifer. Sewerage and soapy waters, and other types of outflows have been shown to take little time in reaching the Liberia aquifer groundwater level. Therefore, the recommendation is made for drilled wells to tap only the Bagaces aquifer while sealing off Liberia due to possible pollution (SENARA, 2000).

2.2   Quality of Water Resources

Evaluation of water quality in Costa Rica has focused on surface waters. Typical studies assess physical and chemical characteristics of water bodies. Recently, biological assessments have also been included, providing for broader evaluations of the resource. Recent legislation provides for more comprehensive assessments of surface and drinking waters (see section 3).

Access to drinking water

In Costa Rica, 74 per cent of the population with domestic water supplies receives drinking water (although its potability is at issue; see below). The service is delivered through 2018 pipeline systems. Of these, 172 are operated and managed by ICAA, the national public operator, 1614 systems are delegated by ICAA to rural communities (CAARs), 225 are municipal aqueducts, and 7 systems belong to the Public Utilities Company of Heredia (ESPH), one of the country's seven provinces (ICAA, 2000a) (see Table 12.3).

Table 12.3   Water agencies and population served

Managing agency	Total population served nationwide	Coverage nationwide (%)	Population served with drinking water	Coverage with drinking water (%)
ICAA	1 637 967	42	1 483 998	91
Municipalities	1 003 272	26	657 109	73
ESPH	154 919	4	153 370	99
CAARs	900 851	24	459 434	51
Others	126 000	3	n.d.	n.d.
Total	3 823 009	100	2 829 190	74

Source: ICAA (2000a).

Sources of pollution

As a whole, water bodies in the country are being affected by material inflows from sediments, sewage, industrial, agricultural or animal husbandry wastes, and agrochemicals. Among the major pollutants affecting water quality are large amounts of solids in suspension (resulting from soil erosion), high densities of fecal coliforms, heavy metals, and nitrates. Tárcoles-Virilla is the most damaged watershed, receiving approximately 67 per cent of the organic load, followed by the Reventazón and Térraba watersheds (with 11 per cent and 8 per cent of the load, respectively) (Astorga and Coto, 1996).

Despite a very high percentage of the population having access to drinking water and wastewater collection systems, no more than 25–35 per cent of wastewaters of the country are being treated, according to public officials (González, 1999).[2] Except for deficient treatment plants in the provincial capitals of Alajuela and Heredia, sewers throughout the country discharge directly into rivers or the sea (in the case of coastal towns), significantly affecting water quality (Boyce et al., 1994). Raw discharges produce disturbances in receptor waterways, such as dissolved oxygen depletion and disappearance of aquatic species. To make the problem worse, water from the Grande de Tárcoles Basin flows into the most populated coastal zone of the country, the port of Puntarenas and the Gulf of Nicoya, where a significant portion of the fishing catch is located.

Detergents, broadly used throughout the country, are not biodegradable and therefore affect aquatic life, producing eutrophication of the waters and adverse aesthetic effects in major riverbeds and waterways. Liquid wastes from industrial activity, geographically clustered in the GMA (within the Central Valley), are spilled with little or no treatment into rivers and streams close to the rainwater catchments or into the sewage system.

Agricultural activity also affects major watersheds of Costa Rica quite significantly. Crops such as coffee, bananas, sugar cane, and rice make use of agrochemical products very intensively. These reach rivers and runoff waterways. Coffee milling is the chief pollutant of the country's rivers. In the coffee picking and processing season, from November through February, daily biological oxygen demand (BOD) levels of up to 260 tons have been reported for the Grande de Tárcoles River, equivalent to a population of 47 million inhabitants (Astorga and Coto, 1996), more than 20 times the actual population.

A comprehensive analysis on the Grande de Tárcoles basin and the Reventazón basin, where most of the country's population reside, included evaluation of the acute toxicity of industrial effluents and river sediments, as well as their chronic toxicity (based on an analysis of their impact on chironomidae and macrobenthic organisms). Larger correlations were found than those discovered in rivers of the European nations (Astorga and Coto, 1996).

An official ICAA survey of the Tárcoles-Virilla watershed (ICAA, 2000b), conducted in 1999, revealed improved quality of water flows in the Grande de Tárcoles basin, particularly regarding its organic load (chemical oxygen demand – COD, BOD, and total organic carbon – TOC). This is probably due to major technological changes introduced by coffee mills that have diminished their polluting impact (see the section below on policy response).

However, levels of bacteriological pollution, phosphates, ammonium, detergents, nitrates, and other parameters typical of household residual waters, show a sustained upward trend because there are no treatment processes for this kind of effluent. The survey concluded that most receptor basins of the Tárcoles-Virilla watershed exceed minimum quality parameters set forth by the European Union (TOC at 2.5 to 3 mg/L, BOD less than 5 mg/L, COD less than 10 mg/L), and cannot be used in conventional processes to make water potable, except in the upstream portions of the respective basins where levels of degradation are below these thresholds (ICAA, 2000b). A further source of concern is that the monitoring programme itself has been suspended, given a lack of 'true interest in making use ... of the information for decision-making and environmental management of pollution in this watershed', according to the report (ibid., p. 5).

Groundwater pollution

Degradation of surface waters in Costa Rica is even more worrisome when the possible repercussion of it on groundwater is considered. As indicated above, groundwater is the main source of supply for drinking water. Reynolds has found isotopic similarity between the water of five major Central Valley rivers and the water of nearby aquifers (Reynolds, 1996), in support of previous findings reported by Darling et al. (1989, in Reynolds, 1996) of close associations between surface water and groundwater in the Central Valley.

The most common groundwater pollutant is nitrogen in nitrate form (or 'nitrate-N'). It generally comes from human or animal wastes that reach the soil due to inadequate sewage treatment, or from the application of fertilisers. Reynolds (1991) found nitrate-N concentrations of 18.9 milligrams per litre during a two years sampling period in 14 sources and wells of the Virilla River basin. This almost doubles the maximum 10 milligrams per litre set forth by the United States Environmental Protection Agency, USEPA (Boyce et al., 1994). Further research from the same author predicted nitrate concentrations would exceed USEPA thresholds in major aquifers in the years 2000 to 2004 (Reynolds, 1996).[3] One potential source of nitrates is nitrogen-based fertilisers applied to crops. The greatest coffee growing activity is located in the central highlands of the country. This endangers the three most important aquifers: Upper Colima, Lower Colima and Barva. Water-borne nitrates leaching through coffee growing soils are estimated to take around 20 years in reaching an aquifer located at a depth of 70 meters (Reynolds, 1996). Current nitrate pollution rates due to use of fertilisers and household sewage are significantly on the rise and only worsen the problem into the future. This same process is also affecting aquifers under banana plantations in the Caribbean, the northern aquifers, and those under rice fields in the Arenal-Tempisque irrigation district.

Another possible source of pollution to groundwater is saltwater intrusion. This problem occurs when a coastal aquifer is exploited at an inadequate flow rate and sea water flows into the overexploited wells. This changes water quality and makes it non-potable. Currently, SENARA is performing research in seashore and beach area aquifers on the Pacific coast (Flamingo-Potrero, Panamá, and Jacó). Still, studies of this problem are just beginning.

2.3 Pressures on Water in the Greater Metropolitan Area: A Threat to Human Security

The Greater Metropolitan Area (GMA) – mostly within the Tárcoles-Virilla watershed – currently houses 1.9 million people (around 60 per cent of the country's population), and is expected to grow by 0.5 million by the year 2005 (Proyecto Estado de la Región, 1999). Several factors are exerting pressure in the GMA, affecting the availability and quality of drinking water. The most important of these pressure factors are outlined below.

Loss of forest cover
Loss of vegetation and forest cover increases runoff and hinders or blocks off the filtering and percolation processes that feed aquifers. The rate of deforestation in Costa Rica is among the highest in Central America, reaching values from 40 000 to 60 000 hectares per year, while reforestation hardly approximates 8 per cent of annual felling (Vargas, 1996). On the whole, loss of forestland is accompanied by change in land use to crops using inadequate technology. This worsens erosion processes and favours loss of organic matter and soil fertility. One indicator of this phenomenon is the land use rationality index (developed by Gutiérrez-Espeleta), which shows the ability of a country to make current use fit potential soil and land use. When the index tends to zero this implies abusive land resource use to the detriment of forest use. In making a comparison among Central American countries, El Salvador and Costa Rica get the lowest values, 0.1 and 0.3, respectively.

Pollution from agrochemicals
Agricultural activities on the upper watersheds of the Central Valley – where the GMA lies – pollute both surface runoff and infiltration water with agrochemicals and syrup ferment wash water from coffee mills. Further downstream, where industrial and urban activities concentrate, surface and groundwater are polluted with chemicals, toxic waste, household waste, and solid waste.

Among the major polluting activities, cultivation of coffee, plants and flowers for export should be mentioned, given their localisation on top of the main aquifers in the valley. In the case of coffee, for example, estimates are that some 56 per cent of coffee land in Costa Rica lies on the Tárcoles River watershed, with 27 per cent of this territory occupied by coffee plantations (Boyce et al., 1994). These are predominantly volcanic soils, with geologic fissures and faults that produce a high infiltration potential: some studies conclude that more than 40 per cent of rainfall in the watershed reaches its underlying aquifers.

In the early 1990s, 30.4 per cent of imported pesticides in Costa Rica were on UNEP's list of prohibited, severely restricted, cancelled or unregistered substances, and 23 per cent were highly or extremely toxic. Of these, 50 different pesticides were used in coffee cultivation: paraquat, copper hydroxide and terbufos were among the most widely used, and are highly or extremely toxic, with very significant acute and chronic impacts, including cancer (Boyce et al., 1994). Pesticide imports have since been deregulated, so the current situation could be considerably worse. Nevertheless, systematic monitoring activities to establish the risks of agrochemical pollution in surface waters and aquifers are just beginning (see section 3).

Concentration of the population and urban development

Population concentration and urban development processes also create pressures on water resources, causing demand to rise and increased soil waterproofing. Demand for drinking water services has risen sharply in the last five years. The number of water connections to the mains provided by ICAA in the greater metropolitan area grew from 224 225 in 1995 to 254 675 in 1999. This accounts for an average annual growth rate of 3 per cent, which is 25 per cent higher than the average growth rate of the population nationwide for the same period (2.4 per cent), indicating an increasing concentration of demand in this area. ICAA has recently announced the drilling of 60 new wells distributed in two fields (Campo Norte and Potrerillos) to meet projections of growing demand in the GMA (Gómez, 2000).

In 1996, ICAA officials estimated that GMA aquifers were being used at a rate of 1.3 m^3/s, while total potential was calculated at 8 m^3/s (Vargas, 1996). As mentioned above, SENARA officials estimate current groundwater extraction in the GMA at 5 m^3/s (Morera, 2000). Although the danger of overexploiting these aquifers is not yet under public scrutiny, such estimates certainly suggest this is a distinct possibility: extraction rates for the GMA have risen from 16 per cent to 62.5 per cent of available groundwater in scarcely four years. Assessing this information with parameters proposed by the World Meteorological Organisation (WMO), groundwater consumption in the GMA appears to have evolved – in WMO terms – from 'moderate' water stress conditions (10–20 per cent withdrawals over total availability) to a 'high' stress situation (more than 40 per cent withdrawals), in the company of such water-stressed nations as Egypt, Libya, the Arab peninsula and the

Middle Eastern states (UNEP, 1999). Current announcements of new studies to reassess groundwater potential and vulnerability in the Central Valley (see section 3) might be indicative that public officials are aware of such possibilities. Yet the fact that new drillings are being planned implies a presumption of high groundwater availability.

The risk is compounded when exploitation of private springs and wells is also considered, where levels of extraction are generally unknown. In addition, the increase in urban infrastructure, housing and roads, waterproofs large surfaces that work as catchments and recharge areas to local aquifers, thereby diminishing the availability of water. In these cases, rainfall water can only run off over the surface into the rivers, thus contributing to lower water tables.

3   WATER MANAGEMENT IN COSTA RICA THREATENS THE FUTURE OF THIS RESOURCE

No integrated management of water resources exists in Costa Rica. Agencies governing water resources operate in a dispersed and fragmented manner, under the mandate of several different laws and with no decision-making unity or coherence for policymaking and implementation. This disarray and disorganisation has resulted in a duplication of functions and rivalry between agencies, so that measures taken do not achieve the desired impact in the management and conservation of water resources.

Legal and institutional framework

The 1942 Water Act established technical guidelines for the development of water resources, including their assignment to the public domain and different procedures for their utilisation, delivery and protection. The law creates the notion of 'easement', provides for the conservation of trees along riverbanks, and defines areas of protection for several watersheds. This law regulates activities in the management and protection of water in both rural and urban areas.

The 1949 Construction Act authorises municipalities to grant licences to any soil use activity, and to extend building permits and permits to carry out commercial and industrial activities. However, this law does not have any provision for the regulation and control of buffer zones and watershed protection areas. In the absence of local development plans and regulations, the 1968 Urban Planning Act places in the hands of the Costa Rican Housing and Urban Development Institute (INVU) all activities associated with infrastructure and hydraulic works. In areas declared as 'rural', the 1973 General Health Act empowers the Ministry of Health to approve permits for the use of territory in industrial activities. One 1980 INVU regulation by decree establishes industrial zoning for the greater metropolitan area and classifies industries according to their pollution levels.

The 1996 Organic Law of the Environment makes a constitutional amendment to Article 50, proclaiming the right to a sound and healthy environment. The new Law for the Conservation of Wildlife forbids the deposition of residual waters or any polluting substance into streams or rivers. It also requires industries and agro-industries to put in place treatment plants for their residual waters, granting them two years to do so.

In 1992, ICAA, the Health Ministry and the national public services regulatory agency, in partnership with the Costa Rican Coffee Institute, required coffee processing plants to reduce by 80 per cent their organic matter discharges into rivers and streams by 1995 (Boyce et al., 1994). In 1996, the Regulation for Residual Water Disposal and Recycling was put into effect, requiring coffee processors to meet a quality standard for chemical oxygen demand (COD) of 1500 mg/L and biological oxygen demand (BOD) of 1000 mg/L, and the restricted use of one cubic metre of water per 'fanega' (46 kilogram sack) of processed coffee. Enforcing this ruling with coffee processors was vital because the greatest polluting discharge load into the Tárcoles Basin came from them. By 1998, their discharges were reduced from 65 per cent to 45 per cent of the total pollution load in the Tárcoles-Virilla watershed (Proyecto Estado de la Región, 1999). Subsequent stages in the 1996 regulation will require treatment for bacteria, phosphates, ammonium, detergents, nitrates and other parameters.

The 1996 regulation was coupled in 1997 with the country's first *Drinking water quality regulations*, establishing parameters to be enforced in four phases. The first phase, which entered into force immediately, was focused on rural aqueducts serving populations below 10 000, with controls for water odour, colour and residual chlorine. The second phase came into effect in 1999 as a 'basic analysis programme', controlling for phase-one parameters plus fecal coliforms, turbidity, colour, conductivity, concentration of hydrogen ions and temperature. The third and fourth phases, in force since 2000, are conceived as 'normal' and 'advanced' programmes, and include basic analyses plus controls for hardness and several chemicals: chlorides, sulphates, calcium, magnesium, sodium, potassium, zinc, aluminium, copper, nitrates, nitrites, ammonium, iron, manganese, fluoride, hydrogen sulphide, arsenic, cadmium, cyanide, chrome, mercury, nickel, lead, antimony, selenium, disinfectants and their sub products, and 'organic substances relevant to health (pesticides)'. At the time of writing, ICAA completed the first annual progress report on phases 3 and 4 (Sequeira, 2000).

Other policy instruments

In addition to legal provisions, other instruments are in place that operate on a more voluntary basis and contribute to the protection of water in the country. Among these, the Ecologic Banner Programme rewards industries working with 'clean technologies', while payments for 'environmental services' (already in place in the forestry sector, and under discussion as a bill in parliament) set a financial compensation for conservation and reforestation along watersheds that deliver significant environmental services, such as hydroelectric power generation or ecotourism. Also, citizen and consumer initiatives can be articulated within existing regulations for the protection of sources of water and health; some examples will be briefly discussed below.

Watershed management

Land zoning and watershed management initiatives are growing in the country (Fernández-González and Aylward, 1999). One major effort involves 31 municipalities and 152 districts which jointly developed the 1982 Regional Plan for the Greater Metropolitan Area (Brenes, 1996). This plan establishes protection zones for rivers with the greatest drainage in major GMA cities (Reventazón, Tiribí, María Aguilar, Torres, Bermúdez, Virilla, Grande de Tárcoles, Grande de Térraba, and others). The plan also places farmlands under protection, such as the Itiquís irrigation district and the agricultural district north of Cartago. It includes further protected areas in several volcanoes and national parks, and areas with scenic value (among others, Irazú, Barva, and Poas volcanoes; Prusia and Braulio Carrillo national parks, and La Carpintera, Pico Blanco, Salitral, and Las Palomas mountains). Recent evaluations indicate the plan has been ineffective, due to a fragmentation of mandates (Proyecto Estado de la Región, 1999). Another recent effort is the Coordinating Commission for the Grande de Tárcoles River Basin, institutionalised in 1993 through an executive decree, and comprising a voluntary coalition of non-governmental organisations, municipalities and public agencies.

Reassessment of Central Valley aquifers

In August 2000, a joint project by SENARA and ICAA was announced to reassess the potential and extraction of Central Valley aquifers. The last such study was done in conjunction with the British Geological Service in 1988. Information from new drillings and climate data are expected to help reassess the aquifers and learn more about their physical characteristics, recharge and discharge zones, and the volumes available for exploitation. Parallel to this research, a risk analysis of pollution to Central Valley aquifers will be made. This includes plotting a vulnerability map (physical and mechanical characteristics of aquifers) and a map of threats or polluting loads produced by human, industrial, urban, tourism, and agricultural development. These maps are essential tools to define areas for protection and also to be used in land use planning and zoning.

4   FUTURE PROSPECTS: WATER AND HUMAN SECURITY IN COSTA RICA

Typically, Costa Rican citizens have felt their drinking water is 'safe': it is both potable and abundant. Since the late 1960s, ICAA has extended its coverage to the whole country, and potability has been equated with chlorination (see, for example, ICAA, 2000a). Notwithstanding the 1996 and 1997 regulations on residual waters and drinking water quality, the public has felt at ease both with the availability and the quality of its fresh water resources.

Yet there are signs of impending danger. Bottled drinking water has been a middle-class commodity for many years, but recent imports from Italy, Spain and Brazil, as well as widespread consumption of retail water, suggests a change of mind, and a new perception of risk.

Other developments point at rising conflicts over water, most of them legal in nature, but not all. In many suburban localities, the availability of water is at stake, and local committees are confronting real estate developers (in a competition for scarce resources) or public agencies (in a claim for equal access). The quality of water is also becoming a matter of contention. In October 1999, a rural community in the Central Valley successfully sued a coffee grower for polluting their drinking water with agrochemicals, claiming the equivalent of several hundred thousand dollars in damages. While the court ruling is still being challenged, public sector officials provided key testimony, and it marks a turning point in Costa Rican environmental law (UNEP, 2000). And not all disputes follow such conventional avenues. The Central American Water Tribunal – non-official in nature – held its first public audience in late 2000, judging on 11 cases; two were from Costa Rica, and both had to do with contamination of major Central Valley aquifers. In 1992, the International Water Court at The Hague (also a non-official tribunal) had set a precedent, judging that the Standard Fruit Company (producer of *Chiquita* brand bananas) had in effect violated human and environmental rights when it polluted waters with agrochemicals on Costa Rica's Caribbean coast. And that same year, a young man from Puntarenas, near the Pacific coast, beheaded three men who were illegally using toxic compounds to fish in the Guacimal River, which he and his family used downstream as their drinking water source (Boyce et al., 1994).

These examples of conflict over water indicate that there is growing insecurity. The availability and quality of drinking water is complicated by its double role of source and sink. Given further population growth, as well as urban, industrial, and agricultural development, greater exploitation and contamination of surface waters and groundwater is expected to continue, not only in the greater metropolitan area, but in remaining regions of the country.

• This commands a more comprehensive and integrated vision of the nation's water resources, in order to mitigate future conflicts over water. The different agencies and organisations dealing with water policy and management need to converge into coordinated and coherent decision-making for planning, management, and conservation of the resource. This in turn does not necessarily entail a process of centralisation, as some may think: pluralistic, participatory approaches are not only possible, but are presently being experimented with (Fernández-González and Aylward, 1999).

To reduce human insecurity on water, the establishment of adequate treatment systems for residual water is urgent, given current signals of surface water pollution affecting aquifers. The 1996 Law for Residual Water Disposal and Recycling has helped to improve the water quality of the Tárcoles Basin, insofar as organic load reduction is concerned. Yet, much remains to be done in terms of regulation, enforcement, and monitoring. The 1997 drinking water quality regulations on chemical contaminants must be systematically enforced and monitoring results publicised and assessed.

Re-utilisation of treated waters is an important option for increased water availability in the future. No country can allow its drinking water supply to be diverted. Clean water, coming directly from pure springs or aquifers, should be used only for human consumption, leaving treated residual water for industrial use or irrigation.

To protect groundwater, forest cover needs to be extended over aquifer recharge land and, in cases where waterproofing has occurred, rehabilitation programmes with relocation of infrastructure need to be put in place. Payment for environmental services and full-cost pricing policies must be fundamentally aimed at groundwater protection.

In major hydrographic basins, watershed authorities should be installed, so that regulations and activities follow provisions agreed to between their dwellers and users. Also, systematic monitoring should be performed, in a participatory manner, to ensure compliance with parameters set forth in the Law for Residual Water Disposal and Recycling and the drinking water quality regulations.

NOTES

*   The authors gratefully acknowledge the contribution of the experts cited in the references, and the collaboration of our former research assistant at the Observatory, Viviana Blanco.

1. The term 'availability' is not to be confused with 'quantity'. Ground water availability is the propensity or susceptibility of an aquifer to be exploited pursuant to user requirements and depends on the characteristics of the aquifer itself, such as permeability, storage coefficient, conductivity, porosity, and recharge (Gómez, 2000).
2. The estimate is high compared to the general situation in Latin America and the Caribbean. A 1995 survey by the Pan American Health Organization revealed that – on average – not more than 13 per cent of residual waters are being treated (Argentina, 10 per cent; Colombia, 5 per cent; Brazil, 20 per cent; Mexico, 13 per cent) (PAHO, 1998).
3. The USEPA standard is 10 mg/l of nitrate-N (nitrogen in nitrate form) or 44 mg/l of nitrogen as nitrate (NO_3^{-1}). The standard in Costa Rica, according to the 1997 drinking water quality regulations, is 50 mg/l nitrate (NO_3^{-1}), but did not come into effect until 2000–2001 (see section 3). ICAA hydrogeologist Alicia Gómez reports that the Authority's laboratory measurements for Santo Domingo exceed the standard (values of almost 50 milligrams per litre of NO_3^{-1}) (Gómez, 2000).

REFERENCES

Astorga, Y. and J. Coto, 1996, 'Situación de los recursos hídricos en Costa Rica' [Situation of water resources in Costa Rica], in Jenny Reynolds Vargas, ed., *Utilización y manejo sostenible de los recursos hídricos* [Utilization and sustainable management of water resources], Editorial Fundación UNA.

Boyce, J., A. Fernández-González, E. Fürst and O. Segura-Bonilla, 1994, *Café y desarrollo sostenible: del cultivo agroquímico a la producción orgánica en Costa Rica* [Coffee and sustainable development: from agrochemical cultivation to organic production in Costa Rica], Heredia, Costa Rica: Editorial Fundación UNA.

Brenes, J., 1996, 'Problemas urbanos y costeros nelacionados con el recurso hídrico en Coasta Rica' [Urban and coastal problems related to water resources in Costa Rica], in Jenny Reynolds Vargas (ed.), *Utilización manejo sostenible de los recursos hídricos* [Utilization and sustainable management of water resources], Editorial Fundación UNA.

CCAD (Comisión Centroamericana de Ambiente y Desarrollo), 1998, *Estado del ambiente y los recursos naturales en Centroamérica 1998* [State of the environment and natural resources in Central America], Costa Rica.

Chacón, Olman, 2000, Interview with the Systems Operations Director of the Costa Rican Water and Sewage Authority (Instituto Costarricense de Acueductos y Alcantarillados – ICAA).

Chaves, Gonzalo, 1996, 'La administración de los recursos hídricos' [Water resource management], in Jenny Reynolds Vargas, ed., *Utilización y manejo sostenible de los recursos hídricos* [Utilization and sustainable management of water resources], Editorial Fundación UNA.

Coto, Marvin, 2000, Interview with Director of Operations of the National Groundwater, Irrigation, and Drainage Authority (Servicio Nacional de Aguas Subterráneas, Riego y Avenamiento – SENARA).

Darling, W.G., J.M. Parker, H.V. Rodríguez and A.J. Lardner, 1989, 'Investigation of a volcanic aquifer system in Costa Rica using environmental isotopes', in *Proceedings of a regional seminar for Latin America on the use of isotope techniques in hydrology*, Mexico and Vienna: IAEA, pp. 215–28.

Fernández-González, A. and B. Aylward, 1999, 'Participation, pluralism and polycentrism: reflections on watershed management in Costa Rica', *Unasylva*, No.

199 (Vol. 50), pp. 52–9.

Foster, S., 1998, 'Las aguas subterráneas del Valle Central de Costa Rica: reconocimiento de su calidad y vulnerabilidad a la contaminación', *Informe técnico*, No. 361. ICAA y BGS-SENARA [Groundwater of Costa Rica's Central Valley: recognition of its quality and vulnerability to pollution; Technical Report].

Gómez, Alicia, 2000, Interview with the hydrogeologist of the Costa Rican Water and Sewage Authority [Instituto Costarricense de Acueductos y Alcantarillados – ICAA].

Gómez, Alicia, 1996, 'Condiciones hidrogeológicas en Costa Rica' [Hydrogeologic conditions in Costa Rica] in Jenny Reynolds Vargas, ed., *Utilización y manejo sostenible de los recursos hídricos* [Utilisation and sustainable management of water resources], Editorial Fundación UNA.

González, Edgar, 1999, Interview with the Adviser to the Chief Executive Officer of the Costa Rican Water and Sewage Authority [Instituto Costarricense de Acueductos y Alcantarillados – ICAA].

ICAA (Instituto Costarricense de Acueductos y Alcantarillados), 2000a, *Información sobre calidad del agua en Costa Rica, Enero 1999–Marzo 2000* [Information about water quality in Costa Rica, January, 1999–March, 2000].

ICAA, 2000b, *Estado de contaminación en la cuenca 24 Virilla-Tárcoles* [State of pollution in basin 24 Virilla-Tárcoles].

ICAA, 1997, *Reglamento de calidad del agua potable* [Quality of drinking water regulation].

ICAA, 1990, *Plan maestro de abastecimiento de agua potable de la Gran Área Metropolitana* [Master plan for delivery of drinking water to the Greater Metropolitan Area].

Morera, Sigifredo, 2000, Interview with the hydrogeologist of the Groundwater Area of the National Groundwater, Irrigation, and Drainage Authority (Servicio Nacional de Aguas Subterráneas, Riego y Avenamiento – SENARA).

PAHO (Pan American Health Organisation), 1998, *Health in the Americas. 1998 Edition*, Volume 1, Scientific Publication No. 569, Washington, DC: Pan American Health Organisation.

Proyecto Estado de la Región, 1999, *Informe Estado de la Región en Desarrollo Humano Sostenible*, San José: Proyecto Estado de la Nación.

Reynolds Vargas, J., ed., 1996, *Utilización y manejo sostenible de los recursos hídricos* [Utilization and sustainable management of water resources], Editorial Fundación UNA.

Reynolds Vargas, J., 1991, 'Soil nitrogen dynamics in relation to groundwater contamination in the Valle Central, Costa Rica', PhD diss., Michigan University.

SENARA (Servicio Nacional de Aguas Subterráneas, Riego y Avenamiento), 2000, *Boletín de aguas subterráneas*, Número 2, September [National Groundwater, Irrigation, and Drainage Authority].

Sequeira, Marcos, 2000, Personal communication from a laboratory official at the Costa Rican Water and Sewage Authority (Instituto Costarricense de Acueductos y Alcantarillados – ICAA).

UNEP, 1999, *Global Environmental Outlook*, London: Earthscan.

UNEP (United Nations Environment Programme), 2000, *GEO Latin America and the Caribbean Environment Outlook*, San José: UNEP.

Vargas, Carlos, 1996, 'La perspectiva del manejo de cuencas' [The basin management perspective], in Jenny Reynolds Vargas, ed., *Utilización y manejo sostenible de los recursos hídricos* [Sustainable management and use of water resources], Editorial Fundación UNA.

Index